CONCISE
DICTIONARY OF
MANAGEMENT

**Simple Definitions of Business Management Terms for
Entrepreneurs, Managers, Students & Interested Readers**

I0084631

Editorial Board

V&S PUBLISHERS

Published by:

V&S PUBLISHERS

F-2/16, Ansari road, Daryaganj, New Delhi-110002
☎ 23240026, 23240027 • Fax: 011-23240028
E-mail: info@vspublishers.com

Branch : Hyderabad
5-1-707/1, Brij Bhawan (Beside Central Bank of India Lane)
Bank Street, Koti, Hyderabad - 500 095
☎ 040-24737290
E-mail: vspublishershyd@gmail.com

Branch Office : Mumbai
Godown # 34 at The Model Co-operative Housing, Society Ltd.,
"Sahakar Niwas", Gound Floor, Next to Sobo Central, Mumbai - 400 034
☎ 022-23510736
E-mail: vspublishersmum@gmail.com

Follow us on: t f in

All books available at www.vspublishers.com

© **Copyright:** **V&S PUBLISHERS**
ISBN 978-93-505712-3-1
Edition: 2014

Printed at: Param Offsetters, Okhla, New Delhi

Publisher's Note

The appreciative response received from the market to the dictionaries published by us earlier on science and commerce subjects has encouraged us to take up yet another dictionary commanding an upsurge in demand - **Concise Dictionary of Management**. Like earlier dictionaries, this again is a concise version. This edition is expected to fulfil the requirements of students, educationists, researchers, scholars, and writers.

Innumerable dictionaries are available in the market for use as a reference manual. Quite a number of these dictionaries come replete with jargon-filled terms; and therefore readers find it difficult to comprehend them. On top of that, many of them fail to include new management-related *terms* that keep finding their way into regular usage every other day. Absence of freshly coined *terms* contributes to difficulty in keeping up to date with definitions and explanations of new words.

Unlike other reference dictionaries that take readers' understanding of management *terms* for granted; and make short passing references while alluding to another *term* in the text, we have tried to be more specific and to-the-point. This has been written with the belief that an average reader is interested only in knowing the meaning of a management *term* without getting lost in incomprehensible explanation.

For easy reference *terms* have been arranged alphabetically. *Terms* that have come into the reckoning lately have also been incorporated; and suitably explained such that a student can grasp them easily. Illustrations and examples, where appropriate, have been added. Even for an average interested reader, who has not made a special study of commerce subjects, explanations of management *terms* will be found to be reasonably comprehensible.

We would be happy to have your views and comments for improving the content and quality of the book.

Contents

A

360 survey
An employee feedback programme whereby an employee is rated by surveys distributed to his or her co-workers, customers, and managers. HR departments may use this feedback to help develop an individual's skill or they may integrate it into performance management programmes.

401(k) Plan
An employer-sponsored retirement plan that has become an expected benefit and is therefore important in attracting and retaining employees. A 401(k) plan allows employees to defer taxes as they save for retirement by placing before-tax dollars directly into an investment account. Employers also contribute to the plan tax-free, for instance by matching contributions. Some plans enable employees to direct their own investments. These plans can be expensive and complex to manage. It is common for companies to outsource all or part of their plan.

Abandonment rate
Number of incomplete transactions (or abandoned shopping carts). Can be caused by misleading ads, such as promoting low prices, but requiring customers to purchase a different or more of a product to get that price.

Above the line
Marketing and advertising through mass-media, such as television, radio, newspapers, magazines, Internet, etc., which is less personal than Below The Line Marketing. Companies usually use advertising agencies for ATL marketing.

Abram's law
Construction industry theory relating to concrete strength as determined by the ratio of water to cement.

Absenteeism policy
A policy about attendance requirements, scheduled and unscheduled time off, and measures for dealing with workplace absenteeism. Repeated absenteeism can lead to termination.
1. **Scheduled time off:** Excused absences from regular work hours scheduled in advance by an employee for such things as vacation, medical appointments, military service, jury duty, etc.
2. **Unscheduled time off:** Absence from work during regular work hours that was not scheduled in advance by the employee (e.g. sickness). Absences are generally accepted and sometimes compensated if their frequency and rationale fall within an organization's attendance policy.

Absolute advantage
One country enjoying total lower costs of production than another country (ies).

Abstract
A brief summary covering the main points of a written article or research project.

Accelerator
A company which supplies office space, marketing services, etc., in exchange for payment, to help get new companies started.

Acceptance bonus
The amount paid to an employee who agrees to perform a difficult task.

Accessibility
The extent to which a contractor's or employer's facility is readily approachable and does not inhibit the mobility of individuals with disabilities, particularly such areas as the personnel office, worksite and public areas.

Accounts
An individual's or company's financial records. Also an arrangement to keep money with a financial institution, e.g., a bank, building society, etc.

Accretion
Growth or increase in the value or amount of something.

Accrual
The accumulation of payments or benefits over time.

Acid test
A stern measure of a company's ability to pay its short term debts, in that stock is excluded from asset value. (liquid assets/current liabilities) Also referred to as the Quick Ratio.

Across the board
The involvement of, or affect on, everyone or everything in an industry or company.

Acting out
Activities engaged in by consumers during purchase decision-making, such as feeling the weight of the product, inspecting ingredients, and reading instructions. Savvy marketers must anticipate these expectations as part of the product utility.

Actuals
Real costs, sales, etc., that have occurred, rather than estimations or expectations.

Ad hoc
Created or done for a particular purpose as necessary and not planned in advance.

Ad rotation
Describes the rotation of advertisements on a web page-each time a user clicks on a different page or returns to a page they've viewed previously in the same session, a different advert appears on the screen.

Adaptation
Goods or service adapted in either product, distribution or advertising form to take account of unique conditions in any one country(ies).

Added value
Enables and justifies a profit in business.

Addendum
An added section of information in a letter or report.

Adjunct
A thing which is added or attached as a supplementary, rather than an

essential part of something larger or more important.

Administrative services only (ASO)

The hiring of a firm (usually a health care vendor) to handle certain administrative tasks. The firm does not assume any risk but merely carries out the specialized functions that the employer cannot or does not want to do. For example, an employer funds its own dental insurance claim payments but pays the ASO firm to process the claims.

Adoption curve

A graph showing the rate at which a new piece of technology is bought by people for the first time. It is based on the idea that certain people are more open for adaptation than others.

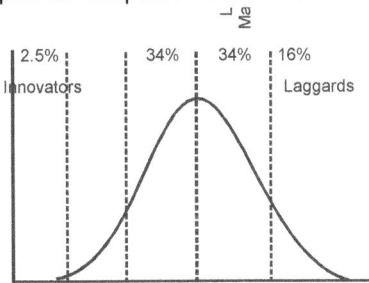

Adverse event

Term used when a volunteer in a clinical trial has a negative or unfavourable reaction to a drug, etc.

Advertising

Paid form of a non-personal communication by industry, business firms, nonprofit organizations, or individuals delivered through the various media. Advertising is persuasive and informational and is designed to influence the purchasing behavior and thought patterns of the audience. Advertising

may be used in combination with sales promotions, personal selling tactics, or publicity.

Advertising elasticity

Change in sales that result from each monetary unit spent on advertising. Formula: ("Q)/(Q)÷("A)//(A) Q is quantity sold A is ad expenditure "Q is change in quantity sold "A is change in ad expenditure Ex: Rockwell Tools leveraged ad elasticity and increased sales by 25%.

Advertising metrics

Ways and means to evaluate, compare, and contrast the effectiveness and efficiency of Internet promotions: Click-through, click-through rate (CTR), conversion rate, cost-per-click (CPC), cost-per-action (CPA), customer acquisition costs, hits, hybrid models, impressions, page view, pay per click (PPC), pay per lead (PPL), pay per sale (PPS), site stickiness, surround session, unique visitors, and website traffic.

Advertising network

Intermediary between advertisers and publishers that sells web properties (space) to advertisers. Often an efficient way to reach social media audiences.

Advertising slogan

Catchy words or phrases that help consumers remember a particular product or service. They tend to reflect the product's sustainable competitive advantage or unique selling proposition in simple 2-3 word phrases or jingles. Through repetition over time, a marketer can establish top of mind awareness and recall.

Advertising standards authority (ASA)

The UK self-regulatory body funded by the advertising industry for ensuring that all advertising adheres to ASA standards, notably not to offend or mislead people. Equivalents named the same exist in other countries.

Advertorial

An advert in a magazine or newspaper that is written like an article giving facts rather than appearing as an advertisement for a product.

Advocacy advertising

Communication aimed at espousing a point of view, usually about controversial issues. Ads can be directed at specific targets, such as political activists, media, consumer groups, government agencies, or competitors.

Affidavit

A sworn signed statement of fact used as evidence in court whose signature has been witnessed by a commissioner of oaths or other authorised officer, for example a notary. Medieval Latin for 'he has stated on oath', from affidare, meaning to trust.

Affiliate

A company or person controlled by or connected to a larger organisation. In web marketing an affiliate normally receives a commission for promoting another company's products or services.

Affiliate marketing

Using a network of partners to market a company—usually internet-based in which a company rewards or compensates an affiliate for each customer directed to it. Affiliates can include blogs, shopping sites, and comparison sites.

Affinity diagram

A tool used to organize ideas, usually generated through brainstorming, into groups of related thoughts. The emphasis is on a pre-rational, gut-fell sort of grouping, often done by the members of the group with little or no talking. Also known as the KJ method after its creator, Kawakita Jiro.

Affinity marketing

Any number of marketing activities targeted to individuals sharing common interests.

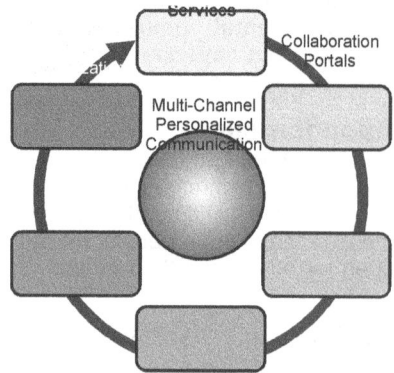

Ex: an auto accessories manufacturer targeting readers of motoring magazines.

Affirmative action

Proactive policies aimed at increasing the employment opportunities of certain groups (typically, minority men and/or women of all racial groups). Title 5, Section 503 of the Rehabilitation Act requires that affirmative action be taken in employment of persons with disabilities by Federal contractors. Affirmative action was designed to rectify past discrimination but has been controversial since its inception.

Affirmative action plan (AAP)

A written set of specific, results-oriented procedures to be followed. Intended to remedy the effects of past discrimination against or underutilization of women and minorities. The effectiveness of the plan is measured by the results it actually achieves rather than by the results intended and by the good faith efforts undertaken.

Ageism
Unfair prejudice or discrimination on the grounds of a person's age.

Agent
A channel institution which represents one or more suppliers for a fee.

Agent (insurance)
An employee who sells the products owned by the company, in contrast to a broker, who sells the insurance products of several companies.

Aggregate
A whole consisting of the combination of smaller separate elements.

Aggregate planning
The process of planning and developing the best way of producing the right amount of goods, at the right time and at the minimum cost, based on the total number of items which need to be produced, and the amount of materials, equipment and workers necessary for production.

Aggregation
Form of segmentation that assumes most consumers are alike.

Aggressive exporter
An organisation which develops clear marketing strategies for what it intends to do in a foreign markets.

Aggressive growth fund
A high risk investment fund in which shares are expected to increase in value very quickly in the hope of making large profits.

Agile development method
A type of business development which gets things moving quickly and adapts during the development, as distinct from conventional planning and project management implementation.

Agile marketing
Term used for marketers that handle/adjust to the dynamic (ever-changing) shift or change in attitudes and behavior among various target markets due to changes in the environment, technology, economy, and competition. Ex: Facebook acknowledges the value of instant messaging and videos that can be uploaded within minutes.

Agile organization
Also known as agile manufacturing, this is a term applied to an organization that has created the processes, tools, and training to enable it to respond quickly to customer needs and market changes while still controlling costs and quality.

Agio
The percentage charged by a bank for exchanging one form of currency or money, into another that is more valuable.

Agitprop
Political propaganda (published ideas designed to motivate people into certain political views or actions) typically in art, music, literature, etc., a portmanteau word combining the original Russian words agitsiya (agitation) and propoganda, where the term grew from the state department responsible for disseminating communist ideas and information to its people in the 1930s. In the west the term is more associated with publication of left-wing or socialist ideas, often targeted

against a governing right-wing authority.

Agribusinesss
Farming industry on a large corporate scale.

AIDA
Attention, Interest, Desire, Action - an early and fundamentally useful model/process for effective communications. Also called the 'hierarchy of effects' - we all buy things, and decide to change something, after passing through these four key stages.

A-list
A list of the most celebrated or sought-after companies or individuals, especially in show business and entertainment.

Alpha test
The first stage of testing a new product, especially computer software or hardware, carried out by a developer under controlled conditions.

Alternate dispute resolution (ADR)
An informal process to resolve disputes. Involved parties meet with a trained third party who assists in resolving the problem by arbitration, mediation, judicial settlement conferences, conciliation or other methods. Though usually voluntary, ADR is sometimes mandated by a judge as a first step before going to court.

Amalgamate
When two or more companies combine or unite to form one large organisation.

Ambush marketing
A covert promotional strategy used by a non-sponsoring organizations to capitalize on the popularity and prestige of its product or service by giving the false impression that it is a sponsor. Nike and Pepsi piggybacked on the atmosphere during the World Cup during which their ads gave the illusion that they were sponsors of the event, even using some of the players in their ads.

Americanization
Conformation to American standards and practices by foreigners or immigrants to the United States. This shift towards the American culture has an impact on mainstream entertainment, consumer trends, and consumer needs. With targeted marketing practices, Americanization can also take place in other countries outside of the United States.

Americans with disabilities act (ADA)
Title I of the Americans with Disabilities Act of 1990 is part of a federal law that prohibits discrimination against someone with a disability, defined as "a physical or mental impairment that substantially limits a major life activity." Disability is decided on a case-by-case basis and does not include conditions such as substance abuse. This law applies to the whole employment cycle, from application through advancement and termination.

Amortize
To gradually reduce and write off the cost of an asset in a company's accounts over a period of time.

Anchor tenant
The first and most prestigious tenant, typically a store in a shopping centre, that will attract other tenants or shoppers.

Ancillary staff

People who provide necessary support to the primary activities and work of an organization, e.g: schools, hospitals.

Annual report

The write-ups and financial statements given every year to investors and inquiring members of the public concerning a corporation's business.

Annuity

Often used to provide a pension. An annuity is a fixed regular payment payed over a number of years to a person during their lifetime.

Antediluvian

An interesting and humorous metaphorical description of something (for example a product or service or concept) that is obsolete, old-fashioned or primitive, or devised a long time ago. 'Ante' is Latin for 'before', and 'diluvian' is from Latin 'diluvium' meaning 'deluge', so the overall literal meaning is 'before the flood', being the biblical flood and Noah's Ark, etc. Antediluvian is therefore a clever way to say that something is (so old as to be) 'out of the Ark'.

Anthropology

The discovery of beliefs, motives and values through the study of a society's overt and covert behaviour.

Anthropomorphic/ anthropomorphism/ anthropomorphous

Also called personification - this refers to giving human characteristics to an non-human thing, such as an animal, or a tree, or the Sun, Moon, a god, cartoon character, etc., for dramatic, visual, metaphorical, and amusing effect, etc. It's a very very old concept. Anthropomorphic characterizations have been found on ancient scuptures dating back more than 30,000 years. The word is Greek, originally from athropos, human, and morphe, form.

Appellant

A person appealing to a higher court against a decision of a lower court or other decision-making body.

Apple box

Used in films, TV, etc. Wooden boxes of various sizes which are used to elevate actors and celebrities.

Applicant tracking system (ATS)

A software application that began as a way to electronically handle recruitment needs but has since expanded to the entire employment life cycle. Onboarding, training and succession planning capabilities now exist, for example. An ATS can be implemented on an enterprise level or small business level, depending on the size and needs of the company. Applicant Tracking Systems may also be referred to as Talent Management Systems. An ATS saves time and increases efficiency and compliance for those tasked with managing human capital.

Application service provider (ASP)

Other common terms are SaaS (software as a service), on-demand or Web-based services. A business that provides computer-based services to customers over a network, as opposed to installing the software on a company server (hosted). This is a cost-effective solution for small and medium-sized businesses, who may find it hard to keep up with the increasing costs of specialized software, distribution and upgrades. Smaller, periodic payments replace one-time lump sum pricing. The ASP can be accessed from any location via the Internet. HRmarketer.com is an example.

Appraisal
A review of performance, capability, needs, etc., typically of an employee, in which case the full term is normally 'performance appraisal'.

Arbiter
A person who settles a dispute or has the ultimate authority to decide the outcome of a matter.

Arbitrator
An independent person or body officially appointed to settle a dispute.

Archive/archives
A collection of records no longer active. Also pluralized-archives- meaning the same, and referring to the place of storage.

Area organisation
A form of international organisational structure used by highly marketing oriented organisations with stable products.

Articles of association
The document which lists the regulations which govern the running of a company, setting out the rights and duties of directors and stockholders, individually and in meetings.

Aspirational brand
A brand or product which people admire and believe is high quality, and wish to own because they think it will give them a higher social position.

Asset
A resource of money value, including cash, accounts receivable, inventory, real estate, machinery, collectibles, and securities.

Asset stripping
Buying a stricken company and selling off its assets with no thought for the future of the company or its people, customers, etc.

Assets
Anything owned by the company having a monetary value; eg, 'fixed' assets like buildings, plant and machinery, vehicles (these are not assets if rentedand not owned) and potentially including intangibles like trade marks and brand names, and 'current' assets, such as stock, debtors and cash.

Assorting
Putting together a variety of products to give a target market what it wants, as in selecting various or different item for a gift basket or first aid kit.

Attention
A momentary attractions to a stimulus, something someone senses via sight, sound, touch, smell, or taste. Attention is the starting point of the perceptual process in that attention of a stimulus will either cause someone to decide to make sense of it—or reject it.

Attitude
A person's point of view toward something (feelings, values, mores).

Attitudes and values
A predisposition towards a person or object based on cultural mores and values which is a precursor of behaviour.

Attributes data

Data that is counted in discrete units such as dollars, hours, items, and yes/no options. The alternative to attributes data is variables data, which is data that is measured on a continuous and infinite scale such as temperature or distance. Charts that use attribute data include bar charts, pie charts, Pareto charts and some control charts.

Attrition

A gradual voluntary reduction of employees (through resignation and retirement) who are not then replaced, decreasing the size of the workforce.

Attrition

The process of reducing the number of employees in an organisation by not replacing people who leave their jobs.

Auditor

A qualified person who officially examines the financial records of a company to check their accuracy.

Auteur

An artist or creative, for example a film director, whose personal style is recognizable because he/she keeps tight control over all aspects of the work.

Autocratic

Offensively self-assured or given to exercising unwarranted power. Expecting to be obeyed and not caring about the opinions and feeling of others.

AV

Anti-Virus, a common abbreviation referring to virus protection software/services for computer and internet use.

Availability

A product or service's ability to perform its intended function at a given time and under appropriate conditions. It can be expressed by the ratio operative time/total time where operative time is the time that it is functioning or ready to function.

Avant garde

New or original and often unconventional techniques, concepts, products, etc, usually associated with the arts and creative areas.

Avatar

An identity, often in cartoon form, which can be chosen from a selection or created by the person using it to represent themselves in a website chatroom, etc.

Average chart (X-bar chart)

A control chart in which the average of the subgroup, represented by the X-bar, is to determine the stability or lack thereof in the process. Average charts are usually paired with range charts or sample standard deviation charts for complete analysis.

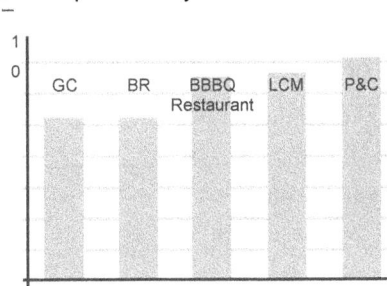

Average daily rate

In the hotel industry a calculation of the average price at which a hotel room is booked each night based on total daily revenue divided by the number of rooms sold.

B

B2b

Business to business. This refers to a commercial trading model by which a business supplies other businesses, and by implication does not generally supply consumers, i.e., domestic private customers. A B2B provider is therefore a provider of business services or products, for example: company auditors, manufacturers of industrial machinery, conference organizers, corporate hospitality, advertising agencies, trade journals, wholesalers, warehousing and logistics, management consultancies, mining, farming, industrial chemicals, papermills, etc.

B2c

Business To Consumer – Business conducted between companies and individual consumers rather than between two companies. A retailer such as Walmart is an example of a B2C company.

B2g

Businesses that sell products and services (or information) to government or government agencies. U.S. Federal Government spends approximately $530bn annually for a wide range of products and services.

Back shift

A group of workers or the period worked from late afternoon until late at night in an industry or occupation where there is also a day shift and a night shift.

Back with music

In the entertainment business, films, TV, etc., dialogue which is spoken over music.

Back-end load

A fee or commission paid by an individual when they sell their shares in an investment fund.

Background Screening / Pre-employment Screening

Testing to ensure that employers are hiring qualified and honest employees and that a prospective employee is capable of performing the functions required by the job. The screening can involve criminal background checks, verification of Social Security numbers, past addresses, age or year of birth, corporate affiliations, bankruptcies, liens, drug screening, skills assessment and behavioral assessments. If an employer outsources pre-employment screening, the federal Fair Credit Reporting Act requires that there must be a consent and disclosure form separate from an employment application.

Backscratching

Informal term for reciprocity or returning favours, as in the term 'you scratch my back and I'll scratch yours'.

Back-to-back loan
A loan in which two companies in separate countries borrow each other's money at the same time for a specific period at an agreed upon interest rate.

Backward integration
Actions taken to acquire greater control over suppliers. Ex: Starbucks formerly purchased coffee beans from a supplier in Colombia; it now operates its own farm in China to control the quality and cost of its beans.

Bait and switch
Dishonest and illegal tactic to attract potential buyers based on attractive special promotional offers (bait); then attempt to sell a more expensive product (switch).

Balance of payments
A measure of all economic transactions between one country and all other countries.

Balance sheet
The Balance Sheet is one of the three essential measurement reports for the performance and health of a company along with the Profit and Loss Account and the Cashflow Statement. The Balance Sheet is a 'snapshot' in time of who owns what in the company, and what assets and debts represent the value of the company. (It can only ever be a snapshot because the picture is always changing.) The Balance Sheet is where to look for information about short-term and long-term debts, gearing (the ratio of debt to equity), reserves, stock values (materials and finsished goods), capital assets, cash on hand, along with the value of shareholders' funds. The term 'balance sheet' is derived from the simple purpose of detailing where the money came from, and where it is now. The balance sheet equation is fundamentally: (where the money came from) Capital + Liabilities = Assets (where the money is now). Hence the term 'double entry' - for every change on one side of the balance sheet, so there must be a corresponding change on the other side - it must always balance. The Balance Sheet does not show how much profit the company is making (the P&L does this), although pervious years' retained profits will add to the company's reserves, which are shown in the balance sheet.

Balanced scorecard
A strategic planning and management system that is used to tie business activities to the vision and strategy of the organization, improve internal and external communications, and monitor performance against goals. Developed in the early 1990's by Drs. Robert Kaplan and David Norton, the balanced scorecard measure four areas of business: internal business processes, financial performance, customer knowledge, and learning and growth.

Balloon
Describes a long term loan in which there is a large final payment when the loan matures.

Bancassurance
The selling of both insurance and banking services, usually by a major bank.

Bandwidth
In computing, the amount of information that can be transmitted through a communication channel over a given period of time, usually measured in 'bits per second' (bps).

Bank loan
A loan made by a bank to an individual, company, etc., for a fixed term, to be repaid with interest.

Bank run
Lots of sudden and heavy cash withdrawals at the same time from a bank or banks, because customers believe the banks may become insolvent.

Bankers hours
A short working day, often with a long lunch break.

Bankruptcy
A term that describes the legal process governed by the U.S. bankruptcy code for companies unable to meet financial obligations.

Bar chart
A chart that compares different groups of data to each other through the use of bars that represent each group. Bar charts can be simple, in which each group of data consists of a single type of data, or grouped or stacked, in which the groups of data are broken down into internal categories.

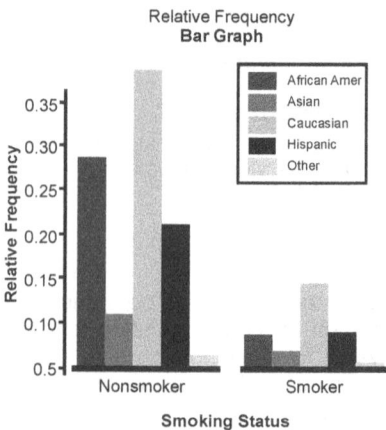

Relative Frequency
Bar Graph

Barista
A person who is a professional speciality coffee maker, for example, cappuccino, latte, espresso, etc.

Barter
Process of exchanging goods or services for other goods or services without the exchange of money. Often used by small business with limited cash flow or limited lines of credit.

Base 2
Also known as the binary system, which is the basis of computer logic. Normal counting is based on 0-9. Binary just has 0-1, which means a new column is started after two, not nine. Binary counting does not go 1, 2, 3, 4, etc. It goes 0, 1, 10, 11, 100, 101, etc. Other than for computing it's not very practical.

Base wage rate (or base rate)
The monthly salary or hourly wage paid for a job, irrespective of benefits, bonuses or overtime.

Basis trading
The difference to new york futures, either on or off.

Bathtub curve
A U-shaped graph, often long horizontally-resembling a bathtub-representing high incidence or measure at the beginning and finish (far left and far right of graph) of a life-cycle or lifetime or period, with much lower incidence over a relatively long middle period (middle of graph), for example when measuring engineering failures in a product over time, in which early development teething problems produce high failure rates, tending to reduce to lower failure rates due to uncommon random faults, with failure rates again peaking at the end of product life, due to natural

'wear and tear'/exhaustion/erosion of components and construction. A Bathtub Curve may also equate to a U-shaped graph, for example in describing a type of recession which contains a prolonged period at the lowest point, i.e., a U-shaped recession.

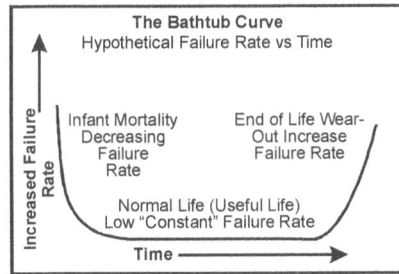

The Bathtub Curve
Hypothetical Failure Rate vs Time

Increased Failure Rate

Infant Mortality
Decreasing
Failure
Rate

End of Life Wear-
Out Increase
Failure Rate

Normal Life (Useful Life)
Low "Constant" Failure Rate

Time

Bean counter
An informal derogatory term for an accountant, especially one who is perceived or suggested to be overly concerned about expenditure detail.

Beanfeast
Also known as a beano-an annual party, dinner, or outing given by an employer for its employees.

Bear market
In the stock market a period of declining prices in which investors continue selling shares, expecting the prices to fall further.

Bear raid
The practice, in the stock market, of attempting to push the price of a stock lower by selling in large numbers and often spreading unfavourable rumours about the company concerned.

Behavioral competency
The behavior qualities and character traits of a person. These act as markers that can predict how successful a person will be at the

position he/she is applying for. Employers should determine in advance what behavioral competencies fit the position and create interview questions to find out if the candidate possesses them.

Behavioral risk management
The process of analyzing and identifying workplace behavioral issues and implementing Programmes, policies or services most suitable for correcting or eliminating various employee behavioral problems.

Behavioral targeting
Practice of targeting and ads to groups of people who exhibit similarities not only in their location, gender or age, but also in how they act and react in their online environment: tracking areas they frequently visit or subscribe to; subjects or content or shopping categories for which they have registered. Google uses behavioral targeting to direct ads to people based on the sites they have visited.

Behavioral-based interview
An interview technique used to determine whether a candidate is qualified for a position based on their past behavior. The interviewer asks the candidate for specific examples from past work experience when certain behaviors were exhibited.

Behaviorally anchored rating scale (BARS)
An appraisal that requires raters to list important dimensions of a particular job and collect information regarding the critical behaviors that distinguishes between successful and unsuccessful performance. These critical behaviors are then categorized and appointed a

numerical value used as the basis for rating performance.

Behemoth
A large and powerful organisation. (originally from Hebrew, behemoth-beast)

Bell curve
Survey/sample distribution term. 'Bell curve' is the common informal term for a graph with a large rounded peak in the middle, sloping sharply to the right and left and then tapering more gently at the extreme ends of the graph. It's a bell-shape, hence the name.

IQ Score Distribution

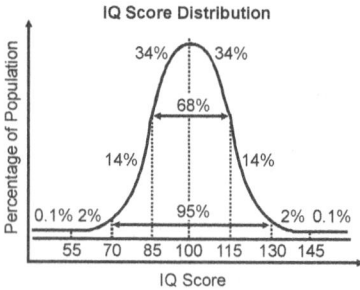

The term 'bell curve' refers also to this sort of statistical distribution, even if it is not actually graphed. Technically in probability theory, mathematics and marketing, etc., the 'bell curve' is 'normal' distribution or Gaussian distribution (after German mathematician ohann Carl Friedrich Gauss). The bell curve is very commonly exhibited in sampling and surveys, where the vast majority of results/subjects/data tend to concentrate towards the average score, with incidence of variation above and below the average (shown graphically right and left) being roughly equal to each other, and much less than the incidence/results towards the average and majority. Business people often refer to a 'bell curve' when anticipating/explaining a situation where the vast majority of

members of an audience or market are very similar, and only a very small minority is outside of the 'norm' or average. This terminology is helpful in emphasizing the needs or tendencies of the big majority, and avoiding distraction by or over-estimating the effect of minority interests/needs, which can cause projects to be distorted unnecessarily. There is a broad correlation between the notion of a 'bell curve' and Pareto theory, also known as the '80-20 Rule', i.e., both concepts highlight the significance of concentration and distribution when assessing opportunity, risk, effectiveness, and the targeting of communications, resources, etc.

Bells and whistles
Extra features added often more for show than function, especially on computers, cameras, etc., to make the product more attractive to buyers.

Below the line
BTL. Describes marketing which has a short-term duration, such as non-media advertising, direct-mail, e-mail, exhibitions, incentives, brochures, etc., which is targeted directly at the consumer/customer. Often used by companies on a limited budget.

Bench warrant
An order issued by a judge for an absent defendent to be arrested and brought before a court.

Benchmark job
A job commonly found in the workforce for which pay and other relevant data are readily available. Benchmark jobs are used to make pay comparisons and job evaluations.

Benchmarking
A technique using specific standards to make comparisons between

different organizations or different segments of the organizations, with the intent of improving a product or service.

Benefit

A desirable attribute of a good or service, which customer<u>s</u> perceives that they will get frompurchasing and consuming/using it. Whereas vendors sell features ("a high speed 1/2" drill bit with tungsten-carbide tip"), buyers seek the benefit (a 1/2" hole).

Benefit principle

A taxation principle which states that those who benefit more from government expenditure, financed by taxes, should pay more tax for the product or service than those who benefit less.

Benefit segmentation

Use of data to define (often narrow) target market segments according to similarities or differences in their unmet needs.

Benefits (benefits package)

Benefits are a form of compensation paid by employers to employees over and above the amount of pay specified as a base salary or hourly rate of pay. Benefits are a portion of a total compensation package for employees.

Benefits administration

Software that helps companies manage and track employee participation in benefits Programmes such as healthcare, flexible spending accounts, pension plans, etc. This software helps automate and streamline the complex and otherwise time-consuming tasks of benefits administration.

Benefits realisation

Also Benefits Realisation Management, or if you prefer the US

English it would be Benefits Realization. This refers to the translation of projects into real and perceived positive effects, seemingly a concept devised originally in the field of IT and ICT (Information and Communications Technology) project management, where projects are notoriously difficult to manage successfully and generate clear end-user appreciation.

BEP

Break even point – sales quantity at which the firm's total cost will equal its total revenue.

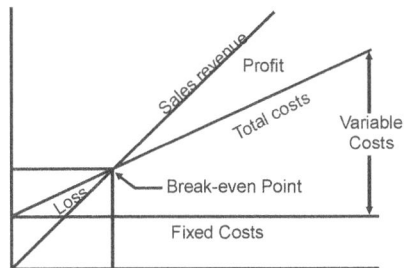

Bereavement leave

Paid or unpaid time off following the death of an employee's relative or friend. This time, generally ranging from one to three days, is given so that the employee can make arrangements, attend the funeral and attend to other matters related to the deceased. Many organizations are flexible in terms of how much time an employee takes off.

Best boy

The person on film sets, TV, etc., who is the assistant to the electrician.

Beta

The indicator used by *Value Line* to measure a stock's risk relative to the market, in this case the NYSE Index. The market's beta is always 1.0 (Based on past statistical records, a beta higher than 1.0 indicates that when the market rises, the stock will rise to a greater extent than that of the market; likewise, when the market falls, the stock will fall to a greater extent. A beta lower than 1.0 indicates that the stock will usually change to a lesser extent than that of the market. The higher the beta, the greater the investment risk.).

Beta test
The second test of a product, such as computer hardware, software, or even a website, under actual usage conditions, before the final version is used by or sold to the public.

Bid bond
A sum agreed to be paid by a company that wins a contract if the work is not carried out.

Bid price
The price one is willing to pay for a security.

Big bang
Occurred (UK) on 27th October 1986, when major technology changes took place on the London Stock Exchange chiefly to replace manual systems with electronic processes.

Bilateral
Agreement or involvement or action by two parties, people, companies, countries, etc.

Bill of lading
The receipt given by the shipping company to the shipper for goods accepted for carriage by sea. (as opposed to an airway bill of lading for goods carried by air).

Bills of exchange
An unconditional order in writing, addressed by one person (drawer) to another (drawee), signed by the person giving it (drawer), requiring the person to whom it is addressed (drawee) to pay on demand, at a fixed or determinable future date, a sum in money to, or to the order of, a specific person (payee) or to bearer.

Biometrics
The biological identification of human features, such as eyes, voices and hands, increasingly used to identify individuals, e.g., in laptop computers, entry systems and passports.

Bit part
In films and TV, a supporting actor who has at least one line of dialogue, and who is usually listed in the credits.

Black economy
Money earned in private cash transactions, which is untraceable, and therefore untaxable.

Black knight
A company which makes a hostile takeover bid for another company that does not want to be bought.

Black market (Underground economy)
Business transactions between sellers and buyers of goods or services that are often not recorded on a financial statement. Thus, an illegal action. Ex: The recent release of Apple's iPhone5 motivated some Chinese to purchase the new products and travel to China where they were resold on the street for hundreds more than the U.S. price.

Black swan/black swan theory
A 'black swan' refers to a random unpredictable and highly influential event (upon economics, society, politics, life, etc) whose potential/ significance is generally only appreciated after it has happened,

and even then is commonly rationalized (by commentators and leaders, etc) to have been predictable and part of a predictable pattern of some sort, which actually is not so, or it would have been. The tendency for many people to be in denial as to the true nature of black swan event unpredictability and impact is an important part of the black swan theory itself. Examples of 'black swans' are events such as the September 11 attacks on the US by al-Qaeda; the 1986 Chernobyl disaster; and the 2008 global financial/credit collapse. Black swans can instead be of a more positive nature, for example, the invention of the internet, or the fall of the Berlin Wall. The black swan term/theory was introduced by Nassim Taleb, a highly regarded Lebanese-American professor, author and theorist, in his best-selling 2001 book Fooled by Randomness: The Hidden Role of Chance in Life and in the Markets, and reinforced by his follow-up 2007 best seller The Black Swan: The Impact of the Highly Improbable. The 'black swan' metaphor alludes to both to the rareness of black swans, and to early beliefs that the creatures did not exist - which relates to general attitudes towards the real nature of 'black swan' events. The word 'black' also suggests negative consequences, which commonly result from black swan events. 'Grey swan' is a related expression, also coined by Nassim Taleb in his books, which refers to a predicted or known event which has uncertain outcomes.

Blamestorming

Portmanteau term contrived from Brainstorming and Blame, referring to meetings or discussions seeking to allocate responsibility for a failure or disaster. Popularised in the late 1990s by viral emails which listed amusing office terminology.

Blatherskite

A person who talks at great length without saying anything useful. Originally a Scottish 16thC expression adopted into American slang from the song Maggie Lauder during the US War of Independence.

Blended workforce

A workforce is comprised of permanent full-time, part-time, temporary employees and independent contractors.

Blind test

Research method in which people are asked to try a number of similar products which are not identified by brand name, to decide which product is the best.

Blind trial

A trial, with two groups of people, to test the effect of a new product, especially in medicine. One group is given the real product while the other group is given a placebo or 'sugar pill', which does not contain any medication.

Bloatware

In computing, software that needs so much computer memory that it takes a long time to load and therefore does not function properly.

Blog

A Web log written for and posted to the Internet using such software as www.blogger.com. Readers access the blog through the Web (e.g., http://hrmarketer.blogspot.com/) or subscribe to the blog's RSS (Really Simple Syndication) feed and receive alerts when there is a new posting. Blogs are becoming increasingly important to HR suppliers in order to increase their company's visibility, communicate with customers, and promote their products or services to establish themselves as thought leaders.

Blue chip
On the stock market, shares of a large company with a good reputation, whose value and dividends are considered to be safe and reliable.

Blue law
In the US, a law which regulates and limits activities for religious reasons, such as Sunday working or shopping.

Blue ocean strategy
Creating new market space that attempts to make a competitor irrelevant.

Blue-sky law
In the US, a law designed to protect the public from buying fraudulent securities.

Blue-sky thinking
Open-minded, original and creative thinking, not restricted by convention.

Bluetooth
Wireless technology which allows data to be transferred over short distances between laptop computers, mobile phones, digital cameras, etc.

Bodhisattva
From Buddhism, a person who seeks enlightenment for the good of, and motivated by a compassion for, other people. In Western thinking we could see this to be similar to Maslow's notion of 'trancendence' in the pursuit of self-actualization, notably helping others to self-actualize. Not an easy concept to explain; in the spectrum of human behaviour it's about as far away that can be imagined from the pursuit of a merchant banker's bonus or the Presidency of Europe, if you'll forgive the clichés.

Boilerplate
A section of standard text, especially a contract clause, inserted into legal documents, or instead increasingly referring to a standard section of code inserted into computer Programmes or other digital applications. The main sense of the 'boilerplate' meaning is that the text/code is already existing and available to use, is quite fixed, needing little or no alteration, and by implication has a proven and trusted validity or suitability, and is therefore an aid to saving effort and cost compared with originating an equivalent clause or section of code from nothing. Usage and origins of the term boilerplate have become varied and confused, which perhaps helped popularize the term itself because this has made its meanings more flexible and widely applicable. The term 'boiler plate' or 'boiler-plate' seems to have two main original meanings: Firstly, plates of pre-cut/pre-formed metal used in constructing industrial boilers, and scondly, a much smaller plate or metal label attached to a boiler to identify the maker and other important details about the boiler. This latter sense is more iconically meaningful because of the visibility and imagery of steam engines and old industrial machinery. There is also a theory (not especially well-proven) that the term was initially applied metaphorically in traditional printing to the occasional use of hard durable steel printing plates for repeatedly used text/graphic sections, to save time and wear compared with the 'hot metal' and related methods of assembling printing plates from individual print blocks made from much softer metal.

Bold-faced names
Informal term for celebrities, used mostly in the USA.

Bond
The financial meaning of a bond is normally a debt/investment instrument issued by a company or country for a period of more than a year, with fixed interest rates and a firm and full repayment date. Typically a bond will pay a stipulated rate of interest at fixed times, and the debt is repaid at a specified time, i.e., the investor is guaranteed to be repaid the amount loaned/invested in full. More loosely the word bond can refer to a mortgage in some parts of the world, for example South Africa. A bond may also refer to a legal deed or agreement by which one person or party is bound to make payments to another; or to an insurance contract; or (notably in the US) to a sum of money paid as bail. The specific and more general meanings of bond logically derive from the older and original sense of bond, meaning fasten together, or the tie/festening itself.

Bonded warehouse
A warehouse in which imported goods are stored under bond, until the import taxes are paid on them.

Bonus
An extra sum of money given to an employee on top of their salary, often for achieving targets.

Bonus culture
Term used when companies give their executives huge bonuses in addition to their large salaries, even if their performance has been poor, especially leaders of financial institutions.

Book depreciation
A decrease or loss in value of a company's assets, as recorded in the company's finances.

Book value per share
The accounting value of a share of common stock, determined by dividing the company's net worth by the number of shares that are circulating.

Bookkeeping
The recording of a business's transactions, such as sales, purchases, payments, income, etc.

Boomlet
A small period of rapid growth in trade and economic activity.

Bootstrapping
Starting a business from scratch and building it up with minimum outside investment.

Bossnapping
Believed to have started in France, the unlawful imprisonment of a boss, in the offices of a company or on the site of a corporation, by employees who are protesting against redundancy, closure of the company, etc.

Bottom fishing
Buying the cheapest investments available which are unlikely to fall much further in value.

Bounce
In economics a bounce is a small quick partial recovery of the economy after a recession, which may subsequently continue upwards in growth, or plateau neither growing or contracting, or descend back into recession.

Bounce rate
Number of visitors to an e-commerce website. Tells web owners if visitors

are finding what they want and whether they're sufficiently interested to click for more content. A bounce occurs when a web site visitor only views a single page on a website, that is, the visitor leaves a site without visiting any other pages before a specified session-timeout occurs. There is no industry standard minimum or maximum time by which a visitor must leave in order for a bounce to occur. Rather, this is determined by the session timeout of the analytics tracking software.

Bounty hunter
In the US, someone who pursues criminals or fugitives and brings them to the police in exchange for a monetary reward.

Boutique
A small shop or outlet typically selling fashionable and expensive items such as clothing. The term 'boutique' is also now increasingly applied as a descriptive word in various other sectors and products to denote an outlet/supplier of small-scale, highly individual, bohemian, quirky, or hand-made quality, for example Boutique Hotels, below.

Boutique hotel
A small individual hotel, commonly within a historic building, with luxurious stylish themed and furnished rooms, typically independently owned.

Bracket creep
Slowly moving into a higher tax bracket with small pay increases over a period of time.

Brain drain
The loss of highly skilled people to another region, country or industry, where they can work in a better environment and/or earn more money.

Brainstorming
A tool used to encourage creative thinking and new ideas. A group formulates and records as many ideas as possible concerning a certain subject, regardless of the content of the ideas. No discussion, evaluation, or criticism of ideas is allowed until the brainstorming session is complete.

Brand
A unique design, sign, symbol, words, or a combination of these, employed in creating animage that identifies a product and differentiates or positions it from competitors. Over time, this image becomes associated with a level of credibility, quality, and satisfaction in consumers' minds. Thus brands stand for certain benefits and value. Legal name for a brand is trademark and, when it identifies or represents a firm, it is called a brand name.

Brand
A unique identifying symbol, trademark, company name, etc., which enables a buyer to distinguish a product or service from its competitors.

Brand architecture
Method by which a marketer can organize and manage various brands (often terms "sub brands"). Ex: In addition to Coke's various flavored colas, it also owns Sprite and Odwalla.

Brand association
Something or someone which make people think of a particular product.

Brand equity
Value of brand's overall strength in the market as measured in loyalty (those who will not switch).

26

Brand licensing

Process of creating and managing contracts between brand owners and individuals (often middlemen such as wholesalers and retailers) who wish to use the brand in connection with their product or service for a fixed period of time, or within a defined marketing territory.

Brand loyalty

When a consumer repeatedly buys a particular brand of product and is reluctant to switch to another brand.

Brand positioning

A distinctive position of careful manipulation of the marketing mix so that a brand adopts to ensure that its target market can set the brand apart from competitors. Ex: Loreal's original USP: "Costs more, but you're worth it," using a higher price point to connote quality.

Branded entertainment

Blending or exposure of products into various TV, movie, or web entertainment Programmes/sites. Ex: TV show 30 Rock poked fun at product placement, such as Outback Steakhouse.

Branding

Promoting a product or service by identifying and then marketing its key differentiators from competitors. The differentiator/s often inspire the name, phrase or logo for which the product or service becomes known.

Bread and Butter

The main source of income of a company or an individual.

Break even

To make enough money to cover costs. In business, the point at which sales equals costs. To make neither a profit or loss.

Breakthrough thinking

A management technique which emphasizes the development of new, radical approaches to traditional constraints, as opposed to incremental or minor changes in thought that build on the original approach.

Bridging/Bridging loan/ Bridge

A short term loan, normally at high rates of interest calculated daily, which 'bridges' a period when funds are unavailable, typically when payment has to be made before finance can be released from elsewhere to cover the transaction.

Brinkmanship

The practice of pursuing a tactic or method to the point of danger or damage, typically employed in competitive situations in which it is felt that the tactic will unsettle or cause the withdrawal of the adversary/ies. Dervies from the word brink, meaning the edge of a cliff or other dangerously high point.

British standards institution

BSI. An organisation which sets out formal guidelines to help businesses, etc., produce or perform more efficiently and safely. The BSI operates in more than 25 countries, and represent UK interests in other organisations, such as the ISO - International Organisation For Standardization.

Broadbanding

A pay structure that exchanges a large number of narrow salary ranges for a smaller number of broader salary ranges. This type of pay structure encourages the development of broad employee skills and growth while reducing the opportunity for promotion.

Broker

A channel institution which puts a specific buyer(s) and seller(s) in contact with one another in one or more commodity(ies) or service(s) with a view to achieving a sale or benefit. In general a broker is an independent agent used extensively in some industries. A broker's prime responsibility is to bring sellers and buyers together and thus a broker is the third-person facilitator between a buyer and a seller. An example would be a real estate broker who facilitates the sale of a property.

B-roll

Promotional tactic designed to enhance and increase exposure for a marketer's product or service. Video clips are often provided to media outlets (TV, satellite, Internet news sources) for use when covering stories or events. This can also include photos (screenshots), used as background images as the newscaster is reading the story.

Brown goods

Household electrical entertainment appliances such as televisions, radios and music systems.

Brownfield

Previously developed land, either commercial or industrial, which has been cleared for redevelopment.

Brown-noser

Insulting slang term for a sychophant, originally 1930s US military slang (brown-nose). Brown-nosing describes crawling or creeping to please a boss; an amusingly disturbing interpretation of various expressions which juxtapose the head of the follower with the backside of the boss, as in the rude slang metaphors: kissing arse/ass, arse-licking, bum-licker, etc.

Brussels nomenclature

An international convention aimed at grouping articles, mainly according to their material composition, into a simplified classification system for tariff administration.

Bubble economy

An unstable boom when the economy experiences an unusually rapid growth, with rising share prices and increased employment.

Budget

In a financial planning context the word 'budget' (as a noun) strictly speaking means an amount of money that is planned to spend on a particularly activity or resource, usually over a trading year, although budgets apply to shorter and longer periods. An overall organizational plan therefore contains the budgets within it for all the different departments and costs held by them. The verb 'to budget' means to calculate and set a budget, although in a looser context it also means to be careful with money and find reductions (effectively by setting a lower budgeted level of expenditure). The word budget is also more loosely used by many people to mean the whole plan. In which context a budget means the same as a plan. For example in the UK the Government's annual plan is called 'The Budget'. A 'forecast' in certain contexts means the same as a budget - either a planned individual activity/resource cost, or a whole business/corporate/organizational plan. A 'forecast' more commonly (and precisely in my view) means a prediction of performance - costs and/or revenues, or other data such as headcount, percentage performance, etc., especially when the 'forecast' is made during the trading period, and normally after the plan or 'budget' has been approved. In simple terms: budget = plan or a cost element within a plan; forecast = updated budget or plan. The verb forms are also used, meaning the act of calculating the budget or forecast.

Built to flip
Companies which have been sold soon after they have been created, so that money can be made quickly.

Bull market
On the Stock Market, a prolonged period in which share prices are rising and investors are buying.

Bullet point
A symbol, e.g. a dot or a square, printed at the beginning of each item on a list.

Bullying (workplace bullying)
Workplace bullying is "repeated, health-harming mistreatment, verbal abuse, or conduct which is threatening, humiliating, intimidating, or sabotage that interferes with work, or some combination of the three."

Bumping
Giving long-standing employees whose positions are to be eliminated the option of taking other positions within the company that they are qualified for and that are currently held by employees with less seniority.

Bundling
Combining products as a package, often to introduce other products or services to the customer. Ex: AT&T offers discounts for customers by combining 2 or more of the following

services; cable television, home phone service, wireless phone service, and internet service.

Business angel
Also known as Private Investor. A, usually wealthy, individual who invests money in developing (often high risk) companies, and who provides their advice, skills, knowledge and contacts in return for an equity share of the business.

Business continuity planning
Broadly defined as a management process that seeks to identify potential threats and impacts to the organization, and provide a strategic and operational framework for ensuring the organization is able to withstand any disruption, interruption, or loss to normal business functions or operation.

Business name
These are a very vague terms indeed. Precise interpretation may depend on the actual legal definitions of these terms in the territory/state/country concerned. And also the way a business perceives and interprets the terms, and whether they fill in the forms/checkboxes correctly. Generally business names and trade/trading names may be registered and licensed. A lot depends on the interpretation of the term 'Business name'. Business name can refer to a trade/trading name, or also could refer to the the over-arching or parent or holding company, which is ultimately responsible for a trade/trading name within or of the business. A trade name is normally a division or branded operation/service, or product brand, within/of a (legally titled) business, but the terms are very broad and it's difficult to be specific because

circumstances and legal interpretations vary. Be careful to avoid applying a strict definition to such loose terms and certainly if serious implications stem from interpretation then seek expert local clarification.

Business plan
A written document which sets out a business's plans and objectives, and how it will achieve them, e.g. by marketing, development, production, etc.

Business process outsourcing (BPO)
The managing of an organizations business applications by a technology vendor.

Business process redesign or Reengineering
A management method which stresses the fundamental rethinking of processes, questioning all assumptions, in an effort to streamline organizations, and to focus on adding value in core processes.

Button ad
A small advertisement on a website, typically measuring 120 x 90 pixels.

Buy and sell orders
An intent to buy or sell a security.

Buy-and-hold
A strategy in which the stock portion of one's portfolio is fully invested, including dividends reinvestments, at all times.

Buy-in
Purchase of a company where outside investors buy more than 50% of the shares, so they can take over the company.

Buzz marketing
A viral marketing technique that attempts to make each encounter with a "prospect" appear to be a personal, spontaneous interaction instead of an obvious marketing pitch. For example, the advertiser reveals information about their new product to a few opinion leaders within their target audience. In theory, these opinion leaders then talk about your product with their peers, thus beginning a word-of-mouth campaign where other buyers are flattered to be included in the group of those "in the know". A typical buzz marketing campaigns is initiated in chat rooms, where marketing representatives assume an identity appropriate to their target audience and pitch their product.

Buzzword
A word or phrase which has become fashionable or popular, or sounds technical or important and is used to impress people.

C

CE mark
Conformite Europeenne (European Conformity). A symbol on many products sold in the European Union indicating that they have met health, safety and/or environmental requirements, ensuring consumer and workplace safety.

CIF
A contract of sale "cost, insurance freight" of the documents of title, not the goods, whereby the buyer is under an obligation to pay against the shipping documents irrespective of the arrival of the goods.

Cafeteria plan
A plan in which an employer offers employees a variety of different benefits. The employee is able to choose which benefits would fit their individual needs. Examples of benefits offered in the cafeteria include group-term life insurance, dental insurance, disability and accident insurance, and reimbursement of healthcare expenses.

Calculated risk
A risk which has been undertaken after careful consideration has been given to the likely outcome.

Call account
A bank account, which usually pays a higher rate of interest, from which investors can make instant withdrawals.

Call option
The right given a buyer to buy stock at a specified price within a certain time period.

Callable
Usually applies to bonds or convertible securities which can be bought back, at an agreed price, before maturity, by the company or government which sold them.

Callable bond
A bond that can be officially repaid by the issuer prior to .its maturity date (Out of courtesy, a premium is usually paid when the bond is repaid.)

Cannibalization
Occasions when a new product will take market share away from an older brand, as in the addition of a diet soda product to a previously existing brand line of sodas. The new diet soda will compete with and perhaps eat away at the profits of the previously existing products. Cannibalization may also be said to occur when product sales fall at a particular sales outlet or set of retail outlets as the result of the opening of a new store, because sales at the new outlet are eating away at sales at the older ones.

CAN-SPAM Act (Controlling the Assault of Non-Solicited Pornography and Marketing Act)

Congressional legislation that regulates commercial emails (i.e. commercial advertisement or promotion) and sets clearly defined opt-out standards. Any billing, warranties, product updates or customer service information is not included in this act. E-mail newsletters that are not considered advertisements are also exempt.

Cap and collar

The upper and lower limits of interest rates on a loan, usually fixed for a specific period of time.

Capital

The net worth of a business, including assets, cash, property, etc., which exceeds its liabilities (debts). The amount of money invested in a business to generate income.

Capital allowance

Money spent by a company on fixed assets, such as buildings, vehicles, machinery, which is deducted from its profits before tax is calculated.

Capital employed

The value of all resources available to the company, typically comprising share capital, retained profits and reserves, long-term loans and deferred taxation. Viewed from the other side of the balance sheet, capital employed comprises fixed assets, investments and the net investment in working capital (current assets less current liabilities). In other words: the total long-term funds invested in or lent to the business and used by it in carrying out its operations.

Capital flight

The sudden movement of money from one country or investment to another in order to reduce risk, such as high inflation, or to increase profit.

Capital gain

An increase from the purchase price to the selling price of common stock or any other capital asset; profit from the sale of investments or property (A capital gain that persists for one year or less is called a short-term capital gain. Likewise, one that persists for more than one year is called a long-term capital gain.)

Capital gains tax

Tax payable on profit made on the sale of certain types of assets by a company or individual.

Capital loss

A decrease from the purchase price to the selling price of common stock or any other capital asset; a loss from the sale of investments or property.

Capital outlay

Money which is spent for the acquisition of assets, such as land, buildings, vehicles, machinery.

Capitalization issue

When a company converts its spare profits into shares, which are then distributed to existing shareholders in proportion to the amount of shares they already hold.

Capitated pricing

Vendors deliver contracted services for a set amount of money per employee per month. This can be a risky strategy for vendors whose profitability is directly tied to how much the services are or are not used (e.g., EAPs).

Capitialism

When an economic system of a country is controlled and profited by private individuals and corporations, rather than the government.

Capped-rate

Interest rate, usually on a loan, which cannot rise above the upper set level but can vary beneath this level.

Caption

Usually appears in the form of text added to help explain the features or benefits that accompany an illustration or photograph in an advertisement.

Carbon credit

Allows the right to emit a measured amount of harmful gases, such as carbon dioxide, into the air, and can be traded between businesses and countries.

Care mapping

Medical procedure for a particular diagnosis in a diagrammatic form that includes key decision points used to coordinate care and instruct patient.

Carey street

To be heavily in debt or bankrupt. Originates from Carey Street in London where the bankruptcy court was situated.

Carload

A shipment of goods which, typically by weight, qualifies for a lower shipping rate. The term 'Less than carload' refers to a shipment which is below the given size/weight necessary to qualify for such a rate. The term originated from USA railway freight car transportation and also applies to other methods of freight transport, notably shipping containers, hence similar terms containerload and 'less than containerload'.

Carnet

An international official permit which allows you to take certain goods, e.g. for display or demonstration, into another country, duty free, for a specific period-usually 12 months.

Carpet bomb

To send an advertisement to a large number of people by e-mail or onto their computer screens.

Carrier

A vendor in the employee benefits space. More commonly used in reference to health care. Carriers (e.g., Met Life, Blue Cross, Aetna, etc.) sell their products through Brokers & Consultants, but may also sell to an employer directly.

Cartel

A group of separate companies or nations which together agree to control prices and not compete against each other. Also known as a Price Ring.

Carve-out

The elimination of coverage of a specific category of benefit services (e.g. vision care, mental health/ psychological services, or prescription drugs). The employer opts out of certain services with one vendor and contracts another to deliver them.

Cash call

A request by a company to its shareholders to invest more money.

Cash cow

A steady dependable source of income which provides money for the rest of a business.

Cash flow forecast

Also called Cash Flow Projection. An estimate of the amounts of cash outgoings and incomings of a company over a specific time period, usually one year.

Cash flow per share

Earnings after taxes and depreciation, divided by the number of a firm's shares.

Cashflow

The movement of cash in and out of a business from day-to-day direct trading and other non-trading or indirect effects, such as capital expenditure, tax and dividend payments.

Cashflow statement

One of the three essential reporting and measurement systems for any company. The cashflow statement provides a third perspective alongside the Profit and Loss account and Balance Sheet. The Cashflow statement shows the movement and availability of cash through and to the business over a given period, certainly for a trading year, and often also monthly and cumulatively. The availability of cash in a company that is necessary to meet payments to suppliers, staff and other creditors is essential for any business to survive, and so the reliable forecasting and reporting of cash movement and availability is crucial.

Casting vote

The deciding vote cast by the presiding officer to resolve a deadlock when there are an equal number of votes on both sides.

Casual employment

The practice of hiring employees on an as-needed basis, either as a replacement for permanent full-time employees who are out on short and long-term absences or to meet employer's additional staffing needs during peak business periods.

Catch-22

Much misused expression, it refers properly only to a problem whose solution is inherently self-defeating. Wrongly it is used to describe any insurmountable or difficult problem.

Category killer

Large companies that put smaller and less efficient competing companies out of business.

Cattle call

Term used in the entertainment industry for a large number of actors, etc., who are all auditioning for the same job.

Cause & effect diagram

A tool used to analyze all factors (causes) that contribute to a given situation or occurrence (effect) by breaking down main causes into smaller and smaller sub-causes. It is also known as the Ishikawa or the fishbone diagram.

Cause-related marketing

Joint funding and promotional strategy in which a percentage of a firm's sales are linked to a charity or other public cause. Unlike philanthropy, money spent in cause-related marketing is considered an expense and is often expected to show a return.

Caveat emptor

When the buyer takes the risks and is responsible for checking the condition or quality of the item purchased.

Central counterparty

Acts on behalf of both parties in a transaction, so that the buyer and seller do not have to deal with each other directly.

Central reservation system (CRS)
A computer database system used by a chain of hotels (and other services providers) enabling availability and rates to be monitored and bookings to be made.

Certificate of deposit (CD)
An interest-bearing bank receipt for a specified amount of money (CD's usually mature between three months and three years. The interest rate depends on the amount of money and length of time of the deposit.).

Chain of command
A system in a business, or in the military, in which authority is wielded and delegated from top management down through every level of employee. In a chain of command instructions flow downwards and accountability flows upwards.

Chamber of commerce
A group of business owners in a town or city who form a network to promote local business.

Change management
A deliberate approach for transitioning individuals or organizations from one state to another in order to manage and monitor the change. Change management can be conducted on a continuous basis, on a regular schedule (such as an annual review), or when deemed necessary on a Programme-by-Programme basis.

Channel of distribution
Also known as Distribution Channel. A means of distributing a product from the manufacturer to the customer/end user via warehouses, wholesalers, retailers, etc.

Channels
Any series of firms or individuals that participate in the movement/flow of goods and services from producer to final user.

Characteristic
Distinguishing feature or attribute of an item, person, or phenomenon that usually falls into either a physical, functional, or operational category.

Check sheet
A customized form used to record data. Usually, it is used to record how often some activity occurs.

Check the gate
A term used in the film industry after a shot is taken on a film set. The gate, or opening in front of the camera, is checked to make sure that there is no dirt, hair, etc., present.

Checklist
A list of important steps that must take place in a process or any other activity. A list of things to do.

Churn rate
Rate of customers lost (stopped using the service) over a specific period of time, often over the course of a year. Used to compare against new customers gained.

Clapper boy
On a film or TV set, the person who holds the clapperboard (which has information on it, for example film title, shot number, etc) in front of the camera for about one second at the start of each shot after the camera starts rolling.

Class a spot
In the media, commercials which are run on a prime time network.

Class action
A lawsuit in which one person makes a claim and sues on behalf of a large group of people who have similar legal claims, usually against a company or organisation.

Clicklexia
Ironic computing slang for a user's tendency to double-click on items when a single click is required, often causing the window or utility to open twice.

Clicks and mortar
Also known as Clicks and Bricks. Refers to businesses which trade on the Internet as well as having traditional retail outlets, such as shops.

Clickstream
A record of an internet user, including every web site and web page which have been visited, and e-mails sent and received.

Click-through
When a person clicks on an advertisement on a web page which takes them to the advertisers website.

Clinical practice guidelines
A general term for statements of accepted medical procedure for a particular diagnosis.

Clip-art
Ready made pictures of computerised graphic art which can be copied by computer users to add to their own documents.

Close company
In the UK, a company which is controlled by five or less directors.

Cluster analysis
A technique for grouping similarities or differences between a set of objects or persons.

Clusters
Customer profiles based on lifestyle, demographic, shopping behavior, or appetite for fashion. Example: Ready-to-eat meals may be heavily influenced by the ethnic make-up of a store's shoppers, while beer, wine, and spirits categories in the same store may be influenced predominantly by the shopper's income level and education.

CMSA
Consolidated Metropolitan Statistical Area - (adjacent to MSA/PMSA with 1 million population).

Coaching
A method of training an individual or group in order to develop skills or overcome a performance problem. Coaching can be between a manager and a subordinate or an outside professional coach and one or more individuals. There are many coaching methods and models, but close observation, accountability and feedback on progress and performance are usually included.

Co-branding
An agreement between two brands to work together in marketing a new product, such as Dreyer's Ice Cream flavored with Baby Ruth candy pieces (promoting both brands on the label).

Code-sharing
An arrangement between different airlines in which they all agree to carry passengers on the same flight using their own flight numbers.

Co-employment
The relationship between a Professional Employer Organization (PEO), or employee leasing firm and an employer, based on a contractual sharing of liability and responsibility for employees.

Coercion
Forcing someone, by some method or other, to do something or abstain from doing something against their will.

Cognitive ability testing
A testing instrument used during the selection process in order to measure the candidate's learning and reasoning abilities.

Collective bargaining
One or more unions meeting with representatives from an organization to negotiate labour contracts.

Combined ratio
In insurance, a way of measuring how much profit has been made by comparing the amount of money received from customers to the amount paid out in claims and expenses.

Commercial monopoly
The control of a commodity or service by one provider in a particular market, virtually eliminating competition.

Commercial paper
An unsecured and unregistered short-term agreement in which organizations can borrow money from investors who cannot take the assets from the organization if the loan is not repaid.

Commercialization
Stage in product development process where the decision to order full-scaleproduction and launch is made. The act of exchange, buying, selling of a commodity on a large scale for profit. This also describes the flow of goods and services from producer to consumer.

Commission
A broker's fee is given for assisting in buying or selling securities.

Commission
In finance, a payment based on percentage of transaction value, according to the local interpretation of value (e.g., based on total revenue, or gross profit, etc).

Commission broker
A person who buys and sells shares, bonds, etc., on a commission basis on behalf of their clients.

Commoditization
When mature industries, slowing innovation, excessive supply, or fickle price-conscious consumers push margins to the floor. Often occurring when products lack differentiation or strong brand identities.

Common causes
Inherent causes of variation in a process. They are typical of the process, not unexpected. That is not to say that they must be tolerated; on the contrary, once special causes of variation are largely removed, a focus on removing common causes of variation can pay big dividends.

Common stock
Shares in a company that represent part ownership of that company.

Companies house
A government agency in the UK which is responsible for collecting and storing information about limited companies. The companies must file annual accounts or face penalties.

Comparative advantage
One country enjoying a lower production ratio (input to outputs) than another country under total specialisation.

Comparative advertising
Promotional messaging in which there is specific mention or presentation of

competing brands, and a comparison is made or implied. Cellular companies often compare their features or advantages, as in this example of Verizon Wireless using a U.S. map to show 5 times more coverage than AT&T for its 3G network.

Comparative analysis
Comparing the same set of statistics within a category of one country with another for the purpose of estimating potential demand.

Compensation
Pay structures within an organization. It can be linked to employee appraisal. Compensation is effectively managed if performance is measured adequately.

Compensation fund
A fund set up by a company or organisation from which to pay people who have suffered loss or hardship which has been caused employees or members of the company or organisation.

Compensatory time-off plan
The practice of giving employees paid time off that can be used in the future in lieu of paying them overtime for hours worked in excess of 40 per week. While an acceptable practice in the public sector, the FLSA places very strict limitations on the use of compensatory time off for private sector employers.

Competency modeling
A set of descriptions that identify the skills, knowledge, and behaviors needed to effectively perform in an organization. Competency models assist in clarifying job and work expectations, maximizing productivity, and aligning behavior with organizational strategy.

Competency-based pay
Competency-based pay, alternately known as skill-based and knowledge-based pay, determines compensation by the type, breadth and depth of skills that employees gain and use in their positions.

Competition
A product, organisation or individual, in either the same or another category which can be directly substituted one for the other in fulfilling the same needs or wants.

Competition law
Known as Antitrust law in the US, regulates fair competition between companies, including the control of monopolies and cartels.

Competitive advantage
In the context of Human Resources, competitive advantage refers to the quality of the employees, as a competing organization's systems and processes can be copied but not its people. All other things being equal among competing companies, it is the company with better employees that has the competitive advantage.

Competitive cost advantage
An advantage that a firm has over competitors, allowing it to generate greater sales margins and/or retain more customers. It supports the firm's cost structure, product offerings, distribution network and customer support.

Competitive intelligence
Process of gathering actionable information on your business' competitive environment. Ex: In 2006, after extensive research to diversify and move into the organic fish market

(available at Whole Foods), Walmart bought all the organic fisheries so it would have no competition, and could keep prices low in sync with its USP.

Competitive strategy
The adoption of a specific target market and marketing mix stance in the market place.

Competitor
A business rival, usually one who manufactures or sells similar goods and/or services.

Competitor analysis
Also called Competitive Analysis. A company's marketing strategy which involves assessing the performance of competitors in order to determine their strengths and weaknesses.

Compliance officer
A corporate official whose job is to ensure that a company is complying with regulations, and that its employees are complying with internal policies and procedures.

Compound interest
Interest which is calculated on not only the the initial loan, but also on the accumulated interest.

Compounding
The paying of interest on the accrued interest as well as on the principal.

Compulsory purchase
When an organisation has the legal right to force the sale of land, property, etc., usually to build motorways or railways.

Concentrated marketing
A growth strategy in which a firm's resources are focused on a well-defined market niche or population segment.

Concept
A thought or notion. An idea for a new product, advertising campaign, etc.

Concierge
An employee of e.g. an hotel who provides a service to guests, such as handling luggage, delivering mail and messages, making tour reservations, etc.

Conciliation
To bring two disputing sides together to discuss the problem with the aim of reaching an agreement.

Concordance
In publishing, a concordance is an alphabetical list of the key words from a text showing their meanings. Concordances are rare in old large books because of the time and effort required to compile them, but more commonly arise in modern computer-generated applications.
A concordance is a sort of cross-referenced index, but in (sometimes very much) more detail than the standard index of chapters and subjects typically shown before the main content. There are other more complex and different meanings of the word concordance relating to various technical applications (mathematics, genetics, etc) where often the meanings concern duality or cross-referencing of some sort.

Condition of employment
An organization's policies and work rules that employees are expected to abide by in order to remain continuously employed.

Conditional sale
A purchasing arrangement, usually where the buyer pays in instalments but does not become the legal owner

of the goods until the full purchase price has been paid.

Conference call
A telephone call which allows three or more people to take part at the same time.

Confidentiality agreement
An agreement between an employer and employee in which the employee may not disclose proprietary or confidential information.

Conflict of interest
A much overlooked, under-estimated, yet highly prevalent factor in the execution of any responsibility or activity, where an organization/group/individual is subject to incompatible demands, opportunities, incentives, or responsibilities, etc., and especially where there is potential for one demand to distort the proper honest diligent execution of responsibility in achieving the second demand, i.e.., the incompatibility is competing and mutually unhelpful. A conflict of interest produces divided loyalties, for example where a person represents two different competing businesses, or an employee is responsible for managing family members or personal friends.

Conformance
Meeting requirements or specifications.

Conglomerate
A corporation which consists of several smaller companies with different business activities.

Conservator
In law, a guardian or protector appointed by a court to manage the affairs, finances, etc., of someone who is too ill or incapable of doing so themselves.

Consortium
A group of businesses, investors or financial institutions working together on a joint venture.

Constructive dismissal
An employer's behaviour (either one serious incident or a pattern of incidents) creates a negative work environment, leading to an employee's resigning. Such behaviour is considered a breach of contract and gives the employee the right to seek compensation in court.

Constructive spending
Helping the local economy by buying home produced goods, holidaying in your own country, etc., rather than buying imported goods and holidaying abroad.

Consultants
An outside individual who supplies professional advice or services to companies for a fee. Large HR consulting firms include Aon, Mercer, Hewitt and Watson Wyatt. Large HR consulting firms typically work with companies who have more than 1,500 employees.

Consumer
A purchaser of a good or service at retail, or an end user not necessarily a purchaser, in the distribution chain of a good or service (gift recipient).

Consumer credit
Also called Personal Credit or Retail Credit. Loans given to consumers by financial institutions for household or personal use.

Consumer debt
Money owed by people in the form of loans from banks or purchase agreements from retailers, such as 'buy now pay later'.

Consumer panel

A group of selected people, usually a cross-section of a population, whose purchasing habits are monitored by an organization, in order to provide feedback on products, services, etc., which are used.

Consumer price

The price which the general public pays for goods and services.

Consumer price index

A measure of inflation which involves regularly monitoring the change in price for everyday goods and services purchased by households.

Consumer protection

Laws which protect consumers against unsafe or defective products, deceptive marketing techniques, dishonest businesses, etc.

Consumer watchdog

An independent organization that protects the rights of individual customers and monitors companies to check for illegal practices.

Consumer-to-business (C2B)

A system in which consumers use online agents (middlemen) to look for a product or service that suits their needs.
Examples include Priceline.com and shopbot.com.

Consumption tax

Tax paid which is based on the price of services or goods, e.g. value added tax.

Contango

A situation in which the price of a commodity to be delivered in the future exceeds the immediate delivery price, often due to storage and insurance costs.

Contextual advertising

Method of deciding and posting specific advertising offers on websites. A contextual ad system scans the text of a website for keywords and returns ads to that webpage based on what the user is viewing (as in sports-related products on a physical fitness site).

Contingency fee

In law, a fee that is payable to the lawyer out of any damages which have been awarded to the client by a court. There is no payment if the case is unsuccessful.

Contingency recruiting (search)

Contingency recruiters conduct frontline talent searches and represent either employers or individuals seeking placement. Contingency firms are not paid unless a candidate is successfully placed.

Contingent liability

This is recorded as a debt on a company's accounts which may or may not be incurred, depending on the outcome of a future event, such as a court case.

Contingent staff

Temporary staff that supplements a companys workforce. Contingent staff may be hired through a staffing firm. Businesses that have fluctuating seasonal staff demands or are in need of temporary call center representatives often use contingent workers.

Continuous improvement

On-going improvement of any and all aspects of an organization including products, services, communications, environment, functions, individual processes, etc.

Contra entry

In accounting, an amount entered which is offset by another entry of the same value, i.e., a debit is offset by a credit.

Contraband

Goods prohibited by law from being exported or imported. Smuggling.

Contract for services

An agreement with a self-employed person for a specific job.

Contract of employment

A contract between an employee and an employer which specifies terms and conditions of employment, such as hours to be worked, duties to perform, etc., in return for a salary, paid benefits, paid holiday, etc., from the employer.

Contract of purchase

Also called Purchase Agreement. A legal document which states the terms and conditions, including price, of the sale of an item.

Contract of service

Another term for employment agreement.

Contract worker

A person who is hired by a company (but not as an employee), often through an employment agency, for a specific period of time to work on a particular project.

Contractor

An individual, company, etc., who agrees to provide goods and/or services to another individual or company under the terms specified in the contract.

Control account

An account which a company keeps in addition to its official accounts, in order to cross-check balances, etc., to ensure that the official accounts are accurate.

Control chart

A chart that indicates upper and lower statistical control limits, and an average line, for samples or subgroups of a given process. If all points on the control chart are within the limits, variation may be ascribed to common causes and the process is deemed to be "in control." If points fall outside the limits, it is an indication that special causes of variation are occurring, and the process is said to be "out of control."

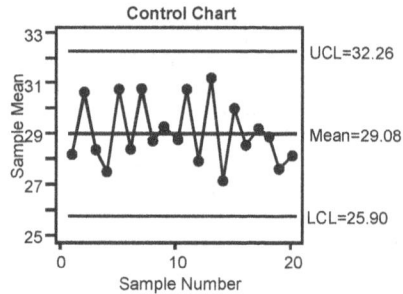

Control Chart

Control limit

A statistically-determined line on a control chart used to analyze variation within a process. If variation exceeds the control limits, then the process is being affected by special causes and is said to be "out of control." A control limit is not the same as a specification limit.

Controlling interest

The ownership of more than 50% of the voting shares in a company, which enables the owner of these shares to make decisions, direct operations, etc.

Convene

To gather together for an official or formal meeting.

Convention

A large formal meeting of politicians, members, delegates, sales people, etc.

Conversion rate

A conversion rate is defined as the relationship between visitors to a web site and actions considered to be a 'conversion', such as a sale or request to receive more information. Search optimization (SEO) is far less expensive than an aggressive paid search campaign and gets you the same amount of traffic. Plus, the effects are longer lasting, and conversions are frequently in the same range (or even higher) than paid ads on engines.

Conversion rate

Percentage of customers to purchase a product or service. Also includes percentage of website visitors to sign up for a newsletter, register for membership, or apply for a credit card.

Convertible

Refers to a security (bonds or shares) which can be exchanged for another type of security in the same company.

Convertible currency

Currency which can be quickly and easily converted into other countries currencies.

Conveyancer

A specialist lawyer who is an expert in conveyancing, i.e., legal work carried out connected to the selling and buying of property.

Cookie

On a computer, coded information that an Internet website you have visited sends to your computer which contains personal information, such as identification code, pages visited, etc., so that the website can remember you at a later time.

Cooling-off period

A period of time after the exchange of contracts, purchasing agreements, etc., during which the purchaser can change their mind and cancel the contract, and usually get any deposit paid reimbursed.

Cooperative

A collection of organisations or individuals, pooling their resources in order to gain commercial or non-commercial advantage in buying, selling or processing goods and/or services.

Cooperative marketing

Also known as Cooperative Advertising. When two companies work together to promote and sell each others products. A manufacturer or distributor who supports, and often pays for, a retailers advertising.

Copyright

An exclusive legal right to make copies, publish, broadcast or sell a piece of work, such as a book, film, music, picture, etc.

Core competencies

The particular set of strengths, experience, knowledge and abilities that differentiate a company from its competitors and provide competitive advantage. Employees should possess these qualities in order to advance business goals.

Core earnings
A company's revenue which is earned from its main operations or activities minus expenses, such as financing costs, asset sales, etc.

Corporate advertising
Also called Institutional Advertising. Advertising that promotes a company's image, rather than marketing its products or services.

Corporate hospitality
Entertainment provided by companies in order to develop good relationships with its employees, customers, other businesses, etc.

Corporate image
The mental image held by others at the mention of a firm's name. It's a compositepsychological impression that's dynamic based on circumstances, media coverage, performance, pronouncements, etc. Similar to a firm's reputation or goodwill, it is the public perception of the firm rather than a reflection of its actual state or position. Large firms use various corporate advertisin techniques to enhance their image to improve their desirability as a supplier, employer, customer, borrower, etc

Corporate ladder
The order of rank, position, etc., in a company from junior to senior, which can be progressed or 'climbed' by employees.

Corporate raider
A term used for an individual or company who purchases large numbers of shares in other companies, against their wishes, in order to gain a controlling interest in the other companies, or to resell the shares for a large profit.

Corporate social responsibility
CSR. An obligation of a company to adhere to legal guidelines in order to meet the needs of its employees, shareholders and customers, and also to be concerned about social and environmental issues.

Corporate veil
A term which refers to the fact that a company's shareholders are not liable for the company's debts, and are immune from lawsuits concerning contracts, etc.

Corporation
A large company or a group of companies which is legally authorised to act as a single entity, separate from its owners, with its liabilities for damages, debts, etc., limited to its assets so that its shareholders and owners are protected from personal claims.

Corporation tax
A tax which limited companies and other organisations, such as societies, clubs, associations, etc., pay on their profits after adjustments for certain allowances.

Correspondence course
A study course using written correspondence, books, etc., which are sent to you by post from learning institutes.

Corruption
Lack of honesty or integrity. Illegal behaviour, such as bribery, by people in positions of authority, e.g. politicians.

Cost accounting
Managerial accounting which calculates, records and controls the operating costs of producing goods or services.

Cost control
A management process which ensures that departments within a company or organisation do not exceed their budget.

Cost cutting
Reducing an individual's, company's, etc, expenditure.

Cost effective
Producing a product, offering a service, etc., in the most economical way to the benefit of the company and the customer.

Cost leader
A company which has a competitive advantage by producing goods or offering services at a lower cost than its competitors.

Cost of debt ratio
Despite the different variations used for this term (cost of debt, cost of debt ratio, average cost of debt ratio, etc) the term normally and simply refers to the interest expense over a given period as a percentage of the average outstanding debt over the same period, ie., cost of interest divided by average outstanding debt.

Cost of goods sold (COGS)
The directly attributable costs of products or services sold, (usually materials, labour, and direct production costs). Sales less COGS = gross profit.

Cost of living
The standard cost of basic necessities which people need to live, such as food, housing and clothes.

Cost of living allowance
COLA. A salary supplement which a company pays to employees because of an increase in the cost of living.

Cost of poor quality
The costs incurred by producing products or services of poor quality. These costs usually include the cost of inspection, rework, duplicate work, scrapping rejects, replacements and refunds, complaints, and loss of customers and reputation.

Cost of quality
Philip Crosby's term for the cost of poor quality.

Cost of sales (COS)
Commonly arrived at via the formula: opening stock + stock purchased - closing stock.
Cost of sales is the value, at cost, of the goods or services sold during the period in question, usually the financial year, as shown in a Profit and Loss Account (P&L). In all accounts, particularly the P&L (trading account) it's important that costs are attributed reliably to the relevant revenues, or the report is distorted and potentially meaningless. To use simply the total value of stock purchases during the period in question would not produce the correct and relevant figure, as some product sold was already held in stock before the period began, and some product bought during the period remains unsold at the end of it. Some stock held before the period often remains unsold at the end of it too. The formula is the most logical way of calculating the value at cost of all goods sold, irrespective of when the stock was purchased. The value of the stock attributable to the sales in the period (cost of sales) is the total of what we started with in stock (opening stock), and what we purchased (stock purchases), minus what stock we have left over at the end of the period (closing stock).

Cost overrun

The amount by which the actual cost of a project, etc., exceeds the original budget.

Cost per click

CPC. The amount of money an advertiser pays to a website publisher every time a visitor clicks on an advert displayed on the publisher's website which links to the advertisers website.

Cost-benefit analysis

The ability to measure the costs associated with a specific programme, project, or benefit. The cost is then compared to the total benefit or value derived.

Cost-centre

Part of a business or organisation such as a marketing department, or quality assurance department, which is a cost to operations and does not produce external customer revenues or profit through trading.

Cost-per-hire

The costs linked to recruiting talent. These costs can include advertising, agency fees, relocation costs, and training costs.

Cottage industry

A small business in which production of goods or services are based in the home rather than in a factory or on business premises.

Count chart (c chart)

An attributes data control chart that evaluates process stability by charting the counts of occurrences of a given event in successive samples.

Counterbid

To make a higher offer than someone else in a bid to buy something.

Counterclaim

In a court of law, a claim made against you (plaintiff) by the person (defendant) you are making a claim against.

Counterpart

A person or position which has a corresponding function in a different organization, country, etc. The corresponding function naturally is also a counterpart. Also a copy of a legal document.

Countersign

To add a second signature, where required, to a document or cheque, in order to make it valid.

Countertrade

An agreement by the customer to buy goods on condition that the seller buys some of the customer's own products in return.

Countervailing duty

An additional tax imposed on certain imported goods which have been produced very cheaply in their country of origin, in order to bring the price of the goods up to the true market price to protect the importing country's producers.

Count-per-unit chart (u chart)

A control chart that evaluates process stability by charting the number of occurrences of a given event per unit sampled, in a series of samples.

Courier

A person who carries and delivers messages, documents, packages, etc., often between companies. A person employed by a travel company as a tourist guide.

Courseware

Computer software designed to be used in teaching or for self-learning.

Covenant

A written promise, sometimes part of a contract, to perform, or not to perform, a particular action.

Cover charge

A fixed fee charged by a nightclub or a restaurant with live entertainment, which covers, or part covers, the cost of musicians, DJs, etc.

Cowboy

A dishonest, often unqualified, business person, especially one who overcharges for bad quality work. Not to be confused with the cowboy of top-shelf publications.

CP

Commonly used process capability index defined as [USL (upper spec limit) - LSL (lower spec limit)] / [6 x sigma], where sigma is the estimated process standard deviation.

CPK

Commonly used process capability index defined as the lesser of USL - m/3sigma or m - LSL /3sigma, where sigma is the estimated process standard deviation.

CPM

Cost Per Thousand – Used by marketers and advertisers to measure the effectiveness of their media expenditures. Derived by dividing the cost of media purchase divided by the number of consumers reached (in thousands).

Cpm

Critical Path Method – Method to break down complex projects into simpler tasks, thus identifying more efficient, easiest, and fastest path to completion.

Crapola

Items of little importance or poor quality.

Crawling peg

A system of frequently adjusting a country's exchange rate by marginal amounts, because of inflation, etc.

Creative director

A person who usually works in the advertising or entertainment industry and is responsible for planning and managing the creative aspects of an advertising or promotional campaign.

Credit

An arrangement in which an item for sale is received by the purchaser and paid for at a later date. A loan. The positive balance in a bank account. An amount entered in a company's accounts which has been paid by a debtor.

Credit analysis

The process of analysing a company's financial records and assessing its ability to repay a loan, etc.

Credit crunch

Also known as Credit Squeeze. This usually precedes a recession. A situation in which loans for businesses and individuals are difficult to obtain, when a government is trying to control inflation, because of the fear of bankruptcy and unemployment. The term 'Credit Crunch' also became a specific informal name for the 2008 global financial crisis and subsequent prolonged recession, which affected western economies particularly, mainly because of their highly leveraged and indebted nature, and the convoluted inter-dependent chains of credit arrangements between banks, some of which failed completely resulting in their effective nationalization or absorption into larger competitors.

Credit history

A record of an individual's or company's debt repayment, used by lenders to asses a borrowers ability to repay a loan, mortgage, etc.

Credit rating

Information (based on interpretation by an official credit rating agency or similar financial services data provider) of a person's or company's or other entity's financial history and circumstances, which assesses and indicates their ability to repay debts, loans, etc. Lenders use this information when making a decision regarding a loan approval, and in larger cases will adjust levels of interest and other financial credit terms according to the perceived risk of the loan situation and client, which may be an individual or a whole country or international federation.

Credit rating agency

A credit rating agency is a company which analyses and issues an official recognized assessment of the quality of a debt or debtor, including corporate, institutional or state debt or debt/credit products (specifically the reliability of repayment/recoverability), such as bonds and tradable securities (debts, equities, mortgages, and derivative complex financial credit contracts), and significantly also of organizations, bodies, and entire countries, by virtue of their credit-worthiness (ability to repay their debts). Ratings are visible, published and officially/internationally recognized, especially for countries. Ratings strongly influence interest rates applied to rated organizations, i.e., poor ratings mean that the low-rated organizations/bodies/nations are charged higher rates of interest by lenders, due to the higher perceived level of risk, and the overall market's response to the rating/risk. Conversely, positively-rated organizations/countries enjoy the lowest possible interest rates when borrowing. The same principle applies to debt products, mindful that many debt products are sold from one lender to another, commonly entailing seriously vast sums of money. Ratings are typically expressed on a scale of AAA ('triple A') as the top/best, which equates to the most reliable and secure debt/debtor, down through AA, A, BBB, BB, etc., to CCC with the lowest being C, although there are variations, including lower case letters, numbers, and + and - symbols. This is a highly significant, pivotal, and controversial area of corporate/global finance, economic management, extending to life and society, because:

1. The sums of money involved/affected by these ratings are extremely big (multi-billions) so there is a lot at stake, for corporations, countries, bankers, brokers, and for societies too.
2. While there are hundreds of small credit rating agencies, historically the market is dominated by just three of them, namely Standard and Poor; Moody's, and Fitch ('The Big Three'), which between them control (at 2013) c.95% of the global market (in ratings and related services, significantly at the highest levels of national and corporate debt/credit).
3. The credit rating industry is inherently and worryingly liable to major conflict of interest because agencies provide important and high-value advisory services to the same

organizations whose products the agencies assess, along with rating the client organizations themselves.
There is also huge potential for conflict of interest and corruption on a vast scale because credit ratings affect interest rates and transactions entailing monumental sums of money, and so there is unlimited temptation and opportunity for incestuous deals between the rate-fixers and those who trade in credit and debt, and financial investments and speculation generally. Sadly, as with much else that happens in the financial sector across the globe, combinations of conflict of interest, extreme 'product' complexity, corporate and personal incentive and greed, together with a lack of sufficient regulation and transparency, tend to produce very big outcomes, trends and economical effects that can be arbitrary, distorted, extremely polarized, so that a few powerful people/organizations/entities achieve massive gains and advantages, while others, especially those in weak positions, suffer massive disadvantages. It is an interesting point of note that despite enormous reliance on credit ratings agencies at the level of global corporations and national governments, credit rating agencies can make large misjudgments, as when for example very positive ratings were given to highly toxic derivative mortgages/debts products whose collapse and virtual irrecoverable value led mainly or substantially to the 2008 global financial disintegration and following recesssion.

Credit rationing
When a bank or money lender limits the amount of funds available to borrowers, or interest rates are very high.

Credit repair
The process of helping to improve a person or company's credit rating, sometimes by disputing or correcting credit history discrepancies.

Credit union
A financial institution, similar to a bank, whose members create the funds from which they can obtain loans at low rates of interest.

Creditor
A person, business, etc., to whom money is owned.

Crib
Plagiarism. To copy someone else's written work and pass it off as your own.

Crisis management
Actions taken by a company to deal with an unexpected event which threatens to harm the organisation, such as a loss of a major customer, bad publicity, etc.

Criterion
A principal or standard by which other things or people may be compared, or a decision may be based.

Critical mass
The minimum amount of customers, resources, etc., needed to maintain or start a business, venture, etc. The point at which change occurs e.g., when a company is able to continue in business and make a profit without any outside help.

CRM
Customer Relationship Management – Broad term that covers concepts used by companiesto manage their

relationships with customers, including the capture, storage, and analysis of customer, vendor, partner, and internal process information.

Cronyism
In business and politics, showing favouritism to friends and associates by giving them jobs or appointments with no regard to their qualifications or abilities.

Crosby, philip
One of the quality guru's. Crosby founded several consulting agencies including Career IV, Philip Crosby Associates, and the Quality College. He has authored several books including Quality Is Free and Quality Without Tears. Crosby is well-known for his theory of "zero defects."

Cross guarantee
Also known as Inter Company Guarantee. A guarantee by a group of companies to be responsible for the debts, etc., of another company in the group if it fails to repay them. The group also use the guarantee to raise capital or take out multiple loans.

Cross merchandising
Also known as Add-On Sales. In retailing, the practice of putting related products together on display in order to encourage customers to purchase several items.

Cross-channel marketing
Use of a single marketing channel (such as direct mail or internet) tosupport or promote another channel (such as retailing).

Cross-training
When employees are trained to perform various jobs by other groups or individuals to improve job performance. Often aimed at creating a diverse working group to combat an "narrow-minded" work force. Also known as conditioning.

Crowdfunding
A method of funding and underpinning a project or business venture which became increasingly popular and visible in the 21st century, whereby users or other interested people are involved as investors at project inception, and therefore agree and commit to support a development of one sort or another. A good example of crowdfunding is the raising capital and support from a local community for the construction of nearby wind turbines, which generally otherwise encounter local hostility instead of support.

Crowdsourcing
Term first coined by Jeff Howe in 2006 in Wired magazine. Crowdsourcing refers to an organisation, group or individual delegating a task to a large number of people via the internet, thereby using the general public or a community of followers, users, experts, etc., to do research, make suggestions, solve a problem, etc., usually without being paid. Their reward is mainly a sense of ownership and real involvement, which is proven to be a very powerful and meaningful force for motivation.

Crown jewel
The most valuable and profitable asset of a company or business.

C-suite
The Chief Officers or most senior executives in a business or organisation.

Cube farm
An open office which is divided into cubicles.

Culpability

Blame or liability for harm or damage to others, from Latin culpa meaning fault.

Culture

The sum total of learned behaviourial characteristics or traits which are manifest and shared by members of a particular society.

Cumulative sum chart

Control chart that shows the cumulative sum of deviations from a set value in successive samples. Each plotted point indicates the algebraic sum of the last point and all deviations since. PathMaker does not support cumulative sum charts.

Currency bloc

A group of countries that use the same currency, for example the Euro.

Currency swaps

A method to gain access to foreign capital at favourable rates comprising contracts to exchange cash flow relating to the debt obligations of the two counterparts to the agreement.

Current account

A bank account which can be used to make deposits, withdrawals, cash cheques, pay bill, etc.

Current assets

Cash and anything that is expected to be converted into cash within twelve months of the balance sheet date.

Current liabilities

Money owed by the business that is generally due for payment within 12 months of balance sheet date. Examples: creditors, bank overdraft, taxation.

Current ratio

The current ratio is an indication of a firm's market liquidity and ability to meet creditor's demands. Acceptable current ratios vary from industry to industry and are generally between 1.5 and 3 for healthy businesses. If a company's current ratio is in this range, then it generally indicates good short-term financial strength. If current liabilities exceed current assets (the current ratio is below 1), then the company may have problems meeting its short-term obligations. If the current ratio is too high, then the company may not be efficiently using its current assets or its short-term financing facilities. This may also indicate problems in working capital management.

Current yield

The amount produced by dividing the annual income, both from interest and dividends, by the current price of the security (Stocks do not gain interest; the current yield for stocks is equal to the dividend yield.).

Customer

Any recipient of a product or service; anyone who is affected by what one produces. A customer can be external or outside the organization, or they can be internal to the organization.

Customer advocate

Individual entrusted by management to study the needs of an organization's customers and help it better satisfy them. A role often cited as problem-solver: addressing customer complaints to protect and enhance the organization's image.

Customer loyalty

Describes when a customer prefers to buy a particular brand or type of product, who prefers a particular shop, or who stays with the same company, such as a bank, insurance company, phone company, etc.

Customer profile

Description of a customer group or type of customer based on various geographic, demographic, and psychographic characteristics; also called shopper profile_(may include income, occupation, level of education, age, gender, hobbies, or area of residence, etc.). Profiles provide knowledge needed to select the best prospect lists and to enable advertisers to select the bestmedia.

Customer relations

The relationship a company has with its customers and the way it deals with them. The department in a company which is responsible for dealing with its customers, for example complaints, etc.

Customer retention

a goal of organizations to keep customers buying their products and services, an essential component to sustaining growth and profitability as it costs more to acquire a new customer than to retain existing customers. Ex: Best Buy has a team that surfs the Internet in search of special offers by competitors on products it offers and make adjustments, as needed.

Customer satisfaction

Customers' state of mind about a company when their expectations have been met or exceeded, most often leading to brand loyalty and product repurchase. Ex: Nordstrom's Department Store emphasizes a 100-year-old customer service philosophy to generate customer satisfaction (best possible service, selection, quality and value).

Customer-centric

An approach to doing business in which a company focuses on creating a positive consumer experiences at the point of sale and post-sale. A customer-centric approach helps organizations to differentiate and position themselves apart from competitors who don't offer the same experiences. Customer-centric organizations are operated from a customers' point of view rather than developing new products and attempting to convince consumers to purchase them.

Customs duty

A tax which must be paid on imported, and sometimes exported, goods, to raise a country's revenue and to protect domestic industries from cheaper foreign competition.

Customs union

A group of nations which have agreed to promote free trade, for example, not to charge tax on goods which they trade with one another, and to set taxes for nations which are not members of the group.

Cutover

Also known as 'Going Live'. The point in time a company or organisation, etc., replaces an old Programme or system with a new one.

Cut-throat

Ruthless and intense competition. An unprincipled, ruthless person.

Cyber monday

In recent times, the busiest online shopping day of the year, in the USA typically the Monday after Thanksgiving Day (the fourth Thursday of November); in the UK typically the first Monday in December.

Cyberspace
Term credited to author William Gibson in 1984 which describes the imaginary place where e-mails, web pages, etc., go to while they are being sent between computers.

Cybersquatting
The illegal activity of buying and registering a domain name which is a well-known brand or someone's name, with the intent of selling it to its rightful owner in order to make a profit.

Cyclical industry
An industry whose success is closely linked to the rise and fall of the general economy (The auto industry is a cyclical industry.).

D

Damage limitation
The process of trying to limit or curtail the amount of damage or loss caused by a particular situation or event.

Dark net
A term for online private websites and networks concealed from and inaccessible to unauthorised users in which materials are shared, normally illegally and anonymously.

Dark store
A retail store adapted or designed for the main or whole purpose of fulfilling online orders. Customers generally do not visit 'dark stores', except where policy/processes allow the collection of pre-ordered goods. The 'dark store' feature of retailing began to emerge seriously in the early 2000s, in which an existing retail store or a purpose-built facility - notably in the supermarkets sector - would be adapted/designed chiefly or entirely for distributing orders placed online, i.e., website sales. Dark stores typically contain similar warehousing/shelving/aisles arrangements to conventional retail stores, but store staff physically pick the products, rather than customers. Orders are then delivered to customers, or (subject to the policy if the retailer) may be collected.

Data
Facts/figures pertinent to a marketing problem.

Data mining (knowledge discovery)
Process of analyzing data from different perspectives or angles for use in such marketing activities as increasing revenue, cutting costs, etc.

Daughter company
A company that is controlled partly or completely by a holding or parent company.

Dawn raid
A sudden planned purchase of a large number of a company's shares at the beginning of a days trading on the stock exchange.

Day player
In the entertainment industry, actors, etc., who are hired by the day.

Day-after recall test
Research method testing consumers' memories a day after hopefully seeing an advertisement. Designed to assess the ad's effectiveness.

Dead cat bounce
A derogatory term used on the stock exchange to describe a huge decline in the value of a stock, usually a

share, which is immediately followed by a temporary rise in price before continuing to fall. From: "Even a dead cat will bounce if it falls from a great height".

Deadbeat
A person or company who tries to avoid paying their debts.

Dear money
Also known as Tight Money. When money is difficult to borrow, and if a loan is secured then it would be paid back at a very high rate of interest.

Debenture
Unsecured certified loan over a long period of time with a fixed rate, based on the trust that payment will be made in the future.

Debriefing
A meeting or interview in which a person or group of people report about a task or mission just completed or attempted.

Debt
Money owed to another person or organisation, such as a loan, mortgage, etc., which is required to be paid back, usually with interest.

Debt exposure
Money that a lender risks losing if the borrower fails to pay it back.

Debt-equity swap
An arrangement between a lender and a debtor, usually a company, in which the lender agrees to reduce the debt in exchange for newly issued shares from the borrower.

Debt-to-equity ratio
The ratio found by dividing long-term debt by the equity (all assets minus debts) held in stock (This is a measure

of financial risk.).

Decentralised plans
A planning system taking into account differences in product/market conditions.

Deceptive advertising (False advertising)
Misleading customers by making claims or promises that are untrue, unproven, or distortions of the truth to promote the sale of goods or services. Often an illegal practice regulated or prosecuted by the secretaries of state.

Decertification
In employment this refers specifically to action taken by workers to disassociate themselves from a trade union which previously represented them. Aside from this the general meaning refers to withdrawal of certification of one sort or another.

Decision consequence analysis
A process for helping decision makers, usually in the pharmaceutical and petroleum exploration industries, decide where resources such as time, money, etc., should be invested.

Decision matrix
A tool used to evaluate problems, solutions, or ideas. The possibilities are listed down the left-hand side of the matrix and relevant criteria are listed across the top. Each possibility is then rated on a numeric scale of importance or effectiveness (e.g. on a scale of 1 to 10) for each criterion, and each rating is recorded in the appropriate box. When all ratings are complete, the scores for each possibility are added to determine which has the highest overall rating

and thus deserves the greatest attention.

Decision tree

A diagram which starts with an initial decision, and possible strategies and actions are represented by branches which lead to the final outcome decided upon.

Decision Tree of Weather

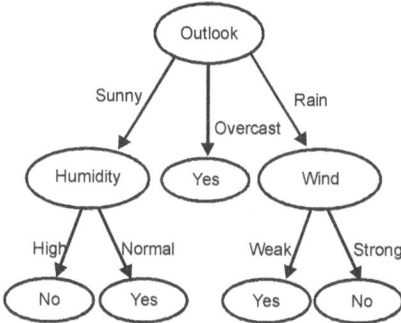

Deed of partnership

A legal document which sets out how a partnership is to be run, and also the rights of the partners. A Deed Of Partnership is not compulsory but it helps to avoid any misunderstandings or disputes in the future.

Deep throat

In business, an anonymous source of top secret information. First used in this sense in the reporting of the US Watergate scandal.

Deep web

Also known as the Invisible Web, said to contain about 500 times more information than the generally accessible world-wide web, the Deep Web comprises data held by secure organizations, for example military and government.

Default

A term that denotes the failure to pay the principal or interest on a financial obligation (such as a bond).

Default risk

The risk that a company will default, or fail to meet its financial obligations, i.e., fail to pay the interest or principal on its bonds.

Defect

An error in construction of a product or service that renders it unusable; an error that causes a product or service to not meet requirements.

Defence document

A document that a company's shareholders receive which explains why an offer to buy the company should be rejected.

Deferred compensation

Payment for services under any employer-sponsored plan or arrangement that allows an employee (for tax-related purposes) to defer income to the future.

Deficit financing

When a government borrows money because of a shortage of funds from taxes. This usually results in pushing up interest rates.

Defined benefit plan

A retirement plan that pays participants a lump-sum amount that has been calculated using formulas that can include age, earnings and length of service.

Defined contribution

A pension plan that clearly defines the amount of contributions, which is usually a percentage of an employees salary. The benefits payable at retirement depend on several factors including future investment return and annuity rate at retirement.

Deflation

Economic decline typified by falling costs of goods and services; falling levels of employment; limited money supply or credit; reduced imports; lower wage increases, often caused by lower personal spending or investment, and/or a reduction in government spending. Deflation is broadly the opposite of inflation.

Delegation
An assignment of responsibility or task, usually by a manager to a subordinate. Separately a delegation refers to a deputation, being a group of people appointed or responsible for representing a nation or corporation or other organization to attend talsk or negotiations, etc.

Deleveraging
An attempt by a company to reduce its debts, for example by selling off assets, laying off staff, etc.

Demand pattern analysis
The analysis of in-country industrial sector growth patterns.

Demerit goods
Products or services such as as alcohol, gambling, drugs, prostitution, etc., which are considered unhealthy or undesirable, and are often subject to extra taxes in order to reduce consumption and potentially to fund remedial actions in response to consumption.

Deming cycle
Alternate name for the Plan-Do-Check-Act cycle, a four-stage approach to problem-solving. It is also sometimes called the Shewhart cycle.

Deming, W. Edwards
Known as the father of quality control. Deming began his work in quality control in the United States during World War II to aid the war effort. After the war, he went to Japan to help in the rebuilding of their country. His

methods of quality control became an integral part of Japanese industry. Deming is a celebrated author and is well-known for his "14 Points" for effective management.

Democracy
Majority rule, by which the biggest proportion of members of a group determine decisions for the whole group. Democracy typically refers to a country's political system, in which government is elected through majority vote.

Demographic profile
Used in marketing to describe a particular segment of the population, for example social class, age, gender, income, etc.

Demographic segmentation
The process of identifying and dividing consumers into groups according to their race, age, gender, religion, etc.

Demographics
Consumer statistics regarding socioeconomic factors, including gender, age, race, religion, nationality, education, income, occupation and family size. Each demographic category is broken down according to its characteristics by the various research companies.

Demonetize
To officially decide that a particular coin or banknote can no longer be used as currency.

Deposition
A sworn statement of evidence by a witness taken outside of the court proceedings before a trial.

Depreciation
The decrease in value due to wear and tear, decay, decline in price, e.g., a new car purchased at $20,000

depreciates to $5,000 in five years.

Depression

A prolonged and very deep economic recession, in a country or wider region. Definitions of an economic depression vary greatly, from two to ten years or more, characterized by extremely deep levels of negative indicators such as unemployment, credit and money supply, living standards, and reduced GDP, etc. Historians and economic commentators commonly disagree about the duration of depressions due to the confused methods of defining precisely what a depression is.

Deregulate

The reduction or removal of government regulations from an industry or business.

Deregulation

The removal or revision of laws that regulate the supply of goods and services.

Derived demand

Desire for something produced as a by-product for another product or service, as in the demand for specialty skilled labour for the auto industry, or inherent value in a sports star's endorsement. Ultimate result is customer fulfillment.

Desk jockey

An informal term for someone who spends their working day sitting behind a desk, and who is concerned about administration.

Desktop publishing

Producing printed documents, magazines, books, etc., using a small computer and printer.

Devaluation

The reduction in the value of one currency vis a vis other countries.

Developmental counseling

A form of shared counseling where managers or supervisors work together with subordinates to identify strengths and weaknesses, resolve performance-related problems and determine and create an appropriate action plan.

Diagnostic journey/Remedial journey

A problem-solving approach in which a problem is investigated by looking first at symptoms, and gradually working back towards root causes. Once root causes have been established, experimentation and tracking are used in the remedial journey - the finding of a cure for the roots of the problem.

Didactic

Describes works of literature or art which are intended to be be informative or instructional, especially morally, rather than entertaining. From the ancient Greek word didaskein, which means to teach.

Differentiated marketing

Sales growth strategy in which several market niches or population segments are targeted with different products for each niche or segment.

Differentiation/product

Differentiation seeks to make a product more attractive by contrasting its unique qualities with competing products. This creates a competitive advantage for the seller when customers view these products as unique or superior.

Diffusion theory

A classification for the adoption of innovation(s) through social phenomenon, characterised by a normal distribution.

Digerati

People who consider themselves to be experts of the Internet and computer industry.

Digital marketing

Use of Internet-connected devices to engage customers with online product and service marketing/promotional Programmes. Includes mobile phones, iPads, and other Wi-Fi devices.

Digital wallet

Computer software used to store a persons bank account details, name, address, etc., to enable them to make automatic payments when they are making purchases on the Internet.

Direct marketing

Direct marketing is a sales method by which advertisers approach buyers directly with products or services. The most common forms of direct marketing are telephone sales, emails and print (e.g., catalogs, brochures). Successful direct marketing also involves renting or compiling / maintaining a database of qualified buyers. According to the Direct Marketing Association, average response rates for print direct mail (flat mail) are 2.73%), catalogs are 2.45% and E-mail is 1.12%. HRmarketer.com research shows emails that offer a compelling "offer" in the form of a free downloadable white paper or research report (on a topic that resonates with your buyer) are significantly more likely to generate a response than promotional offers. In all industries, marketers are shifting their spending from brand building tactics like print advertising to direct response-oriented promotional channels such as direct marketing and interactive marketing (online advertising). The HRmarketer.com research report Trends in HR Marketing (http://www.hrmarketer.com/home/whitepaper_main2.htm) verifies this trend in the HR marketplace.

Direct overhead

A portion of the overheads, e.g. lighting, rent, etc., directly associated with the production of goods and services.

Directives

At an official level, directives are instructions, guidelines or orders issued by a governing or regulatory body. They may amount to law. In a less formal way a directive equates to an instruction issued by an executive or manager or organizational department.

Director

A person appointed to oversee and run a company or organisation along with other directors, In the entertainment industry, the person who directs the making of a film, TV Programme, etc.

Dirty money

Money made from illegal activities which needs 'laundering' so that it appears to be legitimate.

Disability

The inability to perform all or part of one's occupational duties because of an accident or illness. This can be due to a sickness, injury or mental condition and does not necessarily have to have been caused by the job itself.

Disability income insurance
Health insurance that is paid to a policyholder who experiences a loss of income due to an injury or an illness. Disability insurance plans pay a portion of the salary of a disabled worker until his/her retirement age.

Disburse
To pay out money from a large fund, e.g. a treasury or public fund.

Disciplinary procedure
A standardized process that an organization commits to when dealing with an employee who has breached the terms of employment in some way. If this procedure is not standardized and fair, the organization may face discrimination or other legal charges.

Discontinuous innovation
Description of how products and services are displaced by other products and services, reducing their intended utility or in some cases rendering them obsolete. Ex: Computers have virtually replaced typewriters. Will cell phones eliminate the need for a land line? Will iPads/Kindle readers replace college bookstores?

Discount
Reduction off the list price offered by a producer to a buyer; five types of discounts are common: trade, quantity, cash, seasonal and allowances. Marketers issue discounts to increase sales, to move out-of-date items, to reward valuable customers, or use it as a sales promotion.

Discount bond
A bond whose value is less than its face amount.

Discount broker
A stockbroker who charges a smaller commission than other brokers, but provides no counsel in investment.

Discount loan
A loan on which the finance charges and interest is paid before the borrower receives the money.

Discount window
In the US, when banks can borrow money from the Federal Reserve at low interest rates.

Discretionary income
Amount of income after fixed regular expenses (mortgage/rent, car payment, insurance, taxes) have been paid—monies not yet committed and therefore subject to persuasion techniques on the part of marketers. Ex: Take someone living in a $300/month trailer, who eats Ramen noodles as a staple, and often has his electricity or phone shut off for non-payment. But he drives a brand new Chrysler 300 with $3400 21" custom rims. His esteem need is in direct competition with safety/security and physiological needs for his discretionary income.

Discretionary income
The amount of income a person is left with after taxes and living essentials, such as food, housing, etc., have been deducted.

Discretionary order
Permits a broker to buy or sell shares on behalf of an investor in order to get the best price.

Discriminating duty
A variable tax levied on goods depending from which country they were imported.

Discrimination

The favoring of one group of people, resulting in unfair treatment of other groups.

Disease management

An information-based process involving the continuous improvement of care (prevention, treatment and management) throughout the delivery of health care. Effective disease management can mean decreased health care costs.

Dispatch note

Also called Dispatch Advice. A document giving details of goods which have been dispatched or are ready to be dispatched to a customer.

Distance learning

Educational Programmes using instruction via video or audio tapes, computers etc. instead of attending a class in one centralized location.

Distributable profit

A company's profits which are available for distribution among shareholders at the end of an accounting period.

Distributer

An individual or company who buys products, usually from manufacturers, and resells them to retail outlets or direct to customers. A wholesaler.

Distribution

Movement of goods and services through the distribution channel, to the final customer, consumer, or end user, with the movement of payment (transactions) in the opposite direction back to the original producer or supplier.

Distribution channel

An institution through which goods or services are marketed giving time and place utilities to users.

Distribution channel

Path through which goods and services flow from producer to consumer. This can be direct from the vendor to the consumer or may include several intermediaries such as wholesalers, distributors, agents, and retailers. Each intermediary receives the item at one pricing point and moves it to the next higher pricing point until it reaches the final buyer.

Distributive bargaining

A negotiation between competing parties that involves the distribution of resources. One party prevails, to the detriment of the other.

Diversification

modification of a current product or introduction of a completely new product that expands the organization's current market. Usually involves creating a new customer base and often acquiring specialized expertise.

Diversion/product diversion

In marketing and business 'diversion' refers to the unofficial distribution/ availability of branded consumer products. In other words this is the supply of branded products through unautorized stockists or retailers or other suppliers, notably via the web. Diversion does not refer to pirated or counterfeit or 'fake' goods. Diversion refers to official goods being sold through unofficial channels. Also called a 'grey market'.

Diversity

The collective mixture of differences and similarities that may include : individual and organizational characteristics, values, beliefs, experiences, backgrounds, preferences and behaviors.

Diversity training

Diversity training is training for the purpose of increasing participants' cultural awareness, knowledge, and skills, which is based on the assumption that the training will benefit an organization by protecting against civil rights violations, increasing the inclusion of different identity groups, and promoting better teamwork.

Dividend

A dividend is a payment made per share, to a company's shareholders by a company, based on the profits of the year, but not necessarily all of the profits, arrived at by the directors and voted at the company's annual general meeting. A company can choose to pay a dividend from reserves following a loss-making year, and conversely a company can choose to pay no dividend after a profit-making year, depending on what is believed to be in the best interests of the company. Keeping shareholders happy and committed to their investment is always an issue in deciding dividend payments. Along with the increase in value of a stock or share, the annual dividend provides the shareholder with a return on the shareholding investment.

Dividend payout ratio

The ratio found by dividing the annual dividends per share by the annual earnings per share.

Dividend yield

The yield found by dividing the annual dividends per share by the price per share (This yield is an indication of the income from a share of stock. Since return on a stock is comprised of capital gain plus dividends, the total return is comprised of dividend yield plus the capital gains percentage for stock.).

Docking station

A device to which a notebook computer or a laptop can be connected so it can serve as a desktop computer.

Document sharing

Used in video-conferencing. A system which allows people in different places to view and edit the same document at the same time on their computers.

DOE (Design of experiments)

DOE is the science of designing sets of experiments which will generate enough useful data to make sound decisions without costing too much or taking too long.

Dollar cost averaging (DCA)

A system of buying securities at regular intervals, using a fixed amount of cash over a considerable period of time regardless of the prevailing prices of the securities (DCA protects against the risk of losing a sum of money invested all at once at an inopportune time, e.g., right before a price drop.).

Dotcom

an internet business, or the internet business sector.

Double

In the film and TV industry, a person who stands in, or is substituted, for a principal actor.

Double indemnity

A clause in a life insurance policy where the insurance company agrees to pay double the face value of the policy in the event of accidental death.

Double-blind

A method of testing a new product, usually medicine, in which neither the people trying the product nor those administering the treatment know who is testing the real product and who has been given a placebo containing none of the product.

Double-dip Recession

A recession during which there is a brief period of economic growth, followed by a slide back into recession, before final recovery. Also called a W-shaped recession.

Double-dipping

The practice, usually regarded as unethical, of receiving two incomes or benefits from the same source, for example receiving a pension and consultancy income from the same employer.

Double-entry bookkeeping

An accounting method which results in balanced ledgers, i.e., for every transaction a credit is recorded in one account and a debit is recorded in another.

Double-loop marketing

Need for marketers to build offer/share useful information to help consumers make decisions. This is the first loop (and often an enticing free offer), after which a second loop offers other for-profit options. Ex: *Annualcreditreport.com* offers one free credit report with no strings attached; then offers continuing/value-added options such as credit alerts or credit scores for an additional cost.

Doula

A birthing or labour coach, from the greek word doule, meaning female slave.

Dow Jones industrial average

An indicator showing generally how well the market is going, found by averaging the prices of 30 industrial blue-chip stocks trading in the New York Stock Exchange.

Drayage

The fee charged for, or the process of, transporting goods by lorry or truck.

Drip advertising

An advertising campaign in small amounts over a long period of time to ensure that the public is continually aware of a product or service.

Drum-buffer-rope

A method, usually in manufacturing, which ensures an efficient flow of work in a production process by taking into consideration any possible delays or problems which may occur.

Dual labour markets

a situation in an organization where a smaller Core Labour Force and a Peripheral Labour Force co-exist.

Due diligence

In mergers and acquisitions, the process of carefully investigating the details of an investment or purchase to assess risk and potential value and reward.

Dumping

The selling of goods or services in a buying country at less than the production unit price in the selling country, or the difference between normal domestic price and the price at which the product leaves the exporting country.

Duopoly

A market that is dominated by two suppliers to the extent that jointly control pricing of goods or services in a defined market. This way, either seller can exert some control over the output and prices, but must consider the reaction of its sole competitor (unless both have formed an illegal collusive duo Ex: If AT&T merges with T-Mobil for this would this give AT&T and T-Mobil an advantage to reduce risk.

Dutch auction

A type of auction which opens with a high asking price which is then lowered until someone accepts the auctioneers price, or until the sellers reserve price has been reached.

Duty

The actual custom duty based on an imported good either on an ad valorem, or specification amount per unit or combination of these two.

Dvricide

Phenomena of fast-forwarding through TV commercials that consumers see as an inconvenience (as opposed to the Superbowl, in which ads are sometimes watched more than the football game). According to BBC America, commercials have been skipped by 50- 70 percent of viewers. It will be interesting to see how advertisers begin positioning their products into the content of products (ex: Kia car features in episodes of The Glades).

Dynamic pricing

Sudden or frequent pricing fluctuations based on changes in customer demand. Product bidding is often the result, as witnessed on eBay and other "how much would you offer" websites offering coupons, premiums, or contests. Thanks to the Internet, many businesses are finding it essential to remain competitive.

Dysphemism

The substitution of a neutral or positive word/phrase with a replacement word/phrase that has a more negative/pesimistic effect. The opposite or inverse of a dysphemism is euphemism. Both are widely used in press and public relations communications. Extreme examples are unethical at best, and criminally dishonest at worst.

Dystopia

The opposite of Utopia, a society in which conditions are characterised by human misery, depirvation, squalor, disease, etc. The term is said to have been coined by by John Stuart Mill in 1868 in a UK House of Commons speech criticizing the government's Irish land policy.

E

Eap

An employer-sponsored programme that is designed to assist employees whose job performance is being adversely affected by such personal stresses as substance abuse, addictions, marital problems, family troubles, and domestic violence. For every dollar invested in an EAP, employers save approximately $5 to $16. The average annual cost for an EAP ranges from $12 to $20 per employee. Source: US Department of Labour.

Early return to work programme

Modified work programmes designed to get employees who have been out of work due to injury or illness to return to the workforce sooner by providing them with less strenuous alternative jobs until they are able to resume their full regular duties.

Earnest money

Money paid in good faith as a deposit, usually for a property, to show that the buyer is serious about doing business with the vendor.

Earnings before

There are several 'Earnings Before..' ratios and acronyms: EBT = Earnings Before Taxes; EBIT = Earnings Before Interest and Taxes; EBIAT = Earnings Before Interest after Taxes; EBITD = Earnings Before Interest, Taxes and Depreciation; and EBITDA = Earnings Before Interest, Taxes, Depreciation, and Amortization. (Earnings = operating and non-operating profits (eg interest, dividends received from other investments). Depreciation is the non-cash charge to the balance sheet which is made in writing off an asset over a period. Amortisation is the payment of a loan in instalments.

Earnings per share

Earnings found by dividing the net income of the company by the number of shares of common outstanding stock.

Earnings yield

Yield found by dividing the earnings per share for the last 12 months by the market price per share.

Earn-out

An arrangement in which an extra future conditional payment is made to the seller of a business in addition to the original price, based upon certain criteria being met.

Easterlin paradox

A theory that beyond satisfaction of basic needs, increasing wealth of a country does not produce increasing happiness, suggested by US professor of economics Richard Easterlin based on his research published in 1974.

Easy monetary policy

A policy which enables the public to borrow money easily, at low interest rates, in order to expand the economy by investing the money in business activities.

E-business

Electronic Business. Using the internet to conduct business or enable businesses to link together.

E-commerce

Electronic Commerce. The buying and selling of products and services over the Internet.

Econometrics

Using mathematics and statistics to study the economy.

Economic growth

An increase in a region's or nation's production of goods and services.

Economic life

The period of time during which an asset, e.g. property, vehicle, machinery, etc., is expected to be usable, including repairs and maintenance, before a replacement is required.

Economic union

Also known as a Common Market. An agreement between a group of countries which allows the free flow of goods, services, labour, etc., between the member countries and usually has a common currency.

Economies of scale

Reduction in cost per unit resulting from increased production, realized through operational efficiencies of production or reducing the cost of resources.

Economy

The management of money, currency and trade of a nation. The efficient management of resources.

Ecotourism

Nature based travel to unspoilt places in the world with a view to conservation and to bring economic benefit to the local people. Also known as Ecological Tourism.

E-currency

Electronic currency. Used on the Internet for making and receiving payments. Companies which provide this service include Paypal and E-Gold.

Edutainment

Products or media which both educate and entertain at the same time, such as TV, books, computer software.

E-enabled

Being able to communicate and/or conduct business using the internet.

Egalitarian

Believing that everyone is equal and should all have the same rights and opportunities in life.

E-lance

Freelance working using the Internet to sell services or goods anywhere in the world.

Elasticity of demand

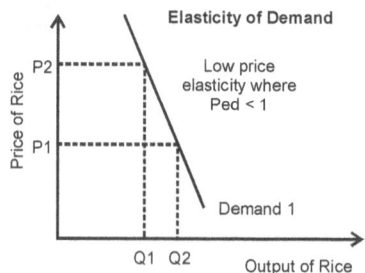

Elasticity of Demand

Low price elasticity where Ped < 1

Demand 1

Price of Rice — P2, P1

Q1 Q2   Output of Rice

The measure of whether people require more or less of a product or service after a price change.

E-learning

E-learning is a method of education via the Internet or other computer related resources. It presents just-in-time information in a flexible learning plan. E-learning can be combined with face-to-face courses for a blended learning approach.

Electronic cottage

A home which has the necessary electronic equipment, such as telephone, computer, etc., from which to run a business.

Electronic data exchange

A means of exchanging documents between businesses using electronic equipment such as computers.

Electronic media

Includes television, radio, internet, DVD (anything not film- or paper-based).

Electronic purse

A type of microchipped smartcard which stores small amounts of money to enable payment for purchases, especially on the Internet, instead of having to use cash.

E-marketing

Activity of promoting a product in electronic media format, such as internet ads, pop up links, e-commerce cell text, or email messages.

Embezzlement

Dishonestly appropriate goods or money from one's employer for personal gain; steal from one's employer, typically by electronic administrative methods, thus abusing a position of trust or responsibility.

Emolument

Total wages, benefits or compensation paid to someone for the job they do or the office they hold.

Emoticon

Used in e-mails, internet chat rooms and text messages, symbols which represent facial expressions, e.g. :-) = smile.

Emotional capital

Emotional experiences, values and beliefs of a company's employees that make good working relationships and a successful business. Low emotional capital can result in conflict between employees, low morale and poor customer relations.

Emotional intelligence I

Based on the book of the same name by Daniel Goleman, Emotional Intelligence is the ability to recognize, assess and manage their own and others' emotions.

Emotional intelligence II

The ability or skill of a person to understand and control their emotions, and to understand and assess and respond appropriately to the feelings and situations of others. Commonly abbreviated to EQ (Emotional Quotient, alluding to the concept of IQ - Intelligence Quotient), Emotional Intelligence theory seeks to enable a sophisticated practical appreciation and application of the concept of intelligence, especially in work, management, leadership and human relationships.

Empirical

Information derived from experience, observation or experiment rather than from theory or subjective opinion. From Greek- empeiros, meaning skilled - in turn from peira, meaning trial or experiment.

Employee

An individual who is hired and paid by another person, company, organisation, etc., to perform a job or service.

Employee assessments

Tests used to help employers in pre-hire situations to select candidates best suited for open positions. These tests can sometimes be taken via the Internet and can provide employees with effective training, assist managers in becoming more effective, and promote people into appropriate positions. Types of assessments include those to determine personality, aptitude and skills.

Employee buyout

A transaction in which employees purchase all or most of a company's shares, thereby gaining control of the company.

Employee engagement

Employee engagement, also called worker engagement, is a business management concept. An "engaged employee" is one who is fully involved in, and enthusiastic about their work, and thus will act in a way that furthers their organization's interests.

Employee involvement

Regular participation of employees in decision-making and suggestions. The driving forces behind increasing the involvement of employees are the conviction that more brains are better, that people in the process know it best, and that involved employees will be more motivated to do what is best for the organization.

Employee ownership

A business model and constitutional framework in which staff hold significant or majority shares of a company, thereby ensuring higher levels of loyalty and commitment, and fairness in the way that business performance relates to employee reward. The John Lewis Partnership is one of the prime and most successful examples of the concept.

Employee relations

Developing, maintaining, and improving the relationship between employer and employee by effectively and proactively communicating with employees, processing grievances/disputes, etc.

Employee retention

Practices and policies designed to create a work environment that makes employees want to stay with the organization, thus reducing turnover.

Employee self service

A programme that allows employees to handle many job-related tasks normally conducted by HR departments including benefits enrollment, and updating personal information. Employees can access the information through the company's intranet, kiosks, or other Web-based applications.

Employee stock option

Allows specified employees the right to purchase shares in the company at a fixed price.

Employer

A person, business, organisation, etc., that pays for the services of workers.

Employment branding

A strategy designed to make an organization appealing as a good place to work. This targeted marketing effort utilizes both print and Internet tactics and attempts to shape the perceptions of potential employees, current employees and the public / investment community.

Employment equity
Promotes equal employment opportunities for everyone, regardless of gender, race, ability, etc.

Employment law
Also known as Labour Law. The branch of the law that deals with the legal rights of employees, e.g. workplace safety, discrimination, compensation, etc.

Empowerment
Giving employees the resources, skills and authority necessary to share power with management and make decisions. Employees are then held accountable for their decisions and rewarded if appropriate. Empowerment is then the process of obtaining these basic opportunities for marginalized people, either directly by those people, or through the help of non-marginalized others who share their own access to these opportunities. It also includes actively thwarting attempts to deny those opportunities. Empowerment also includes encouraging, and developing the skills for, self-sufficiency, with a focus on eliminating the future need for charity or welfare in the individuals of the group.

Encrypt
Convert data into code which cannot be easily understood by people who have no authorisation to view it.

End consumer
An individual who buys and/or uses a product or service.

End marker
Used at the end of a take in a film, TV Programme or audition to cover a mistake or to remind people who the person auditioning was during auditions.

Enterprise
A company or business. A business project, often one which is sometimes difficult and/or risky.

Enterprise application integration
Software technology that links computer Programmes, data bases, etc., within an organisation, so that information can be shared.

Enterprise compensation management (ECM)
The automation of the compensation process to assist organizations in the acquisition, management and optimization of its workforce.

Entrenpreneur
An ambitious person who starts new business ventures in order to make a lot of money, often taking financial risks.

Environmental impact assessment
The effect that a proposed project, such as a new building or development, will have on the environment.

Environmentalist
An individual who is concerned about the protection, conservation and improvement of the natural environment.

E-procurement
Electronic procurement. Businesses using the internet to purchase from, or

sell goods and services to, other businesses.

Equal employment opportunity (EEO)

A policy statement enforced by the Equal Employment Opportunity Commission that states that equal consideration for a job is applicable to all individuals, and that the employer does not discriminate based on race, color, religion, age, marital status, national origin, disability or sex.

Equilibrium price

The price at which the demand of a particular product or service is equal to the quantity supplied.

Equity

(1) Value determined by subtracting debts from assets.
(2) An alternate term for stock or similar securities which denote a partial ownership.

Equity accounting

When a company records, in its financial records, profits which can be claimed from an affiliated company which they part own.

Equity theory

The idea that people desire to be treated fairly and thus compare their own contributions to the workplace—and resulting rewards—against those of their coworkers, to determine if they are being treated fairly.

E-recruitment

Web-based software that handles the various processes included in recruiting and onboarding job candidates. These may include workforce planning, requisitioning, candidate acquisition, applicant tracking and reporting (regulatory or company analytics).

Erisa (employment retirement income security act)

A federal law that governs pension and welfare employee benefit plans. ERISA requires plans to provide participants with plan information including plan features and funding. It also requires that plans provide fiduciary responsibilities for those who manage and control assets. It gives participants the right to sue for benefits and breaches of fiduciary duty.

ERP

Short for enterprise resource planning, a business management system that integrates all facets of the business, including manufacturing, sales, marketing, finance and human resources. This is slightly different than best-of-breed HRIS applications and the industry continues to debate the merits of one versus the other. With the growing popularity of web-based applications (ease of use, lower costs) ERP seems to be losing out, especially in the mid-market.

Escape clause

A condition in a contract which allows the contract to be broken in particular circumstances.

E-tailer

An retailer who uses the internet to sell goods and/or services to the public.

Ethernet

Technology, invented by The Xerox Corporation, which connects computers in a local area network (LAN).

Ethics committee

In medicine, an independent body which is appointed to examine and consider the rights and safety of people taking part in clinical trials.

Ethnic monitoring

Recording and evaluating the racial origins of employees in a company to ensure that all races are represented fairly.

Ethnocentrism

A home country orientation but with export of surplus production.

Euphemism

The replacement of a strong/offensive word or phrase with an alternative word or phrase considered to be milder/inoffensive. Euphemisms are used widely and very wrongly by politicians and business people attempting to avoid responsibility and personal acknowledgment of mistakes, bad decisions and unjustifiable actions, etc. Euphemisms in such situations are part of 'spin', or spinning a story.

Euroland

Also known as the Eurozone. All the countries in the EU (European Union) that use the Euro as currency.

European union

EU. Previously called the European Community. An international, economical and political organisation which brought the nations of Europe together so that people, goods, money, services, etc., can move freely between member nations.

Ex-gratia

Something given or carried out as a favour or gift, rather than as a legal duty.

Ex-officio

Someone who has a right to be included because of their job or position, e.g. to sit on a committee. (Latin - by virtue of office or position)

Ex-stock

Goods which are available for immediate delivery because the supplier has them in stock.

Ex-works

Goods which are delivered to the purchaser at the plant or place where they are manufactured. The purchaser then pays for transporting and insuring the goods from that point.
Ex: Cirque de Soleil expanded beyond the boundaries of traditional circus acts with its themed Vegas entertainment offerings. It has no competitors.

Exchange rate

Also known as Foreign Exchange Rate. The rate, which can vary from day to day, at which a country's currency can be exchanged for another country's currency.

Exchange rate exposure

When a business risks losing money because of the need to change one currency for another of lower value.

Exclusive distribution

Contracting with single channel members to move the product through the commercialization schedule. (Not to be confused with Exclusive exposure: Selling a product only through a single outlet in a particular region or market. Exclusive retail outlets are expected to perform many, if not most of the marketing functions to promote and support sales.)

Execution risk

The risk that a company's plans, or a project, will fail because of changes being made, e.g. entering a new market, bad management, etc.

Executive coaching
Executive coaching is a professional relationship between a coach and an executive, or an executive team. The goal is to assist executives with positive leadership development. It can be provided in one-on-one sessions or via the Internet.

Executive compensation
Also called executive pay, compensation packages are specifically designed for executive-level employees that include items such as base salary, bonuses, perquisites and other personal benefits, stock options and other related compensation and benefit provisions.

Executive director
Also called Internal Director. A person who usually works as a full-time senior employee for a company, and is responsible for the day to day running of the business, and is often a member of the company's board of directors.

Executive search
An agency or organization used by employers to assist them with the selection and placement of candidates for senior-level managerial or professional positions.

Exempt versus non-exempt employees
The difference between exempt and nonexempt employees is who gets paid overtime and who doesn't. The U.S. Department of Labour specifically designates certain classes of workers as exempt, including executives, administrative personnel, outside salespeople, highly skilled computer-related employees, doctors, lawyers, engineers, etc. Managers who hire and fire employees and who spend less than half their time performing the same duties as their employees are typically also exempt employees. In general, the more responsibility and independence or discretion an employee has, the more likely the employee is to be considered exempt. Generally, any worker performing repetitive tasks is most likely nonexempt and must be paid overtime.

Exit interview
The final meeting between management, usually someone in the HR department, and an employee leaving the company. Information on why the employee is leaving is gathered to gain insight into work conditions and possible changes or solutions.

Exit strategy
A plan by an investor to dispose of an investment, such as shares in a company, to make a profit, or a business owner to dispose of their company, e.g., by selling the business, floating it on the stock market, ceasing to trade, handing it over to another family member, etc.

Expatriate
An employee who is transferred to work abroad on a long-term job assignment.

Expectancy theory
A theory of motivation developed by Canadian Victor Vroom, Yale professor of management and psychology, established in his 1964 book, Work and Motivation, which essentially states that motivation

necessarily comprises and is determined by three elements of belief:
1. Effort will produce success.
2. Success will produce reward.
3. These outcomes will be personally satisfying.

Experience curve
In business, when costs fall and production increases as a result of increase in workers skills and lower material costs.

Expert system
A computer software system which can provide expert knowledge for a specific problem when users ask a series of questions.

Export credit
A loan taken out by an importer with a bank in an exporters country, so that the importer can buy foreign goods and pay for them at a later date.

Export credit guarantee fund
A facility, provided by government treasury, to guarantee the development costs of exports or legal claims arising there from.

Export factoring
A facility offered by banks to exporters. The bank is responsible for collecting payments for exported goods, so that the exporter can borrow money from the bank before the goods have been paid for by the customers.

Export processing zone
A zone, designated within the country, enjoying tax privileges or other status, where goods and services can be brought into, reprocessed and re-exported.

Exporting
The marketing of surplus goods produced in one country into another country.

Exposition
A public event at which businesses, that produce related goods, can showcase their products and/or services.

Exposure
Presentation of a sales promotion piece or advertisement to an individual, such as a person viewing a television commercial or a reader opening a magazine to an advertisement page. The number of exposures achieved is an important measure of the effectiveness of an advertisement as measured in conjunction with the quality of the exposures achieved. For example, if a golf club advertisement is exposed to 1000 golfers; it has greater value than if it is exposed to 1 million non-golfers.

Expropriation
The annexation or seizure of national assets as an extreme form of political action.

Extension strategy
A marketing strategy to stop a product going into decline by making small changes to it, reaching new customers or finding new uses for it, e.g. a drink which was sold as an aid to those recovering from illness is now sold as a sports drink.

External competitiveness
Being able to sell goods and services to customers in foreign countries at a competitive price.

External customer
A person or organization outside your organization who receives the output of a process. Of all external customers, the end-user should be the most important.

External debt
Also known as Foreign Debt. Money that is owed by the government, organisations or individuals to creditors in other countries.

External equity
A situation in which an organisation's employees receive similar pay for the same type of work as employees in other organisations, i.e., pay which is equal to market rates.

Extranet
A private computer network to which a company's customers and suppliers can link and communicate using the Internet.

Eye tracking
Research method used in advertising to determine which parts of an advertisement tend to get consumer attention. Accomplished by tracking eye movements.

Eyeballs
Advertising term. A name given to the number of people who visit a website advertisement, which can be counted by the number of click-throughs.

E-zine
An electronic magazine which is published on the internet, or delivered by e-mail.

F

FAS
A contract of sale "free along side" whereby the seller undertakes to place the goods alongside a ship ready for boarding and carry all charges up to that point.

FOB
A contract of sale "free on board" whereby the seller undertakes to place the goods on board a named ship at a named port and berth and carry all charges up to delivery over the ships rail.

Face value
The value printed on the face of a stock, bond, or other financial instrument or document.

Facilitating agent
Firms or individuals that performs any number of distribution or commercialization tasks other than buying, selling, or transferring title of products or services. They perform these services more effectively and/or efficiently than the producer. Ex: Transportation, warehousing, financing, sorting, etc.

Facilitator
Person who helps a team with issues of teamwork, communication, and problem-solving. A facilitator should not contribute to the actual content of the team's project, focusing instead as an observer of the team's functioning as a group.

Facings
Generally a retail term used to describe the number of products displayed vertically on the same shelf. Marketers often provide incentive or pay to gain this exposure.

Factor comparison
A systematic and scientific comparison, that instead of ranking complete jobs, ranks according to a series of factors. These factors include mental effort, physical effort, skill needed, responsibility, supervisory responsibility, working conditions, etc.

Factory floor
The area of a factory where the goods are made. Also the collective name of the ordinary workers in a factory, rather than management.

Factory price
The price charged for goods direct from the factory, not including transport costs, etc. Factory Price is often quoted by retailers or in advertisements to show that products are for sale at a very low price.

Failure mode effects analysis
A technique that systematically analyzes the types of failures which will be expected as a product is used,

and what the effects of each "failure mode" will be.

Fair representation

The duty of fair representation is incumbent upon U.S. labour unions that are the exclusive bargaining representative of workers in a particular group. It is the obligation to represent all employees fairly, in good faith, and without discrimination.

Fairy dust

A term often used in the entertainment business. The final enhancement or touch on a project. The unknown factor which turns something great into something fantastic.

Fallen angel

Term used in finance to describe bonds which once had a good investment value, but have now dropped in value to a much lower rating.

False accounting

A criminal offence. Giving false information in, or destroying, a company's accounts, usually for personal gain. Fraud.

False bottom

On the stock market, selling prices which seem to have already hit their lowest level because of a subsequent price rise then fall through a false bottom because the price falls even lower.

Fast moving consumer goods (FMCG)

Products (and the related industry) which are sold in big volumes by big retailers at low profit margins, at keen prices, to domestic consumers - traditionally foods and groceries, household consumables, etc., and nowadays extending to any products of short life and disposable/consumable nature.

Fast track

Quick route in a career to success and promotion, associated with high ambition.

Fat cat

A wealthy person living off investments or dividends, or a chief executive of a large company or organisation who is on a very large salary, huge pension, etc.

Fault tolerance

Enables a system, especially in computing, to continue to operate properly even though a component in the system has failed.

Feasibility study

A preliminary assessment of a new project, including costs, risks, etc., to determine whether the project will be successful and practical.

Feather-bedding

A term often used in industry describing the practice of hiring more workers than is necessary to carry out a job, often because of a contract with a union.

Feature/accessory

Characteristics that are offered to the potential consumer that are sought out or desired as an attribute of form, time, place, and possession utility. An accessory is not essential in and of itself, but adds beauty, convenience, or effectiveness to what it is attached.

Federation

An organisation which has been formed by the joining together of a group of companies, clubs, etc.

Fidelity bond

Also known as Fidelity Insurance. Protects an employer against any losses incurred because of dishonesty, or damage caused, by an employee.

Fiduciary

Describes an organisation or individual who manages money or property for a beneficiary.

Figurehead

In business, organizations, politics, etc., a person who holds an important position or office but lacks real power or authority; a 'front man'. Derived from the carved painted figurehead models which traditionally were fixed to the front of sailing ships.

Filibuster

A person who attempts to delay or obstruct legislation by giving long speeches, but does not contravene rules concerning proceedings.

Fill or kill

Also FOK, on the stock exchange, an instruction received by a broker from a client to buy or sell specified shares immediately or not at all.

Finance

To provide or obtain funds for a business, commercial project, an individual, etc. The management of money. To sell or provide goods on credit.

Financial engineering

The practice of solving financial problems or creating financial opportunities in a company, by changing the way money is borrowed, debts paid, etc.

Financial equity

The ownership of interest in a company, usually in the form of shares.

Financial planner

An investment professional who helps with financial plans for specific goals and assists in the coordination of financial concerns.

Financial strength

A company's financial condition as seen by its analysts (*Value Line* rates financial strength on a scale from A++ to C.).

Finite capacity scheduling

A process in which a computer Programme organises tasks, matching the resources available to the most efficient way of production.

Firepower

The amount of power, money and/or influence that is available to a business or organisation.

Firewall

A firewall is a software or hardware-based network security system that controls the incoming and outgoing network traffic by analyzing the data packets and determining whether they should be allowed through or not, based on a rule set. A firewall establishes a barrier between a trusted, secure internal network and another network (e.g., the Internet) that is not assumed to be secure and trusted.

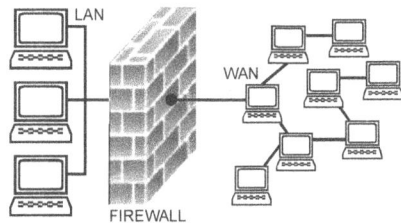

Firmware

Describes the fixed Programmes, which cannot be lost or changed, in electronic devices such as digital cameras, calculators, remote controls, etc.

First mover

A business that gains an advantage by being the first to establish itself in a specific market by producing a new product or offering a new service, or by being the first to use new technology.

First order of business

The most important task to be dealt with.

Fiscal drag

A situation in which wages rise because of inflation but income tax thresholds are not increased, which can push people into higher tax brackets and therefore makes them pay an increased proportion of their wages in tax.

Fiscal policy

A government policy to regulate a nation's annual economic activity by setting tax levels and determining government expenditure.

Fishbone diagram

Another name for a cause & effect diagram, derived from the original shape of the diagram as used by its creator, Kaoru Ishikawa.

Five nines

Refers to the 99.999% of the time that some companies claim their computer systems work properly.

Fixed assets

Fixed assets, also known as "tangible assets" [Dyckman, Intermediate Accounting,Revised Ed. (Homewood IL: Irwin, Inc. 1992),195.] or property, plant, and equipment (PP&E), is a term used in accounting for assets and property that cannot easily be converted into cash. This can be compared with current assets such as cash or bank accounts, which are described as liquid assets. In most cases, only tangible assets are referred to as fixed. International Accounting Standard (IAS) 16, defines Fixed Assets as assets whose future economic benefit is probable to flow into the entity, whose cost can be measured reliably.

Fixed cost

A cost which does not vary with changing sales or production volumes, eg, building lease costs, permanent staff wages, rates, depreciation of capital items.

Fixed parity

In foreign exchange, when the currency of one country is equal in value to the currency of another country.

Fixed term contract

Also known as Temporary Contract. A contract of employment which ends on a specific date, or on completion of a task or project. Fixed term employees have the rights to the same pay, conditions and benefits as full-time employees.

Fixed term employment

An employee agrees to work for a fixed term—until a certain date, at the completion of a project, etc.

Fixer

A person who makes arrangements for someone else, usually for a fee, by using their influence and often underhand, illegal methods.

Flame

To send a rude or unacceptable message by e-mail, or to post a message on an Internet forum which is offensive or inciteful.

Flash drive

A small portable device such as a 'pen drive' which connects to a USB port on a computer and is used to store data which can then be transferred to another computer. The term flash drive derives from 'flash' memory, invented by Dr Fujio Masuoka of Toshiba around 1980. The name flash (apparently, according to Wikipedia, 2010) was suggested by Masuoka's colleague, Shoji Ariizumi, who likened the memory erasure function to a camera flash.

Flash mob

A secretly-planned (usually via modern computerised social networking technology), quickly-formed, organized group of people, assembled to engage in a quirky activity, typically for the amusement and entertainment of the participants. Potentially the term may be applied to similar gatherings organized for more conventional promotional, protest or other publicity/pressure purposes, although this strays somewhat from the usual concept, in which the flash mob event is an aim in itself, rather than part of a wider campaign with a specific purpose. The expression is not new.

Flats

In the entertainment industry, these are painted canvas sheets fixed onto wooden frames used on film sets, etc. for scenery.

Flexecutive

A manager who works flexible hours, often from home using the Internet. A multi-skilled executive who can change tasks or jobs with ease.

Flexible spending accounts (FSA)

FSAs allow employees to set aside a portion of their earnings on a pre-tax basis into separate spending accounts to fund allowable health care and/or dependent day care expenses. The funds must be segregated as per IRS regulations.

Flexible work arrangements

Schedules that allow employees to structure their work hours around their personal responsibilities. Examples include flextime, job sharing, telecommuting and a compressed workweek. Home sourcing has become a popular flexible work concept in recent years. In this arrangement, employees work full-time from their homes.

Flexitime

A work system in which employees work a set number of hours each week or month, but they decide when they are going to start and finish each day, usually between a range of given working hours.

Flight capital

The movement of large sums of money from one of investment to another, or from one country to another, to avoid high taxes or financial instability due to political unrest.

Flighting

A cost effective method of advertising. A commercial is scheduled to appear on TV, usually when viewing figures are high (flight). There are periods in between the flights when the commercial does not appear on TV (hiatus). During the TV hiatus the product being advertised will often appear in newspapers or magazines, so the public is continually aware of it.

Floor limit

In retailing, the highest amount of money for a sale for which a debit or credit card can be used by a customer without authorisation from the customer's bank.

Floor trader

Also known as a Local. An investor who is allowed on the trading floor of a stock exchange, to buy and sell shares, etc., for their own account.

Flotation

The process of financing a company by selling shares on the stock exchange for the first time.

Flowchart

A graphical representation of a given process delineating each step. It is used to diagram how the process actually functions and where waste, error, and frustration enter the process.

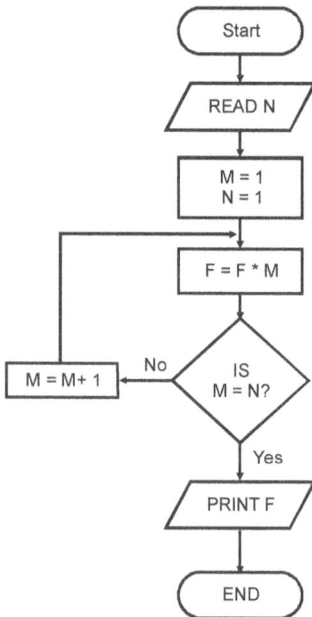

Flyback

Also known as a Callback. A series of screening interviews for a job during which a person, usually a student, is interviewed several times, often on the same same day, by the prospective employer.

Flynn effect

Research showing that the results of IQ (Intelligence Quotient) tests in various countries (i.e. internationally) have risen consistently over several decades, (after political scientist James R Flynn).

FOB - 'Free on board'

The FOB (Free On Board) abbreviation is an import/export term relating to the point at which responsibility for goods passes from seller (exporter) to buyer (importer). It's in this listing because it's commonly misunderstood and also has potentially significant financial implications. FOB meant originally (and depending on the context stills generally means) that the seller is liable for the goods and is responsible for all costs of transport, insurance, etc., until and including the goods being loaded at the (nominated FOB) port. An importing buyer would typically ask for the FOB price, (which is now now often linked to a port name, eg., FOB Hamburg or FOB Vancouver), knowing that this price is 'free' or inclusive of all costs and liabilities of getting the goods from the seller to the port and on board the craft or vessel. Logically FOB also meant and still means that the seller is liable for any loss or damage up to the point that the goods are loaded onto the vessel at the FOB port, and that thereafter the buyer assumes responsibility for the goods and the costs of transport and the liability. From the seller's point of view an FOB price must therefore include/recover his costs of transport from factory or warehouse, insurance and loading, because the seller is unable to charge these costs as extras once the FOB price has been stated. The FOB expression originates particularly from the meaning that the buyer is free of liability and costs of transport up to the point that the goods are loaded on board the ship. In modern times FOB also applies to freight for export by aircraft from airports. In recent years the term has come to be used in slightly different ways, even to the extent that other interpretations are placed on the acronym, most commonly 'Freight On Board', which is technically incorrect. While technically incorrect also, terms such as 'FOB Destination' have entered into common use, meaning that the insurance liability and costs of transportation and responsibility for the goods are the seller's until the goods are delivered to the buyer's stipulated delivery destination. If in doubt ask exactly what the other person means by FOB because the applications have broadened. While liability and responsibility for goods passes from seller to buyer at the point that goods are agreed to be FOB, the FOB principle does not correlate to payment terms, which is a matter for separate negotiation. FOB is a mechanism for agreeing price and transport responsibility, not for agreeing payment terms. In summary: FOB (Free On Board), used alone, originally meant that the transportation cost and liability for exported goods was with the seller until the goods were loaded onto the ship (at the port of exportation); nowadays FOB (Free On Board or the distorted interpretation 'Freight On Board') has a wider usage - the principle is the same, ie., seller has liability for goods, insurance and costs of transport until the goods are loaded (or delivered), but the point at which goods are 'FOB' is no longer likely to be just the port of export - it can be any place that it suits the buyer to stipulate. So, if you are an exporter, beware of buyers stipulating 'FOB destination' - it means the exporter is liable for the goods and pays transport costs up until delivery to the customer.

Focus list

A list of companies, recommended by an investment firm, whose shares are worth buying or selling.

Footer

In a report or document, a line or block of text that appears at the bottom of every page which is printed from a computer.

Footfall

The extent or measure of numbers of people who visit a business or shop or other retail/leisure/entertainment venue during a given period of time. Footfall is a crucial factor in retailing methods, and also in promotion and advertising which focuses on the physical presence on foot of consumers at a particular location.

Force field analysis

A tool, developed by social psychologist Kurt Lewin, which is used to analyze the opposing forces involved in causing/resisting any change. It is shown in balance sheet format with forces that will help (driving forces) listed on the left and forces that hinder (restraining forces) listed on the right.

Force majeure

A clause in a contract which exempts the contracting party (e.g., insurer) from liability in the event of an unforeseen intervention or catastrophe which prevents fulfilment of contractual obligations, such as war, act of God, etc. The term force majeure is French, meaning loosely 'superior strength'.

Forced ranking

Also known as a vitality curve, this is a system of work performance evaluation in which employees are compared against each other instead of against fixed standards. Based on the "20/80 Rule" idea, that 20 percent of employees do 80 percent of the meaningful, productive work, the top 20 percent of workers are rewarded and, oftentimes, the bottom 10 percent are fired.

Foreign exchange

Facilities' business across national boundaries, usually expressed in foreign currency bought or sold on the foreign exchange market.

Forex

Also called FX, refers to Foreign Exchange, in which foreign currencies are bought and sold.

Fortune 500

Published by Fortune magazine, an annual list of the 500 US corporations with the largest revenue.

Forward integration

A business strategy whereby a company takes control of its distributors, therefore guaranteeing the distribution of the controlling company's products.

Forward rates

A mechanism whereby the risk of changes in exchange rates can be covered by obtaining a new rate quote for a future exchange of currencies.

Forwarding company

Also called a 'freight forwarder', a company specialising in transfer of freight from businesses or individuals by finding an appropriate transporter of the goods.

Four-colour process

In printing, the use of four ink colours -yellow, magenta, cyan and black - which are combined together to produce the whole spectrum of colours.

Fractional ownership

An arrangement where a number of people or companies each buy a percentage of an expensive asset, such as a property. The individual owners then share the asset, and when it is sold the profits are distributed back to the owners.

Fragmentation

Ability to break up or identify various media that target specific audiences, allowing marketers to more effectively target segments and niches.

Franchise

An authorisation or license - effectively a business, which can be bought - enabling someone (franchisee) to use the franchisor's company name and trademarks to sell their products services, etc., and usually to receive certain support, in a particular area of a country. A franchise for a whole country is typically called a master franchise.

Free collective bargaining

A situation in which workers and union members meet with employers to discuss working conditions, pay, etc., in talks that are not limited by law or government.

Free enterprise

An economic system in which private businesses have the freedom to compete with each other for profit, with minimal interference from the government.

Free market

A market in which prices of goods and services are affected by supply and demand, rather than government regulation.

Free on board

Maritime trade term. The supplier delivers the goods to a ship at a specified port. The supplier then pays the shipping costs after obtaining official clearance. Once they have been put on board, the buyer is then responsible for the goods.

Free port

A port where goods can be brought and stored temporarily, without custom duties having to be paid, before being shipped to another country.

Free rider

A person or organisation that enjoys benefits and services provided by others, and doesn't pay their fair share of the costs.

Free zone

An area in a country where importers can store foreign goods, prior to further transportation, without having to pay customs duties or taxes on them.

Freeconomics

A situation in which companies provide certain goods and services for free, and those businesses who don't follow suit are likely to fail.

Freedom of association

The right of workers to join a union and to bargain collectively. This right is protected by the Universal Declaration of Human Rights and the Human Rights Act of 1993.

Freedom of association

The right of individuals to join together to form, or join an existing, group or organisation, including a union.

Freemium

(Combination of *free* and *premium*) When a product or service, such as a digital application for a smart phone or tablet, is provided free of charge, but a premium is charged for advanced features or functionality.

Freeware

Computer software that is copyrighted by the author and offered, usually on the Internet, free of charge.

Frequency

Number of times an advertising message is presented within a given time period. In general, number of times something occurs within a specified period of time. Frequency may refer to the issues of a periodical, the purchases made by a customer over time, or the number of times a commercial or an advertisement is aired or printed or reaches its audience.

Frequency distribution

An organization of data, usually in a chart, which depicts how often an different events occur. A histogram is one common type of frequency distribution, and a frequency polygon is another.

Frequency words

Terms use in marketing plans or proposals that contain bias—unless followed by data (numbers, percentages, indices, etc.). The following require data: usually, constantly, mostly, frequently, typically, generally, continually, sometimes, occasionally, sporadically, intermittently, rarely, seldom, hardly ever. The two exceptions: always (100%) and never (0%).

Frictional unemployment

Unemployment of people who are temporarily between jobs, changing careers, changing location, etc.

Fringe benefit

A benefit given to employees in addition to their salary, such as a company car, pension scheme, paid holidays, etc.

Front-end load

A fee charged for an investment, for example an insurance policy, limited partnership, mutual fund, etc. The fee is made with the initial payment, and subsequent payments are therefore lower.

Frontstage technology

Innovative advances embraced by consumers that provide convenience and confidence relative to usage and purchasing decisions. Example: 24/7 banking/ATMs at your fingertips (Internet). It's technology that makes it easier for consumers to satisfy needs.

FTSE

An abbreviation of the Financial Times Stock Exchange (Index), commonly referred to verbally as 'footsie'. There are various FTSE indices (indexes), including most notably the FTSE 100, which is the index of the top 100 shares on the London Stock Exchange, whose movement is regarded as an important indicator of national (and wider) economic health and buoyancy. The FTSE 100 represents about 80% of the market capitalization of all shares listed on the London Stock Exchange, which is interesting considering over 3,000 companies are listed in total.

Fulfilment

In the context of business and retailing, fulfilment refers to the processing of a (consumer or commercial) customer's purchase/order - i.e., a 'sale'. Fulfilment is generally considered to happen after the order is placed and usually payment is made, completing on confirmation of safe and correct delivery to the customer. Payment/ invoicing is generally separate from the fulfilment process/provider. In most cases fulfilment entails the warehousing, stock management, product 'picking', order assembly/ compiling, packaging and delivery, then confirmation of safe delivery, of products/orders for which payment has already been made. Fulfilment may be an internal activity of the selling organization, or may instead be contracted to an external provider of fulfilment services.

Fulfilment house

A provider of order-processing fulfilment services to a 'selling' company, typically processing sales/ orders of the selling company, through to the delivery of products to the purchaser. Specific activities of a fulfilment house generally include warehousing, stock control, order picking, packaging, distribution/ delivery to the customer (and confirmation thereof), and typically a degree of direct customer communications, and potentially handling returns.

Full-time contract

A permanent or ongoing contract of employment in which the employee works at least the standard number of hours in a working week, usually 35.

Full-time equivalent (FTE)

A value assigned to signify the number of full-time employees that could have been employed if the reported number of hours worked by part-time employees had been worked by full-time employees instead.

Functional job analysis

Developed by the U.S. Department of Labour, functional job analysis is a method of gathering specific and detailed job information. This information can be used to write job descriptions.

Fundamental analysis

An analysis of stocks based on fundamental factors, such as company earnings, growth potential, etc., to determine a company's worth, strength, and potential for growth.

Fungible

Fungible is the property of a good or a commodity whose individual units are capable of mutual substitution, such as sweet crude oil, shares in a company, bonds, precious metals, or currencies. It refers only to the equivalence of each unit of a commodity with other units of the same commodity.

Future

A legally binding contract to deliver/take delivery on a specified date of a given quality and quantity of a commodity at an agreed price.

G

Gaffer

In the entertainment industry, a member of a film crew who handles the lighting equipment.

Gag clause

Refers to the employment contract restrictions used as a means of protecting the organization's trade secrets or proprietary information.

Gagging clause

An informal term which has become generally used in formal business/ employment language, a 'gagging clause' is a clause in an employment contract, or more commonly a termination contract, which prevents an employee from disclosing certain information about the company or employing organization (typically extending to related organizations/ interests) to the press, union officers, authorities, etc., and by implication also extending to the police. Often an employer agrees or enforces a payment with/upon the employee to secure the signature to the gagging clause or contract which contains it.

Gagging order

A legal order issued by a court to prevent the public reporting of a court case.

Gainsharing

Also called profit sharing. An incentive system which enables employees to have a share in a company's profits.

Game theory

Sometimes called Games Theory, this is a potentially highly complex branch of mathematics increasingly found in business which uses the analysis of competing strategies (of for example market participants) and their effects opon each other to predict and optimise outcomes and results. Relates strongly to cause and effect and chaos theory. Game Theory may also arise in military strategy.

Gamification

Use of gaming concepts to motivate or drive certain behaviors from a target audience. Much like continuity Programmes, organizations offer awards, points, and other specific offers when customers check in on their websites. It's an incentive, or reward, for multiple visits.

Gamification

Use of gaming concepts to motivate or drive certain behaviors from a target audience. Much like continuity Programmes, organizations offer awards, points, and other specific offers when customers check in on their websites. It's an incentive, or reward, for multiple visits.

Gantt chart

A bar chart that shows planned work and finished work in relation to time. Each task in a list has a bar corresponding to it. The length of the bar is used to indicate the expected or actual duration of the task.

Gap analysis
Enables a company to assess the gap between its actual performance and its potential performance, by comparing what skills, products, etc. are available to what is required to improve performance, output, etc.

Garden leave
Also called Gardening Leave. Term used when an employee's contract has been terminated but they are instructed by the company to stay away from work, on full pay, during their notice period. Often to prevent them from working for competitors during that time.

Garnish
To take part of someone's wages, by law, to pay their debts, e.g. child support, alimony.

Gatekeeper
A person in an organisation who controls access to the people in the organisation, and/or controls access to information or goods, or even a market. Microsoft could be described as a gatekeeper to the computer industry. Google could be described as a gatekeeper to the internet industry.

Gazelle
A US term for a fast growing company that creates a lot of job opportunities, and which has grown by at least 20% in the last four years.

Gazump
In selling and buying property, a term used to describe when a purchaser has an offer accepted by the vendor but is then gazumped because someone else makes the vendor a higher offer which the vendor then accepts instead of the first person's offer.

Gearing
The ratio of debt to equity, usually the relationship between long-term borrowings and shareholders' funds.

Geek speak
Technical language often used by computer experts which doesn't make sense to non-technical people.

General agents
General agents are middleman for carriers and brokers and usually focus on the 250 employee market. Usually an individual appointed by a life or health insurer to administer its business in a given territory. GAs are important for companies who sell to small employers or brokers e.g., benefits administration software providers.

General agreement on tariffs and trade (GATT)
An institutional framework producing a set of rules and principles with the intention of liberalising trade between member countries.

General creditor
A person or company that lends unsecured money, so that the creditor is unlikely to recover much of the loan if the debtor goes bankrupt or does not pay it back.

General strike
Widespread withdrawal of labour by a nation's workforce, which aims at bringing the country to a standstill because of a disagreement over pay and/or working conditions.

Generalist
A person who has a broad general knowledge at a high level, and/or many skills.

Generation I
The term used to describe children born after 1994 who are growing up in the Internet age.

Generation X
A term used for people born during the 1960s and 1970s, who are often described as disaffected and irresponsible.

Generation Y
The term used to describe individuals born between 1985 and the present.

Genetic-based Discrimination
The practice of requesting or requiring genetic testing information during the hiring process or using genetic testing information to base any other employment decisions or actions.

Geocentrism
A world orientation with world market strategies.

Geodemographics
Study of where potential customers live, their ages, income levels, education, and how it affects spending. Data are used to create clusters that help marketers identify and define potential target markets—those who might be intrigued to know more about their products.

Geographic information system (GIS)
demographic databases, digitized maps, and computer software designed to help marketers interpret data and define potential markets.. Ex: Metropolitan Life employs GIS to target customers and boost profits.

Geographical differential
The variance in pay established for same or comparable jobs based on variations in labour and costs of living among other geographic regions.

Geographical segmentation
a defined market segment defined or divided according to geographic units, such as nations, states, regions, counties, cities, or neighborhoods. McDonalds' burgers in India are made from lamb, and in Mexico, chili sauce is added to the beef.

Geotargeting
Ability to target a marketing or advertising campaign based on defined set of target customers within a defined geographic territory.

Gerontocracy
A government or political system which is ruled by old men.

Get all your ducks in a row
A term for getting organised, having everything in order and making sure all the small details are accounted for before embarking on a new project.

Get go
From the start, the earliest stage of something. Used in the phrase 'From the get go.'

Gift tax
A tax payable on gifts over a certain annual value made during the lifetime of the giver.

Giro
A system, used in some countries, of transferring money from one bank or post office account into another using a central computer.

Giveback
An agreement in which employees accept a wage reduction or fewer benefits as a gesture of goodwill, usually because of an economic

downturn. The employees are often offered wage rises and new benefits at a later date.

Glamour stock

A company's shares, which are very popular with investors, because they have performed well on the stock exchange.

Glamping

A portmanteau word meaning 'glamorous camping', for example staying in a posh serviced yurt (a large Mongolian-style nomadic tent) and eating luxury hamper foods.

Glass ceiling

An invisible barrier in the workplace which prevents women and minority groups from advancing to positions of leadership in a company, although some do manage to 'break through' the glass ceiling.

Glass wall

An imaginary barrier in the workplace which prevents women and minority groups from being employed in other sectors of business or industry.

Glitterati

Combination of Glitter and Literati. Glamorous, rich, famous people, often connected to show business.

Global environment

All semi or uncontrollable factors which a marketer has to account for in carrying out global operations.

Global evaluation

A four stage organisational development process evolving from first stage; domestic focus to a fourth stage; global marketing strategy of extension, adaptation and creation of market opportunities.

Global market

A universal market that can be viewed as a total global economy in which organizations target markets that extend beyond local borders; hence, globalization.

Global marketing

Marketing on a worldwide scale reconciling or taking commercial advantage of global operational differences, similarities and opportunities in order to meet global objectives.

Global products

Products designed to meet global market segments.

Global village

A term used to describe the whole world as a single community, connected by electronic communication systems, such as the Internet.

Globalisation

The process of integrating nations, economically and socially, through free trade, international business activities, technology (for example the Internet), etc.

Glocalisation

Global Localisation. A term used when an international company adapts its manufacturing methods, products or services to suit local conditions.

Goal setting

Assigning specific, attainable goals to a person, team or organization. Goal setting is a motivational technique, as workers often rise to the challenges given them.

Going public

An expression used to describe the first public selling of shares of an institution that previously sold shares privately.

Gold reserve

The amount of gold bullion or gold coins held by a country's central bank to support its currency and provide security for its international debts.

Golden handcuffs

Financial incentives or benefits given to a valued employee to ensure that they continue working for a company, and to discourage them from wanting to leave to work for another company.

Golden handshake

Usually offered to high-ranking executives in a large company. A clause in their contract which provides them with a large sum of money and/or other benefits in the event of them losing their job or retiring.

Golden parachute

A company's agreement with an employee, usually a top executive, which promises a significant amount of money and/or benefits if the employee is forced to leave their job, usually because of a change of company ownership, outside of the control of the original employer company.

Gone to the wall

Describes a business which has failed.

Good faith bargaining

A requirement of the Employment Relations Act of 2000 that all parties to a contract conduct negotiations with a willingness to reach an agreement on new contract terms.

Goodwill

The difference or premium which a purchaser pays, or which a seller asks, for a business or company compared to the 'book value' of its assets, typically representing intangibles such as brand value, intellectual property, talent, market relationships, etc., and which tend to reflect the overall value and appeal with which the purchaser regards the target acquisition. Over-estimating goodwill value, sometimes to an extraordinarily stupid degree, is a surprisingly common downfall of many big corporate takeover deals, when arrogance and blindness to market trends of the acquiring CEO and takeover team can lead to a reckless waste of shareholder funds and ruthless cost-cutting, post-acquisition, when performance, synergies and return on investment fail to reach required levels.

Googlewhack

Two proper words (found in a dictionary) which together produce just a single result from a normal Google search. A googlewhack tends not to retain its status indefinitely, and sometimes only fleetingly, because due to the strange popularity of the effect, googlewhacks are likely to be published on the web when discovered, which immediately produces a second occurrence.

Grace

A period of time given to a debtor to enable them to pay an overdue bill or loan, or extra time given in a contract for a piece of work to be finished.

Grandfather clause

A provision in a new law which allows the person or business already engaged in the activity, which may have been made illegal, to continue to be so engaged.

Graphology

The study of handwriting, often used as a way of analysing a person's character.

Grass roots

The ordinary people in a business or organisation, rather than the management or the decision-makers.

Gratis

Gratis is the quality of an action where the action is willingly provided without any requirement by the provider for compensation or monetary remuneration. It is often referred to in English as free of charge (FOC), complimentary, or on the house.

Graveyard market

A term used on the Stock Exchange to describe a Bear Market in which share owners are reluctant to sell because they face substantial losses, and buyers are reluctant to buy because the financial outlook is poor. Those who are in it can't get out, and those who are on the outside have no desire to get in.

Gravy train

A business activity which makes a large profit for an individual or an organisation without much effort. To have it easy.

Green audit

Also called Environmental Audit. An official assessment which shows the effect that an organisation or a company has on the environment.

Green card

In the US, a legal document which allows an immigrant to become a permanent resident, to work legally and to become eligible for citizenship.

Green marketing

Promotional activities aimed at reflecting the level of its concern for renewable/recycled resources and well-being of the community. For example, Nestle Waters is touting its Eco-Shape bottle as one of the lightest half-liter plastic bottles available.

Green taxes

Also called Ecotax. Taxes which are levied on companies, businesses, etc., to discourage activities which will harm the environment.

Greenback

An informal term for US paper money, i.e., the dollar, derived from the colour of the money.

Greenwashing

Organizations that spend more time and money claiming to be "green" through promotional Programmes than actually implementing business practices that minimize environmental impact. Ex: Hotels that ask guests to reuse sheets or towels; this does little to reduce water and energy.

Grey knight

A third person, or company, who makes an unsolicited bid in a corporate takeover, and who takes advantage of any problems which arise between the first bidder (White Knight) and the company being acquired.

Grey market/gray market

In marketing and business a grey market (gray market in US-English) is the supply of official goods through unofficial channels, for example the availability of branded consumer products on the internet from unauthorized stockists. Also called a parallel market orproduct diversion. These terms do not refer to counterfeit goods. The reference is to the unofficial, sometimes illegal, distribution and availability of official branded original goods. The term alludes to the older expression 'black market', and is used or analysed most

91

commonly from the standpoint of manufacturers, who generally regard grey markets as threatening to their marketing distribution and pricing strategies. The term grey market extends widely and includes notably the substantial availability of products which have been diverted from one international marketing territory to another.

Grey swan

a marketing/economics/probability expression about random events with big consequences, a 'grey swan' refers to a major predicted or known event of national or more usually international significance, which has uncertain outcomes and unquantifiable effects on society, economics, etc.

Grievance

a complaint by an employee due to an alleged violation of law or collective bargaining or dissatisfaction with work conditions.

Grip

In the film and TV industry, a member of the film crew who makes sure that the lighting is right for a scene. They also move scenery and set up large pieces of equipment.

Gross domestic product

Commonly abbreviated to GDP, Gross Domestic Product is a very frequently used term in business and economics, and basically refers to a nation's total production at market values. GDP is however not easily explained or understood at a detailed and precise level. GDP may be calculated in different ways. Each method requires some qualification of precise definition, and then comprises quite complex formulae, mainly to ensure there is no double-counting, and no ommissions. The main methods seem to be as follows, although each nation has its own rules, and various institutional bodies produce other rules and standards for calculations and definitions. Ordinary people can reasonably regard fully detailed definitions of GDP very confusing. Lots of experts do too.

Gross misconduct

An action so serious that it calls for the immediate dismissal of an employee. Examples include fighting, drunkenness, harassment of others and theft.

Gross national product (GNP)

The market value of all goods and services outputted by residents of a country in one year including income from aboard.

Gross profit

Sales less cost of goods or services sold. Also referred to as gross profit margin, or gross profit, and often abbreviated to simply 'margin'.

Gross profit margin

Expressed as a percentage, what is left from a company's sales after cost of goods sold is paid out. Gross profit margin is obtained by dividing gross income by net sales.

Group dynamics

The way that people interact within a group that determines how it functions and how effective the group is.

Growth strategy

Strategy aimed at winning larger market share, even at the expense of short-termearnings, such as diversification, product development, market penetration, and market development (from the Marketing Opportunity Grid).

Guerrilla marketing

Unconventional methods of performing marketing activities (primarily promotion) on a low budget. It is up to the "guerrilla marketer" to be creative to generate product publicity. It can take many forms, such as social media (pop-up ads on Facebook and Twitter or video clips on YouTube). These tactics are utilized by both small and large-scale companies.

Guru

An influential teacher or an expert in a particular subject who shares their knowledge, often by writing books.

H

Hacker
Nowadays the word hacker commmonly refers to a person who breaks into or 'hacks' into the secure computer systems of an organization, especially websites and online systems, using online connection, often just as a technical challenge, or potentially with intent to steal, destroy, vandalise information, websites, etc. Originally however the terms hack and hacker referred to a person who enjoyed exploring and experimenting-perfectly legitimately and legally - with computer code and related computing systems, out of curiosity or for purposes of technical challenge and improvement, discovery, etc. This is an example of how language and meanings evolve over time, particularly when a term becomes distorted for dramatic effect by mass media. Be aware in this case therefore, that some people - especially original 'old-school' hackers and computer code enthusiasts could be offended and unjustly maligned by the criminal implication of the common illicit hacking interpretation. Incidentally among coding enthusiasts the original technical term for a criminal 'hacker' was a 'cracker'.

Haggle
Negotiate with someone over the price of something until an agreeably mutual price is reached.

Haircut
A percentage subtraction from the market value of an asset, typically on a large scale, enforced by a powerful institution or authority in response to debt/liabilities incurred by the asset owners/investors, producing an effective devaluation of the asset. The 'haircut' term became a more general description for a tax or levy imposed on ordinary savings accounts with reference to the EU-imposed tax on Cyprus bank deposits in 2013, although the underpinning principle/cause was consistent with the technical meaning of the term.

Hall test
A term used when a group of people are gathered together at a particular location and asked to take part in market research.

Halo effect
Where the image or reputation of a person (or group or organization or brand or other entity) is enhanced by influence from or association with the quality of another situation. A halo effect typically refers to an unreliable indicator of good quality (ethics, goodness, honesty, value, benevolence, etc) but might rarely instead refer to an unreliable indicator of negative quality.

Handbill
A small printed advertisement, usually on one sheet, often given out to people by hand.

Hands-free
Term used when a telephone can be used without having to be held in the hand.

Hands-off
A term often applied to managers who do not directly participate when dealing with a situation in the workplace by letting the people involved decide what they want to do.

Hard selling
An aggressive type of selling which puts a lot of pressure on a prospective customer to buy a product or a service.

Harvesting
A term used when a product is still being sold, although it is no longer being invested in, prior to being withdrawn from the market.

Hashtag
A type of tag (here a prefix used with a word/term/reference/etc via electronic keypads, computing, smartphones, etc) in the social networking website Twitter and similar short messaging systems, so that a word preceded by the hash symbol (#) may be found subsequently or otherwise organized, analyzed, displayed, etc. The symbol is generally called the pound sign in the US, since it is used commonly instead of the traditional British £ symbol in referring to sterling currency.

Hawthorne effect
The theory that organizations can motivate their employees as much or more by expressing concern for problems as by actually improving their work conditions. This personal interest results in increased performance, according to the observations of productivity researcher George Elton Mayo.

Hawthorne effect
Specifically the inclination of a group of workers to change their behaviour positively because they were being studied, irrespective of whether they were subjected to 'positive' or 'negative' conditions. First observed in studies by Elton Mayo at the Western Electric plant in Chicago, beginning 1928. The Hawthorne Effect basically established that attitude was more influenced by emotional rather than economic factors.

Headhunt
To find a person who is specialised in a particular job, usually for a senior position in a company, and then persuade them to leave their present employment.

Health and safety
Concerned with the protection of employees from risks and dangers in the workplace.

Health care flexible spending account (FSA)
A benefit plan designed to allow employees to set aside pre-tax dollars to pay for eligible medically related expenses, such as medical, vision or dental exams, copays and deductibles, as well as other out-of-pocket expenses.

Health savings accounts (HSA)
A tax-free account that can be used by employees to pay for qualified medical expenses. To be eligible for a Health Savings Account, an individual must be covered by a High Deductible Health Plan (HDHP), must not be covered by other health insurance, is not eligible for Medicare and can't be claimed as a dependent on someone else's tax return.

Heat map

Graphic representation of data where varying degrees of a single metric appear by color, such as tracking clicks on a marketer's website.

Heatseeker

A person who, without fail, always buys the most up to date version of an existing product as soon as it comes onto the market.

Heavy-up

Short period of concentrated advertising in a media schedule. Advantageous when a product is more likely to be used at one specific time. Ex: With an approaching summer, Water Babies Sun Screen will be touting its protection when families will soon be lounging at the beach.

Hedge fund

A type of investment fund, which is unregulated and usually very high risk, used by individuals and organisations (not the general public) with large amounts of money to invest.

Hedging

A mechanism to avoid the risk of a decline in the future market of a commodity, usually by entering into futures markets.

Heterogeneous markets or products

Geographic markets or products the marketer or customer sees as different. This term also applies to markets, in that a heterogeneous market is unique or different from others. As regards the need for winter snow blower equipment, Minneapolis and Houston would be heterogeneous (dissimilar winter weather).

Hierarchy of effects

Series of 7 steps that prospective customers move through, from initial product awareness to trial. These steps are divided into cognitive (knowledge about), affective (feelings about), and conative (action tendencies towards purchase) dimensions.

Hierarchy of needs

The ordering of a person's needs into hierarchy of relative potency such that as lower order needs are fulfilled higher, unfulfilled order needs emerge, which require fulfillment.

High context culture

Minimum reliance on explicit verbal or written conversations, more on the "implied".

Hire purchase

HP. A contract between a buyer and seller in which the buyer takes possession of an item and then pays for it in regular instalments, usually monthly, and does not become the owner of the item until the final payment has been made. Also referred to as 'Buying on the never-never'.

Histogram

A specialized bar chart showing the distribution of measurement data. It will pictorially reveal the amount and type of variation within a process.

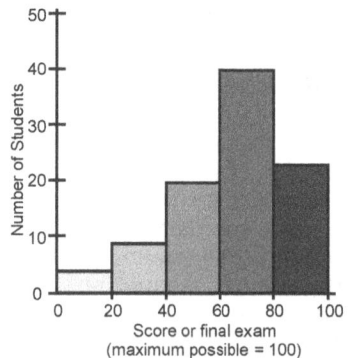

Score or final exam
(maximum possible = 100)

Holding company
A company which is formed for owning and holding controlling shares in other companies.

Holding period return/yield
The yield calculated by dividing the income plus price appreciation during a specified time period by the cost of the investment.

Hole in the wall
An informal term for a cash dispensing machine, also called an ATM (automated teller machine).

Homeostasis/homoeostasis
Homeostasis is a powerful and illuminating concept. Technically, yet somewhat unhelpfully, the OED (Oxford English Dictionary) defines homeostasis as "The tendency towards a relatively stable equilibrium between interdependent elements, especially as maintained by physiological processes". Homeostasis is perhaps more easily understood initially via its Greek roots, meaning 'similar' and 'standing still'. Homeostasis refers scientifically to the act of 'self-balancing' or 'internally self-compensating' in ecological/ biological systems.

Homogeneous markets or products
Geographic markets or products the customer sees is basically the same (sharing similar attributes, or easily substitutable products). Homogeneous markets share similar traits or conditions. As regards the need for winter snow blower equipment, Minneapolis and Cleveland would be homogeneous.

Horizontal integration
Distribution strategy in which one company establishes ownership or control of another company's production, transportation, manufacturing, distribution, or retail outlet. Ex: .Most guitar companies do not manufacture their own low-end guitars. They contract Samick Guitars, the largest guitar manufacturer in the world (Indonesia). Samick can produce them much cheaper than these companies can produce themselves. Samick controls the low-end production channel for these products.

Horizontal integration
The joining together of businesses which produce similar goods or offer similar services, or are involved in the same stage of activities, such as production or selling.

Horizontal sector/horizontal market
Horizontal market sector-Often called simply a 'horizontal'-this refers to products/services which can be supplied to or 'across' a number of 'vertical' sectors, for example, office cleaning services to various industries (verticals), or transport services to different industries (verticals).

Hoshin kanri
Japanese term for hoshin planning, a form of interactive strategic planning which aids the flow of information up and down the organizational layers in a systematic, productive way.

Hoshin planning
A method of strategic planning for quality. It helps executives integrate quality improvement into the organization's long-range plan. According to the GOAL/QPC Health Care Application Research Committee, "Hoshin Planning is a method used to ensure that the mission, vision, goals, and annual

objectives of an organization are communicated to and implemented by everyone, from the executive level to the 'front line' level."

Hot desking

In an office, the practise of having a pool of desks, which are usually equipped with phone and computer links, so that workers can use them when they are required, rather than having their own individual desk.

Hothouse/hothousing

Informal term for an intense development environment or method, or the verb equivalent, typically applied to training people or developing ideas or ventures; a metaphor alluding to a heated greenhouse for growing plants.

HR audit

A periodic measurement of human resources effectiveness, conducted by internal staff or with the use of an HR audit system.

HR generalist

An individual who is able to perform more than one diversified human resources function, rather then specializing in one specific function.

HTML banner ad

Form of Internet promotion featuring information or special offers for products and services. These small space "banners" are interactive: when clicked, they open another website where a sales can be finalized. The hosting website of the banner ad often earns money each time someone clicks on the banner ad.

Human capital

The collective skills, knowledge and competencies of an organization's people that enables them to create economic value.

Human capital management

The challenge of recruiting and retaining qualified candidates, and helping new employees fit into an organization. The goal is to keep employees contributing to the organizations intellectual capital by offering competitive salary, benefits and development opportunities. The major functions of human capital management include Recruitment, Compensation, Benefits and Training.

Human resource information system (HRIS)

Business software systems that assist in the management of human resource data (e.g. payroll, job title, candidate contact information). Some of the larger HRIS platforms include SAP and Peoplesoft.

Human resource outsourcing (HRO)

A contractual agreement between an employer and an external third-party provider whereby the employer transfers responsibility and management for certain HR, benefit or training-related functions or services to the external provider.

Human resources

HR. The people who are employed by and operate a business or organisation. The department within a company which deals with recruitment, training, employee benefit, etc.

Hunt and peck

Inexpert slow typing on a keyboard using only one or two fingers.

Hush money

A bribe or payment, which is often illegal, given to someone to stop them from disclosing information, usually to prevent bad publicity or to hide a crime.

Hushmail

An internet service offering encypted email, file storage, etc.

Hyperbole

(Pronounced 'hy-per-bollee' - emphasis on the 'per' syllable)- Hyperbole is an extreme and figurative exaggeration or overstatement, which in strict grammatical terms is not generally expected to be taken seriously or interpreted literally, for example, "I've been waiting for ever for a bus," and yet where hyperbole is used for motivational or persuasive effect in business or politics, the technique very often intends to convey maximum impact on an audience, for example, "You'll never have another opportunity like this..." The word derives ultimately from the Greek root words: huper, over, and ballein, to throw.

Hyperinflation

An extraordinarily high rate of economic inflation during which a country's prices rise and currency loses its value uncontrollably in a vicious cycle, usually occurring during severe political instability or war. Normally inflation is measured in terms of a few percentage points increase per year-typically below 10% and sometimes approaching 20%. By contrast hyperinflation may be at a rates of tens of percentage points increase per month, and in extreme rare cases hundreds of percentage points per month. In this event, where prices can be doubling and currency values halving every few weeks (or days, in very rare situations), a country is forced to issue new banknote denominations of ludicrously high values, and within living memory news stories have featured workers collecting their wages in wheelbarrows.

I

Idea showers
Usually called Brainstorming. A method of problem solving involving members of a group meeting and sharing ideas.

Identity theft
A crime in which someone obtains another person's personal information, such as passport, credit card details, etc., and poses as that person in order to steal money, get benefits, make purchases, etc.

Ideology
An individual's organisation or country's political belief.

Idle time
The time that a piece of equipment or a machine, such a as computer, is available, but is not being used.

Image advertising
Attempt to create a favourable mental picture of a product or firm in mind of consumers to associate the advertised product or firm with certain lifestyles or values. Ex: In some markets, McDonalds' golden arches image is being changed to appear more upscale.

Impeach
To charge somebody, usually a government official, with serious misconduct. To cast somebody out of public office, for example a president or courtroom judge because of a serious crime or misdemeanor.

Imperfect market
A market in which buyers do not have access to enough information about prices and products, and where buyers or sellers can have an influence over the quantity and price of goods sold.

Import duty
A tax charged on certain goods which are brought into a country.

Impound
To seize and hold property, funds, etc., in custody (typically by a state-empowered authority), often during legal dispute.

Impression
Singlular display or viewing of a particular ad or web page. Some search engine ad fees are based on the number of impressions; others are PPC (number of clicks).

Impression
Singlular display or viewing of a particular ad or web page. Some search engine ad fees are based on the number of impressions; others are PPC (number of clicks).

Inbound marketing
(where the customer comes to you) Passive sales technique the relies on

the customer to find a product (as opposed to marketer-directed promotional efforts to communicate with potential customers). Achieved through website content personalization, media monitoring, and lead nurturing.

Inbound marketing

(where the customer comes to you) Passive sales technique the relies on the customer to find a product (as opposed to marketer-directed promotional efforts to communicate with potential customers). Achieved through website content personalization, media monitoring, and lead nurturing.

Incapacity benefit

A state benefit in the UK which is paid to people below pensionable age who have made National Insurance contributions, and who are too ill or disabled to work.

Incentive marketing

The offering of rewards or gifts to sales people as an incentive to get more orders from dealers or customers. To offer customers rewards for buying products or services.

Incentive pay

Additional compensation used as a motivational tool to exceed specified work goals.

Incidence rate

Indicates the number of workplace injuries/illnesses and the number of lost work days per 100 employees.

Income elasticity measurements

A description of the relationship between the demand for goods and changes in income.

Income fund

An investment fund with high returns which pays the owners a regular income.

Income per capita

The market value of all goods and services outputted by a country divided by the total number of residents of that country.

Income statement

The financial statement of a firm that presents both revenues and expenses during a specified time period.

Income tax

A tax paid by individuals to the government, the amount of which is dependent on how much a person earns from their salary and/or other sources of income.

Incubator

An organisation or company which provides support to new businesses to help them develop and grow.

Indemnify

To insure and offer financial protection against loss, damage or liability.

Independent contractor

A self-employed person who works for another person or organization on a contract basis.

Independent financial advisor

(IFA) Someone who works independently, i.e., not for a particular company, and offers people advice about financial matters and recommends where to invest their money.

Index

A quantity whose variation represents market fluctuation (The Standard & Poor's 500 index measures the overall change in the value of 500 stocks of the largest firms in the US.).

Index-linked

Concerning salaries, pensions, investments, etc. If they are Index-Linked it means that the payments or income from these may vary according to the rate of inflation.

Indicator

Quantitative measure of performance. Indicators are usually ratios comparing the number of occurrences a certain phenomenon and the number of times the phenomenon could have occurred.

Indict

To formally charge someone with a crime.

Indirect compensation

Compensation that is not paid directly to an employee and is calculated in addition to base salary and incentive pay (i.e., health/dental/vision insurance, vacation, retirement benefits, educational benefits, relocation expenses, etc.).

Indirect materials

In accounting, products or services, such as electricity, cleaning materials, chemicals, etc., which are used in the production of goods but are not part of the end product.

Individual employment agreement

A written document that describes the legal relationship between an employer and employee.

Induction

The introduction and training of a member of staff in a new job or position in a company.

Industrial action

Also called a strike in the UK. Known in the US as Job Action. A protest by employees during which they refuse to work, usually because they want better wages and/or better working conditions.

Industrial psychology

Applied psychology concerned with the study of human behavior in the workplace and how to efficiently manage an industrial labour force and problems encountered by employees.

Industrial relations

A field of study that examines the relationship between employer and employees, particularly groups of workers in unions.

Industrial tribunal

An independent judicial body which deals with disputes between employers and employees.

Industrialist

A person who owns or runs a large industrial enterprise. They are often referred to as a Business Magnate.

Industry rank

Value Line's ranking of a company within its own industry.

Inflation

Normally referring to the economy of a country, inflation is the gradual increase in the price of goods and/or services, and the consequential devaluing of the national currency. Inflation is typically up to 10%, or more unusually approaching 20% per year. Minimising inflation is normally a high priority within national fiscal policy since higher levels of inflation cause a variety of economic and business problems.

Inflation risk
The uncertainty of the future real (after-inflation and -tax) value of an investment.

Inflection point
In business, when important significant changes take place in an organisation.

Infomediary
An agent who works on behalf of a business, collecting information on, and developing profiles of, individual customers.

Infomercial
Information Commercial. A long television commercial presented in the form of a documentary or TV Programme. This format is used so that it does not appear to be selling a product or service.

Information superhighway
Communications network, notably the Internet, which provides high speed access to information in the form of sound, text, images, etc.

Information system
A system for gathering, analysing and reporting data aimed at reducing uncertainty in business decision making.

Information technology
Information technology (IT) is the application of computers and telecommunications equipment to store, retrieve, transmit and manipulate data, often in the context of a business or other enterprise. The term is commonly used as a synonym for computers and computer networks, but it also encompasses other information distribution technologies such as television and telephones. Several industries are associated with information technology, such as computer hardware, software, electronics, semiconductors, internet, telecom equipment, e-commerce and computer services.

Inheritance tax
Also called Death Duty in the UK. Known as Death Tax in the US. A tax imposed by the government which much be paid on the total value of the estate of a deceased person.

Initial public offering
An Initial Public Offering (IPO being the Stock Exchange and corporate acronym) is the first sale of privately owned equity (stock or shares) in a company via the issue of shares to the public and other investing institutions. In other words an IPO is the first sale of stock by a private company to the public. IPOs typically involve small, young companies raising capital to finance growth. For investors IPOs can risky as it is difficult to predict the value of the stock (shares) when they open for trading. An IPO is effectively 'going public' or 'taking a company public'.

Injunction
An official court order which demands that someone must refrain from carrying out certain actions.

Innovation
The introduction of new ideas, goods, etc., or new methods of production. A new way of doing something.

Inorganic
A term used to describe the growth of a business from mergers or takeovers, rather than from the increase in productivity or activity of the company's own business.

Inside information

Information about a company which is known only by the owners, management and/or employees, and not the general public. The use of Inside Information for the buying and selling of shares is usually illegal.

Inside track

An advantageous position in a company or organisation. To know about something before others get to hear about it.

Insolvency

Not having enough finances or assets available to pay all your debts.

Instant access account

A bank or building society account which allows you have instant access to your money without any penalties.

Institutional advertising

Promotional messages aimed at creating, improving, or reinforcing an organization's image: reputation enhancement, goodwill, advocating ideas. Such efforts are not intended to promote sales; rather, it's a form a corporate advertising, often aimed at vested publics with an interest in how the organization conducts business (stockholders, elected officials).

Insurance adjuster

Also known as a Claims Adjuster. An independent person who investigates insurance claims for an insurance company and evaluates the damage caused and decides whether the claims are valid, and if they are, how much should be paid in settlement to the insured party.

Intangible asset

A company's assets which do not physically exist, such as brand name, trademarks, copyrights, etc.

Intangible rewards

A subjective benefit that has no monetary value, such as praise for excellent performance.

Integrated marketing

Strategy aimed at unifying different marketing mix elements/tactics, such asmass marketing, one-to-one marketing, and direct marketing. It complements and reinforces themarket impact of each method in product development, pricing, distribution, promotional Programmes, and customer service.

Intellectual capital

The skills and knowledge of a company's employees, which can be used to make the company more successful than its competitors.

Intellectual property

Commonly abbreviated to IP, an idea or creation, e.g., artwork, writing, etc., that belongs to an individual or organisation, which has commercial value and therefore cannot be copied or sold without the owner's permission.

Intensive distribution

Selling a product through all responsible and suitable wholesalers or retailers who will stock or sell the product.

Intentional destruction

Situation or circumstances requiring organizations to break down the existing structure of its operations to properly research future potential and restructure itself to face the realities of a dynamic marketplace. Generally brought on by advancements in technology and innovation.

Inter alia

Latin for 'among other things' - a traditional term which typically precedes a list of examples, and is found in official or formal text or various sorts. Inter alios means 'among other people', but is much less used.

Interactive plans
A planning system whereby headquarters sets a policy and framework and subsidiaries interpret these under local conditions.

Interest rate
A fee which is charged for borrowing money, e.g., a loan from a bank or financial institution, lease arrangement, goods bought through hire purchase, etc.

Intermediary
A mediator or agent who negotiates between two parties who are unable or unwilling to reach an agreement by themselves.

Intermediate good
Physical resources applied to or used in the creation of a final product. For example, sugar may be consumed directly or used in the manufacturing of ice cream. (Changing the shape or form of a resource in the creation of another product is call a transformation.

Internal customer
Someone within your organization, further downstream in a process, who receives the output of your work.

Internal equity
In a company or organisation, ensures the pay each employee receives is determined fairly by the type of job they do.

International monetary fund
A fund, with world wide country membership, (united nations) which lends money to countries on a short term basis to assist them balance of payments problems.

International organisation for standardization
ISO. A non-government organisation with over 150 member nations, which promotes international standards in trade, technology, science, economy, etc.

International product life cycle
A model which suggest that products go through a cycle whereby high income, mass consumption countries go through a cycle of exporting, loss of exports to final importers of products.

International products
Goods or services seen as having extended potential into other markets.

Internesia
Relating to the Internet. Being unable to locate a particular website which you found interesting or on which you saw a useful piece of information.

Internet cafe
Also called a Cybercafe. A public place where people can use a computer, usually for a fee, to check e-mail, access the Internet, etc. These places often sell drink and food, like a regular cafe.

Intervention price
A guaranteed minimum price set by a government for a product, usually farm produce. If the price falls below this then the government, or agency, will buy the produce at the Intervention Price.

Interventionism
The policy of a government to intervene and manipulate a country's (often its own) affairs and/or economy.

Intestate
Without leaving a will, as used in the phrase, 'to die intestate'.

Intrapreneur
A person employed by a large company to work independently to develop new projects and business within the company.

Intrinsic value
The actual or real value of a business, commodity, asset, etc., rather than the market value or share price.

Invention
A new device, process, product, etc., which has been created and developed by an individual or a group.

Investment
Money or capital that is invested in a business or in an account with a financial institution in order to make a profit or earn interest.

Investment adviser
A professional who, for a fee, manages an investment portfolio.

Investment boutique
A small company which offers specialist advice about investments and business.

Invisibles
'Invisible' services of a country, such as banking, tourism, insurance, etc, of which the buying and selling are from international trade.

Involuntary liquidation
When a company is forced into bankruptcy by its creditors, so that its debts can be paid.

Ishikawa diagram
Another name for the cause & effect diagram, after its inventor, Kaoru Ishikawa.

Ishikawa, kaoru
One of Japan's quality control pioneers. He developed the cause & effect diagram (Ishikawa diagram) in 1943 and published many books addressing quality control. In addition to his work at Kawasaki, Ishikawa was a long-standing member of the Union of Japanese Scientists and Engineers and an assistant professor at the University of Tokyo.

Island position
An advertisement or commercial which is surrounded by text, or placed between TV Programmes, with no other advertisements, so it has no competition.

Iso 9000
A set of internationally-accepted standards, created by the International Organization for Standardization, for quality management and quality assurance. These standards apply uniformly across all industries and company size. Companies can receive ISO 9000 certification for meeting these standards.

Iso 9001, 9004
Developed by the International Organization for Standardization (ISO), it is a set of standards for quality management systems that is accepted around the world. Organizations that conform to these standards can receive ISO 9000 certification. The standard intended for quality management system assessment and registration is ISO 9001.

Issue price
On the Stock Exchange, the price at which a new share, stock, etc., is offered to the public.

Issuer
One who under writes (issues) and distributes a company's securities.

J

Jasdaq
Japanese Association of Securities Dealers Automated System. Japanese securities exchange, the headquarters of which are situated in Tokyo.

Jingle
A short song used in a promotional announcement, usually mentioning a brand name

Job accommodation network (JAN)
A service provided by the US Department of Labour's Office of Disability Employment Policy (ODEP), JAN's mission is to facilitate the employment and retention of workers with disabilities by providing employers and people with disabilities with information on job accommodations, entrepreneurship, and related subjects.

Job analysis
The process of gathering information about the requirements and necessary skills of a job in order to create a job description.

Job board
An online location that provides an up-to-date listing of current job vacancies in various industries. Applicants are able to apply for employment through the job board itself. Many job boards have a variety of additional services to help job seekers manage their careers and their ongoing job search processes.

Job classification
A method of evaluation used for job comparisons, which groups jobs into a prearranged number of grades, each having a class description and a specified pay range.

Job costing
A system of calculating the cost of each individual job or project carried out by a business, includes time, labour, materials, etc.

Job description
A written statement that explains the responsibilities and qualifications of a given job, based on a job analysis. The job description usually includes specific required tasks as well as an overview of the position and whom the employee reports to.

Job evaluation
A comparison of one job with other jobs in a company for the purpose of assessing fair compensation.

Job lock
A situation in which a person feels they cannot leave their job because they are afraid of losing benefits connected to the job.

Job protected leave
Allows people to officially take time off from their work for a longer period

without the fear of losing their job, often because of illness or pregnancy.

Job sharing

A work schedule in which two or more people voluntary do one full-time job, sharing the work and dividing the hours between them.

Johari window

A leadership disclosure and feedback model used primarily in self-help groups and corporate settings as a heuristic exercise which can be used in performance measurement and features the four quadrants (windows) of "knowing."

Joint consultation

An organisational decision-making process in the UK, where managers and employees representatives, usually from unions, meet to discuss matters relating to the employees working conditions, etc.

Joint stock company

A company or organisation owned by joint shareholders, which is a type of corporation and partnership. The stockholders run the company and share its profits and debts.

Joint ventures

An enterprise in which two or more investors share ownership and control over property rights and operations.

Jumble display

Mixture of often dissimilar products on a single display—usually promoted as clearance items.

Junk bond

Also known as High Yield Bonds. A high risk bond with a high interest rate, often used by companies to raise finances in order to take over other companies.

Just-in-time

JIT. A manufacturing system in which materials and components are delivered immediately before they are required, in order to increase efficiency, reduce waste and minimise storage costs.

Just-in-time instruction

Training given as needed for immediate application, without lag time and the usual loss of retention.

K

Kaizen

Japanese for 'improvement'. When implemented in the workplace, kaizen activities help to improve the running of a business.

Kanban

Japanese for 'visible record'. In industry, a manufacturing system which is regulated by the use of cards or boards which contain specifications and instructions for the production process of goods.

Keiretsu

In Japan, an alliance of companies or organisations which own shares in one another as a means of security, but each individual company operates independently.

Kerb market

In the US, the buying and selling of shares in companies which are not listed on the stock exchange. In the UK, the buying and selling of stocks and shares outside official trading hours.

Kettling

Term which is used to describe the police tactic of penning protesters into an area by forming a barrier around them and refusing to let them out.

Key account

In business, a company's main client or customer, who represents a large percentage of the company's income.

Key performance indicators (KPIS)

Tasks that are central to the success of a business and show, when measured, whether the business is advancing toward its strategic goals.

Keyword advertising

Used on the Internet. When a user types in a particular 'keyword', an advertisement which is linked to a business relevant to that word, is displayed alongside the search engine results.

Keyword effectiveness index

Compares the number of searches for a key word, providing Internet marketers the ability to include these terms/words on their websites.

Keyword effectiveness index

Compares the number of searches for a key word, providing Internet marketers the ability to include these terms/words on their websites.

Kickback

A bribe or illegal payment made to someone in exchange for a successful referral for a job or transaction.

Kidult

An adult who enjoys films, games, TV, clothes, etc., which are deemed more suitable for children or much younger people.

Killer app
Short for Killer Application. Derives from the computer industry. A new product or service which is the first in its category and therefore dominates that particular market, creating huge returns on the initial investment.

Kitemark
In the UK, the official mark of approval by the British Standards Institution, to show that a product or service is safe, reliable and of good quality.

KJ method
Another name for the affinity diagram, after its inventor, Kawakita Jiro.

Knocking copy
In advertising, the criticism or attacking of a competitor or a rival product.

Knock-off
An unauthorised copy of a product, usually designer clothing.

Knowledge
A customer's understanding or relationship with an notion or idea. This applies to facts or ideas acquired by study, investigation, observation, or experience, not assumptions or opinions.

Knowledge base
A knowledge base or knowledgebase (also KB or kb) is a special kind of database for knowledge management. A knowledge base is an information repository that provides a means for information to be collected, organized, shared, searched and utilized. It can be either machine-readable or intended for human use.

Knowledge worker
Also known as an Intellectual Worker. A person who is employed by a company to use their brain and intellect to work with information, rather than performing manual tasks.

Ksas
The Knowledge, Skills and Abilities an employee needs to meet the requirements of a job.

Kudos
Common management term meaning positive recognition, praise or fame- from the Greek word kydos, meaning glory.

L

Labeling
Description, instructions, and warnings printed on products and packaging as required by law or as an aide to the consumer.

Labour certification
Labour certification is a statement from the U.S. Department of Labor (DOL) that a particular position at a particular company is "open." It is the first step in the process of obtaining a green card.

Labour force participation rate
The ratio between the labour force (all those currently employed or seeking work) and the nation's total working-age population.

Labour intensive
A job requiring a lot of work, and often a lot of workers, in comparison to the costs of materials, equipment, etc.

Labour law
Also known as Employment Law. Legislation which defines the legal rights and obligations of employees in the workplace.

Labour law posting
Federal and state regulations requiring employers to post in conspicuous places a variety of labour law posters with information regarding employee rights

Labour market
A geographical region (local, national or international) in which labour transactions occur—employers find workers and workers find work.

Lading
Freight or cargo carried by a large vehicle. The act of loading cargo onto a ship.

Laffer curve
Named after US economist Arther Laffer (b.1940), the Laffer Curve refers graphically to notional/optimal government revenues according to changing levels levels of taxation, on the basis that at each extreme, i.e., 0% and 100% taxation, government revenues are zero, and that somewhere in between, a certain taxation % level (for which no general standard exists or can be applied) will produce optimal government revenues.

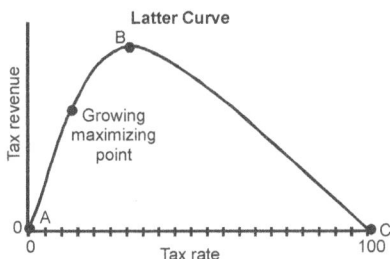

The expression was popularized in the mid-1970s after discussions between Laffer and government officals Don Rumsfeld and Dick Cheney, seemingly to advance Laffer's counter-intuitive argument that lower taxation would increase tax revenues. Laffer attributed the underpinning curve concept theory to Ibn Khaldun and John Maynard Keynes.

Lagniappe (native to Southern Louisiana and Southeast Texas: pronounced "lan-yap")

A little something extra; an unexpected surprise; gifts given to customers at the time of purchase. Ex: It's getting your car washed and vacuumed at no charge when taking it for service at the dealership. Or the chocolate chip cookie at check-in at Doubletree hotels.

Laicisation

The defrocking of a minister or priest. The changing to lay status.

Laid-off

In industry, etc., when workers lose their jobs, sometimes temporarily, because there is no work for them.

Laity

Usage is typically 'the laity' ('lay-ity'), an old traditional alternative word for lay people/members, typically used in relation to church organization and council, but applicable widely to ordinary people, as distinct from professional or qualified folk.

Landing page

A website page used to collect relevant data from those interested in the content featured on that page. Also known as Lead-capture page. Often used for invitation-only and special offer promotional Programmes that feature exclusive offers or discounts. A unique method to evaluate effectiveness of Internet marketing Programmes.

Larceny

The crime of unlawfully taking someone else's property or money. Theft.

Large cap

On the Stock Exchange, a company that has a large market capitalisation, i.e., a high total value of shares.

Law of one price

The rule that without trade barriers and transportations costs, identical products would cost the same worldwide using the appropriate exchange rate of currency.

Lay (people/person/member)

Also layman, or laywoman. Lay means non-professional, non-expert-ordinary member(s), of the public or of an organization, typically referring to religious communities, often relating to professions such as law and medicine, but potentially in any situation where non-professionals/ experts are differentiated from qualified/professionals. The term may have an arrogant or patronising implication where expert, qualified, learned professionals discuss the general public or members who lack expertise.

Layaway

Often referred to as Lay-By. A means of purchasing an item by paying a small deposit to reserve it and then paying the balance in installments. When the total purchase price has been paid the customer can then take delivery of the goods.

Lead user

Term introduced by economist Eric von Hippel in 1986. Lead users are individuals or companies who greatly benefit from being the first to use or adapt a product for a particular need, often months or years before the general public or other businesses are aware of the need for the product.

Leader
Someone who leads, sets example, inspires, motivates, etc-technically having the personal qualities which attract followers for given situations.

Leadership
A person or number of people responsible for leading a team or group of people, usually in some sort of organized body or company, or the direction of a smaller team in a specific project or situation.

Leadership development
Activities, whether formal or informal, that enhance leadership qualities

Leading indicator
A particular measure of a country's economic activity, used to predict near future economic trends.

Lean
Also known as the Toyota Production System or Just-In-Time Production. A system used in management, production, manufacturing, etc., to decrease waste and increase efficiency, especially with the use of automated assembly lines in the motor industry.

Learning curve
A graph depicting the rate at which a person learns a new skill. A steep learning curve shows that a person is learning quickly, and a shallow learning curve means that a person is slower and taking more time to learn.

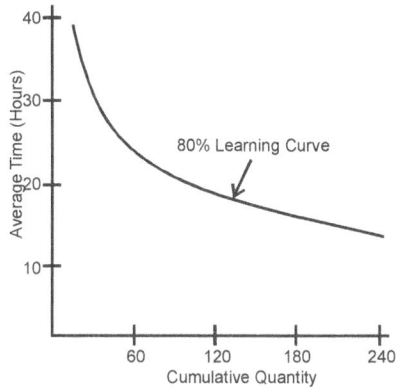

Learning management software and systems
A software platform for businesses and organizations designed to train and educate employees. Components typically include content delivery and other tools needed to administer, measure, track, and report / analyze the effectiveness of a company's training initiatives. Modern learning management systems (LMS) are often cloud-based solutions, allowing access to training and other LMS content & features online using a standard web browser.

Learning style
Learning styles are overall patterns that provide direction to learning and teaching. They involve educating methods, particular to an individual, that are presumed to allow that individual to learn best.

Lease purchase
A finance agreement in which an item, usually a car, is leased for a certain period of time with an option to purchase at the end of the contract.

Leaseback
An arrangement between a purchaser of a property and the vendor in which

the vendor immediately leases the property back from the purchaser.

Leave of absence
The period of time which a person is permitted by their employer to be absent from their job.

Leave-behind
A premium left with prospective customers by a sales person to remind them of the product or service being sold.

Legal aid
Legal assistance provided , usually by the state, for people or organisations who cannot afford to pay for solicitors or legal advice.

Legal entity
An individual or organisation who has the legal right to enter into a contract or an agreement, is responsuble for its actions, and can sue or be sued if the terms of the contract are broken.

Legal reserve
The minimum amount of money, required by law, that a bank, insurance company, etc., must set aside in order to be able to operate.

Legal tender
In day-to-day language the term generally refers to coinage or banknotes which have not been withdrawn or demonetised by the Bank of England and so are valid, but technically the term the UK refers to forms of currency which by law must be accepted by a creditor in payment of a debt.

Lemon
A defective product which is poor quality and fails to function as promised. Particularly used in the automotive industry, specifically for a poor-quality second-hand car, or a sub-standard new vehicle.

Lender of last resort
A country's central bank which loans money to other banks or financial institutions which cannot borrow money from anywhere else and do not have enough reserves to cover cash withdrawals by their customers.

Letter of comfort
A letter of approval written to a bank by a parent company on behalf of a subsidiary company which needs financial backing.

Letter of indemnity
A document in which an individual, company, etc., guarantees to protect another from costs, liability, etc., as a result of certain actions which may be carried out.

Letters of credit
These mechanisms are used by exporters and importers, and usually provided by the importing company's bank to the exporter to safeguard the contractual expectations and particularly financial exposure of the exporter of the goods or services. (Also called 'export letters of credit, and 'import letters of credit'.) When an exporter agrees to supply a customer in another country, the exporter needs to know that the goods will be paid for. The common system, which has been in use for many years, is for the customer's bank to issue a 'letter of credit' at the request of the buyer, to the seller. The letter of credit essentially guarantees that the bank will pay the seller's invoice (using the customer's money of course) provided the goods or services are supplied in accordance with the terms stipulated in the letter, which should obviously reflect the agreement between the

seller and buyer. This gives the supplier an assurance that their invoice will be paid, beyond any other assurances or contracts made with the customer. Letters of credit are often complex documents that require careful drafting to protect the interests of buyer and seller. The customer's bank charges a fee to issue a letter of credit, and the customer pays this cost. The seller should also approve the wording of the buyer's letter of credit, and often should seek professional advice and guarantees to this effect from their own financial services provider. In short, a letter of credit is a guarantee from the issuing bank's to the seller that if compliant documents are presented by the seller to the buyer's bank, then the buyer's bank will pay the seller the amount due. The 'compliance' of the seller's documentation covers not only the goods or services supplied, but also the timescales involved, method for, format of and place at which the documents are presented. It is common for exporters to experience delays in obtaining payment against letters of credit because they have either failed to understand the terms within the letter of credit, failed to meet the terms, or both. It is important therefore for sellers to understand all aspects of letters of credit and to ensure letters of credit are properly drafted, checked, approved and their conditions met. It is also important for sellers to use appropriate professional services to validate the authenticity of any unknown bank issuing a letter of credit.

Letters of guarantee

There are many types of letters of guarantee. These types of letters of guarantee are concerned with providing safeguards to buyers that suppliers will meet their obligations or vice-versa, and are issued by the supplier's or customer's bank depending on which party seeks the guarantee. While a letter of credit essentially guarantees payment to the exporter, a letter of guarantee provides safeguard that other aspects of the supplier's or customer's obligations will be met. The supplier's or customer's bank is effectively giving a direct guarantee on behalf of the supplier or customer that the supplier's or customer's obligations will be met, and in the event of the supplier's or customer's failure to meet obligations to the other party then the bank undertakes the responsibility for those obligations. Typical obligations covered by letters of guarantee are concerned with: 1. Tender Guarantees (Bid Bonds) - whereby the bank assures the buyer that the supplier will not refuse a contract if awarded. 2. Performance Guarantee - This guarantees that the goods or services are delivered in accordance with contract terms and timescales. 3. Advance Payment Guarantee - This guarantees that any advance payment received by the supplier will be used by the supplier in accordance with the terms of contract between seller and buyer. There are other types of letters of guarantee, including obligations concerning customs and tax, etc, and as with letters of credit, these are complex documents with extremely serious implications. For this reasons suppliers and customers alike must check and obtain necessary validation of any issued letters of guarantee.

Levy

A tax imposed by government, to meet a specific objective.

Liabilities

General term for what the business owes. Liabilities are long-term loans of the type used to finance the business and short-term debts or money owing as a result of trading activities to date . Long term liabilities, along with Share Capital and Reserves make up one side of the balance sheet equation showing where the money came from. The other side of the balance sheet will show Current Liabilities along with various Assets, showing where the money is now.

Libertarian/libertine

A person who believes in the freedom of speech and thought, and that people should be able to do whatever-within reason-they wish with minimal interference from government. The words derive from the Latin root liber, meaning free, like the word liberty, meaning freedom.

Licensing

A method of foreign operation cooperation whereby an organisation in one country agrees to permit a firm in another country to use the manufacturing, processing, trademark, know-how or some other skill provided by the licensor.

Lien

A legal right to take and keep another persons property until a debt has been paid by the property owner.

Life tables

Also called Mortality Tables. Tables which show peoples life expectancy, depending on their age, lifestyle, etc., often used by insurance companies.

Lifeboat

An emergency loan offered to a company or bank which is in financial trouble.

Lifestyle business

A business set up and run so as to fit with the wider life needs of the business owner(s) which might be called 'life balance', or happiness or wellbeing. Typically this will mean that the business can be established and operated with very simple, relatively small-scale, and easily manageable: infrastructure, overheads, inbound supply-chain (if any), premises (typically in a home), legal issues, administration products/ services range, ambition, marketing and advertising, technology and ICT, staffing, and demands on workload, time, and generally work pressures. Given these criteria, certain types of businesses do not make naturally good lifestyle businesses, because they imply/require a more burdensome degree for one or a number of the features listed above. Businesses that do not naturally make good lifestyle businesses would be for example: manufacturing.

Lifo (last in, first out)

A method of determining who should be laid off in which the most recent hires are laid off first.

Lightning strike

A sudden strike by workers, with little or no warning. These strikes are often short in duration and usually without official union backing.

Like-gate

Online barrier that requires a user to first "Like" a brand's page before being able to access specific content that could include special limited time offerings, special sales, and other promotions, thus allowing the brand marketer to stay in touch with target customers.

116

Likeonomics

Phenomena that consumers buy products from companies they like. Underlying principle: The more people like you, the more they will buy from you, and thus the more profit the company makes (attributed to Advertising Guru David Ogilvy).

Limit order

An order to buy stock once the price has dropped below the price limit.

Limited company

In the UK, a company that has a name ending in 'Ltd.' The owners of these companies have limited liability if the company gets into debt.

Limited liability

In law, the owners and/or shareholders of a limited company only lose the amount they have invested if the company gets into debt.

Linchpin

The most important person or thing in a business or organisation.

Line authority

In business, the power given to management allowing them to give orders and to control subordinates.

Liquidate

The closing down of a business by selling its assets to pay its debts.

Liquidated damages

The fixed amount agreed upon by parties to a contract, to be paid to one party in the case of a breach of contract by the other party.

Liquidity

The ability or ease with which assets can be converted into cash; also the degree to which one can obtain the full cash value of an investment.

Liquidity ratio

Indicates the company's ability to pay its short term debts, by measuring the relationship between current assets (ie those which can be turned into cash) against the short-term debt value. (current assets/current liabilities) Also referred to as the Current Ratio.

List price

Known as 'Sticker Price' in the US. The advertised or recommended retail price (RRP) of a product.

List rental

The renting, from an organisation, of a mailing list which has potential customer names and addresses, for a one-off mailing.

Litigant

A person or party who is involved in a court action or lawsuit.

Litigate

To legally settle a dispute in, or take a claim to, a court of law.

Litigious

To routinely or enthusiastically take legal action to settle disputes.

Litotes

A language term referring to understatement, used for emphasis, often ironically, in which the negative-opposite is used instead of the positive expression, for example, "It wasn't the best presentation I've ever given," when the speaker means that they considered it to have been a particularly poor one. Another example is the commonly used "Not bad," or "Not half Bad," when referring to something very good. The word litotes comes from Greek, litos, meaning single, simple or meagre.

Living trust

A trust created in which assets can be transferred to someone while the grantor (the person who owns the assets) is still alive. Living Trusts avoid dealing with the legalities of a will.

Loan shark

A loan shark is a person or body that offers loans at extremely high interest rates. The term usually refers to illegal activity, but may also refer to predatory lending with extremely high interest rates such as payday or title loans. Loan sharks sometimes enforce repayment by blackmail or threats of violence. Historically, many moneylenders skirted between legal and extra-legal activity. In the recent western world, loan sharks have been a feature of the criminal underworld.

Local content measure

Where a business or investor is required to purchase a certain amount of locally sourced materials to be used in the manufacturing, etc., of their product.

Local products

Goods or services seen only suitable in one single market.

Lockout

A term used during an industrial dispute, when management closes down a workplace and bars employees from entering until they agree to certain terms and conditions.

Locus standi

(Latin-place of standing) The right or capacity of a litigant to be heard or to bring an action in court.

Logistics

Process of planning, implementing, and controlling the efficient and effective flow and storage of goods, services, and related information from point of origin to point of consumption for the purpose of conforming to customer requirements, internal, and external movements, and return of materials for environmental purposes.

Logotype (logo)

Graphic element used to identify a company, or its products and services. Typically trademarked to legally protect ownership and usage rights so others cannot use it.

Long grass

To 'Kick something into the long grass' means to push a problem aside in the hope that it will be ignored or forgotten.

Long position

A situation in which an investor or dealer holds onto shares, etc., which they have purchased, expecting them to rise in value in the future.

Long term liability

Taxes, leases, loans, etc., which are payable over a period greater than one year.

Long-term care insurance

Helps provide for the cost of long-term care beyond a predetermined period, and is generally not covered by health insurance, Medicare, or Medicaid.

Long-term debt

A debt owed over a relatively long period of time.

Loophole

An unintentional mistake in a contract or a law which allows people to evade an obligation in the contract, or to get round the law without actually breaking it.

Looping

In films, TV Programmes, etc., the process of dubbing the original film footage by synching (lining it up) with new or replacement dialogue.

Loss leader

Products sold at or below cost to stimulate other profitable sales. Often, popular items are priced below cost to entice customer visits to a retailer's store of website. Can be highly profitable, should customers purchase several other items at the same time.

Loss leader

In retail, a product which is offered at a very low price to attract customers who will then buy other goods which will produce more profit for the retailer.

Low context culture

High reliance on explicit verbal or written communications or other explicit format.

Low hanging fruit

A term used in business for something which is easily obtainable and highly visible, and provides a quick easy way to making a profit.

Low yield

A term used to describe investments which are low risk and do not produce a high level of income.

Loyalty card

A card given to customers by a retailer which gives the customer points, etc., every time they shop there. These points convert into vouchers which the customer can spend at the store at a later date.

Luddite

A derogatory term for someone who opposes or disapproves of new technology and/or new methods of working, often because the changes threaten jobs. From the Luddite rioters of 1811-16, who in defence of labourers' jobs in early industrial Britain wrecked new manufacturing machinery.

Lump sum payment

A single large payment given to an employee, usually instead of more and smaller pay increases.

M

Machine code
Also known as Machine Language. A computer language, which consists only of numbers, that can be read and interpreted by a computer's central processing unit (CPU).

Macro
In a computer, a single instruction which results in a complete series of more detailed instructions being put into effect.

Macromarketing
Study of marketing processes, activities, institutions, and results from a broad perspective such as a nation, in which cultural, political, and social interaction are investigated. It is marketing in a larger context than any one firm: the delivery of a standard of living.

Magalog
A catalogue which appears to be a magazine, used for marketing purposes.

Magic bullet
A simple effective solution to a serious or complex problem, especially in medicine, for example a cure for a disease. The simplicity is for users, not necessarily for the developers.

Magnetic media
Disks and tapes which are used to record and store computer data.

Mail merge
The process of automatically personalising a customised letter or document by using a list of individual names and addresses, so the same letter can be sent to many people.

Mail order
The purchasing or selling of goods over the Internet, telephone, from catalogues, etc., which are delivered to the customer by mail.

Mainframe
Also known as 'Big Iron'. A large powerful central computer to which a network of smaller computers are connected, used commonly by large organisations.

Mainstream
A term applied to activities, ideas, products/services, etc., that are used/followed/supported by most people. Mainstream basically means 'commonly used by people'. Mainstream as a marketing term is the opposite to 'niche' or specialised. Interestingly while 'mainstream' seems like a relatively modern word, it's actually existed in this sense since about 1830.

Majority interest
Owning more than 50% of the total shares in a company, and therefore more than 50% of the voting interest.

Make to stock
In manufacturing, products which are made and stocked before customers orders have been received.

Makegood
In advertising, a free advertising slot given to a company by a TV station, magazine, etc., if the company's advert was previously run incorrectly.

Maladministration
In business or government, the act of incompetence or running a system in a dishonest way.

Managed care
A health care system in which the provider manages the care of the individual for a fixed fee. The opposite of this preventive intervention (or, population-based) approach is fee-for-service. Managed care emphasizes wellness and prevention.

Managed economy
An economy in which goods, allocation of resources and prices are determined by the government.

Managed hosting
A type of Internet hosting in which the hosting supplier deals with technical issues and problems related to the website, in addition to the basic hosting of the website.

Management buy-in
When a management team from outside a company acquires more than 50% of the company, so they become the majority shareholders, and then manage the company themselves.

Management buy-out
MBO. The purchase of all or part of a company by the company's existing managers.

Management by exception
A management style in which managers give employees the authority to run projects, etc., by themselves and managers only become involved if the employees fail to meet certain criteria or standards.

Management by objective (MBO)
A process of defining objectives within an organization so that management and employees agree on the overall goals and objectives for the organization. The employees determine and set goals for themselves based on the overall goals and objectives for the organization.

Manager
A person who is in charge of a project, department, group, team, etc.

Mandate
Technically a legal or official document giving an order or instruction. More loosely it refers to a permission or approval. In politics or democratic situations such as trade unions it refers to an authorisation for leadership to act based on election or vote. Derived from Latin mandatum meaning 'something commanded', from manus (hand) and dare (give). Mandate is also a verb, meaning to empower someone to take action.

Mandatory convertible bond
Bonds that must be redeemed in shares by the company which issues them, usually by a specified date.

Margin
The difference in the price of producing a product and the price it sells for, calculated as a percentage, i.e., profit margin.

Margin account

An account held by an investor with a broker in which the broker lends the investor money to purchase shares, etc., which are then used as collateral against the loan.

Margin call

A demand by a broker for an investor to bring his margin account up to the minimum level required by depositing additional money, shares, securities, etc.

Marginal productivity

The additional output of a product, etc., which is produced as a result of adding one unit of a resource, for example labour input, in the production process.

Markatainment (marketing + entertainment)

Using other goods and services to entertain customers at the point of purchase. Ex: Best Buy stores a free outdoor screening of the as-yet-unreleased Harry Potter movie for those waiting in line for doors to open for Black Friday sales. This is a form of publicity and sales promotion.

Market

Economic system bringing together the forces of supply and demand for a particular good or service. A market consists of customers, suppliers, and channels of distribution, and mechanisms for establishing prices and effecting transactions where exchanges take place. Often, marketers will define primary, secondary, and even tertiary markets to help it allocate its limited resources in the most effective and efficient manner.

Market basket

A way of measuring the cost of living. A collection of products or services which consumers buy on a regular basis, and the prices which are paid for them.

Market capitalization

The value found by multiplying the number of outstanding common stock shares by the share price; indicates firm size and total value held in stock.

Market clearing price

The price of a product or service at which the level of demand equals the level of supply.

Market control

A situation in which the quantity and/or price of goods or services is influenced by buyers or sellers.

Market development

Addition of new geographic markets in which to offer the existing mix of products and services—those NOT currently served by a firm.

Market economy

A situation in which businesses operate in a free market, i.e., they are in competition with each other and are not under government control.

Market entry

The way in which an organisation enters foreign markets either by direct or indirect export or production in a foreign country.

Market forces

Influences, such as the availability of raw materials for the production of goods, or customer numbers, which affect supply, demand and prices of products and services.

Market holding price

The charging of a price at what the market can bear in order to hold market share.

Market leader
A company or brand which has the highest sales of a particular product. A best-selling product.

Market order
An order to purchase or sell stock at a current price.

Market orientation
A business strategy whereby a company focuses on meeting the customers needs and wants regarding products and services.

Market penetration price
A low price at which a new product is offered when it first comes onto the market, in order to attract customers, after which the price is usually increased.

Market positioning
The adoption of a specific market stance, either leader, challenger, follower, flanker or adopter, vis a vis competition.

Market research
The process of gathering and analysing information about customers, competitors, etc., in order to make decisions and solve problems connected with selling products or services.

Market risk
The movement of a stock price relative to the overall market; indicated by beta.

Market saturation
The point at which a market is no longer generating new demand for a firm's products, due to competition, decreased need, obsolescence, or other uncontrollable variables.

Market sector
Competing businesses which produce or buy similar goods and/or services. The customers for which certain goods and services are marketed.

Market segment
A subgroup within a larger market in which people share certain characteristics and require similar products or services.

Market segmentation
Targeted market or audience for a given product is divided into categories (segments) based on geographic, demographic, or psychographic variables, such as demographic segmentation, geographic segmentation, and psychographic (behavioral) segmentation.

Market share
Percentage of sales volume captured by a brand, product, or firm in a given market.

Market test
The testing of a product or service in several areas of the country to see if customers will like it and want to buy it.

Market testing
Risk-reduction effort based on planning and executing a regional or local marketing strategy before rolling out nationally. Markets are selected based on demographics that mirror the total potential target market. Also used to test awareness and recall of advertising messages.

Market timing
The selecting of the best time for leaving or reentering the market in order to achieve the maximum result.

Marketing
Planning, executing and controlling the conception, pricing, promotion and

distribution of ideas, goods and services in order to build lasting, mutually profitable exchange relationships satisfying individual and organisational objectives.

Marketing analytics
scientific process for identifying patterns and relationships in survey data that will increase effectiveness of marketing activities. For example, after more than 40 years the GAP changed its logo, which set off negative postings on various blogs. So much so that the company went back to its original logo. When companies change parts of their strategy without consulting long-time faithful fans, it can cause an uproar and loss of loyalty by loyal customers. (Of course, the other side of this action is that the GAP received lots of free publicity.)

Marketing blitz
Intensive fast-paced campaign (attack), designed to build up business clients. Examples include face-to-face campaigning and intensive media ad spending. Several books on the topic: check out Guerilla Marketing by

Marketing channels
Connected system of exchange relationships of wholesalers and retailers, developed to build lasting bridges between buyers and sellers. It is based on their ability to perform marketing activities more effectively and efficiently than the producer.

Marketing concept
Goal-oriented risk-reducing integrated philosophy practiced by producers of goods and services that focuses efforts on satisfying the needs of consumers by allocating resources to satisfy that need, and making a profit by doing so. For example, a successful marketing concept in the perfume industry is about selling dreams, sex, and romance the benefits derived from perfume, not the perfume itself (its ingredients and packaging).

Marketing environment
Range of uncontrollable variables related to competitive, economic, political/legal, technological, and social/cultural variables that impact the target market and marketing mix.

Marketing hyperopia
Condition or situation when consumer willpower against acquiring a product or service is overshadowed or exaggerated by desire, pleasure, or indulgence to have it—often apart from the expense or actual need fulfillment. Often occurring in Maslow's Belonging and Esteem need levels.

Marketing mix
Combination of marketing elements used in the sale of a particular product, sometimes called the 4 Ps: product, price, place, and promotion.

Marketing myopia
When a business is being shortsighted regarding the needs of its customers, only focusing on its products or short range goals and missing marketing opportunities.

Marketing objectives
What an organization wishes to achieve (the end result). They focus on existing products in existing markets, new products for existing markets, existing products for new markets and new products for new markets (Marketing Opportunity Grid). Most importantly, they can be measured in terms of sales volume, sales value, market share, profit, percentage of penetration outlets, awareness and esteem. Savvy

marketers also add timelines and assign responsibilities to individuals to assure accountability.

Marketing plan
Set of specific goals (measurable), timelines (when goals are to achieved), and actions required (assignment of responsibility) to successfully implement a marketing strategy.

Marketing PR
Marketing PR is the combining of what are traditionally two separate departments, public relations and marketing, to one integrated front whereby all marketing and PR activities focus on reaching buyers directly. Marketing PR incorporates both traditional marketing and PR tactics with social media and other Internet-based initiatives that support the measurable goals of online publicity, increased web site traffic, search-optimization (SEO) and, lead generation. A key difference between traditional PR and Marketing PR is the use of a press release. Traditional PR writes and distributes a press release for the sole purpose of securing media placements. Marketing PR does this as well but also uses the press release to enhance website SEO, increase web site traffic and generate qualified sales leads.

Marketing research
Process of gathering, analyzing, and interpreting information (data) about a market, product, or service; or about past, present and potential customers' characteristics, such as pricing, spending habits, location, and needs; or about the industry as a whole and its competitors.

Marketing scorecard
A reporting approach that aligns marketing outcomes with objectives. Allows organizations to set, monitor, and adjust results to reduce risk. EX: Some oil companies use a scorecard to evaluate effectives of their service suppliers. During the life of a project, the supplier is graded on any number of factors; an overall score at the end may well determine whether it will be asked to bid on a future project.

Marketing strategy
Plan allowing the organization to concentrate its limited resources on the greatest opportunities to increase sales and achieve a sustainable competitive advantage. It is comprised of a target market and marketing mix.

Marketing-oriented company
An organization that aligns or adjusts the allocation of its resources to product development, distribution, pricing, and promotional message channeling as dictated by the demands, interests, and needs of its target market. This approach reduces risk and enhances sustainability of the organization.

Market-to-market
The process of valuing a security, share, etc., on a daily basis to assess its current price, rather than its acquisition price or book value.

Mark-up
Dollar amount added to the cost of products to get the selling price (can include incentives such as discounts and allowances), expressed as a percentage of the new selling price. Applies to each channel member.

Mark-up chain
Sequence of mark-ups used at different stages in a channel to help

determine the price structure among all channel members. This is helpful to marketers when analyzing the profitability of a new product or service.

Marque
A brand name or model of a well-known manufactured product, especially an expensive car.

Mass customization
Extension of one-to-one marketing exposure for customizing products and services on a mass scale via personalizing buying interactions for each customer.

Mass market
Describes products or services which have mass appeal and are aimed at large numbers of people or a whole population.

Mass marketing
Broad unfocussed attempts to appeal to an entire geographic market with one basicmarketing strategy utilizing mass distribution and mass media. Also called undifferentiated marketing.

Master franchise
Allows companies or individuals the right to purchase a sub-franchise business which can be developed in a particular area or country.

Material requirements planning
The use of computer software to plan and manage a production process, for example the amount of materials or parts required, calculation of workload, delivery schedules, etc.

Maternity leave
The time a pregnant employee is entitled to take off from her job before and after the birth of her baby.

Entitlement to Maternity Leave depends on how long the woman has been with her employer.

Maternity pay
An employee benefit paid to pregnant women when they take time off from their job to have their baby. Entitlement to Maternity Pay depends on how long they have worked for their employer and varies from country to country.

Mates rates
To sell a product or service to a friend or family member at a discounted or reduced rate on the normal price.

Matrix management
Also known as Dotted Line Responsibility. A system of management in which people from different departments in an organisation work together, so that each individual employee has two bosses, one functional and one operational. This is common in project management.

Matrix organisation
A complex form of organisational structure bringing together the competencies of geographic knowledge, product knowledge and know how, and functional competencies - financial, production and marketing - and a knowledge of the customer, industry and its needs.

Matrix organization
Used primarily in the management of large projects, a horizontal authority structure in which teams are created from various departments and report to more than one boss.

Maven
An expert, often self-proclaimed, in a particular field.

Maverick
An independent thinker who does not conform to accepted opinion on certain matters and takes a stand from other people.

Mean
The average of a group of measurement values. Mean is determined by dividing the sum of the values by the number of values in the group.

Mean wage
The average wage for a worker in a specified position or occupation, which may be skewed up or down if there are a few extreme examples in the sample.

Media
Any paid for communication channel including television, radio, posters etc..

Media scheduling
A timetable for the allocation of advertising messages in the media over a given time horizon.

Mediagenic
A tendency (for a person or activity, etc) to convey a favourable impression when reported by the media.

Median
The middle of a group of measurement values when arranged in numerical order. For example, in the group (32, 45, 78, 79, 101), 78 is the median. If the group contains an even number of values, the median is the average of the two middle values.

Median wage
The margin between the highest paid 50 percent and the lowest paid 50 percent of workers in a specific position or occupation. It is often more representative of the average wage than a mean would be, as it can account for extreme outliers.

Mediation services
The use of a trained third party to settle an employment dispute. The third party has no legal authority and so must use persuasion to settle the dispute.

Medical savings account (MSA)
A savings account funded by employees in which tax-deferred deposits can be made for use as medical expenses, co-payments, or deductibles.

Meltdown
A situation in which something, or someone, suddenly dramatically ceases to function properly.

Meme
Originally a biological term referring to a behavioural characteristic which transfers non-genetically between people, meme increasingly refers more widely to other non-human characterstics or examples which arise as imitations of or variations on a particular theme.

Memo
Usually used for communication within an organisation. Memos can be formal letters or informal notes to colleagues.

Memorandum and articles of association
A legal document drawn up when a company is formed containing details such as company name, type, objectives, and number and value of shares, etc.

Memorandum of understanding
A sometimes informal written agreement between two or more parties which establishes each party's responsibilities and requirements.

Menial (work, job, task)
Unskilled typically poorly paid work.

Mentor
Someone who is experienced and gives guidance and support to a person less experienced to help them develop and grow and achieve their goals.

Mentoring
An informal training process between a more experienced person and a junior employee.

Menu bar
On a computer screen, the strip at the top of each open window that contains pull down menus with functions, for example file, edit, etc.

Mercantile
Relating to trade or commerce.

Mercantilism
A nationalist doctrine of one nation prospering at the expense of another nation.

Merchandising
The practice of promoting and selling goods. Commercial products which are associated with a film, pop group, TV show, celebrity, etc., such as toys, clothing, food products, household items, etc.

Merchant bank
Known in the US as an Investment Bank. A financial institution which offers financial advice and services to large businesses and wealthy individuals.

Merge-purge
The process of combining two or more lists or files of names and addresses etc., typically databases, and removing duplicated and/or unwanted items, to produce one new clean list or database.

Merger
Buying or combining companies financially using cash and/or stocks. Ex: Bank One and JPMorgan Chase bank form one strategic brand that builds on brand loyalty, and helps both lower risk and obtain more control over financial markets.

Merit pay
Performance-related pay which provides bonuses or base pay increases for workers who perform their jobs effectively, according to measurable criteria.

Meritocracy
In business, a system in which people advance because of their abilities rather than their connections or wealth, etc.

Merlin
TV/Movie term for a visual mistake in a film or TV show, derived from the accidental inclusion of a beer can in a TV drama scene featuring Merlin, in the days of King Arthur and the Knights of the Round Table.

Mesne profits
Compensation or penalty charges instead of, or 'in lieu' of, rent claimed by a landlord against a person illegally occupying land or property and subsequently evicted, commonly arising from a court order.

Message
An informative communication about a product or service placed in a communication channel.

Meta/metatags/metadata

Meta means an additional useful part of the whole thing, usually data or communication of some sort, and usually hidden or underlying and coded. The original sense is from the Greek word meta, loosely meaning 'with' and arises now commonly as a prefix in computing and communications terminology, for example referring to meta tags (increasingly 'metatags') within website or computer code, which are typically hidden in normal use but which carry useful or vital information about the material or functionality concerned-specifically useful for computerised automated functions and analysis, data search, retrieval, organization and display, etc. The similar term meta data (increasingly 'metadata') refers more generally to information or code which is usually hidden in normal use or communications but which carries important meaning towards understanding or using the whole message or instruction, or other form of data.

Metacraftsmanship

Metacraftsmanship is a term used to tie together the many ideas shared by quality improvement, reengineering, management, leadership, and customer-driven production. Although these theories have much in common, they are often treated as separate and disparate approaches to improving a business. Metacraftsmanship focuses on overcoming the losses to society which are engendered by specialization, and suggests ways of getting complex organizations to work the way a single craftsman would.

Metamarkets

Markets that are similarly associated with a product or service. They can also be different products spread across different industries, but are closely related in the minds of consumers.

Mezzanine finance

A high interest, usually unsecured, loan in which the lender often has the right to obtain shares in the business which has acquired the loan. Sometimes used in management buy-outs.

Microblogging

A type of blogging allowing users to post or broadcast pictures and/or short messages or articles typically in the range of 140-200 characters.

Microcap

In the US, small companies on the stock exchange that have shares which are very low in total value.

Microcredit

The loaning of very small sums of money to entrepreneurs, especially in the developing world, typically enabling the start-up of small business activities, especially social enterprise.

Microeconomics

A branch of economics which studies individual parts of the economy, such as households, industries and businesses, and how they make decisions about spending money, use of goods and services, etc.

Micromarketing

Practice of tailoring products and marketing Programmes to the needs and wants of specific individuals and local customer groups.

Microsite

A small separate part of a larger website which is designed to be used for a particular purpose, e.g., advertising or selling. Often co-branded or 'white label', i.e., run by a larger website organisation for a smaller website acting as an agent or affiliate.

Middle management

In organisations and business, managers who are in charge of small departments and groups of people while reporting to upper management.

Middleman

Any person or business entity that plays a marketing role between producer and consumer in a distribution system (buying, selling, transportation, storing, sorting/assorting, grading, financing, research/data sharing). Examples include real estate brokers, banks, insurance companies, trucking/warehouse firms, and auto dealers.

Midsession

On the stock exchange, the middle period of trading during the day, usually around noon.

Milk round

In the UK, a term used when large companies visit universities each year to advertise job opportunities to students.

Mindshare

In advertising, the development of consumer awareness of a product or brand.

Minimax strategy

In Game Theory and strategy generally, a method which seeks to minimise the maximum potential losses, which usually equates to 'playing safe'.

Minimum wage

The lowest amount an employer can pay an hourly employee. This rate is set by the federal government.

Minimum wage

The legal lowest wage an employee can be paid by an employer.

Minion

A low-ranking loyal and often favoured servant or worker.

Minister without portfolio

A government minister who has not been appointed to any specific department, and who has no specific departmental responsibilities. Also refers metaphorically to an executive or director or manager in an organization who has authority and rank but no responsibility for specific activity.

Minority business enterprise

A business which is at least 51% owned, operated and controlled on a daily basis by one or more African American, Asian American, Hispanic American, or Native American citizens.

Mirror site

On the Internet, an exact copy of a popular website. This is done so that some of the traffic can be diverted from the original website to the Mirror Site when the original site becomes very busy. Alternatively a copy website whose purpose is to attract and direct additional visitors towards the original site, regarded as unacceptable SEO (search engine optimisation) or 'cheating' by most search engines.

Misery index

Created by economist Arthur Okun, an economic indicator of a country which adds the inflation rate to the unemployment rate.

Mission creep

Originally applied to military operations, a gradual expansion of a project that goes beyond original aims, so things turn out differently than planned, often resulting in undesirable consequences.

Mission statement
A written declaration of the purpose of an organization or project team. Organizational mission or vision statements often include an organizational vision for the future, goals, and values.

Mitigate
To make something less severe or dangerous, e.g., using 'Mitigating Circumstances' as an excuse to try to make an offence seem less serious than it appears.

Mixed economy
A country's economic system which has both private and state owned enterprises in operation.

Mnemonic
A technique or mechanism for helping to remember something, such as an acronym or rhyme.

Mob
A crowd of people-usually unruly and agitated. Mob is actually a shortened version of the full Latin phrase, mobile vulgus, meaning excitable crowd. The term was abbreviated in English first as 'mobile', in the 1600s. In more recent times the meaning of mob has become much wider-notably slang for gangsters (hence 'mobsters'), and in modern times to expressions such as 'flash mob', whose full technical meaning (aside from its earliest underworld meaning) is a secretly planned, surprising and quickly-formed excitable crowd.

Mobile marketing
Use of mobile technology (iPhone, iPads, netbooks/notebooks) for promotional purposes. A way for companies to connect with customers—anytime and anyplace. The concept is a fairly new form of permission marketing.

Mobile recruiting
Using mobile technologies to find and connect with people (candidates) who use mobile devices (e.g., phone).

Mode
The most frequently occurring value in a group of measurements.

Modem
From MOdulate and DEModulate. An electronic device which is used to connect computer systems using a telephone line for transmitting data.

Moderator
An arbitrator or mediator. Someone who presides over a debate. On the Internet a person who presides over a website forum to make sure that rules and guidelines are adhered to.

Mogul
Also called a tycoon. A very rich, powerful business person.

Mondeo man
A derogatory term used to describe the average British man, who is depicted as boring, living in a semi-detached house in Kent with a wife and two children. Also used to describe travelling salesmen, a large number of who drive Mondeo cars.

Monetary base
Also known as Narrow Money in the UK. The total amount of a country's currency which is in circulation, for example, coins, notes, etc. held by individuals and in bank deposits.

Money at call
A loan or debt which must be paid upon demand.

Money spinner
A product or project that generates a lot of earnings.

Money-market fund
A type of mutual fund that invests in short-term securities such as Certificates of Deposits and Treasury Bills.

Monopoly
A situation in which one company or organisation has complete control of all, or nearly all, of the market for a particular type of product or service.

Monopsony
Also known as Buyers Monopoly, a market in which there is only one customer for a product or service being sold by several sellers.

Mooc
Acronym for 'Massive Open Online Course' conceivably the future of most higher/further education globally.

Moore's law
Founder of Intel Gordon Moore's theory that the power of computing has the potential to double every two years (often quoted as every 18 months).

Moppers
Mobile shoppers who use cell phones and other devices such as iPads to browse on-line stores, comparison shop, and get recommendations from friends.

Moppers
Mobile shoppers who use cell phones and other devices such as iPads to browse on-line stores, comparison shop, and get recommendations from friends.

Moral hazard
The situation in businesses and organisations when people are protected, e.g. by insurance cover, so they are more likely to take risks.

Mortgage
A loan acquired from a bank, building society, etc., with which to buy property or land, usually to be paid back with interest over a specified number of years at regular monthly intervals. To borrow money from a bank, etc., using your property as collateral, giving the lender the right to own your property if the loan is not repaid.

Mothball
In business, to stop using a piece of equipment or building, etc., for a period of time, but keep it in good condition for when work can resume.

Motherboard
Also known as the Logic Board. The main circuit board of a computer which has all the components to make everything in the computer work together, such as the monitor, keyboard, mouse, DVD drive, etc.

Motivation
Implies an emotion or desire that causes the customer to think and act. It's a driving force arising from personal temperament or constitution that can be stimulated through incentives applied to an external influence (as an expected reward) inciting action. In marketing, it's the energy/fuel that drives the thought process, designed to result in a specific action by the consumer (purchase).

Motivational research
A type of market research used to investigate the reasons why people buy specific products or brands.

Motivational theories
Psychological models that attempt to explain what motivates people. These theories can help employers design incentive strategies.

Mountweazel
A fictitious entry in a reference source or listing, traditionally an act of mischief, but also used to catch copyright cheats or those who obtain and use a database without a licence or a fee. Logically mountweazel entries are removed from legitimate authorized versions. Mountweazel is supposedly named after a false entry Lillian Virginia Mountweazel in the 1975 New Columbia Encyclopedia. Also called a nihilartikel, from the Latin nihil meaning nothing, and the German word artikel. A fictitious 'trap street' is the equivalent used to combat map copyright theft.

Mousetrapping
Use of Internet browser tricks to keep a visitor captive at a site, often by disabling the "Back" button or generating pop-up windows (not too marketing-oriented, for sure).

Msa
Metropolitan Statistical Area – City > 50k population, or urban center with 100k population.

Mulct
A fine or financial penalty, or the verb form, to cheat or swindle someone out of money or penalize someone by imposing a fine, from the Latin word multare, to fine.

Multichannel distribution
Occurs when a producer uses several competing channels to reach the same target market, perhaps using several middlemen to sell directly (sometimes called dual distribution).

Multinational corporation
MNC. Also known as Transnational Corporation. A company which operates in several countries outside the country in which it is based.

Multinational products
Goods or services adapted to the perceived unique characteristics of national markets.

Multiple factor indices
A measure of potential demand indirectly using, as proxies, variables that either intuition or statistical analysis suggest can be closely correlated with the potential demand for the product under view.

Multivariate testing
Research method of analyzing effect of multiple variables in a controlled situation/scenario. Example: Inputting relevant factors that a home buyer might debate when choosing a financial institution for his loan. This enables marketers to quickly identify an appropriate marketing strategy for the home buyer.

Murketing
Blurring the lines between branding and everyday life. Ex: Axe body care products promote an "effect" (socialization) rather than a means of hygiene.

Murphy's law
Humorous saying: Anything that can possibly go wrong will go wrong.

Mutual company
A type of organisation, business, etc., which is owned by members and has no shareholders. The members usually have a share of the profits.

Myers-briggs type indicator

(MBTI) A psychometric questionnaire or personality test in which people answer questions about themselves, which helps identify strengths and personal behavioural/behavioral preferences.

Mystery shopper

A person hired by market research companies or manufacturers, etc., to visit or telephone shops or service providers anonymously in order to assess the quality of goods, helpfulness of staff, layout of premises.

N

Nagware
Also known as Begware. Computer shareware that periodically displays messages on your computer screen prompting you to register for a product and/or pay a fee.

NAICS (North American Industrial Classification System)
Standard used by Federal statistical agencies in classifying business establishments for the purpose of collecting, analyzing, and publishing statistical data related to the U.S. business economy. A complete and valid NAICS code contains six digits and applies to businesses in the United States, Canada, and Mexico each to have country-specific detail. The first two digits designate the economic sector, the third digit designates the subsector, the fourth digit designates the industry group, the fifth digit designates the NAICS industry, and the sixth digit designates the national industry.

Naked debenture
Also known as Uncovered Debenture. A company's loan or debt which is not backed by any security, i.e., the company's assets.

Narrow branding
Ways/methods by which brands present themselves differently to different customer segments (a more customer-centric approach to marketing). Ex: Food companies that address those who "live to cook" (affinity in the belonging and esteem needs), and those who "cook to live" (basic physiological or safety/security need set).

Narrow money
Also called M1. A country's money supply which can be exchanged, for example coins, bank notes, bank cheques, travellers cheques, etc.

National association of securities dealers automated quotations system (NASDAQ)
A "virtual stock exchange"—that is, a stock market without a trading floor whose orders are made through a computer network.

National brand
A brand or product which is available nationwide rather than a local brand which is available in only one area of the country.

National debt
The total amount of money owed by a nation's government.

Nationalism
The assertion of indigenous culture by an individual, organisation or country.

Natural wastage

In business, the process of reducing the number of employees by not replacing those who have left their jobs, rather than by redundancy or dismissal.

Needs

Basic forces that motivate a person to think about and do something/take action. In marketing, they help explain the benefit or satisfaction derived from a product or service, generally falling into the physical (air > water > food > sleep > sex > safety/security) or psychological (belonging > esteem > self-actualization > synergy) subsets of Maslow's Hierarchy of Needs. A mouthwash or toothpaste might be used to rid the mouth of germs (safety/security), or combat bad breath and yellow teeth (esteem).

Negative certificate of origin

A document which states that goods, or any part of the goods, were not produced in a country from which the buyer refuses to accept goods or produce.

Negative equity

A term commonly used in the property market during a recession when a property is worth less in value than the outstanding balance of the loan with which it was purchased. This usually only affects the borrower if they need to sell the property during this time.

Negative growth

A term used to describe a recession. The opposite of economic growth.

Negative inventory

A situation where a mistake in the ordering system or transactions of a business shows the stock to be less than zero. Sometimes this is done deliberately to reduce costs.

Negotiating table

Describes formal discussions where agreements are trying to be reached.

Negotiation

Bargaining between two or more parties with the goal of reaching consensus or resolving a problem.

Neologism

A word or expression which has been newly invented but is not yet in common use, or an old word which has a new meaning. There are a few in this very dictionary listing.

Nepotism

In business and organizations, nepotism refers to those in power showing favouritism towards friends and family, for example by giving them jobs because of their relationship rather than their abilities. The word came into English from French in the mid-1600s and originally derives from the Italian nipote, nephew, and the tradition of giving privileges to the 'nephews' of popes, who were typically actually illigitimate sons.

Nest egg

A sum of money which someone has saved for the future.

Net assets

Total assets (fixed and current) less current liabilities and long-term liabilities that have not been capitalised (eg, short-term loans).

Net current assets

Current Assets less Current Liabilities

Net lending

The total amount of funds lent by a bank or building society over a certain period, minus any repayments made by borrowers.

Net present value (NPV)

NPV is a significant measurement in business investment decisions. NPV is essentially a measurement of all future cashflow (revenues minus costs, also referred to as net benefits) that will be derived from a particular investment (whether in the form of a project, a new product line, a proposition, or an entire business), minus the cost of the investment. Logically if a proposition has a positive NPV then it is profitable and is worthy of consideration. If negative then it's unprofitable and should not be pursued. While there are many other factors besides a positive NPV which influence investment decisions; NPV provides a consistent method of comparing propositions and investment opportunities from a simple capital/investment/profit perspective. There are different and complex ways to construct NPV formulae, largely due to the interpretation of the 'discount rate' used in the calculations to enable future values to be shown as a present value. Corporations generally develop their own rules for NPV calculations, including discount rate.

Net price

The price payable for goods or services after any deductions, discounts, etc., have been taken off.

Net profit

Net profit can mean different things so it always needs clarifying. Net strictly means 'after all deductions' (as opposed to just certain deductions used to arrive at a gross profit or margin). Net profit normally refers to profit after deduction of all operating expenses, notably after deduction of fixed costs or fixed overheads. This contrasts with the term 'gross profit' which normally refers to the difference between sales and direct cost of product or service sold (also referred to as gross margin or gross profit margin) and certainly before the deduction of operating costs or overheads. Net profit normally refers to the profit figure before deduction of corporation tax, in which case the term is often extended to 'net profit before tax' or PBT.

Net profit margin

A measure of a company's profitability and efficiency, calculated by dividing a measure of net profits (operating profit minus depreciation and income taxes) by sales.

Net sales

Amount of sales found by subtracting returns and allowances from money collected for goods and services.

Net worth

Value found by subtracting all liabilities from all assets.

Net yield

The profit from an investment after taxes, costs and all other expenses have been deducted.

Net-centric

Activities, communities, services, information, etc., interconnected by the Internet.

Netiquette

Proposed code of proper behaviour when communicating via the Internet, not only with email, but for comments posted on social networking sites. Of concern to those whose postings might be judged by employers, customers, and suppliers.

Networker

A person who meets and builds relationships with other people in order to make business or social contacts.

New issue
On the Stock Market, a share or bond which is offered to the public for the first time.

New product
"New" means substantially changed or altered in form. Technically, "new" has a shelf life of 6 months before it has to be removed (or the product altered again). Simply changing the packaging does not constitute the word "new" being placed on the product, other than to say "New Packaging."

New York stock exchange (NYSE)
The largest stock exchange in the U.S. located in New York City (Also known as "Wall Street," this stock exchange carries stocks of well-established companies on its trading floor.).

New York stock exchange index
A market-value-weighted measure that indicates stock market changes for all NYSE stocks.

Newbie
A newcomer or novice at something, especially on the Internet.

Next-generation
Term used to describe a product or technology which has been improved or upgraded so that the newest version is much more advanced than previous versions.

Niche
Particular specialty in which a firm has garnered a large market share. Often, the market will be small enough so that the firm will not attract much competition. For example, a company that makes a line of specialty chemicals for exclusive use by the petroleum industry is said to have a niche in the chemical industry.

Niche market
A specialised market in which a specific product is sold to a particular type or group of customers. A product or service for which there is sometimes little demand and often little or no competition.

Nielsen rating
In the US, a system which measures TV audiences, i.e., which Programmemes are watched by which type of person. Companies use this information to decide when to advertise their products, and TV companies use this information to set prices for advertisement slots.

Nih syndrome
Not Invented Here. A term used for companies who reject ideas or products which are not theirs because they originated from outside the company.

Nikkei index
A share price index for the 225 stocks traded on the Tokyo Stock Exchange in Japan.

Noise
In the context of quality management, noise is essentially variability. For example, if you are making ketchup, noise in the process comes from variations in the quality of incoming tomatoes, in changes in ambient temperature and humidity, in variations in machinery performance, in variations in the quality of human factors, etc.

No-load fund

A fund which does not impose a sales or commission fee on the investor for the buying and selling of stocks and shares.

Nominal group technique

Technique used to encourage creative thinking and new ideas, but is more controlled than brainstorming. Each member of a group writes down his or her ideas and then contributes one to the group pool. All contributed ideas are then discussed and prioritized.

Non tariff barriers

Measures, public or private that cause intentionally traded goods or services to be allocated in such a way as to reduce potential real world income.

Non-callable

Also known as Bulletbond. A bond or stock which cannot be redeemed by the issuer before a particular date or until maturity.

Non-compliance

Failure or refusal to obey or comply with a rule, regulation or standard, which can commonly result in serious action by an inspector or ombudsman.

Non-departmental public body

Also known as Quangos (Quasi-Autonomous Non-Governmental Organisations) In the UK, organisations which are not government departments but are accountable to Parliament and are financed by the government to deal with public matters, e.g., Health Trusts.

Non-disclosure

A signed formal agreement in which one party agrees to keep certain information secret. Often used in business when products or projects are being developed.

Non-executive

In business, a member of a board of directors or a consultant who is not an employee of a company but who gives independent advice.

Non-executive director

Also called Outside Director. A person who is an independent member of a company's board of directors, i.e., they are not an employee of the company and are therefore not responsible for the day to day operations of the company but monitor the activities of the full time executives.

Nonfeasance

Failure to perform a duty or carry out an act when under legal obligation.

Nonprofit marketing

Marketing of a product or service in which the offer itself is not intended to make a monetary profit for the marketer.

Non-recourse debt

A type of loan or debt in which the borrower is not personally liable to the lender. If the borrower fails to make repayments the lender can only take back what was bought with the loan and none of the borrowers other assets.

Non-tariff barrier

(NTB) A type of non-tax trade restriction on imported goods which is used to make it difficult for certain goods to be taken into a country.

Nosedive

A sudden drop or plunge in prices, values, etc.

Not enough bandwidth

Term which is used when there are not enough people and/or enough time to get a job done.

Notary

A notary is a lawyer or person with legal training who is licensed by the state to perform acts in legal affairs, in particular witnessing signatures on documents. The form that the notarial profession takes varies with local legal systems.

Notebook

A very small portable computer.

Notice of deficiency

In the US, an official document sent to a taxpayer which shows that they owe more tax than has been declared on their tax form.

Notice period

The period of time during which an employee must work between resigning from and leaving their place of work.

Not-spot

An area of poor or lack of coverage in cellphone service or similar communications technology.

No-win no-fee

Conditional Fee Agreement. An agreement with your solicitor in which you don't have to pay their fee if your court case is not successful.

Np chart

A control chart indicating the number of defective units in a given sample.

Number cruncher

An accountant or person who's job is working with numbers, and who is able to do large calculations. A computer which can perform complex calculations in a short time.

Numbered account

Often called a Swiss Bank Account. An account, offered by certain banks, which can only be identified by a number, so the account holder is known only to a restricted number of the bank's employees.

O

O*net (occupational information network)

A free online database that contains thousands of occupational definitions to help match job seekers with jobs, which is administered and sponsored by the U.S. Department of Labour's Employment and Training Administration.

Objects clause

A section in a company's Memorandum Of Association which sets out the objectives of the company.

Observation interview

A method of assessing job requirements and skills by observing the employee at work, followed by an interview with the employee for further assessment and insight.

Obsolescence

The state of becoming obsolete or out of date. Old-fashioned.

Occam's razor/ockham's razor

A guiding principle or maxim for theorists, writers, communicators, etc., which asserts that the most effective (and arguably most reliable) explanations and theories employ minimal assumptions. In other words, in choosing between competing theories or explanations for uncertain things, the most reliable theory will be that which entails the least use of assumptions and other unknowns. More generally the term is used in reminding/guiding us of a need for prudence, economy and simplicity in describing, justifying, or explaining ideas and concepts, etc. The 'razor' term seems first named and recorded by Sir William Hamilton in 1852, after the 14th-century English logician and Franciscan friar Father William of Ockham (c.1285-1349), who was a notable early advocate of the principle. Philosophers and scientists throughout history (including Einstein, Russell, Newton) have described similar and basically supportive versions of the Occam's Razor principle, moreover many great thinkers have also demonstrably put the principle into practice in their own work, from which we can derive a reasonable degree of confidence in the validity of the concept itself. It's a very memorable and teachable idea the theme itself, its Ockham derivation, and the metaphorical allusion to 'shaving' away unnecessary or unsubstantiated aspects of a written or spoken theory or explanation.

Occupational hazard

Aspects of a job which can be dangerous or pose a high risk of injury.

Occupational psychology

Also called Organisational Psychology. The study of peoples behaviour at work, covering personal relations, mental health, employee selection and training, safety, etc.

Ochlocracy

Mob rule. Also known as Mobocracy. Ocholocratic groups are typically prone to extreme actions and not very clever decisions, which may be a reflection of vengeful motivation, weak intelligence, lack of organization, or any/all of these. An ochlocracy is usually an example of ineffective democracy, and of the so called 'wisdom of crowds' not working very well. Often mob rule results from a reaction against oppressive leadership. A popular metaphor which criticizes mob rule is: 'the lunatics have taken over the asylum'. Ochlocracy derives from the Greek word okhlos meaning mob. An ochlocrat is one who advocates or participates in mob rule.

Odd lot

A lot that is less than 100 shares, or less than a round lot.

Off-balance sheet

(OBS) Refers to items such as assets or debts which are not recorded on a company's balance sheet.

Offer by prospectus

A description of a company, for example financial structure, prospects, aims, etc., used when new shares are offered to the public, or when the company is for sale.

Offer document

A document which a prospective buyer of a company sends to the company's shareholders giving details of the offer in the hope of persuading them to sell their shares.

Office of fair trading

(OFT) In the UK, a non-ministerial government organisation, established in 1973, to protect consumers and ensure that competing businesses deal fairly, and to prohibit cartels, rogue trading, etc.

Official strike

A work stoppage by employees that has the backing and approval of a union.

Offline

Refers to a computer which is not connected to the Internet.

Off-market

Refers to the buying and selling of shares outside the Stock Market.

Off-peak

A time period when a service, e.g. phone network, travel, electricity, gas, etc., is being used less frequently by consumers, therefore prices and rates are cheaper at this time.

Offshore

Refers to accounts, investments, banks, etc., which are in countries where there are lower taxes and/or little government control.

Offshoring

The act of moving work to an overseas location to take advantage of lower labour costs. Offshoring usually involves manufacturing; information technology and back-office services like call centers and bill processing. Companies can build its own work center abroad, establish a foreign division, or create a subsidiary in remote locations.

Off-the-books

A payment which is not officially recorded, usually to avoid tax.

Off-the-charts
Something way below or way above normal expectations.

Off-the-grid
A person who does not wish to be in 'the system' (for example has no bank account, employment or tax identification, no fixed address, etc). May instead refer to a person who lives self-suffiently in terms of gas, electric, water, sewerage services, etc. Or someone not connected to the internet.

Off-the-peg
Known in the US as Off-the-Rack. Describes merchandise, usually clothing, which is made in standard designs and sizes, rather than made-to-measure, and is available in stock at retail outlets.

Oligarchy
A small, elite group of usually wealthy people or families who control a government or organisation, and who are unwilling to share their power.

Oligopoly
Condition/situation in which a market is controlled by a small group of firms (at least 2 different organizations, as opposed to monopoly in which there is only one firm).. Ex: In many cities, airlines or mass merchandisers compete against each other for sales. It's all about exerting control over a large part of a defined market.

Ombudsman
A government official who investigates complaints from the general public about companies, government officials, the media, etc.

Omnishambles
Severe chaos, typically in several areas of organizational responsibility, and typically where a person or organization is expected to be well-organized.

Onboarding
The process of moving a new hire from applicant to employee status ensuring that paperwork is done, benefits administration is underway, and orientation is completed. One of the great quality gurus, and, like Deming, an early student of the work of Walter Shewhart at Western Electric. His work has specialized in linking management to quality engineering. Dr. Juran is the founder of the Juran Institute which has long been the vehicle of his work in quality management and is well-known for espousing "the quality trilogy" of quality planning, quality control, and quality improvement. Juran has authored many books and other works in an effort to spread awareness of quality management ideas and applications.

One-stop
Describes a retail establishment which provides an extensive range of goods and services, so the customer can purchase everything they need without having to go elsewhere.

One-to-one marketing
Personalized customer management approach employed by organizations desiring to tailor its offerings based on individual customer needs, often accomplished through private/personalized counseling and customized on-line offerings.

Online
Refers to a service or product which is available to use or buy on the Internet. A computer which is connected to the Internet.

Onshore accounts
Bank accounts or investments held in countries which have normal rates of tax and strict government control.

Open account
An arrangement between a vendor and buyer in which the vendor allows the buyer to pay at a later date for goods received.

Open border
A border which allows the flow of unrestricted goods and people between countries.

Open cheque
Also known as an Uncrossed Cheque. A cheque which does not have to be paid into an account, and can be cashed at the bank of the person who wrote it. Also means a cheque which has been signed but no amount has been filled in.

Open communication
In business, a situation in which employees have full information about the organisation, and are encouraged to exchange ideas and objectives with management.

Open market
A market which operates without restrictions, in which anyone can buy and sell.

Open offer
Also known as Entitlement Issue. An offer to existing share holders of a company, which entitles them to purchase new shares at a fixed price, usually lower than the current market price, in order to raise money for the company.

Open shop
A business or factory which does not require employees to be members of a trade union.

Open source
Describes computer software for which the original source code is freely accessible to everyone, so that anyone can modify or copy the Programme without paying a fee.

Open-book management
A management strategy emphasizing employee empowerment and individual impact on the success of the company by making the organization's financial data available to all employees so they can make better decisions as workers.

Open-ended investment companies
Limited investment companies which manage mutual investment funds. An OEIC can issue more shares if there is a demand from investors. The fund reduces if investors sell their shares back to the company.

Operating costs and expenses
The costs and expenses necessary to operate a company; includes manufacturing, marketing, research and development operating costs.

Operating income
The income derived after subtracting operating costs and expenses from net sales.

Operating lease
An arrangement in which a business leases equipment, cars, buildings, etc., for a period of time which is less than the expected useful life of the asset.

Operating margin
A measure of a company's profitability and efficiency, calculated by dividing a measure of operating profit (sales minus cost of producing goods and

operating expenses) by sales.

Operation process chart
Used in manufacturing, a chart which shows each stage of a production process, including when materials are needed, how much time is to be allocated for each job, how many people are required to carry out the work, etc.

Opinion leader
A high-profile, influential public figure, such as a celebrity or business person, whose opinions and tastes are respected and/or copied by the general public.

Opportunism
The practice of exploiting and taking advantage of opportunities which present themselves, with no regard for other people or eventual consequences.

Opportunity cost
Term which refers to the value or benefit of something which will be lost in order to achieve or pursue something else.

Optimise
To get the most out of something. To use something in the best possible way.

Option
A bilateral contract giving its holder the right, but not the obligation to buy or sell a specified asset at a specific price, at or up to, a specific date.

Ordinary capital
The amount of capital invested in a company by shareholders.

Ordinary creditor
A creditor who has no priority or security if a company which owes them money goes bankrupt. Therefore, they will be paid only after other creditors have been paid.

Ordinary interest
Interest paid which is calculated based on a 360 day year, or 12 months of 30 days.

Ordinary resolution
A resolution accepted and passed by a company's shareholders by a simple majority, i.e., more than 50%, at a shareholders meeting or by a signed postal resolution which has been sent to the shareholders.

Ordinary share
Also called Common Stock. A share in a company which entitles the owner to a share in the company's profits, and the right to vote at shareholders meetings.

Organic growth
Describes when a company develops and expands by increasing output and/or sales through its own activities, rather than by a merger or acquisitions (buying other companies).

Organic search results
Search results returned by search engines that are based purely on the content of the pages and page popularity. Organic search results are not categorized directory results, or pay-per-click advertising results. According to MarketingSherpa.com, total money spent on search engine optimization represents only 12% of what is spent on pay-for-click advertising (PPC). What makes this statistic so startling is that it is that organic search engine results (those that show up in natural "free" listings) are better noticed, read, and clicked on than the paid listings.

Organigram
Also called Organisation Chart. A diagram which shows the structure of a business or organisation, showing connections between departments, jobs, etc.

Organised labour
Employees who are members of a Trade Union.

Organizational culture
The values, attitudes, beliefs and behaviors that characterize an organization. It is the unwritten workplace ethos that is picked up by new employees.

Organizational development
A planned organization-wide effort to improve and increase the organizations effectiveness, productivity, return on investment and overall employee job satisfaction through planned interventions in the organization's processes.

Orientation
Introducing new hires to the organization and its policies, benefits and culture. Training and familiarization with each department are sometimes included.

Orphan product
In medicine, a test, device, drug, etc., which may be useful for certain rare diseases or disorders but is not financially viable, so is therefore not developed for commercial use.

Orphaned technology
A term which refers to computer products, Programmes, etc., which have been abandoned or not marketed by their developers.

Osha
The Occupation Safety and Health Administration, an agency of the U.S. Department of Labour. The agency's goal is to promote health and reduce accidents, injury and death in the workplace.

Outbid
To offer more money than a rival for something, especially at an auction.

Outbound telemarketing
When a company calls prospective customers on the phone in order to sell them goods or services, compared to Inbound Telemarketing where the customer calls a company for assistance or to purchase goods.

Outdoor advertising
Out-of-home advertising (or outdoor advertising) is made up of more than 100 different formats. Outdoor advertising is essentially any type of advertising that reaches the consumer while he or she is outside the home.

Outgoings
Term used in the UK to describe money being paid out on a regular basis by an individual or a company.

Outlay
The total amount of money which has to be spent to acquire an asset or start a project, including costs, taxes, delivery charges, etc.

Outplacement
A benefit offered by a downsizing employer to assist former employees in re-entering the job market. Assistance can include job training, resume workshops, interview practice and career counseling.

Output tax
In the UK, the amount of VAT (Value Added Tax) a company or business adds to the price of its products or services.

Outside shareholder
A shareholder who doesn't own more than 50% of a company's shares.

Outsourcing
Contracting out non-core functions, such as payroll, benefits administration or manufacturing, to save money and focus on what the company does best.

Outstanding shares
Also called Outstanding Stock. A company's ordinary shares which have been issued and are owned by investors.

Outward investment
Investments which are made abroad.

Overage
A company's surplus, such as money or goods, which is available but exceeds the amount needed or required.

Overallotment
On the Stock Market, the offering for sale of more shares, etc., than are actually available, in the anticipation that some orders will be cancelled.

Overbought
On the Stock Market. a situation in which there has been too much buying of shares, etc., which has therefore caused prices to rise too high.

Overcapitalised
Refers to a business which has been provided with more money than it needs. To overestimate the capital value of a business.

Overdraft
Refers to the amount of money that is owed to a bank because withdrawals from an account exceed deposits. An arrangement in which a bank extends credit to a customer, usually up to a maximum amount.

Overhead
An expense that cannot be attributed to any one single part of the company's activities.

Overmanned
A situation in which there are more workers than are needed for a job.

Overproduction
Overproduction, oversupply or excess of supply refers to excess of supply over demand of products being offered to the market. This leads to lower prices and/or unsold goods along with the possibility of unemployment. The demand side equivalent is underconsumption; some consider supply and demand two sides to the same coin – excess supply is only relative to a given demand, and insufficient demand is only relative to a given supply – and thus consider overproduction and under consumption equivalent.
Overproduction is often attributed as due to previous overinvestment – creation of excess productive capacity, which must then either lie idle (or under capacity), which is unprofitable, or produce an excess supply.

Overriding commission
A commission paid to an agency office manager based on business created by agents who work at that office.

Over-the-counter market
A communications network, supervised by the National Association of Securities Dealers (NASD), which trades bonds, non-listed stocks, and other securities.

Overtime
Overtime is the amount of time someone works beyond normal working hours. Normal hours may be determined in several ways:
1. by custom (what is considered healthy or reasonable by society),
2. by practices of a given trade or profession,
3. by legislation,
4. by agreement between employers and workers or their representatives.

Overtrading
A situation which occurs when a company expands its business too quickly and does not have enough capital to pay expenses, such as debts, wages, etc., which often results in liquidation.

Own brand
Known as House Brands in the US and Home Brands in Australia. Products which are sold by a retailer under the retailer's own name, rather than the name of the manufacturer.

Owner-operator
A self-employed commercial truck or lorry driver who uses their own vehicle to run a business.

P

P and P (P&P)
Postage and Packing. In the UK, The cost of packing and sending goods, usually added to the price of mail-order goods.

P/E ratio (price per earnings)
The P/E ratio is an important indicator as to how the investing market views the health, performance, prospects and investment risk of a public company listed on a stock exchange (a listed company). The P/E ratio is also a highly complex concept - it's a guide to use alongside other indicators, not an absolute measure to rely on by itself. The P/E ratio is arrived at by dividing the stock or share price by the earnings per share (profit after tax and interest divided by the number of ordinary shares in issue). As earnings per share are a yearly total, the P/E ratio is also an expression of how many years it will take for earnings to cover the stock price investment. P/E ratios are best viewed over time so that they can be seen as a trend. A steadily increasing P/E ratio is seen by the investors as increasingly speculative (high risk) because it takes longer for earnings to cover the stock price. Obviously whenever the stock price changes, so does the P/E ratio. More meaningful P/E analysis is conducted by looking at earnings over a period of several years. P/E ratios should also be compared over time, with other company's P/E ratios in the same market sector, and with the market as a whole. Step by step, to calculate the P/E ratio:
1. Establish total profit after tax and interest for the past year.
2. Divide this by the number of shares issued.
3. This gives you the earnings per share.
4. Divide the price of the stock or share by the earnings per share.
5. This gives the Price/Earnings or P/E ratio.

Package deal
A set of several products which are offered for sale and must be bought in a combined package.

Packaging
Promoting the product on the shelf and protecting the product during shipment. Designing a package also includes consideration or size and weight to make transportation and storage more effective and efficient (as in sizing containers to fit neatly onto pallets).

Page break
On a computer screen, a mark which indicates where a new page will be printed in a document.

Page traffic
In computing, the number of times a web page has been visited.

Paid-up capital
The total amount of money which has actually been paid in full by shareholders for their shares.

Paid-up policy
An insurance policy on which no more premiums are required, and the policy is considered paid in full and still remains in force.

Paid-up share
A share for which the shareholder has paid the full amount, as stated in the contract.

Palm top
A small computer which fits into the palm of the hand.

Pan-european
Relating to all, or most of, the countries in Europe.

Pants
Street slang now mainstream, referring to anything of very poor quality. Interestingly the term first appeared in the late 1800s, based on the word 'knickers' as an expression of contempt or ridicule.

Paper loss
In business, a loss which has occurred and appears in a company's accounts, but has not yet been realised until a transaction has been made, e.g. the sale of an asset which has lost value.

Paper profit
A profit which has been made but has not yet been realised until a share, etc., has been sold.

Paper-pusher
An office worker who has a boring job dealing with paperwork all day.

Par value (bond)
The face value of a bond, usually $1,000 for corporate bonds, and generally higher denominations for many government bonds.

Paradigm
A way of thinking about a given subject that defines how one views events, relationships, ideas, etc. within the boundaries of that subject.

Paradigm shift
Term first used by Thomas Kuhn in 1962 to describe when an important or significant change occurs in the perception of things. A sudden change in point of view.

Paralegal
A legal assistant who is not a qualified lawyer, but who is trained to work in or with the law.

Parallel market
A country's separate market which deals in goods and currencies outside the country's normal official government controls.

Parastatal
In certain countries, a company or organisation which is partially or fully owned and controlled by the government.

Parent company
A company or organisation which owns more than 50% of the voting shares in another company, therefore the Parent Company controls management and operations in the other (subsidiary) company.

Pareto chart
A quality assurance tool that ranks information, like reasons for certain problems, in descending order. The goal is to identify the most serious

problems so improvements can be made.

Pareto Chart

Dollars   Percent

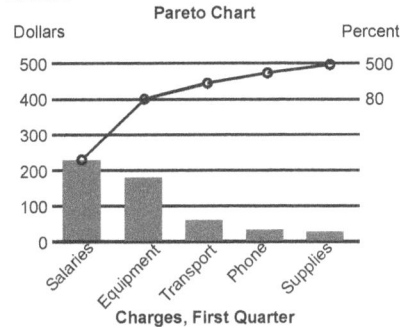

Charges, First Quarter

Pareto principle

The idea that a few root problems are responsible for the large majority of consequences. The Pareto principle is derived from the work of Vilfredo Pareto, a turn-of-the-century Italian economist who studied the distributions of wealth in different countries. He concluded that a fairly consistent minority, about 20% of people, controlled the large majority, about 80% of a society's wealth. This same distribution has been observed in other areas and has been termed the Pareto principle. It is defined by J.M. Juran as the idea that 80% of all effects are produced by only 20% of the possible causes.

Parkinson's law

A humorous and generally true observation by Cyril Northcote Parkinson (British historian 1909-1993) that capacity or time is inevitably filled, for example: 'Work will expand so as to fill the time available for its completion'.

Part exchange

Known in the US as Trade-In. A payment method, usually when purchasing a car, in which the buyer gives something they own, for example a car, as part payment to the vendor

for the more expensive item. The balance is usually paid in cash or with a loan.

Participating performance share

A type of share/stock which gives a company's shareholder the right to receive dividends and also extra payments relating to the company's profits.

Partnership

A business which is owned by two or more people, all sharing the profits and responsibility for managing the business.

Part-time worker

Someone who works less hours than a full time employee on a permanent basis for a company, usually for a set number of hours a week.

Party plan

Also called Party Selling. A method of marketing in which agents host parties, usually at someone's home, to demonstrate and sell products to invited potential customers.

Pascal

A computer language which is used to write Programmes, also used in teaching Programmeming.

Passing trade

Describes customers who go into a shop, public house, etc., because they notice it as they are passing by.

Passive exporter

An organisation which awaits orders or comes across them by choice.

Patent

An official document which grants an inventor or manufacturer sole rights to an invention or product.

Patent pending
A phrase sometimes printed on goods to show that a patent has been applied for but not yet granted.

Paternity leave
The right of male employees, to take time off from his job following the birth of his baby. Entitlement to Paternity Leave depends on how long they have been with their employer.

Paternity pay
An employee benefit paid to husband of pregnant women so that he can take time off from his job after the birth of the baby to give support to the mother. Entitlement to Paternity Pay depends on how long the person has been with his employer.

Patron
A person who purchases goods or services, often on a regular basis, from a shop or company. A benefactor or sponsor who supports and/or gives money to an individual or an organisation, such as a charity.

Pawnbroker
A money lender who lends cash at a high rate of interest in exchange for the borrowers personal possessions, such as jewellery, as security, which is returned when the loan is fully paid. If the loan is not repaid the Pawnbroker sells the item.

Payable to bearer
A cheque, security, etc., which can be exchanged for money by the person in possession.

Pay-as-you-go
Refers to a method of paying for a service as you use it, such as mobile phone credit. Also can be used to pay debts as they are incurred.

Paye
Pay As You Earn. In the UK, a system of paying income tax, which is deducted from an employees salary by an employer and paid to the government.

Paying agent
An agent, usually a bank, that makes dividend payments to shareholders on behalf of the issuing company.

Payment by results
A system of paying employees according to the amount of work they do. Therefore, the bigger the volume of work output, the bigger the salary.

Payout ratio
The ratio found by dividing the dividends per share by earnings per share (Shows how well earnings support dividends, or how secure the dividend is. The lower the ratio, the more secure the dividend.).

Pay-per-click
Internet ad model used to direct traffic to websites. Advertisers pay the website owner when the ad is clicked. Search engines provide advertisers the opportunity to bid on keyword phrases relevant to their target market.

Pay-per-click
Online advertising payment model in which payment is based on qualifying click-throughs. A typical PPC agreement has the advertiser paying for clicks to the destination site based on a prearranged per-click rate. Popular PPC advertising options include search engines (right sidebar on Google). Paying per click is different than paying per impression which generates lower-quality traffic/ leads.

Pay-per-impression
Online advertising payment mode in which payment is based on how often the "publisher" (e.g., web site where you purchase a banner ad) shows your banner ad on their web site (e.g., an "impression"). Typically, prices are set per one thousand exposures.

Payroll
Documentation created and maintained by the employer containing such information as hours worked, salaries, wages, commissions, bonuses, vacation/sick pay, contributions to qualified health and pension plans, net pay and deductions.

PDA
Personal Digital Assistant. A small hand-held electronic device that is used for storing information and can serve as a telephone, diary, alarm clock, fax, etc.

Pecking order
The hierarchy in businesses, organisations, etc, i.e., the order of people at different ranks.

Pecuniary
Relating to, or involving money.

Peer appraisal
A performance assessment given by an employee's peers who have observed the employee's job performance.

Peer group
A social group of equals, for example, in age, social class, education, etc. A group of products or businesses which are similar.

Peer-to-peer
Computer systems which act as servers and are connected to each other via the Internet, allowing people to share share files, so there is no need for a central computer.

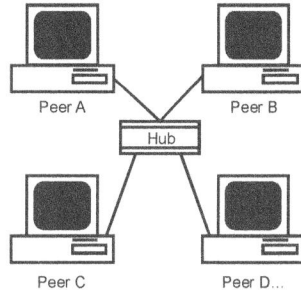

Peer A   Peer B

Hub

Peer C   Peer D...

Pen portrait
A description of a person, a 'character sketch in words', now commonly a person-profile used for audience targeting purposes (marketing, recruitment, etc), although the expression dates back to the 1800s, originally referring to a description of a person, so as to produce a picture in the mind. 'Pen Picture' was an early alternative term.

Penalty clause
A clause in a contract which states that a specified sum of money must be paid by the party who breaks the contract.

Penetration
Process by which the marketers attempts to increase sales of an existing product in existing markets, thus minimizing risk. It's also a pricing strategy designed to price a product or service at the lowest potential price to break into a market. Often, it's slightly below that of the lowest-price competitor's product, or at a level that's perceived as low.

Penetration price
The charging of a low price in order to gain volume sales conducted under

conditions of little product uniqueness and elastic demand patterns.

Penetration pricing
The practice of charging a low price for a new product for a short period of time in order to establish a market share and attract customers.

Penny share
Describes shares which have a very low value and therefore appeal to speculators.

Pen-pusher
An employee with a boring job whose work consists of dealing with unimportant documents, paperwork, etc.

Pension
A private or government fund from which regular payments are made to a person who has retired from work, or who is considered too ill to carry on working.

Pension fund
A fund set up to collect money on a regular basis from employers and employees, which pays the employees pension when they retire from work.

Peppercorn rent
In the UK, a very low or nominal payment, which was originally a single peppercorn, made to secure a lease.

Per capita
For each person in the population.

Per diem
Latin for 'Per Day'. Often refers to money paid to employees for daily expenses or reimbursements.

Percent chart (p chart)
A control chart that determines the stability of a process by finding what percentage of total units in a sample are defective.

Perception (perceptual process)
A process by which consumers make sense of stimuli they get from not only marketer's promotional messages, but also unmet needs (such as a growling stomach to remind them to eat). There are 3 steps in the process: sensing (getting the attention of the customer), selecting (deciding to figure out what it means), and interpreting (assignment meaning and whether to take action).

Perfect competition
Describes a market in which no one can influence prices because there is enough information about a product to prevent control by an individual or a single organisation.

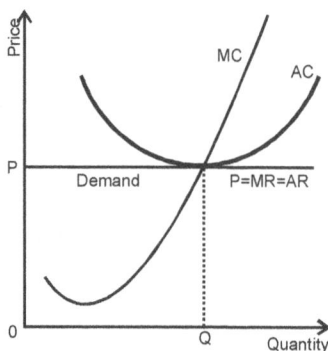

Perfect storm
Coincidentally arising circumstances combining to produce a disastrous effect. This is an allusion to weather factors, commonly applied to economic or trading situations, but applicable to any disaster or chaotic outcome resulting from forces or effects whose combination and timing has not been thought likely or anticipated at all.

Performance Evaluation Review Technique (PERT)
A management scheduling tool which charts the tasks involved in a project, showing the sequence of the work, the time needed for each task, etc.

Performance appraisal
A periodic review and evaluation of an individual's job performance.

Performance improvement
A plan to improve an employee's performance in which the performance problem is identified, modified and monitored.

Performance management
The process of maintaining or improving employee job performance through the use of performance assessment tools, coaching and counseling. The ultimate goal is to better meet organizational objectives.

Performance planning
An organization-wide plan to manage employees and their performance wherein goals are set for employees, departments and the organization as a whole.

Performance-related pay
A scheme set up in the workplace in which the employees get paid according to how well they perform in their job.

Peripatetic
Working or travelling from place to place, staying at different locations for a short period, such as, and especially as a teacher does, in working at more than one school. The teacher analogy is apt since the word derives from the Greek peripatetikos, and the earlier peripatein, which referred specifically to the teaching style of Aristotle (384-322 BC, Greek philosopher, student of Plato, teacher of Alexander the Great), who walked about while he talked. The ancient Greek prefix peri means around, or round, and patein means to tread.

Perishability
products and services that worsen in quality over time, thus reducing their value. In addition to fresh vegetables, fruits, bread, and milk, consider airline ticket fare promotions with an expiration/ending date.

Perishables
Describes food, such as fruit, meat, fish, dairy products, etc., which will decay or spoil rapidly.

Perjury
The criminal offence of knowingly telling a lie (with intent to influence the outcome of the hearing) in a court of law after having taken an oath or affirmation. It closely relates to and is often implicit within the offence of perverting the course of justice, which in the UK technically carries a maximum penalty of life imprisonment. The word perjury derives from Latin perjurium, meaning false oath, similar to jury which comes from jurare, meaning to swear.

Permatemp
A person who works for an organisation on a long-term contractual basis, but who is not a permanent employee.

Permission marketing
Building an ongoing relationship of increasing depth with customers based on approval to send or receive email newsletters, catalogs, and other promotional incentives to gain brand recognition and status. Mostly used by on-line marketers to invite

consumers to take part in defining the range of services to be offered.

Permission marketing

Building an ongoing relationship of increasing depth with customers based on approval to send or receive email newsletters, catalougs, and other promotional incentives to gain brand recognition and status. Mostly used by on-line marketers to invite consumers to take part in defining the range of services to be offered.

Personal action

A type of court case in which an individual claims damages for personal injury, damage to his property, etc.

Personal allowance

Known as Personal Exemption in the US. The amount of income an individual can earn in a year before paying tax.

Personal assistant

PA. A person who works for one person, often an executive, in an organisation, performing secretarial and administrative duties.

Personal day

When an employee is permitted to have time off work to deal with personal matters.

Personal development

Also called Self-Development. Acquiring abilities, skills, knowledge, etc., in order to enhance one's performance and self-perception.

Personal information manager

Computer software which handles personal information, such as names, addresses, memos, lists, e-mails, etc.

Personal liability

An individual's legal responsibility in the event of injury to someone, damage to property and/or the debts of their own company.

Personnel

The people who work for a business or organisation. An administrative department in an organisation which deals with employees and often liaises between departments.

Persuasion/The three modes of Persuasion

Aristotle's 2,300 years-old three principles model for communications which successfully move an audience to action or change: 1 Ethos: The integrity of the communicator. 2. Pathos:The emotional effect (of communicator and message) on the listener/reader/audience. 3. Logos: The relevance and strength of the message content.

Pest analysis

Political Economical Social and Technological Analysis. A business tool which is used in strategic planning and helps to understand the environmental influences on a business or orgasnisation.

Peter principle

Formulated by Canadian author Laurence J Peter (1919-1990): 'In a hierarchy, every employee tends to rise to his level of incompetence'. The theory that employees rise in rank in an organisation until they are finally promoted to a level, and remain there, at which they do not have the ability to do their job.

Petrodollar

Term coined by professor of economics Ibrahim Oweiss in the 1970s which describes the large amounts of money earned by oil production in OPEC

(Organisation of the Petroleum Exporting Countries) countries.

Petty cash
A small amount of cash kept by a business to pay for small purchases.

Phablet
A tablet computer that is also a phone. Or a phone that is also a tablet computer. This term emerged in 2012/13 with the launch of the technology to which it refers. A word formed like this (i.e., a combination of parts of the two words/things it refers to - in this case, phone and a tablet) is called a phablet.

Pharmaceutical
Relating to or engaged in the process of making and selling medicinal drugs.

Philanthropy/philanthropist
Promotion of the welfare of others, typically through financial provision (a philanthorpist is one who does this). From the Greek philanthropos, meaning man-loving.

Philology
The branch of knowledge which deals with the study of the history of language and literature. Historical linguistics.

Phishing
A type of fraud carried out on the internet by sending people legitimate-looking e-mails asking for their personal information, such as bank account details, passwords, etc., and using them to steal their money.

Photocall
A planned and announced occasion during which celebrities, politicians, products launches, etc., have photographs taken by the press and other media for publicity purposes.

Physical capital
Refers to a company's assets which are used in a production process, such as machinery, buildings, materials, etc.

Physical distribution
Transporting and storing of goods as a part of the commercialization schedule. This is not to be confused with Exposure, which is where the customer wants/expects the product to be available for possession utility

Picket
A person, or persons, posted at the entrance of a place of work which is affected by a strike, in order to stop people entering the premises.

Pictogram
Also called a Pictograph. A graphic symbol or diagram which represents a concept, an amount, an activity, etc., in pictures.

Pie chart
A chart that compares groups of data to the whole data set by showing each group as a "slice" of the entire "pie." Pie charts are particularly useful for investigating what percentage each group represents.

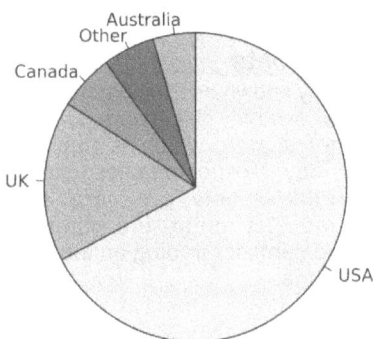

Piece rate

A payment system in which employees are paid a fixed rate for each item they produce.

Piecework

Work in which payment is based on the amount of work done regardless of the time it takes to do it.

Piggyback

A system which rides on the back of an existing system, e.g. a loan or mortgage or an advertising campaign.

Pin

Personal Identification Number. A number given by a bank to a customer so the customer can access their bank account using an ATM (cash machine), or use their credit/debit card in retail outlets.

Ping

Packet INternet Groper. An Internet Programme which is used to check if another computer on a network is working. To contact someone on a computer.

Pink collar

Describes jobs which were once traditionally done by women, such as nursing, secretarial, teaching, etc.

Pink sheets

Formally known as Pink Quote. In the US, a system displaying over-the-counter shares, which is published every day. Most companies listed on the Pink Sheets are very small and do not meet the minimum requirements for trading on the Stock Exchange.

Pink slip

In the US, an official notice of job termination given to an employee.

Pinning

Every time an individual pins an article or image, it gets shared with others that have chosen to follow that account. Followers can then "like" a pin and continue sharing.

Piracy

The unauthorised copying of CDs, DVDs, computer Programmes, etc., in order to sell them or give them away.

Pixel

Short for Picture Element. The smallest element of an image displayed on a computer screen. The quality of the image depends on the number of pixels per square inch, i.e., the more pixels the higher the resolution.

Place mix

Those activities involving distribution (moving the product from producer to consumer through channel members called wholesalers and retailers) and exposure (researching and delivering the product where the customers wants or expects it to be available). Marketers enroll channel members based on their ability to perform marketing activities more effectively and efficiently than they can.

Plain language

Represented notably by the Plain Language Movement, and the Plain Language Information and Action Network (PLAIN), in the late 1900s, Plain Language became a generally recognized technical term for the advocation and use of clear explanations, descriptions, instructions, etc., in official documents and other communications, which frequently use goobledegook or 'officialese', i.e., language which is overly complex and/or containing confusing jargon and abbreviations, etc.

Plaintiff

A person who brings a lawsuit against someone else in a court of law.

Plan sponsor

An entity that has adopted and has maintained an employee-benefit plan. The plan sponsor is often an employer, but may be a union or a professional association. The Plan Sponsor is responsible for determining employee participation and the amount of benefits involved.

Plan-Do-Check-Act (PDCA) cycle A four-step improvement process originally conceived of by Walter A. Shewhart. The first step involves planning for the necessary improvement; the second step is the implementation of the plan; the third step is to check the results of the plan; the last step is to act upon the results of the plan. It is also known as the Shewhart cycle, the Deming cycle, and the PDCA cycle.

Planned economy

A country's economic system controlled by the government, which makes all the decisions about production, distribution and consumption of goods and services.

Planogram

In retailing, a drawing or diagram which shows when and how products should be displayed in a store.

Plasma

Interestingly, in physics, plasma is the often overlooked fourth state of matter, aside from solid, liquid and gas. Plasma is ionized gas containing free electrons, making it responsive to electromagnetism, and conductive of electricity, in turn enabling it to take a very visible physical shape unlike other forms of gas. The stars are made of plasma; so is lightening and the Northen Lights (Aurora Borealis). Plasma display screens also basically employ this effect.

Plenary/Plenary session

Plenary essentially means full or complete. In the context of formal organized gatherings it means fully attended by everyone together. The term 'plenary session' is very commonly used in business and management to refer to a session which all attendees attend at a conferences or other event, notably to differentiate from smaller sessions of sub-groups concerened with different topics and held in different locations/rooms. Separately plenary refers to something or someone having a complete or absolute quality, such as an official with plenary (full and complete) power.

Plimsoll

Named after merchant Samuel Plimsoll. International Load line or Waterline on the hull of every cargo ship, which indicates the maximum depth to which a ship can be safely loaded with cargo.

Plutocracy

A government which is controlled by wealthy people.

PMI

Purchasing Managers Index. Published every month, an economic measure relating to manufacturing. A PMI over 50 indicates industry is expanding.

Poison pill

A business strategy used by a company to avoid being taken over by another company, e.g., the selling of assets, shares, etc., to make the company look less attractive to the potential buyer.

Poisoned chalice
A job or situation which seems good at first but soon becomes unpleasant or harmful.

Policy deployment
Another name for hoshin planning.

Political correctness
The practice of not using words, expressions, actions, etc., which could cause offence to minority groups. PC could also stand for Political Claptrappers - People who insist on political correctness from everyone at all times, even in their private lives.

Polycentrism
A host country orientation on a subsidiary basis.

Polymath
A person of great knowledge and varied learning. Loosely from Greek poly, many, and manthanein, learn.

Ponzi scheme
Named after Charles Ponzi, a fraudulent investment scheme, similar to a Pyramid Scheme, in which people are offered high returns, while their money is used to pay earlier investors, so that later investors often end up with little or no return because new investors can't be found.

Poorgeoisie
People who are rich but pretend they don't have much money.

Population
Total set of items from which a sample set is taken.

Pop-under
On a computer, an advertisement, etc., which comes up on the screen behind the web page which is being viewed, and does not appear until the page is closed.

Pop-up
On a computer screen, a small window containing an advertisement, etc., which appears on a page on top of the content which is being viewed.

Pork barrel
A US political term used when government funds are used for projects which benefit certain local groups or constituents, and show their political representative in a good light.

Port of entry
A place in a country where people and/or goods can officially leave or enter.

Portal
On the Internet, a website, which is the point of entry to other websites, and offers services such as e-mail, news, shopping, etc.

Porter's generic strategies
Named after economist Michael Porter. Describes strategies used by companies to achieve a strong advantage against competitors.

Portfolio
A collection of investments, such as shares, bonds, etc., which are owned by an individual or organisation.

Portfolio career
Concept attributed to guru Charles Handy in the 1990s. A career in which a person pursues several jobs at the same time, rather than working full-time for one particular company.

Portmanteau word
A word formed from parts of two separate words, whose combination

generally produces the meaning also. Many new management and business words, especially slang and jargon, enter the language in this way, and some become popular and well-established.

Pos
Point of Sale or POP (point of purchase) – Business or market where products and services are transacted. Also used to convey temporary displays used by marketers to showcase products. Soda companies use POP/POS in advance of sporting or holiday events to feature their products in other parts of the store or warehouse. Another example is gas station pump toppers that advertise daily food or drink specials inside the store.

Positioning
Term used to describe the way a company, product, service, etc., is marketed in order to make it stand out from the competition by choosing a niche according to brand, price, packaging, etc.

Positioning (or Framing)
How potential buyers see the product, relative to the position of competitors. It happens in the minds of the target market. It is the aggregate perception the market has of a particular company, product, or service in relation to their perceptions of the competitors. Repositioning involves changing the identity of a product, relative to the identity of competing products, in the collective minds of the target market. It's also physical product placement/location in stores.

Positive language
Art of using words or phrases to create a positive image about a product, service, or organization. It tells customers what you CAN do rather than can't do.

Positive sum game
A win-win situation in which both sides involved in a business transaction, etc., can profit.

Postage and packing
Called Postage and Handling in the US. The cost of wrapping an item and sending it by post. Often used for mail order goods.

Post-date
To insert a future date on a cheque or document at the time of writing, so it becomes effective at that later date.

Post-fordism
Also called Flexible Modernity. An industrial production system which has changed from mass production in large factories, such as Ford Motors, and moved towards smaller flexible, more specialised manufacturing systems.

Power brand
A brand of goods, etc., which is well known and has a large share of the consumer market for a long period of time.

Power lunch
A business meeting held over lunch in which important decisions may be made, or high level discussions carried out.

Power nap
A short nap. usually lasting about 20 minutes, taken during the day, that refreshes a person so they can carry on working.

Prairie dogging

This occurs when someone who works in an open office, which is divided into cubicles, drops something or shouts and everyone else pops their heads above the dividing walls to see what is happening.

Precedent

A past act or decision which is used as an example to decide the outcome of similar subsequent acts.

Predatory lending

The often illegal practice of lending money to people who the lender knows are unable to pay back the loan, such as low-income house-owners, who subsequently may lose their homes which they have used as security against the loan.

Predatory pricing

Occurs when a firm charges extremely low prices for a product with the intent of driving competition out of business or out of a specific market. Prices then tend to return to normal once the competitor has been eliminated. While illegal and unethical, it's difficult to prove in court.

Predatory pricing

Also known as Destroyer Pricing. A situation where a company charges very low prices for goods or services in order to put its competitors out of business, after which prices will be raised.

Preemptive marketing

Building relationships with consumers/clients BEFORE they need your services. This can include introducing an organization's products/services towards building preference, loyalty, even conviction of not having to search for alternatives when the need arises.

Preference share

Also called Preferred Shares. A type of share which pays the owner a fixed dividend before other share owners are paid their dividends. Preference Shareholders do not usually have the right to vote at shareholders meetings.

Preferential creditor

A creditor who has the right to receive payment of debts, before other creditors, from a bankrupt company.

Preferred stock

Stock whose holders have precedence over common stock in claiming dividends and assets.

Pre-market

On the Stock Market, trading which takes place between members before the official opening time.

Premium bond

A bond whose value is greater than its face value.

Premium income

The revenue recieved by an insurance company from its customers.

Premium only plan (POP)

Section 125 is part of the IRS Code that allows employees to convert a taxable cash benefit (salary) into non-taxable benefits, so they may pay for qualified benefit premiums before any taxes are deducted from their paychecks. The Premium only plan allows for certain employee paid group insurance premiums to be paid with pre-tax dollars.

Present value

The amount invested at a certain interest rate.

Presenteeism
The opposite of Absenteeism. A situation where employees work very long hours or come to work when they are ill and their performance is below standard, which can have a negative effect on the business.

Press agent
A person employed to arrange publicity for an individual or organisation, for example in newspapers, on television, etc.

Press conference
Called A News Conference in the US. A meeting held by a business, organisation, individual, etc., to which journalists are invited to hear a public announcement, and usually to ask questions.

Pressure group
An organised group of people, or lobbyists, who campaign to influence businesses, governments, etc., to change their policies.

Prestige pricing
Setting a high price based on the quality and the demand for which consumers are willing to spend. For example: Starbucks gives a feeling of a high end product by its packaging, delivery and product promise, based on years or consistent promotion in its iconic coffee houses as "creating a product of excellence."

Price
The amount of money required to purchase something or to bribe someone. The amount agreed upon between the buyer and seller in a commercial transaction.

Price bundling
Selling 2 or more goods or services as a single package, as in Taco Bell offers 2 hard tacos, a burrito, and a drink in a package for 1 price (usually a saving if you add up the pricesof each individual item).

Price ceiling
The maximum price which can be charged bearing in mind competition and what the market can bear.

Price control
Maximum and minimum price limitations, often during periods of inflation, which a government puts on essential goods and/or services.

Price discrimination
The practice of a provider to charge different prices for the same product to different customers.

Price escalation
The difference between the domestic price and the target price in foreign markets due to the application of duties, dealer margins and/or other transaction costs.

Price fixing
The, often illegal, practice of prices being fixed, by agreement, by competing companies who provide the same goods or services as each other.

Price floor
The minimum price which can be charged bounded by product cost.

Price gouging
Controversial strategy that sellers sometimes use to charge higher than normal prices for products and services, especially when there is little or no competition.

Price mechanism
Describes the way prices for goods and services are influenced by the

changes in supply and demand. Shortages cause a rise in prices, surpluses cause a fall in prices.

Price mix
Those objectives and strategies marketers apply to setting and managing profits for itself and each channel member. Pricing policies vary among organizations based on internal goals, ROI(return on investment), cost of goods, etc.

Price support
A system in which a minimum price is set by a government, and sometimes subsidised, for a product or commodity.

Price tactic
Justifying the use of low price as the principle reason why consumers will buy a product, as opposed to sustainable features or benefits. A short term remedy vs. strategy.

Price taker
A company or individual whose selling or buying of goods and services has little or no influence over prices.

Price-earnings ratio (P/E)
The ratio found by dividing market price per share by earnings per share (This ratio indicates what investors think of the firm's earnings' growth and risk prospects.).

Price-earnings ratio to earnings per share growth
The ratio found by dividing a stock's price-earnings ratio by its earnings per share growth rate, indicating the company's profits relative to investors' expectations.

Price-earnings relative
The relative amount found by dividing a stock's price-earnings ratio by that of the market as given by a widespread market yardstick such as the S&P 500 or the Value Line index (This relative suggests to the investor whether his investment's price is reasonable compared to the market. Also can be used for historical comparison with P/E relatives of recent years.).

Price-to-book ratio
The ratio found by dividing a stock's market price per share by its book value (defined as being assets minus all liabilities) per share (This ratio measures the stock's value relative to its net assets. A high ratio, for instance, might suggest that a stock is overvalued.).

Price-to-cash-flow ratio
The ratio found by dividing a stock's price per share by its cash flow per share (This ratio, similar in type to the price-earnings ratio, serves as a measure of investors' expectations on a firm's future financial success.).

Pricing
To evaluate the price of a product by taking into account the cost of production, the price of similar competing products, market situation, etc.

Primary data
Data which is collected by a company, business, etc., itself for its own use, using questionnaires, case studies, interviews, etc., rather than using other sources to collect the data.

Primary demand
Consumers demand for a generic product rather than a particular brand.

Primary market
Group of consumers targeted to receive the major share of a marketer's

attention, resources, and media expenditures.

Primary research
Also called Field Research. The collection of new or primary data through questionnaires, telephone interviews, etc., for a specific purpose.

Prime cost
In manufacturing, etc., the cost of direct materials and labour required to make a product.

Principal
In finance, principal (the principal, or the principal sum/amount) refers to an amount of money loaned or borrowed. The term is used particularly when differentiating or clarifying an amount of money (loaned/borrowed/invested) excluding interest payments. Separately, more generally, in business the term 'the principal' refers to the owner of a business or brand, as distinct from an agent or representative, such as a franchisee.

Private brand
Also called House Brand. A product which is owned by a retailer, and therefore has its own brand label on it, rather than the manufacturer or producer.

Private company
Called A Private Corporation in the US. A company whose shares are not offered to the general public on the open market.

Private corporation
A corporation which does not offer stock for public sale (Private corporations are not required by law to provide information about their financial conditions.).

Private equity
Describes companies shares which are not available for investors to buy and sell on the Stock Market, because the company is unlisted.

Private sector
The part of a country's economy which is owned and run for profit by private businesses rather than being government controlled.

Privatise/privatize
(UK/US English spelling) To change or sell a government controlled business or industry to privately owned companies.

Privity
A legal relationship between two parties in a contract.

Pro
Public Relations Officer. Also known as a Chief Communications Officer. A person whose job is to promote and establish a good relationship between their client- an organisation or an individual - and the public.

Pro bono
Short for Pro Bono Publico (Latin for 'The Public Good'). Work carried out in the public interest for no fee or compensation, e.g. by a lawyer.

Pro forma invoice
An invoice prepared by a supplier describing goods, price, quantity, etc., which is sent to the buyer before the goods are supplied.

Pro rata
In proportion to. Refers to the division of costs, profits, income, etc., depending on the size of each persons share in the whole amount.

Pro tem
Temporarily. For the time being.

Probation
A trial period during which an individual's suitability for a job or membership to a club, etc., is tested.

Probationary arrangement
An agreement between an employer and employee that the employee will work for a set amount of time on a trial or probationary period.

Probity
Complete integrity. Having strong moral principals and total honesty.

Process capability
1. A statistical measure indicating the inherent variation for a given event in a stable process, usually defined as the process width divided by 6 sigma.
2. Competence of the process, based on tested performance, to achieve certain results.

Process capability index
Measurement indicating the ability of a process to produce specified results. Cp and Cpk are two process capability indices.

Proctor
Someone who supervises students, etc., taking exams to prevent cheating. Also a person or agent employed to manage the affairs of another person.

Procurement
Process (acquisition) of obtaining goods (materials) and services (expertise) from middlemen/suppliers. This is a major component of the "Marketing Concept: define customers" unmet needs; allocate resources; make a profit.

Product
Whatever the customer thinks, feels, or expects from an item or idea. From a "marketing-oriented" perspective, products should be defined by what they satisfy, contribute, or deliver vs. what they do or the form utility involved in their development. Ex: A dishwasher cleans dishes but it's what the consumer does with the time savings that matters most.

Product adoption curve
Explains that product and services are first purchased and evaluated by innovators and early adopters, after which by early and late majority, and finally laggards.

Product development
Creation of products with new or different characteristics than those already offered. This may involve modification of an existing product or formulation of an entirely new product that satisfies a newly-defined set of customer wants or desires.

Product differentiation
Attributes/qualities that make one product stand apart from both competitors and easily-substitutable alternatives. These may not always be favorable, as in the choice of how to finance a purchase or select a course of treatment for a disease. A major component of a marketer's product mix, usually focusing on a product's unique feature.

Product evangelist
A person who is committed to a promoting a product through demonstrations, talks, blogging, etc.

Product liability
Area of the law in which a manufacturer or retailer is legally responsible for

any damage or injury caused by a defective product.

Product life cycle
The normal stages that a product passes through from development to decline until it becomes obsolete, usually because it has saturated the market because everyone who wants it has purchased it.

Product mix
All of the products or product lines offered by a firm. Some companies have a wide product mix geared toward a diverse consumer group. For example, Procter & Gamble has a product mix that includes detergents, toothpaste, Procter bar soap, deodorants, disposable diapers, coffee, household paper goods, and food products. Some companies have a narrow product mix geared toward a particular market segment, such as the Williams Sonoma catalog that sells gourmet cooking accessories. A product mix is also one of the 4 Ps or the marketing strategy. It includes the product idea (features, accessories, installation, warranty, and product lines), packaging, and labeling.

Product organisation
A form of international organisational structure whereby executives in functional areas are given global responsibility.

Product placement
Also called Embedded Marketing. A type of advertising where a company pays a fee to have one or more of its products used as props in a film or television show.

Product portfolio
A variety of products which are manufactured or distributed by a company or organisation.

Product strategy
A set of decisions regarding alternatives to the target market and the marketing mix given a set of market conditions.

Productivity
The rate at which goods are produced based on how long it takes, how many workers are required, how much capital and equipment is needed, etc.

Professional employer organization (peo)
A staffing service that is contracted to assume the employers responsibilities and risk for his/her workforce. Employees are legally co-employed by the PEO. The PEO is responsible for such actions as the preparation of accurate payroll checks, the remittance of payroll taxes to federal and state jurisdictions and the preparation of various tax information.

Professional liability
The legal liability of a professional, such as a doctor, accountant, lawyer, etc., who causes loss, harm or injury to their clients while performing their professional duties.

Profit
What remains after all costs (direct & indirect) have been covered from the initial selling price.

Profit and loss account (P&L)
One of the three principal business reporting and measuring tools (along with the balance sheet and cashflow statement). The P&L is essentially a trading account for a period, usually a year, but also can be monthly and cumulative. It shows profit

performance, which often has little to do with cash, stocks and assets (which must be viewed from a separate perspective using balance sheet and cashflow statement). The P&L typically shows sales revenues, cost of sales/ cost of goods sold, generally a gross profit margin (sometimes called 'contribution'), fixed overheads and or operating expenses, and then a profit before tax figure (PBT). A fully detailed P&L can be highly complex, but only because of all the weird and wonderful policies and conventions that the company employs. Basically the P&L shows how well the company has performed in its trading activities.

Profit margin

The margin found by dividing a firm's post-tax net earnings by sales (Profit margin measures how well a firm can earn money from sales relative to others.).

Profit sharing

An incentive scheme in which a business shares some of its profit , usually in cash or shares, with its employees.

Profit squeeze

A situation in which a company or business makes less profit over a period of time because of rising costs and/or falling prices.

Profit-centre

A business division or department or unit which is responsible for producing a profit, for example a shop unit within a chain of shops, or a branch within a network dealerships. Significantly a Profit-centre business unit will use a 'Profit and Loss Account' as a means of managing and reporting the business. A profit centre is involved in selling to customers.

Profiteer

An organisation or individual who makes excessive profits by charging very high prices for goods which are in short supply.

Programme trading

On the Stock Market, the buying and selling of large amounts of shares by computer, the Programme of which is triggered when trading reaches a certain level of volume.

Prohibitive

Preventing or discouraging something, for example people are discouraged from buying a product because the price is prohibitive, i.e., too high.

Project

A very general term for a task or objective of some complexity and duration, such that it needs properly planning, organizing, resourcing and managing. A small project can easily be part of a person's usual work duties. A large project can be as big as starting a new business, or constructing a skyscraper, or putting a spacecraft on Mars. Typically large projects are established as being separate to usual operational duties and responsibilities of workers, although any job can at any time be extended to include responsibility for the management of a project within it. A project differs from conventional 'work' mainly in being far more firmly structured, scheduled, resourced, and proactive, etc., whereas conventional 'work' is less predictable and tends to be of a more passive, responsive, reactive and flexible nature. Projects may be opportunistic and proactive (such as new product developments, or building something new, or some sort of exploratory research), or a necessary response/reaction to problems, emergencies, failures, etc., (for example a product recall, or a disaster recovery or investigation, or a re-training requirement). Large projects almost inevitably involve a degree of people-management.

Project management
The process of managing and planning a successful project from start to finish, which includes controlling, organizing, managing resources, people, budgets, etc.

Project manager
A person responsible for planning and delivering a large stand-alone task, objective, venture, etc., (a large and complex 'project') or a professional who is skilled in doing this, which generally includes using suitable project management tools and systems, and people-management skills where appropriate. N.B. A person who is instructed to plan and manage a project within his/her conventional work duties is not necessarily, in the usual meaning of the term, a 'project manager'. The term 'project manager' usually refers to a person whose primary responsibility is to manage a stand-alone project which by definition falls outside of conventional and normal operational work duties.

Project sponsor
A person in an organization who instigates or proposes a project, and creates/establishes/agrees the necessary executive approval, funding, resourcing, etc., typically extending to the appointment of the project manager. A project sponsor is usually and crucially responsible for developing and presenting the financial justification for the project, which generally entails outcomes and timescales, and assuming personal accountability for the success of the project.

Prom
Programmemable Read Only Memory. In a computer, a permanent memory chip which can only be recorded on once, by the computer user, not the manufacturer, after which the data is stored and cannot be changed.

PROM
A promotional broadcast on television, radio, etc., advertising a product, TV show, film, etc.

Promotion
The use of marketing and/or advertising to bring attention to a product, brand, service, company, etc., usually in order to increase sales. The raising of an employee to a higher rank in an organisation.

Promotional mix
Combination of one or more promotional elements that a firm uses to communicate with customers: often a mix of personal selling, mass selling (advertising, public relations, and publicity), sales promotion, and direct marketing.

Prompt note
A document sent to someone to remind them when a payment is due on a purchase.

Proof copy
The printed pages of a book, magazine, etc., which is read and corrected (e.g. spelling mistakes) by a Proof Reader before the final printing of all the copies.

Propaganda
Politically motivated publication or writing designed to influence thinking or action, usually in a misleading way.

When carried out by a government or other authority this may also be referred to in more modern terms as 'spin'. The word derives from the Latin name of a Roman Catholic committee responsible for 'propagation of the faith' in the 1600s.

Proprietary trading
The buying and selling of shares, bonds, etc., by a securities firm with its own money for its own profit, rather than for its customers.

Proptype
An original design or working model of something, often used in demonstrations.

Prosecute
To bring a criminal charge against someone in a court of law.

Prospectus
A document published by a company which is offering its shares for sale, disclosing information such as the company's activities, objectives, finances, etc. A book published by a university or school containing information about courses, etc.

Prosumer
Profession/Producer Consumer. A consumer who is involved in the specification of products, or has professional tools and is involved in the the design and manufacture of products.

Protectionism
The policy of a country protecting its own industries against foreign competition by imposing taxes, etc., on imported goods.

Protocol
In computing, a set of rules which determine the way data is transmitted between computers. The code of conduct in an organisation, etc.

Provident fund
A form of retirement savings. An employer and employee pay regular, usually equal, amounts into an investment fund, which is then paid to the employee upon retirement, often in a lump sum.

Proviso
A clause in a contract which makes a condition or stipulation.

Proxy
A person who has been given the authority to act for another person.

Prudence
Aside from its usual general meaning of carefulness in judgment and decision-making, prudence particularly refers to caution in commercial/financial/economic risk-taking, and to the typically great caution exercised by financial folk (accountants and bankers notably) in planning, budgeting, forecasting, granting loans, extending credit, defining standards and policies, and accounting practice as a whole, etc.

Pseudo
Pronounced 'sudo', this is a prefix which can be put before many different words to represent a fake or false quality which often attempts to imitate or behave as the real thing. From Greek pseudos, meaning falsehood.

Pseudonym
a false name, commonly adopted by a writer seeking to hide their true identity.

Psychographic segmentation
The process of identifying and dividing consumers into groups according to

their interests, attitudes, social class, values, personality, etc.

Psychographics
Criteria for segmenting consumers by lifestyle, attitudes, beliefs, values, personality, buying motives, and/or extent of product usage—in essence: activities, interests, and opinions. For example, the market for shampoo may consist of various psychographic segments described by their primary purchase motives (beauty, health, grooming), usage styles (daily, weekly, salon-only), or lifestyle (frequent travelers, parents with young children, empty-nesters). Research studies might focus on what magazines they read, which TV shows they view, and their opinions on the importance of "good grooming."

Psychological contract
Usually expressed as 'the Psychological Contract', this is the understanding between employee(s) and employer as to their mutual expectations arising from the employment relationship. The expectations involve a complex balance of inputs and rewards, including contractually clear elements such as hours and pay, and extend to implications and assumptions about security, loyalty, and other highly subjective factors. The Psychological Contract is a two-way notional agreement between employee and employer, typically analysed from the employee perspective.

Psychological pricing (price ending)
Practice based on a theory that the display of certain types of prices impact retail sales. Often expressed as "odd/even," prices ending in 99-cents drive greater demand to non-rational consumers.

Psychometric test
A test which measures a person's personality, mental ability, knowledge, etc., often used to ascertain whether a potential employee is suitable for a job.

Public company
A company whose shares are traded on the Stock Market.

Public corporation
A corporation which offers stock for public sale (Public corporations are required by law to provide information about their financial condition, operations, and such.).

Public debt
Also known as National Debt. The total amount of money owed by a country's national and local governments.

Public domain
Something that is not protected by copyright and is openly available for anyone to use, look at, etc.

Public employee
A person employed by the government.

Public enterprise
A business or economic activity owned and controlled by the government.

Public issue
When a company offers shares for sale to the public for the first time.

Public liability
When the owner of a business, etc., is responsible for any injury or harm inflicted on a member of the public because of negligence or unsafe products, etc., against which an insurance policy can be obtained by the business.

Public relations
Form of communication that is primarily directed toward gaining

understanding and acceptance by vested groups of what the marketer is doing. It often tends to deal with issues rather than specifically with products or services. PR also cannot be controlled by the organization because it is not purchasing the time or space in the media, but it offers legitimacy that advertising cannot claim. The practice of PR is used to build rapport with the various (vested) publics a company, individual, or organization may have (employees, customers, stockholders, voters, competitors, or the general population). Publicity releases, employee-training seminars, and company-produced newsletters, (house organs) are examples of instruments used in public relations.

Public works

Buildings and structures constructed by the government for public use, such as roads, bridges, schools, hospitals, etc.

Publicist

A publicity or press agent who publicises organisations, people, etc.

Publicity

Involves supplying information that is factual, interesting, and newsworthy to media not controlled by the organization (radio, television, magazines, newspapers, and trade journals). It is an uncontrolled method of placing messages in the media because the source does not pay the media for placement. Publicity typically generated from an organization's public relations department and its goal is to gain media coverage. Examples of news-worthy events that may receive media coverage, or publicity, include ground-breaking ceremonies, press conferences, organized protests, or ceremonial appointments or awards.

PR/publicity is "doing good — and getting caught."

Puff

In advertising, to exaggerate the qualities of a product, etc., without actually breaking the law.

Pull strategy

Used in marketing to create a demand for a product by means of advertising and promoting to the end consumer, rather than through the marketing channel. To 'pull' the product through from distributor to final consumer.

Pump and dump

The illegal practice of artificially boosting share prices by false and misleading statements in order to sell the originally cheap shares at much higher prices.

Punitive

Inflicting or concerned with punishment, for example punitive taxes, punitive justice.

Punitive damages

Damages awarded, over and above general damages, by a court of law against a defendant who has committed a malicious act which has resulted in injury to a person or damage to property, in order to deter the defendant from committing similar acts in future.

Purchase ledger

A record of a company's accounts which shows amounts owed to suppliers for items purchased on credit.

Purchasing officer

A company employee who is responsible for the purchasing of equipment, materials and services from suppliers and contractors.

Purchasing power

Also called spending power, the amount of goods or services which can be purchased with a particular currency, or more generally, the amount of money a person or group has available to spend on goods and services. The term may also emphasise a group or organization's ability to achieve heavily discounted prices or rates due to the high buying volumes.

Purchasing power parity

The rate at which one unit of currency will purchase the same amount of goods and services as it bought in an equilibrium period, despite differential rates of inflation.

Pure play

Term that relates to a company which deals in one specific line of business, rather than a range of products, services, etc.

Purpose-based marketing (pro-social movement)

Marketing efforts designed to communicate social responsibility ideas that are shared between an organization and its customers. Ex: Panera Bread's "Bakes before sunrise; donated after sunset" campaign.

Purveyor

A company or person who supplies provisions, especially food.

Push system

In production, a system in which the demand for goods is predicted by the company, so more goods are made to keep up with pre-set levels rather than customer demand.

Push/Pull strategies

Customers "pull" products towards themselves (creating channels that until now did not exist), while a producer "pushes" a product toward customers by promoting (advertising, sales promotion and discounts/allowances) through an existing channel, one channel member at a time.

Put option

The right given a buyer to sell stock at a specified price within a specified period of time.

Put option

An option in a contract giving the holder the right to sell shares, materials, etc., at a specified price at, or up to, a fixed date.

Pyramid scheme

Illegal in several countries, a scheme in which people are paid for recruiting others who pay a fee, part of which goes to the person who recruited them as a commission. In order to get their payment the recruits then have to find new recruits to pay a fee. This goes on until there is no one left to recruit and the people who come into the scheme last end up losing their money. The difference between Pyramid Selling and a Pyramid Scheme is that is that the latter has no product.

Pyramid selling

A system in which people buy the rights (often a franchise) to sell a company's products to other distributors who have been recruited, who then sell the products on to other recruits. This type of selling often ends up with no final buyer for the products. The few people at the top of the pyramid commonly make a lot more money than the many people at the bottom.

Q

QR codes (Quick Response)
Digital graphic links found in magazine ads, webpages, billboards, and practically anywhere a marketer wishes to advertise his business. Read by cell phones and other digital devices with cameras to display additional information or promotional offers to potential customers.

Qualified opinion
A statement written by an independent auditor which accompanies a business's financial statements, saying that the audit has been limited, e.g., because the auditor may not have been able to collect all the information required to carry out a full audit.

Qualifying period
The length of time an employee must serve in a job before being entitled to various benefits, or being able to make a claim against unfair dismissal.

Qualitative
Associated with a thing's quality which cannot be measured, such as feel, image, taste, etc. Describes peoples qualities which cannot be measured, such as knowledge, behaviour, attitude, etc.

Quality
An attribute or level of excellence. The standard of a product, service, etc., as measured against similar products, services, etc. A distinctive characteristic or attribute possessed by someone or something.

Quality assurance
QA. A system in which the delivery of a service or the quality of a product is maintained to a high standard, especially by means of attention to every stage of the process.

Quality audit
An independent investigation and assessment of quality activities and results to determine whether or not the quality plan is effective and appropriate.

Quality circle
Originating in Japan, a group of workers in a company who meet regularly to discuss ways in which to improve working conditions for employees and productivity for the company.

Quality circles
1. Quality improvement teams or groups.
2. In Japan, groups of employees formed for the study of and sharing information regarding quality control issues and theory.

Quality control
The use of techniques and activities that compare actual quality performance with goals and define appropriate action

in response to a shortfall.

Quality function deployment
A technique used to translate customer requirements into appropriate goals for each stage of product or service development and output. The two approaches to quality function deployment are known as the House of Quality and the Matrix of Matrices.

Quality improvement
A systematic approach to the processes of work that looks to remove waste, loss, rework, frustration, etc. in order to make the processes of work more effective, efficient, and appropriate.

Quality improvement team
A group of employees that take on a project to improve a given process or design a new process within an organization.

Quality loss function
An algebraic function that illustrates the loss of quality that occurs when a characteristic deviates from its target value. It is expressed often in monetary terms. Dr. Genichi Taguchi coined this term; his work suggests that quality losses vary as the square of the deviation from target.

Quality management
A system to make sure that a product or service meets standards of excellence, and that the process by which the product or service is created is efficient and effective as well. The three key components of this system are quality control, quality assurance and quality improvement.

Quantitive/quantitative
Related to or measured in numbers. Comparison based on quantity rather than quality.

Questionnaire
A form containing a list of research or survey questions for people to answer, so that information can be gathered for analysis

Quick ratio
Same as the Acid Test. The relationship between current assets readily convertible into cash (usually current assets less stock) and current liabilities. A sterner test of liquidity.

Quota
A specific imported amount imposed by one country on another, when once filled cannot be exceeded within a given time. When a quota is in force the price mechanism is not allowed to operate.

Quoted company
A company whose shares are listed on the Stock Exchange.

R

R&d
Research and Development. Investigative work carried out by a business to improve and develop products and processes.

Race relations act
A British government Act, introduced in 1976, making it unlawful to discriminate against someone because of their colour, race, nationality or ethnic origin.

Race to the bottom
A phrase said to be coined by US Supreme Court Justice Louis Brandeis. A situation in which competition between nations could result in lower standards, cheaper wages, poorer working conditions, etc.

Rack rate
The full price of something before discounts have been offered, especially hotel rooms.

Racketeer
A person who makes money through illegal business or crime, such as extortion, bribery, fraud, etc.

Raid
On the Stock Exchange, a situation where an individual or company makes a hostile bid to take over another company by buying a controlling interest in the company's shares.

Rainmaker
An employee, often an executive, who brings a lot of business and income to a company.

Ram
Random Access Memory. In computing, the place where current data is stored while a computer is being used. The data is removed when the computer is switched off.

Random sample
Often used in research, a method of sampling members of a large group, such as a population, in which everyone has an equal chance of being selected.

Random testing
Employer-administered drug and alcohol tests conducted at random intervals.

Range chart
Control chart in which the range of the subgroup is used to track the instantaneous variation within a process, i.e. the variation in the process at any one time, when many input factors would not have time to vary enough to make a detectable difference. Range charts are usually paired with average charts for complete analysis.

Rank and file
The ordinary members of a group, such as enlisted troops in an army, or

members of a union, who have no power.

Rat

Slang term for an informer, or to inform, typically for personal gain. Rat is also a verb, meaning to inform or betray.

Rat race

The exhausting, competitive struggle and routine of working and living in a large town or city.

Rate card

A printed list of charges and details regarding advertising costs on television, radio, websites, newspapers, etc.

Rate of return

The amount of profit or loss generated by an investment, expressed as a percentage of the total sum invested.

Ratify

To sanction formally. Validate an agreement with a vote or signature.

Rating

Broadcast size of an actual listening or viewing audience for a particular Programme or commercial as compared to the size of the potential audience (all households in a geographic area that have broadcast receivers—whether or not these broadcast receivers are turned on). One rating point represents 1% of the households making up the potential audience. Outdoor advertising estimates the number of persons exposed to an outdoor sign. Each outdoor structure is rated in terms of the number of persons who pass by on a daily basis as compared to the entire population in the area where the structure is located.

Rating agency

A company which assesses and rates businesses on their credit-worthiness and/or their ability to repay debts.

Ratings point

The measure of a size of an audience, i.e., one point equals one per cent of all households watching a television Programme or listening to a radio station at a particular time.

Ratio analysis

A study of a company's financial statements which show the relationships between items listed on a balance sheet and gives an indication as to whether the company can meet its current obligations.

Reach

Size of the audience who listen to, read, view or otherwise are exposed to a particular ad message over a defined time period. Reach may be stated either as an absolute number, or as a fraction of a given population (for instance TV households, men, or those aged 25-34).

Reactive marketing

Describes when companies or businesses wait for customers to contact them in order to buy their products or services.

Ready-to-wear

Describes clothing that is produced in standard sizes and designs and sold as finished products in retail outlets.

Real estate

Also called Realty. Property consisting of land with permanent structures on it, such as buildings, walls, fences, etc.

Real rate of return
The percentage of return on an investment over one year after adjustments for inflation or deflation.

Real time
In computing, systems which receive information and update it at the same time.

Ream
500 sheets of paper. A large quantity of written material.

Rebadge
To change the name , brand or logo of an existing product or business, especially cars.

Reboot
To switch a computer off and restart it again immediately.

Rebrand
Change the name, packaging, etc., of an existing product or business and advertise it as new and improved.

Recall
To ask customers to return a product which they have bought because it has been found to be faulty or dangerous.

Recall (Aided and Unaided)
Ascertaining whether potential customers saw/heard a specific product or service advertisement, often conducted via telephone after showing/playing the ad in test markets. Unaided question: "What ads do you recall from your TV viewing last night?" Aided question (often after negative unaided response): "Do you remember any ads for shampoos?"

Recapitalise
To put more money into a business, often one which is facing bankruptcy.

To reorganise a company's capital structure by exchanging preferred stock for bonds, usually to reduce taxes.

Receivables
Shown as assets on a balance sheet, money which is owed to a company by customers who have purchased goods or services on credit.

Receiver
An independent person appointed by a court to manage and control the finances, property, etc., of a bankrupt company, who usually sells the company's assets in order to pay the creditors.

Recession
The decline of the economy of a country (or other region) over a period of time, resulting in increased unemployment, reduced productivity, reduced GDP (Gross Domestic Product), falling household income and livings standards, etc. Different nations and financial institutions, bodies, etc., have different definitions of a recession. Many economists and business commentators use the term very loosely without regard to a particular definition, other than it being a period of economic contraction with related factors. A common official definition at national/governmental level is broadly that a recession is: "Two consecutive quarters (i.e., total 6mths) of 'negative growth' (or contraction or reduction) in GDP (Gross Domestic Product)". Aside from the euphemistically unhelpful term 'negative growth' (used by UK governments notably) this definition of recession is open to debate because it is calculated over such a short period and is therefore very finely balanced. This definition tends to increase instances of 'double-dip'

or 'triple-dip' recessions (i.e., two or three recessions in very close succession, according to this particular definition of 'recession') when in fact many such 'ups and downs' may be due to seasonal effects and adjustments rather than being actually different recessions. By more general (and some would say sensible and realistic) definitions of a recession, a 'double-dip' or 'triple dip' recession may instead be plainly and simply one long recession, and is historically seen as such.

Recession shape

A common way to describe a recession, in terms of how the recession appears in a graph of GDP movement over time. 'Shapes' are mostly letter-shapes (V, W, U, etc). Here are the most common recession shapes: V-shaped recession - The simplest shape and basic form of recession, namely a broadly straight-lined angled decline to a trough or lowest point, followed by a relatively quick 'bounce' upwards again in a straight-lined angled rise back to the pre-recession level. U-shaped recession - Like the V-shaped recession but with a longer period at the lowest point. Alternatively called a 'Bathtub Curve'. W-shaped recession - Also called a double-dip recession, essentially characterized by a recession whose recovery is interrupted by a further decline into recession, before final recovery. L-shaped recession - A recession which fails to recover for a very long period, typically ten years or longer, or indefinitely, i.e., pre-recession levels of GDP and GDP growth are not seen again for many decades. Also, where extremely severe an L-shaped recession might more traditionally be called a depression. The Japanese recession of the 1990s is gererally

regarded as an example of an L-shaped recession. The recessions in the US and large parts of Europe following the 2007/8 global financial crisis might easily be interpreted as similarly long-term and ominously L-shaped recessions. WW-shaped recession - A recession which lurches from recovery back into recession several times, which given the implication of the need for such a term, contains more ups and downs than a triple-dip recession. As with many of the terms referring to types of recessions, the need for the terminology is produced more by finely balanced definitions of a recession, rather than the ups and downs of economic performance, which are generally happening anyway whether in growth or recession. It's all a matter of degree; i.e., where recessions are defined by very tiny degrees of contraction (as happens in modern times), then 'multiple dip' and convoluted letter-shaped terminology tend to be used more frequently. J-shaped recession - This shape unusually and optimistically refers to a recession which recovers into a boom or period of high growth, i.e., the level of GDP immediately beyond recovery continues to increase strongly and substantially above pre-recesssion levels for a period exceeding the duration of the recession. This sort of recessionary recovery might be fuelled by technology innovation, or discovery and exploitation of new natural resources, etc. Inverted Square Root Sign-shaped recession - Otherwise technically the 'inverted radical symbol-shaped' recession, this term, apparently coined by financier George Soros, is very rarely used, and is included here mainly for curiosity. It refers to an L-shaped recession containing a small bounce (partial initial recovery) before a prolonged or indefinite period of depressed/recessionary-level economic conditions. Confusingly an inverted radical sign, with or without the long horizontal overline, seems not to fit the effect Soros described. A reverse tick or check sign is more apt.

Reciprocal

Loosley meaning 'in return', based on the stricter mathematical sense of the word, found in financial and scientific theories, where reciprocal refers to the number or fraction which when multiplied by a specified other number or fraction will produce the number one. For example a half is the reciprocal of the number two; and a fifth is the reciprocal of the number five. The word derives from Latin 're' (back) and 'pro' (forward).

Reciprocal trade/trading

Exchange of product or services. A simple example might be an accountant providing book-keeping services to a telemarketing company which in return performs telemarketing services on behalf of the accountant.

Reciprocity

Based on the notion of mutuality or return in the term 'reciprocal', reciprocity means give-and-take, such as to achieve a mutually agreeable balance.

Recognition test

Also known as Readership Test. A test carried out after people have read a newspaper, magazine, etc., to see if they have remembered or read a particular advertisement.

Record date

A date set by a company by which an investor must be recorded as owning shares in order to qualify to receive dividends and be able to vote at a shareholders meeting.

Recorded delivery

A postal system for which an extra fee is charged in addition to postage. The sender is given a receipt at the time of posting and the recipient signs a form to confirm delivery.

Recorder

The team member that takes minutes during team meetings to capture team's progress. Once the team is well underway, this role can be rotated through out the group.

Recruit

To seek employees for a business or organisation. To enlist military personnel.

Recruitment

The process of finding and hiring the best-qualified candidate for a position.

Recruitment process outsourcing (RPO)

The outsourcing of the recruiting process to a third party.

Red ink

Term used when referring to a company's financial loss.

Red-circling

The practice of protecting the salary of employees whose jobs have been downgraded because of the restructuring, etc., of the company.

Redundancy

A situation in which an employer intends to cease business, so therefore the workforce lose their jobs, or an employee is made redundant because their job no longer exists in the company they work for. Employees in these situations often qualify for redundancy pay.

Refer to drawer
In the UK, a phrase used by banks when someone's account does not have sufficient funds to clear a cheque which they have written, or the cheque has been written incorrectly.

Reference
A letter/statement written about a person by someone who knows them, detailing their abilities, character, qualifications, etc., which is sent to a prospective employer.

Referral premium
Reward offered to customers that introduce new customers, or to employees that bring in suitable recruits. For example, customers at a Miami car wash can earn $ 3.00 off their next wash for each new customer referred. At the end of the month, the customer with the most referrals gets a $50.00 gift card.

Regiocentrism
A regional market orientation with world market strategies.

Registered capital
Also called Authorised Capital. The maximum value of shares which a company can legally issue.

Registered company
In the US, a company which has filed an SEC (Securities and Exchange Commission) registration, and may issue new shares. In the UK, a company which is listed on the Companies Register as a limited private company, a public limited company, or an unlimited company.

Registered trademark
A distinctive symbol, name, etc., on a product or company, which is registered and protected by law so it cannot legally be used by anyone else.

Registrar
A person in a company or organisation who is in charge of official records.

Registration statement
In the US, a legal document containing details about a company's activities, financial status, etc., which must be submitted to the SEC (Securities and Exchange Commission) before the company can issue shares.

Regression analysis
A statistical technique used to determine the best mathematical expression to describe the relationship between a response and independent variables.

Reinsurance
The practice of sharing insurance risk among several insurance companies, in case of major disasters such as floods, hurricanes, etc.

Relationship marketing
Emphasizing customer retention and satisfaction rather than a point-of-sale transactions by recognizing the long term value of keeping customers.

Reliability
Research study can be replicated and get some basic results (free of errors).

Remunerate
To pay a person for services rendered, goods, losses incurred, etc.

Renewal notice
An advanced notice of payment required to renew insurance cover, subscription, etc., by a certain date.

Rental fleet
Cars, vans, etc., which a business leases from a vehicle leasing

company for its workers to use, usually sales teams, executives, service engineers, etc.

Replacement charts
A tool in succession planning in which current and future job vacancies, as well as the number of employees in currently filled jobs, are visually summarized.

Reporting line
In a business or organisation, employees, managers, etc., who report to the next person higher up, usually their boss.

Repositioning
Changing a brand's status in comparison to competing brands, usually through changing the marketing mix in response to changes in the marketplace, or due to a failure to reach the brand's marketing objectives.

Repossess
To take back property, goods, etc., usually from an individual or organisation who has failed to repay a loan or has defaulted on a repayment plan.

Repudiate
Refusal to perform a contractual duty or repay a debt.

Request for proposal (RFP)
A request sent by a company to a vendor to submit a bid for a product or service. The bid includes a timeline, a description of the good or service, the type of contract, cost and other specifics.

Requisition
An official written request or demand for something.

Rescind
To make void or cancel, for example a law or contract.

Research
The gathering of information, facts, data, etc., about a particular subject.

Reserve currency
A reserve currency (or anchor currency) is a currency that is held in significant quantities by governments and institutions as part of their foreign exchange reserves, and that is commonly used in international transactions. Persons who live in a country that issues a reserve currency can purchase imports and borrow across borders more cheaply than persons in other nations because they need not exchange their currency to do so.

Reserve price
The lowest fixed price at which a seller will sell an item at auction. If the bidding does not reach the reserve price then the item is not sold unless the highest bidder comes to an arrangement with the seller.

Reserves
The accumulated and retained difference between profits and losses year on year since the company's formation.

Residual income
Part of a person's income which is left over after taxes and living expenses, for example mortgage, bills, etc., have been deducted.

Residual value
Also Called Salvage Value. The market value of an asset which is no longer in use or has reached the end of its useful life.

Resource
Economic or productive factors required to accomplish an activity, such as materials, components, land,

and capital. Others include energy, entrepreneurship, information, human skills/management expertise.

Resource allocation
The process of assigning available finances, materials, labour, etc., to a project.

Restitution
Money paid by an offender in compensation for loss, damages or injury. To give something back to its rightful owner.

Restricted funds
These are funds used by an organisation that are restricted or earmarked by a donor for a specific purpose, which can be extremely specific or quite broad, eg., endowment or pensions investment; research (in the case of donations to a charity or research organisation); or a particular project with agreed terms of reference and outputs such as to meet the criteria or terms of the donation or award or grant. The source of restricted funds can be from government, foundations and trusts, grant-awarding bodies, philanthropic organisations, private donations, bequests from wills, etc. The practical implication is that restricted funds are ring-fenced and must not be used for any other than their designated purpose, which may also entail specific reporting and timescales, with which the organisation using the funds must comply.

Restrictive covenant
Also known as a negative covenant; a provision in a contract excluding key employees from working for competitors in a certain geographic area and for a certain length of time.

Restrictive practice
A trading agreement between businesses or industries which prevents free competition. The practice of workers, often trade unions, of protecting their jobs in a manner which limits the freedom of other workers.

Resume
A written summary of a person's education, employment record, qualifications, etc., which is often submitted with a job application.

Retail
Channel members in a distribution network or commercialization schedule that sell directly to the end user. In the U.S., that's where sales tax is collected. If a producer sells direct to consumers, it is a retailer (it charges and collects sales tax.) It's where possession utility takes place.

Retail banking
Also called Consumer Banking. Banking services provided directly to the public, such as savings accounts, credit/debit cards, mortgages, etc.

Retail investor
Also called Small Investor. An individual who buys and sells shares, etc., for themselves, usually in small quantities.

Retail park
Usually situated on the outskirts of a large town, a large retail development consisting of shops, stores, car parking, and often cinemas and restaurants.

Retail price index
RPI. An inflation indicator, usually calculated on a monthly basis, reflected in the retail price of everyday goods, such as food, fuel, fares, etc.

Retail therapy

Shopping which is done for enjoyment and to relieve stress.

Retailer

A channel institution which acts as an intermediary between other channel institutions and the end user and who usually breaks bulk, charging a margin for its services.

Retained earnings

The earnings of a business or company which is used for reinvestment, rather than being distributed to shareholders as dividends.

Retained profits

A business profit, after tax and dividend payments to shareholders, which is retained by the business and often used for reinvestment.

Retainer

A fee paid in advance to someone, such as a lawyer, to engage their services as and when they are required.

Re-targeting

Tracking website visitors, often with small embedded coding on the visitor's computer called "cookies." Then displaying relevant banner ads relating to products and services on websites previously visiting as surfers visit other websites.

Retention ratio

The percent of a firm's earnings kept for investment purposes.

Retention strategy

In order to retain employees and reduce turnover managers must meet the goals of employees without losing sight of the organization's goals, utilizing valence and expectancy theories.

Retrench

To cut down on spending, economise, for example to reduce a workforce.

Return

The sum of the income plus capital gains.

Return on assets

Net income divided by total cost or value of assets. The more expensive a company's assets, the less profit the assets will generate.

Return on capital employed

A fundamental financial performance measure. A percentage figure representing profit before interest against the money that is invested in the business. (profit before interest and tax, divided by capital employed, x 100 to produce percentage figure.)

Return on equity (ROE)

The value found by dividing the company's net income by its net assets (ROE measures the amount a company earns on investments).

Return on investment

Another fundamental financial and business performance measure. This term means different things to different people (often depending on perspective and what is actually being judged) so it's important to clarify understanding if interpretation has serious implications. Many business managers and owners use the term in a general sense as a means of assessing the merit of an investment or business decision. 'Return' generally means profit before tax, but clarify this with the person using the term - profit depends on various circumstances, not least the accounting conventions used in the business. In this sense most CEO's and business owners regard ROI as the ultimate measure of any business or any business proposition, after all it's what most business is aimed at producing - maximum return on investment, otherise you might as well put your money in a bank savings account. Strictly speaking Return On Investment is defined as: Profits derived as a proportion of and directly attributable to cost or 'book value' of an asset, liability or activity, net of depreciation. In simple terms this the profit made from an investment. The 'investment' could be the value of a whole business (in which case the value is generally regarded as the company's total assets minus intangible assets, such as goodwill, trademarks, etc and liabilities, such as debt. N.B. A company's book value might be higher or lower than its market value); or the investment could relate to a part of a business, a new product, a new factory, a new piece of plant, or any activity or asset with a cost attached to it. The main point is that the term seeks to define the profit made from a business investment or business decision. Bear in mind that costs and profits can be ongoing and accumulating for several years, which needs to be taken into account when arriving at the correct figures.

Revaluation

The increase in the value of one currency vis a vis other currencies.

Revenue

Amounts generated from sale of goods or services, or any other use of capital or assetsbefore any costs or expenses are deducted. Also called sales.

Revenue bond

A municipal bond (muni) backed by the revenue gained from a specific project such as the building of a stadium.

Revenue stamp

A stamp or sticker which is put on an item, for example a packet of cigarettes, as proof that a government tax has been paid.

Reverse auction

A type of auction in which there are several sellers and only one buyer. The buyer usually purchases the goods or service from the seller who offers the lowest price.

Reverse billing

A payment method used for messaging on mobile phones in which the recipient pays for the text message.

Reverse merger

When a private company acquires the majority of a public company's shares, therefore enabling the private company to get a public listing on the stock exchange.

Revolving credit

A type of credit agreement, e.g., a credit card, in which a person is given a specified credit limit which can be paid in full or in part, usually on a monthly basis. If the amount owing is paid in full in the first month then usually no interest is charged. When the full credit limit has been reached a payment must be made before the credit card can be used again.

Rider

An attachment which makes amendments or provisions to an original contract or official document. In the entertainment industry, a rider is a list of demands made by a performer, usually before a show, sometimes including particular foods and drinks, hotels and transport, free tickets for friends and family, etc.

Right to manage
The "right" of management to conduct business without having to answer to internal or external forces for their decisions.

Rights issue
The issuing of new shares which are offered to a company's existing shareholders at a fixed price, usually lower than the market price.

Risk
Uncertainty of falling short of goals in a marketing plan. It's also all the unknowns that are uncontrollable by the marketer. That's why researching the needs of the target market is imperative towards reducing risk.

Risk management
The use of insurance and other strategies to minimize an organizations exposure to liability in the event a loss or injury occurs.

Risk/return trade-off
The compromise made between high- and low-risk investments (High-risk investments generally generate more earnings, while low-risk ones generate a lower rate of return.).

Roaming
Roaming is a general term referring to the extension of connectivity service in a location that is different from the home location where the service was registered. Roaming ensures that the wireless device is kept connected to the network, without losing the connection.

Robust
The ability of a product or service to function appropriately regardless of external conditions and other uncontrollable factors.

Robust design
An approach to the planning of new products and services that harnesses Taguchi methods.

Rogue trader
A stockbroker who makes unauthorised, usually high risk, trades on behalf of their employer, often resulting in huge losses.

Rolling contract
A contract which runs for a specific period of time and continues to be renewed for further periods, subject to review.

Roll-on roll-off
Ro-Ro. In the UK, describes ferries which vehicles can be driven onto at one end and driven off at the other end on reaching their destination.

Rotational training
A training method where employees are rotated among a variety of different jobs, departments or company functions for a certain period of time.

Round lot
Also called Normal Trading Unit. A block of shares, usually 100, which is traded on the Stock Market.

Route 128
Also known as Yankee Division Highway. A highway encircling Boston , Massachusetts, which is associated with the technology industry.

Router
A device which connects at least two computer networks and sends data from one to the other.

Royalty
A fee paid for the use of another person's property, for example a copyrighted work, a patent, a

franchise, etc. A payment made to a writer, composer or singer when a book, CD or performance of their work is sold. A share of the profit paid to the owner of the land which an oil or mining company is leasing.

RSI

Repetitive Strain/Stress Injury. Damage caused to hands, arms and neck due to continual computer use, or by repetitive movements while performing a task.

RSS (Real simple syndication)

A commonly used protocol for delivering web-based content such as blogs. RSS is an XML-based format that allows webmasters to provide fresh web content in a succinct manner. It is fast becoming an easy and affordable way to spread content.

Rubber cheque

A cheque which bounces, due to insufficient funds in the account of the person who wrote the cheque for it to be cleared by the bank.

Run chart

Also known as a line chart, or line graph. A chart that plots data over time, allowing you to identify trends and anomalies.

Run Chart Showing Upward Trend

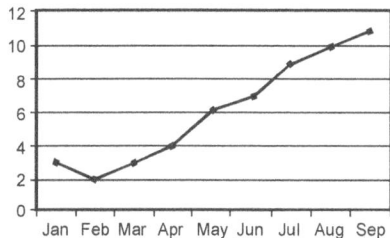

Run of network

RON. Describes when an advertisement is placed on any page on one or more websites and the advertisers have no say where their advert is placed, usually because the advertising rates are cheaper.

Running cost

The day to day running costs of a business, for example wages, rent, utilities, etc.

Rush hour

A rush hour or peak hour is a part of the day during which traffic congestion on roads and crowding on public transport is at its highest. Normally, this happens twice a day—once in the morning and once in the evening, the times during when the most people commute. The term is very broad but often refers to specifically private automobile transportation traffic, even when there is a large volume of cars on a road but not a large number of people, or if the volume is normal but there is some disruption of speed.

Rust belt

Also called The Manufacturing Belt. In the US, an area which contains many old, unmodernised factories, such as steel works, many of which are now closed or not very profitable.

R-value/u-value

Refers to insulation effectiveness in buildings, and to materials used in construction. Either term may be used. U-Value is the reciprocal of R-Value. The higher the R-Value the better the insulation. The lower the U-Value, the better the insulation.

S

Sabbatical

A period of leave which is granted to an employee, sometimes up to a year, in order for them to study, travel, rest, etc.

Sabotage

To deliberately destroy or damage property, tools, or machinery in order to hinder production. To cause an obstruction to something in order to make it unsuccessful.

Safe harbor regulations

Guidelines regulated by the Department of Labour, which, when fully complied with, may reduce or limit the liability of a plan fiduciary, on the condition that the party performed its actions in good faith or in compliance with defined standards.

Safety

Value Line Index's measure of stock volatility (magnitude of beta), measured from 1 to 5, 5 being most volatile.

Safety stock

Also called Buffer Stock. Extra stock kept by a company or business in case of extra demand or late deliveries of new stock.

Salami slicing

The process of carrying out small actions or removing something in very small amounts so that it goes unnoticed, i.e., stealing money.

Salary

An employees wages which are paid on a regular basis for performing their job.

Sale and leaseback

An arrangement in which property, machinery, etc., is sold to a business or individual, who then immediately leases it back to the seller.

Sale or return

An agreement in which unsold goods can be returned to the supplier without the goods having to be paid for.

Sales and marketing

The business of promoting and selling a company's products or services. The department of a business which carries our these activities.

Sales conference

A meeting at which members of a company's sales team(s) are brought together to discuss or review ways of marketing the company's products or services.

Sales ledger

Also known as Accounts Receivable. A company's record of transactions for goods and/or services which have been provided to a customer, and for which money is still owed.

Sales pitch

A salespersons attempts to persuade a potential customer to buy something, often using demonstration and argument.

Sales resistance
The refusal of a potential customer to buy a product or service, often as a result of aggressive selling practices.

Sales tax
A tax based on the cost of a product or service which must be paid by the buyer. This tax does not apply to all goods or services.

Salvage value
Also known as Residual Value. The estimated value of an asset, for example a piece of machinery, which is to be scrapped or removed.

Sample
A subset of a population used to represent the population in statistical analysis. Samples are almost always random, which means that all individuals in the population are equally likely to be chosen for the sample.

Sample standard deviation chart (s chart)
Control chart in which the standard deviation of the subgroup is tracked to determine the variation within a process over time. Sample standard deviation charts are usually paired with average charts for complete analysis.

Sandbagging
In a court of law, the practice by a lawyer of not mentioning a possible error which has occurred during a trial in the hope that it goes unnoticed and the lawyer can then use it as a basis for appeal.

Sandwich course
An educational course, sometimes lasting three or four years, which involves alternate periods of study, e.g. at university, and periods of work experience in business or industry.

Sca
Sustainable Competitive Advantage – A position that a firm occupies in its competitive landscape. A firm possesses an SCA when it has value-creating processes and positions that cannot be duplicated or imitated by other firms over a long term. It takes time and sustained promotional expenditure to establish an SCA. Without both of these criteria, it's probably a USP (unique selling proposition).

Scab
A derogatory term for an employee who refuses to join a trade union, or who continues to work during a strike at their workplace. Also describes someone who accepts work or replaces a union worker during a strike.

Scalability
The degrees to which the system, network, or process of a computer's hardware or software can be expanded in size, volume, or number of users served and continue to function properly. An analogous business model of economic growth refers to a businesses ability to expand to a greater capacity.

Scam
Means of making money by deceit or fraud.

Scarcity value
A situation where the more scarce an item is, the more its worth.

Scatterplot
A tool that studies the possible relationship between two variables expressed on the x-axis and y-axis of a graph. The direction and density of

the points plotted will indicate various relationships or a lack of any relationship between the variables.

Schadenfreude
German word derived from Schaden (damage, harm) and Freude (joy). Malicious pleasure derived from the misfortune and suffering of others. Typically felt by individuals with low self-esteem.

Scheme of arrangement
In the UK, a legal agreement between a company and its shareholders and/or creditors in which the company will pay what debts it can as an alternative to bankruptcy.

Schism
A split or division in a group into opposing factions, caused by differences of opinion.

Scorched-earth policy
A situation in which a company tries to prevent a hostile take-over by selling off its most valuable assets, thereby making the company unattractive to a potential buyer. Derives from a military strategy of 'leaving nothing for the enemy' by burning crops, buildings, etc.

Screen-based activity
A task which is carried out using a computer.

Screening interview
A brief, first interview, sometimes over the phone, with a company looking for potential job applicants. This process weeds out unsuitable applicants, and successful ones go on to the next stage of interviews.

Screensaver
A moving image on a computer screen which appears when there has been no screen activity for a specific time. Screensaver Programmes were originally used to prevent damage to the screen.

Scrip
A certificate which entitles someone to a parcel of shares. An issue of additional shares given to existing shareholders instead of dividends.

SD card
Secure Digital Card. A small memory card used in portable devices such as mobile phones, cameras, etc.

Sealed bid
A bid to buy an item, or a cost estimate for a contract, which is kept secret in a sealed envelope until all the bids have been received and are opened together.

Seaq
Stock Exchange Automated Quotation system. In the UK, a system used on the London Stock Exchange which continuously updates share prices and shows the information on computer screens around the world.

Search
The collection of relevant information by deliberate searching either formally or informally.

Search engine
Google, Bing, Yahoo, etc., are examples of Search Engines which locate, list and rank (according to various crietria and unknown algorithms) relevant websites and website content on the Internet when the user types in key words or phrases.

Second generation
Term which describes an improved product, service, etc.

Secondary action

A sympathy strike. Action which is taken by workers in one industry in support of striking workers in a separate but related industry.

Secondary boycott

An organised protest to prevent or persuade a company from doing business with another company which is involved in a dispute.

Secondary data

Facts and figures already recorded prior to a project. There may be a higher degree of risk due to the length of time that has passed when the data were collected.

Secondary market

On the Stock Exchange, the purchasing of shares from another investor rather than from the issuing company.

Secondary research

Also called Desk Research. The collating and analysis of existing data which has already been collected for another purpose often by an outside source.

Secretary

A person who works for another person , usually in an office, dealing with correspondence, filing, phone calls and other clerical duties.

Securities

A financial that indicated the holder owns a share or shares of a company (stock) or has loaned money to a company or government organization (bond).

Securities and Exchange Commission (SEC)

In the US, a government agency which is responsible for protecting investors against fraudulent and dishonest practices in the securities market.

Securities and futures Authority

Now part of the Financial Services Authority. In the UK, an organisation which regulates the trading in stocks and shares, bonds, etc., and protects investors against dishonest practices.

Securities market(s)

Exchange(s) where investments such a stocks and shares, etc., are traded. Traditionally and originally these exchanges were buildings containing traders and brokers, etc., whereas nowadays such trading is conducted virtually using modern communications and IT systems, usually online, so that markets and exchanges are virtual, i.e., existing mostly through connections between people and organizations and systems, rather than necessarily requiring a physical grouping in a building.

Security

The strict financial meaning of a security is a document that proves ownership of stocks, shares, bonds, etc., or other investments. More loosely securities refer to investments generally, for example in the term securities market.

Security analyst

A person who specializes in evaluating information regarding stocks and bonds.

Security deposit

A sum a buyer pays, which is not usually refundable, to protect the seller if the buyer does not complete a transaction or if a rented item gets damaged.

Seedcorn
Money or assets set aside by a business in order to generate more profit or benefit in the future.

Segmentation
Clusters of people with similar needs that share other geographic, demographic, and psychographic characteristics, such as veterans, senior citizens, or teens.

Seigniorage
Profit made by a government from printing and minting banknotes and coins. The profit being the difference between the cost of issuing the money and the face value of the money.

Selective attention
Term which applies to consumers who only notice, or are aware of, certain pieces of information in advertisements, etc., because that is the only part in which the consumer is interested.

Selective distribution
Contracting with several, but not all available channel members to move the product through the commercialization schedule. Attention is given to those channel members willing to give special attention to the product or service, such as employing a sales force to help sell/move the product to the next channel. (Not to be confused with Selective exposure: Providing several different choices where the customer can obtain possession utility. Often marketers select selective channel members based on their ability to push the product to the next channel member through its own sales force.)

Self reference criterion
Perceptual distortion brought about by an individual's own cultural experience.

Self-employed
A person who earns their income by operating their own business, rather than working for an employer and receiving a salary.

Self-funded (self-insured) plan
A health care insurance Programme in which employers (usually larger companies) pay the specified health care costs of their employees rather than insuring them. Self-funded plans may be self-administered, or the employer may contract a third party administrator (TPA) for administrative services only (ASO).

Self-supporting
Financially independent. Being able to operate without the help of others.

Sell limit order
An order to a stock broker to sell a specific number of shares at or above a specified price.

Seller's market
A situation in which there are more buyers than sellers, often resulting in high prices.

Selling cost
Costs which are incurred for the advertising and distribution of a product.

Selling orientation
A company-centered approach designed to motivate potential customers to buy products and services through various promotional offers, such as quantity discounts, free trial, money-back guarantees, and rebates. This orientation tends to ignore what the customer really needs. (All those extra rolls of toilet paper in your bathroom linen closet probably got there through a selling-oriented

coupon or quantity price discount.)

Seminar
A business meeting for training purposes or for discussing ideas.

Semi-skilled
Having or requiring some skills or special training to perform a job, such as operating machinery.

Semi-structured interview
An informal method of research in which set questions are asked which allow other questions to be brought up as a result of the interviewees response.

Sensitivity analysis
Looks at the effects of the performance of a system, project, etc., by changing the variables, such as costs, sales, production, etc.

Sensitivity training
A form of individual or group counseling geared toward increasing self-awareness of one's own prejudices and sensitivity to others.

SEO (Search engine optimization)
The process of optimizing a web site (e.g., identifying and placing targeted keywords on web pages) to ensure the site places well when queried on search engines. It is important for corporate web sites to optimize their visibility on search engines.

Sequential sampling
A sampling method in which an unfixed number of samples are tested and enough data is collected before a decision can be made.

Sequester
Keeping a jury in isolation, under close supervision and away from the public and media, during a trial.

Sequestrate
To legally confiscate someone's property until a debt has been paid.

Serial bonds
Also called Instalment Bonds. Bonds which are issued on the same date but mature over a period of time, usually at regular intervals, so the issuer can spread the repayment to the investor.

Server
A computer which provides services, such as e-mail, file transfers, etc., to other computers connected to the network.

Service
An intangible economic activity (buying and selling transaction) that is not stored, and does not result in ownership—such as a check-up at the doctor, or being privileged to attend an EMBA marketing class in Houston at Texas Woman's University.

Service economy
Part of a country's economy which provides services, such as banking, tourism, education, retail, etc., rather than manufacturing or production.

Service level agreement
A contract, which can be legally binding, between a service supplier and a user, in which the terms of service are specified.

SET
Secure Electronic Transfer. A safe and confidential way of paying for goods which have been purchased over the Internet.

Set-aside scheme
Introduced in 1988 in the UK to reduce the overproduction of arable crops. Farmers are paid to keep land fallow rather than use it to grow produce.

Settlement date

Term used to describe the date by which shares, bonds, etc., must be paid for by the buyer, or a sold asset must be delivered by the seller.

Seven tools of quality

Quality improvement tools that include the histogram, Pareto chart, check sheet, control chart, cause-and-effect diagram, flowchart, and scatter diagram.

Shadow

To be with someone in the workplace as they perform their job so that you can learn all about it.

Shadow economy

Also called Black Economy. Business activities, including illegal activities, which are carried out without government approval or regulations.

Share

Percentage of a media audience reached with an advertisement among those watching at the time. This is often a misleading term. For example, a 50 share (half of all viewers) means only that half of those watching at that time had the potential to see the ad. But if only half of 2 million TV households in a given market had their TV sets tuned to that Programme, that would equate to 500,000 households (only half of 1 million TV households).

Share

Any of the equal units into which a company's capital stock is divided and sold to investors.

Share buyback

Also known as Stock Repurchase. A situation in which a listed company buys back its own shares from shareholders.

Share capital

The balance sheet nominal value paid into the company by shareholders at the time(s) shares were issued.

Share incentive plan

SIP. A way for employees to invest in the company for which they work. The company gives the employees shares or offers shares for them to buy, enabling the employees to receive some of the company's profit, i.e. in dividends.

Share index

A list of certain companies share prices, which can be compared on a day to day basis, i.e. showing whether prices have risen or fallen.

Shareholder

Also called Stockholder. An individual, business or group who legally owns one or more share in a company.

Shareholders' equity

The sum of preferred and common stock equity held by shareholders.

Shareholders' funds

A measure of the shareholders' total interest in the company represented by the total share capital plus reserves.

Shareware

Copyrighted computer software which is available for a free trial, after which a fee is usually charged if the user requires continued use and support.

Shark

A dishonest business person who cheats and swindles others.

Shark repellent

Measures taken by a company, such as creating different voting rights concerning shares, or requiring certain shareholders to waive rights to capital gains resulting in a takeover, etc., in an attempt to keep a hostile bid from succeeding.

Shark watcher
An individual or company who monitors the stock market for another company and warns them of a potential takeover, e.g., if a lot of their shares are being bought by one person or one company.

Shelf talker
Also known as Shelf Screamer. A sign hung on the edge of a shelf in a shop to attract peoples attention to a product.

Sheriff's sale
In the US, a forced sale of property ordered by a law court, the proceeds of which settle unpaid debts.

Shewhart cycle
Another name for the Plan-Do-Check-Act cycle. It is also sometimes called the Deming cycle.

Shoestring
A very tight, barely adequate budget.

Shop floor
Workers, usually in a factory, as opposed to managers. The area in a factory where production of goods takes place.

Shop steward
A member of a Trade Union, usually in a factory, who is elected to represent other members in meetings with management and personnel officers.

Shopping bot
Also called Price Engine. Computer software which searches the Internet and compares prices from retailers for specific products.

Short covering
The purchase of the same number of shares, bonds, etc. which have been sold short.

Short selling
The sale of shares, etc., which are not owned by the seller but borrowed from a broker, on the understanding that they must be bought back, hopefully at a lower than what they were sold for in order to make a profit, and returned to the broker.

Short-change
Give too little change in a cash transaction, and metaphorically meaning to treat someone unfairly or dishonestly, deprive someone of something, or cheat, usually from a position of control or dominance.

Short-term disability
Disability income insurance designed to replace employee income for a temporary, specified time frame while they are unable to perform their duties due to illness or injury, before they return to work.

Shoulder season
In the travel industry, the time between high and low season.

Shovelware
A derogatory term for content which is put directly on to a web page, e.g. from a magazine, etc., without changing its appearance to make it suitable for the Internet. Also refers to pre-installed Programmes on some computers, which have little value to the user.

SHRM
Their self-definition : "The Society for Human Resource Management (SHRM) is the world's largest

association devoted to human resource management. Representing more than 250,000 members in over 140 countries, the Society serves the needs of HR professionals and advances the interests of the HR profession."

SIC

Standard Industrial Codes for the United States (up to four digits) used from 1930 to 1997. Replaced by the NAICS (National American Industrial Code) in 1997 for North America, 6-digit code.

Sick building syndrome

SBS. Ailments, such as headaches, fatigue, nose and throat irritations, etc., experienced by workers or residents in certain buildings, often believed to be caused by poor ventilation, air conditioning, heating, cleaning chemicals, or the materials from which the building has been made.

Sickout

A type of organised strike in which the employees refuse to work by staying away from the workplace and claiming they are ill.

SIG

Special Interest Group. On the Internet, a place where people can discuss and exchange information about a particular subject. A group or organisation whose aim is to influence political decisions by trying to persuade government officials to act or vote in the group's interest.

Sight unseen

To buy something which has not been available for inspection before the purchase.

Signature loan

Also called Unsecured Loan or Character Loan. A loan which is not backed by any security, and which only requires the borrowers signature.

Silicon alley

An area in Manhattan, New York, which is known for its Internet and multi-media companies.

Silicon valley

An area south of San Francisco, California, which is noted for its computer and high-technology industries.

Silver bullet

A simple extremely effective solution to a very challenging and serious problem. A metaphor alluding to the mythical method of killing a werewolf or similar monster.

Silver surfer

An older person who uses the Internet.

Sim card

From the full meaning, Subscriber Identification/Identity Module. A small removable card which stores personal information on a mobile phone or other small personal computerized device. There are other less serious interpretations of the SIM acronym.

Simple interest

Interest which is calculated on the original amount of money deposited or borrowed, and not on any interest which may have accrued.

Sin tax

A tax on certain goods or services which are considered bad for people, such as cigarettes, alcohol, etc.

Sinecure

A sinecure means an office that requires or involves little or no responsibility, labour, or active service. The term originated in the medieval church, where it signified a post without any responsibility for the "care of souls", the regular liturgical and pastoral functions of a cleric, but came to be applied to any post, secular or ecclesiastical, that involved little or no actual work. Sinecures have historically provided a potent tool for governments or monarchs to distribute patronage, while recipients are able to store up titles and easy salaries.

Single-entry bookkeeping
A simple system of recording a company's finances in which transactions are recorded only once in one account.

Sinking fund
Money set aside on a regular basis by a company, that is used for paying debts, taxes, etc., which are due at a later date.

Situational leadership
A management theory stating that effective leadership varies, but is task-relevant, and the most successful leaders are those that adapt their leadership style to the maturity of their audience.

Six sigma
Six Sigma is a disciplined, data-driven methodology used to improve the quality of process outputs by identifying and removing the causes of defects and minimizing variability in manufacturing and business processes. It also cuts costs from manufacturing by creating a special infrastructure of people that are experts in these methods.

Skimming
Pricing strategy often used in the introductory and growth stages of the product life cycle to target innovators and early adopters that are willing to pay a relatively high price for the product. Over time, the price may be reduced to take advantage of production economies of scale achieved by selling higher volumes. A skimming strategy can attract competitors to the market if the product or technology can be easily duplicated. Luxury perfumes use a skimming strategy that takes advantage of the high perceived value, enabling them to sell perfume at hundreds of dollars per ounce. The term is derived from the concept of "skimming the cream" off unprocessed milk. In this case, the marketer is skimming the cream, or those consumers willing to pay the most, off the market.

Skimming price
The charging of a high price in order to gain maximum revenue conducted under conditions of product uniqueness and inelastic demand patterns.

SKU
Stock Keeping Unit. A unique number which identifies the price, size, manufacturer, etc., which is assigned to a product by a retail store.

Skunkworks
A production development Programme in a company which has the freedom to work outside the usual rules, without the restrictions of company procedures and policies.

Sleeper
Something, such as a film, book, share, etc., in which there is little interest but suddenly becomes a success.

Sleeping partner
Also called Silent Partner. A person who has invested capital in a company but does not take an active part in managing or running it.

Slogan

A catch-phrase used in advertising which is easy to remember so it is associated with a product or company when people hear or see it.

Slotting fees

Fees charged by retailers to obtain exposure (shelf space) for a product. This may take the form of promotional, advertising and stocking fees. Supermarkets often earn more profit from agreeing to carry a marketer's product than from actually selling the product to customers.

Slush fund

Also called Slush Money. Funds which are raised and set aside for dishonest or illegal purposes, e.g., for bribing government officials.

Small claims court

A UK court in which hearings are generally informal, without jury, for the judgment of civil claims for small amounts of money, and where parties commonly represent themselves instead of hiring a solicitor or lawyer, although legal assistance or representation is permitted.

Smoke and mirrors

Term based on a magician's illusions. To cover something up by drawing attention away from it.

SMS

Short Message Service. Allows a text message to be sent from one mobile phone to another.

Snail mail

Mail which is delivered in the traditional way by postal service, rather than e-mail.

Sneakernet

Humorous term describing the transfer of electronic information, such as computer files, by physically taking the disk, cd, etc., from one computer to another.

Social collabouration

Processes that help multiple people within an organization interact, share information to achieve common goals. Globalization and the rise of contingent workforces and telecommuting have given increased importance to social collabouration and social collabouration software.

Social culturism

Uncontrollable variables that relate to values, religion, tradition, age, and ethnicity that impact the effectiveness of marketing strategies and tactics. Ex: Sales of matzah balls increase dramatically during annual Jewish Passover; then level off for the remainder of the year.

Social currency (online)

A measure of a person's power, or influence, within a defined social group. Factors contributing to one's social currency are their visibility, activity and following on social networks like Twitter, LinkedIn, Facebook, Blogs.

Social enterprise

A business chiefly having positive social and/or environmental aims, in which community and staff tend to feature strongly in priorities, and where profit is a means towards social, environmental or community purposes rather being an aim itself for the enrichment of owners or shareholders.

Social HR

The extent to which human resource departments leverage social media tools (Facebook, LinkedIn, Twitter, etc.) to conduct human resource activities (recruiting, employment branding, etc.) aimed at aligning HR goals to the company's business goals.

Social marketing

Seeking to increase the acceptability of a social idea, cause, or practice in a target group or vested public. Ex: Oklahoma State University used social marketing to broaden its image as a conscious global solutions-oriented university. Both enrollment and alumni donations increased. Beyond shortening the distance between friends, Facebook is also an advertising site: Click "like" and you advertise to everyone in your network. Social marketing (social networking) Seeking to increase the acceptability of a social idea, cause, or practice in a target group or vested public. Ex: Oklahoma State University used social marketing to broaden its image as a conscious global solutions-oriented university. Both enrollment and alumni donations increased. Beyond shortening the distance between friends, Facebook is also an advertising site: Click "like" and you advertise to everyone in your network

Social media

Forms of electronic communication (as Web sites for social networking and microblogging) through which users create online communities to share information, ideas, personal messages, and other content (as videos).

Social media background screening

Using publicly available social media profiles of job candidates in the hiring decision process. Typically done after a company has extended or is about to extend and offer to a candidate. Recruiters and employers need to be aware of governing bodies like the Equal Employment Opportunity Commission (EEOC) and the Office of Federal Contract Compliance Programmes (OFCCP) when conducting social media screening to avoid discrimination.

Social media marketing

Various methods of obtaining online traffic and brand exposure through socially-based or driven websites. Blogs, videos, social book marketing sites and other social online communities often go viral (rapid attention and exposure).. Those who work to effectively leverage these efforts are often referred to as social mediologists.

Social networking

The building of online communities of people who have common interests. LinkedIn, Facebook and MySpace facilitate these interconnected systems. HR departments have begun to incorporate social networking into the recruiting process as a means to attract and evaluate candidates.

Social recruitment

The process of recruiting potential job candidates through the use of social networking platforms and/or websites such as Twitter, Facebook and LinkedIn. Social recruitment software is used to search social networks for passive candidate information, manage active social recruiting efforts, as well as distribute job postings and information related to open positions to job posting websites.

Socialism

A belief that a country's wealth should be distributed equally among its population, and to varying extent also that its industries should be under government ownership and control.

Socio-economic grouping

The process if identifying and dividing people into groups according to their social, economic and/or educational status.

Soft loan

Also known as Soft Financing. A loan which has attractive terms for the borrower, such as low or no interest rates and/or a long repayment period, often made by banks to developing countries.

Soft sell

A subtle, persuasive way of selling a product or service, as opposed to Hard Selling.

Software

A general term for Programmes, etc., used to operate computers.

Soldier of fortune

A mercenary. A person, sometimes ex-military, who is hired to work for another person or country. A freelance fighter.

Sole trader

Also called Sole Proprietor. A business which is owned and managed by one person who is responsible for any debts which are incurred, keeping their own accounts, etc.

Solomo

Blend of social, local, and mobile targeting trends to target customers with content designed to be shared via social networks, based on their location (via smartphones, tablets, or other mobile devices).

Solvency margin

The money a business requires in the form of cash or saleable assets, which must exceed the amount needed to pay bills, debts, etc.

Solvent

Having enough funds to pay all your debts.

Sort code

A number which is assigned to a branch of a bank, found on cheques, bank statements, etc., which enables that particular bank's address to be identified.

Sourcing

The developing of lists of potential candidates. Also relates to the task of requisitioning, or creating job descriptions, approval workflows and actual job postings. Most e-recruitment software providers include modules for requisitioning.

Spam

Unsolicited e-mail which is sent to numerous recipients.

Special causes

Causes of variation in a process that are not inherent in the process itself but originate from circumstances that are out of the ordinary. Special causes are indicated by points that fall outside the limits of a control chart.

Special commissioners

In the UK, special commissioners are present at appeals concerning disputes between the Inland Revenue and tax payers.

Special resolution

In business, a resolution which must be passed by a high majority of a company's shareholders, often 75%, as opposed to an ordinary resolution, which only requires more than 50% of the the vote.

Specialised

To be highly skilled in a particular branch of a profession, occupation, activity, etc. Developed or adapted for a particular job or task.

Specification limit
An engineering or design requirement that must be met in order to produce a satisfactory product.

Specimen signature
An example of a person's signature required by a bank, etc., so that it can be compared with the same person's signature on cheques and documents.

Speculate
To risk investment in property, shares, etc., in the hope of making a profit when selling them.

SPHR (Senior Professional in Human Resources)
Senior Professional in Human Resources (PHR) is an industry certification for people working in the human resource management profession, awarded by the Human Resource Certification Institute. It is the senior-most human resources certification for those who have also demonstrated a strategic mastery of the HR body of knowledge.

Spider food
Key words or phrases which are placed, usually invisibly, on a web page in order to attract search engines.

Spiff
Money paid to sales people as an incentive to push/sell certain merchandise or services. It can include such items such as extended warranties, or in the case of auto salesmen, paint protection or window tinting for new car buyers.

Spin
Often a heavily-biased portrayal of an event or situation. Often used in PR campaigns to create and support favorable impressions among vested groups, such as customers, investors, or a specific community. It can also imply disingenuous, deceptive and manipulative tactics.

Spin doctor
A public relations official or press/media spokesperson, in government or corporate work.

Splash page
Branding/introductory page or screen before you enter the main homepage on a website. Usually designed to prompt attention and make the viewer feel that the website has what's needed. It sets the tone and mood of the browsing experience.

Sponsor
A company or individual who helps to support, usually financially, a team, an event, such as a sports meeting or concert, etc., in return for publicity or to advertise their own company or product.

Spot check
A random inspection or examination, often with no warning, of a sample of goods or work performance to check for quality.

Spreadsheet
On a computer, a Programme used for entering, calculating and storing financial or numerical data.

Square mile
A term used for an area of London in which many financial institutions are based.

Staffing
A method of finding, evaluating, and establishing a working relationship with future employees. They may be

current employees or future employees.

Stagflation

A situation in which there is a slow economic growth along with high inflation and high unemployment.

Stakeholder

A person or group, such as shareholders, customers, employees, suppliers, etc., with a vested interest in, and can affect the success of, a company or organisation, or successful completion of a project.

Stamp duty

Called Stamp Tax in the US. A stamp which must be put onto certain documents, contracts, etc., to show that he tax has been paid when property, land, etc., has been sold.

Standard & poor's 500 index (S&P 500)

A well-known, value-rated index of 500 major US companies: 400 industrial firms, 20 transportation firms, 40 utilities firms, and 40 financial firms.

Standardisation

Same goods or services marketed in either product, distribution or advertising form, unchanged in any country.

Standardised plans

A uniform planning system applied globally, based on economics of scale and consumer uniformity.

Standing order

In the UK. an instruction given to a bank to debit a fixed amount of money from an account, usually every month on the same date, to pay a bill, mortgage, etc.

Standing room only

A sales technique in which a company or individual selling a product gives the impression that many people wish to buy the product, encouraging people to purchase it immediately in case it sells out and they don't get another chance.

State benefit

In the UK, money given by the government to people who don't have enough funds to live on and need financial assistance, often because they are unemployed or too ill to work.

State of the art

The highest level of development and/ or technology applied to a product or service which is currently available.

Statistical process control

Analysis and control of a process through the use of statistical techniques, particularly control charts.

Statistical quality control

Analysis and control of quality through the use of statistical techniques, essentially the same as SPC.

Statistician

A person who specialises in or works with statistics.

Status enquiry

In the UK, a request made to a bank asking for a report on a person's financial status, i.e., whether they can repay a loan, mortgage, etc.

Stay interviews

Unlike exit interviews, stay interviews are conducted during employment to help employers understand why good employees stay and what might make them leave.

Staycation
US term for spending one's vacation at home or near to one's home.

Stealth marketing
Also known as Buzz Marketing. A method of advertising a product where customers don't realise they are being persuaded to buy something, e.g., people recommending a product on Internet Chat Forums, without others realising that the person actually works for the company or manufacturer selling the product.

Steering committee
Also called Steering Group. A group of people who are responsible for monitoring a company's operations or project progress, by ensuring it complies with company policies, resources and costs are approved, etc.

Stenographer
A shorthand typist. From Greek: Stenos (narrow) and Graphie (writing)

Sterling
The basic monetary unit of the UK, e.g. the pound.

Stet
Latin for 'let it stand', a term from printing, which extends to proof-reading and copy-checking, editing, etc., to indicate that a word or section marked for deletion (crossed through) within a document or other media is to be retained.

Stevedore
Also called Longshoreman. A person who works on the docks, loading and unloading cargo.

Sticker shock
A US term for the feeling of surprise or shock experienced by some customers when they see that the price of an item they were thinking of purchasing is much higher than they expected.

Stipend
A fixed, often modest, payment, usually made on a regular basis, to someone, e.g. an apprentice, for living expenses during a training period.

Stock
An investor's share of ownership in a company which entitles them to equity in the company, dividends, voting rights, etc.

Stock dividend
A dividend paid in shares of stock as a substitute for cash (Stock dividends allow dividends to make money on themselves.).

Stock exchange
An organised market place where shares in companies are traded by professional stockbrokers.

Stock split
The splitting or dividing of shares to reduce the price needed for the formation of a round lot (To illustrate, in a 2-for-1 split, when 1 shares splits into 2, an investor would receive one additional share for each he formerly owned.).

Stock ticker
A display which automatically updates and shows the current prices and volumes of traded shares on the Stock Market.

Stockbroker
A broker who buys and sells stocks and other securities for his customers, charging commission.

Stockholder
A holder or owner of shares of stock.

Stocktaking

The process of listing all the items, materials or goods which a shop, company, etc., has in stock. An inventory of merchandise.

Stop list/stoplist

Excluded people, organizations, or other items, typically for reasons of disqualification for failing to meet standards or terms stipulated by the organization responsible for the exclusion. This might be customers excluded from a supply by a provider, or people prevented from membership or involvement with an organisation. Often a stoplist refers to customers 'on stop' because of poor credit rating or payment history, and notably payment default. More technically a stoplist may refer the words excluded ('stopwords') in computerized generation of a concordance, which in publishing refers to a detailed cross-referenced index of key words from a text or book or report, etc. Another example might be a schedule of banned substances or ingredients. Basically a stoplist may refer to a roster or schedule of potentially acceptable items/entities/people excluded or barred for reasons of not meeting qualifying standards.

Stop word/stopword

A word or term excluded from a word listing or index, notably from a computer-generated concordance in publishing where the exclusion of common words enables time-consuming cross-referencing processes to move faster.

Stop-limit order

An order placed with a stockbroker to buy or sell at a certain price or better during a limited period of time.

Stop-loss order

An order placed with a stockbroker to buy or sell a designated stock once a designated price has been reached (This order limits the amount an investor can lose on that investment.).

Storyboard

Used in films, TV Programmes, etc., drawings or photographs which are illustrations of the scenes which are to be shot.

Straight rebuy

When a business or individual orders the same goods, in the same quantity from the same supplier.

Strapline

A subheading in a newspaper or magazine. A slogan attached to a well known brand.

Strategic business unit

A self contained grouping of organisations, products or technologies which serve an identified market and competes with identified competitors.

Strategic HRM

Aligning human resource management (HRM) with the strategic goals of an organization.

Strategic industry

An industry which is considered essential to the economy of a region or country.

Strategic management

The process of predicting and assessing a company's opportunities and difficulties, and making decisions so the company can achieve its objectives and gain a competitive advantage.

Strategic planning
The process of considering an organization's future, usually three to five years ahead, and then working backward to create strategic plans and allot resources to realize this desired future state. This includes a hiring strategy.

Stress puppy
A person who seems to thrive on stress, but is always complaining about it.

Stress/stress management
Area of study and corporate/employer responsibility relating to workers' health, well-being, productivity.

Strike
A work stoppage caused by a disagreement between employees and management over working conditions, pay etc.

Strike-breaker
A person who continues to work, or is employed to work, during a strike.

Structural engineer
A professional who researches, plans and designs structures, such as buildings, bridges, etc.

Structural variation
Variation caused by recurring system-wide changes such as seasonal changes or long-term trends.

Sub judice
Term used when a legal case is currently under trial or is being considered by a judge, and any information about the case must not be disclosed to the public.

Subcontract
To hire someone to carry out some of the work that you have been contracted to do.

Subliminal advertising
An illegal form of advertising. An image which is flashed onto a screen, usually for about one second, or a message played at low volume, that can influence the person watching or listening but they are not aware of what they have seen and/or heard.

Subordinate
Someone who is lower in rank than another person, and is subject to the authority of a manager, etc. Less important.

Subpoena
An official summons which requires a witness to attend a court case and testify at a specific time and place. Failure to do so may result in them being punished for contempt of court.

Subrogation
The right of an insurer, who has paid out a claim to an injured party, to sue the person, company, etc., who caused the injury.

Succession planning
The process of identifying long-range needs and cultivating a supply of internal talent to meet those future needs. Used to anticipate the future needs of the organization and assist in finding, assessing and developing the human capital necessary to the strategy of the organization.

Succession planning
The process of identifying suitable employees who can be trained and prepared to replace senior staff when their positions become vacant.

Summary dismissal
The immediate firing of an employee, usually due to an act of gross misconduct.

Summary material modifications

A summary of modifications or changes made to an employee benefit plan that is not included in the summary plan description.

Summary plan description

A document that explains the fundamental features of an employer's defined benefit or defined contribution plan, including eligibility requirements, contribution formulas, vesting schedules, benefit calculations, distribution options, participation, coverage and employee rights for any ERISA-covered benefit plan. ERISA requires that the SPD be easy to understand and that each participant receive a copy within 90 days of joining the plan.

Summons

An official document which orders a person to appear in court to answer a complaint against them.

Sunk cost

A company's past expenditures which cannot be recovered, and should not be taken into account when planning future projects.

Sunset provision

Also called Sunset Clause. A provision which states that a particular law or regulation will expire on a certain date unless further action is taken to extend it.

Superannuation

A pension, for which regular sums are deducted from a person's salary while they are working, which is paid by an employer when the person retires from their job.

Superstitial

A web-based advertisement format that combines flash and other animation

technology with Java Programmeming to deliver video-like commercials.

Superstitial

a web-based advertisement format that combines flash and other animation technology with Java Programmeming to deliver video-like commercials.

Supertax

Also called Surtax. An additional tax on something already taxed, e.g. an income above a certain level.

Supplemental unemployment benefits (SUB)

Pay benefits which are taxable payments that form a fund, which can be combined with state unemployment insurance benefits. Typically found in collective bargaining agreements, they provide a higher level of unemployment benefits during periods of temporary layoff.

Supplier

Anyone whose output (materials, information, service, etc.) becomes an input to another person or group in a process of work. A supplier can be external or internal to the organization.

Supply and demand

Supply is the amount of a product or service which is available, and demand is the amount which people wish to buy. When demand is higher than supply prices usually rise, when demand is less than supply prices usually fall.

Supply chain

A chain through which a product passes from raw materials to manufacturing, distribution, retailing, etc., until it reaches the end consumer.

Supply chain management

Management activities to maximize customer value by ensuring the most effective and efficient commercialization schedule.

Supply Chain Management – Main Component

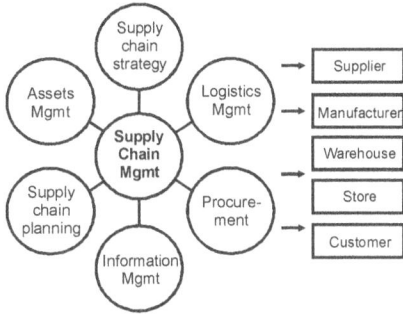

Surface mail

Mail which is transported over land or sea, not by air.

Surveillance

The collection of relevant information which crosses an individual's scanning attention field.

Suspension

An employee is sent home for a period of time, usually without pay, as a disciplinary measure.

Swag ("stuff we all get")

Useful items given to specific groups of people that are designed to reinforce a brand, experience, or theme. Also know as branded logo merchandise, promotional ad specialties — "freebies" used to stimulate thoughts about a product or service.

Sweat equity

Term used to describe a person's investment in a project, etc., by the contribution of their time and effort, rather than their money.

Sweatshop

A place, often a clothing factory, where people work long hours in poor conditions for low wages.

SWOT analysis (Strengths, Weaknesses, Opportunities, and Threat)

Internal and external factors identified in a situation analysis that can be both advantageous and disadvantageous to the organization in its efforts to satisfy the needs of its target market.

Sychophant

A servile person or follower, not necessarily of low rank, who tries to please a (more) powerful or influential person by using flattery, and often by informing on others, from which the word is derived in its original Greek meaning.

Symposium

A meeting or conference at which experts discuss a particular topic, often with audience participation.

Synergy

The working together of two or more individuals, groups, companies, etc., to produce a greater effect than working individually.

Systemic discrimination

A pattern of discrimination that permeates workplace practices, and is not apparent at first glance, but is actually systematic in its application of policies and practices.

T

T/t (telegraphic transfer)
Interntional banking payment method: a telegraphic transfer payment, commonly used/required for import/ export trade, between a bank and an overseas party enabling transfer of local or foreign currency by telegraph, cable or telex. Also called a cable transfer. The terminology dates from times when such communications were literally 'wired' before wireless communications technology.

Table d'hote
Technically 'table d'hôte'-a food menu which offers a full meal with set courses and limited choices at a fixed price, from French 'host's table'.

Tachograph
A device which is fitted to vehicles, especially commercial vehicles, which records the speed, distance and time travelled.

Tag
A word or words assigned to or associated with electronic data, usually on a website, to aid searching, finding, analysis, display, organization, etc., of the data. Used as a verb also, for example, to tag or tagging articles, content, etc., when posted onto a website.

Tag line
Slogan or phrase that conveys important attribute or benefits of the product or service. Often, a theme to a campaign that's defined by the product's unique selling proposition or sustainable competitive advantage. Ex: Nike Just do it; Las Vegas What happens here, stays here; M&M Candies Melts in your mouth, not in your hands.

Taguchi, genichi
Developed a set of practices known as Taguchi Methods, as they are known in the U.S., for improving quality while reducing costs. Taguchi Methods focus on the design of efficient experiments, and the increasing of signal to noise ratios. Dr. Taguchi also articulated the developed the quality loss function. Currently, he is executive director of the American Supplier Institute and director of the Japan Industrial Technology Institute.

Tailor-made
Adapted or made for a particular purpose or individual.

Take-home pay
The amount of money received by an employee after deductions, such as tax, insurance, etc.

Takeover
The purchase of one company by another.

Takeover bid

A bid made by an organisation or individual to acquire a company, usually by offering to purchase the shares of the company's shareholders.

Takeover panel

A panel set up in certain countries to ensure that all company takeovers comply with laws and regulations, and that all shareholders are treated equally and fairly.

Talent management

Also called Human Capital Management, the process of recruiting, managing, assessing, developing and maintaining employees.

Tampering

Dr. Deming cautions against tampering with systems that are "in control." It is very common for management to react to variation which is in fact normal, thereby starting wild goose chases after sources of problems which don't exist. Tampering with stable processes actually increases variation.

Tangible asset

Physical assets, such as machinery, buildings, vehicles, cash, etc., which are owned by a company or individual.

Tangible rewards

Gifts in the form of merchandise, gift certificates, etc. that can be physically held or touched.

Tare

The weight of packaging used in wrapping and protecting goods which is deducted from the total weight of a product in order to ascertain the actual weight of the goods. The deduction in weight of a vehicle used to transport goods in order to determine the actual weight of the goods.

Target audience

TA – Group of persons to which the firm generates advertising or other e-marketing efforts towards gaining exposure of their product.

Target company

A company that another company or organisation wants to acquire.

Target market

Group of persons for which a firm creates and maintains a product mix that specifically fits the needs and preferences of that group. For example, the furniture market can be divided into segments described as Early American, contemporary, or traditional.

Tariff

An instrument of terms of access normally the imposition of a single or multiple excise rate on a imported good.

Task force

A group of people formed to work on a particular project or assignment.

Tax

A fee imposed by a government on personal or corporate income, products, services, etc., in order to raise revenue to pay for public services.

Tax abatement

Also known as a Tax Holiday. An exemption or reduction of taxes by a government for certain companies for a specific period of time, often as an incentive for industrial development.

Tax allowance

The amount of income that can be earned or received in one year before tax has to be paid.

Tax avoidance
Legal ways of paying the minimum amount of tax possible by making use of allowances and exemptions.

Tax bracket
Based on income levels, the higher the income the higher the tax bracket, therefore people earning more money have to pay a higher rate of tax on the part of their income which is below the lower tax bracket allowance.

Tax evasion
Illegally avoidng paying tax, usually by making a false declaration of income.

Tax exile
A person or business who chooses to leave a country to reside or operate in another country, usually called a Tax Haven, where taxes are much lower or there aren't any.

Tax lien
The right of a tax authority to claim assets belonging to a company or individual who default on tax payments.

T-commerce
Television Commerce. The purchasing and selling of products and services using interactive television.

Team building
A philosophy of job design which fosters teamwork to create a work culture that values collabouration. It is a training Programme designed to encourage employees to view themselves as members of interdependent teams instead of as individual workers, in which people understand and believe that thinking, planning, decisions and actions are better when done cooperatively.

Team player
A person in any type of profession who works well as a member of a team.

Teaser ad
A brief advertisement which reveals only a little bit of information about a product, usually not yet available, in order to arouse widespread interest.

Teaser rate
A low rate of interest, for example on a mortgage, loan, credit card, etc., which is below the going market rate and available for only a short period of time in order to attract borrowers.

Techie
A person who is very knowledgable, or an expert, in technology, especially computing.

Technical analysis
The analysis of historical trends of price, volume, and other related market indicators to aid in predicting future trends; commonly includes tables and graphs.

Technical analyst
A stock market analyst who uses charts and computer Programmes to study investments in order to predict the future of share prices, etc.

Technical support
A service provided by the vendor of technology products, such as computers, mobile phones, televisions, etc., which the purchaser can use if they need help using the product.

Telecommunications
Known informally as Telecoms. Communicating over long distances by telephone, e-mail, etc.

Teleconference
A conference involving two or more people at different locations, using telecommunications equipment, such as computers, video, telephone, etc.

Telemarketing
Also known as Telesales. The selling of goods or services by contacting potential customers by telephone.

Teleworking
An arrangement in which the employee works at home and contacts their office or workplace by telephone or computer.

Tenant
An individual or business who pays a fee for the use of land, property, etc., to the owner. An occupant.

Tenant at will
A tenant who continues to rent land, property, etc., past the expiration of the lease. Also a tenant who rents property without a written lease, therefore they can be forced to leave without notice from the owner.

Tender offer
An offer, usually above the market price, made to the shareholders of a company by another company or individual as part of a takeover bid.

Term assurance
A form of life insurance which pays out a lump sum if the policyholder dies within a fixed period of time.

Terminal anchor
TA or (Primary Optical Area / POA) – We learn to read by first scanning the page top left to bottom right. Primary Optical (POA) point is the top left corner, with the Terminal Anchor Point being the last thing we scan at the bottom right (TA).

Terms of access
The conditions imposed by one country which apply to the importation of goods from another country.

Terms of reference
A document which describes the objectives, scope and purpose of a project, committee, meeting, etc.

Terrestrial
Term used to describe broadcasting systems, such as television, which operate on land, rather than from a satellite.

Tertiary industry
Third sector of a country's economy which covers the provision of services, such as transport, schools, financial services, etc., rather than manufacturing or production.

Test case
Term used to describe a court case which establishes legal rights and serves as a precedent for future similar cases.

Test market
Research technique to test consumer behaviour under actual buying conditions before executing distribution on a mass scale to the target market. Involves selecting a metropolitan area with demographic and psychographic characteristics that mirror the target market.

Text message
A written message sent from one mobile phone to another.

Text-to-speech
Describes the converting of text into audible speech on a computer by using speech synthesis techniques.

The big three
The three largest credit ratings agencies: Standard and Poor's; Moody's, and Fitch. There are hundreds of smaller credit rating agencies, but historically 95% of the market is served/controlled by these three companies. As at 2013 their ownership is all American, except 50% of Fitch in French ownership. These companies have an enormous and controversial influence over corporate and international debt and the workings of credit and debt markets, banking, investments, etc., and consequently also on economies and societies around the world. 'The Big Three' are particularly controversial because of their considerable market dominance, considered by most commentators to be monopolistic (or at least a duopoly, given S&P/Moody's 80% market share), together with potential for conflict of interest in the way that the credit ratings industry operates: Credit rating agencies provide extensive high-value advisory services to the same markets/clients that are subject to the ratings issued by the agencies. Despite the heavy reliance on their assessments and pronouncements, the Big Three agencies failed to identify the toxic nature of the mortgage and related derivative debt 'products' prior to and regarded central to the 2008 global financial collapse, and in some cases awarded very positive ratings for these debts which subequently proved largely valueless and irrecoverable.

The daily official list
The daily record setting out the prices of shares that are traded on a stock exchange. The father of statistical process control or statistical quality control. He pioneered statistical quality control and improvement methods when he worked for Western Electric and Bell Telephone in the early decades of the 20th century.

The world bank
Known also as the International Bank for Reconstruction and Development (IBRD). A bank, with world wide country membership, (United nations) which provides long term capital to and economic development.

The big board
An informal name for the New York Stock Exchange on Wall Street.

Theory of constraints
Theory originally developed by Dr Eliyahu Goldratt, which states that every organisation must have at least one constraint that should be overcome by recognising and dealing with the cause of the 'bottleneck', thus enabling the company to achieve its goals.

Theory X
Developed by Douglas McGregor in the 1960s, a theory which states that most people in the workplace do not enjoy work and will take every opportunity to avoid doing their job because they are lazy and need to be closely supervised, threatened and disciplined by management.

Theory Y
Developed by Douglas McGregor. The opposite to Theory X, a method of managing people in the workplace

based on the idea that most workers enjoy their job, are self-motivated and want responsibility, and the managers role is to help the workers realise their full potential by giving them more responsibility, including them in decision-making, etc.

Theory Z
A Japanese management style based on the theory, developed by William Ouchi, that workers like to build relationships with other workers and management, to feel secure in their jobs, develop skills through training, and have their family life and traditions valued.

Think tank
A group or organisation which researches and advises on issues relating to technology, economy, politics and social strategy.

Third line forcing
A situation which occurs when a supplier will only sell a product or service to a customer on condition that it is purchased from a third party nominated by the supplier.

Third party
A person or organisation not principally involved with the other two parties but who has an interest in an agreement or contract. In an insurance policy, the third party is the person whose car, etc is damaged by you in an accident.

Third sector
Part of a country's economy which is non-profitmaking, such as voluntary work, charities, etc.

Third world
Refers to poor, underdeveloped nations in South Africa, Asia and South America.

Third-generation
3G. Describes wireless technology which has been developed to send messages and data over networks using mobile phones, computers, etc.

Third-party administrator (TPA)
An organization that is responsible for the administration of insurance for a self-insured group. It does not have any responsibility for paying claims. The self-insured group is financially responsible.

Thrift
In the US, a savings or loan association. The practice of not spending too much money or using up too many resources.

Through-the-line
(first helps to understand above-the-line: media advertising; below-the-line:traditional mix of promotional events, discounts, coupons and catalogs) Through-the-line is a combination of above- and below-activities for the purpose of building brand image and repeat sales among specific groups of customers.

Ticker symbol
In the US, a set of characters, usually letters, used to identify a particular share on the Stock Exchange.

Tied agent
A sales agent or business who represents or sells and/or offers advice only on one company's products, such as insurance.

Tier pricing
a promotional price-setting tool that generally affords customers unit price savings for purchasing in higher quantities. This is an effective way to

move more merchandise. For example: customers that purchase 3 boxes of printer paper save money. The retailer sign might read: — Buy 2 and save 6% — Buy 3 and save 15% — Buy 5 and save 42%

Time and a Half
Rate of pay which is 50% more than the regular rate, usually for overtime work.

Time and Motion Study
The study and analysis of a specific job within an organisation, the results of which are used to improve efficiency and production.

Time to market
Range or amount of time that precedes the commercialization of an enterprise (time it takes to realize an idea and deliver a product to the marketplace). Often this period of time is used to research, refine, and adapt a product to meet customer needs; in addition, promotion can also be used to introduce and educate customers about what it to come.

Timekeeper
Team member who keeps track of time spent on each agenda item during team meetings. This job can easily be rotated among team members.

Timeliness
Value Line Index's measure of a stock's price performance for the upcoming year.

Timeshare
A lease on a (usually holiday) property jointly owned by several people who have the right to use it during agreed times of the year, usually for one or two weeks. The industry is often associated with high-pressure or unethical selling methods.

Title deed
A legal document which proves a person's rights of ownership of property or land.

Tokenism
The practice of doing the minimum required, especially by law, by making small token gestures, such as employing or including a single person who represents a minority or ethnic group.

Toolbar
On a computer screen, a set of icons or symbols, usually under the menu bar, which allow you to perform different tasks on your computer, such as print documents, change font size, use a paintbrush , etc.

Top brass
The most important people in a company or organisation.

Top dog
The person who has the highest authority and is in charge of a whole operation, business, etc.

Top dollar
The very highest price paid for a product, service, worker, etc.

Top-heavy
Describes a company or business which has too many managers and/or administrators in comparison to the number of workers.

Top-level domain
TLD. The last part of a domain address on the Internet, for example .com (commerce), .gov (government), etc.

Tort
A wrongful act, other than a breach of contract, which is not criminal but harmful to another person, against

which legal action for damages may be taken.

Total assets
The sum found by adding property, plant, and equipment asset values to current asset values.

Total costs
In business, the costs of manufacturing, overheads, administration, etc. i.e., the sum of fixed costs and variable costs. In investments, the price paid for a share, security, etc., plus brokerage fees, taxes, interest due to the seller, etc.

Total debt to total assets
The ratio found by dividing short- and long-term debts by the total assets of the firm (This ratio measures a company's financial risk, showing how much of the firm's property has been financed by debt.).

Total liabilities
The liabilities found by adding current liabilities to long-term debts.

Total quality management
An integrative philosophy of management for continuously improving the quality of products and processes. Practices and systems include: cross-functional product design, process management, supplier quality management, customer involvement, information and feedback, committed leadership, strategic planning, cross-functional training, and employee involvement.

Total remuneration
An employee's complete annual pay package, including benefit and pension plans, bonuses, incentives, and paychecks.

Touch base
To make contact, usually managers who want to communicate with their staff.

Trade
The buying and selling or exchange of goods and services. The buying and selling of shares on the Stock Market. A skilled occupation such as builder, carpenter, plumber, electrician, etc.

Trade agreement
An agreement, usually between countries, to limit or change their policies when trading with one another.

Trade descriptions act
In the UK, a 1968 Act of Parliament which prevents misrepresentation of goods and services to customers by manufacturers, retailers or service providers.

Trade name/trading name
These are vague terms and care needs to be taken if deciding serious matters based on interpretation. Precise interpretation may depend local state/national company law definitions. Generally business names and trade/trading names may be registered and licensed. A lot depends on the interpretation of the term 'Business name' which could refer to a legal/parent/holding company, or merely to a branded product or division. A trade name could be a brand or a division or branded operation/service within/of a (legally titled) business. Avoid applying a strict definition to these terms, and if there are serious implications then seek expert local clarification, or a ruling from your legal department/advisor.

Trade secret

A secret device or formula used by a company in the manufacturing of a product which gives it an advantage over the competition.

Trade war

A conflict between countries in which each country puts up trade barriers in order to restrict or damage the others trade.

Trademark

A symbol, logo, word or phrase which is used exclusively by a company, individual, etc., so their products or services can be easily identified, A Trademark cannot legally be used by anyone else.

Trading floor

An area of a Stock Exchange where dealers trade in stocks, shares, etc.

Trading range

The range of prices within which a stock is normally traded.

Trailblazer

An innovator or pioneer. An individual or company who is the first to do or discover something, and leads where others follow.

Training and development

Providing information and instruction that equips employees to better perform specific tasks or attain a higher level of knowledge.

Training needs analysis

An assessment to determine the training needs of a group of employees, taking into account the employees' prior education and skills and the desired outcome once training is completed.

Tranche

Describes part of a loan, investment, etc., which is a portion of the whole amount.

Transaction costs

The costs that are brought about by the buying or selling of securities, including broker commissions and the difference between dealer buying and selling price (called a dealers' spread).

Transactions

An exchange. What one gives up for something else without any change in form to the object, as in buying a pack of gum at the drugstore vs. having a roll of film developed. The latter involves both a transformation (developing the film and printing photo) and a transaction (paying for processing and printing).

Transfer deed

Also called Deed Of Transfer. A legal document which shows that the ownership of property, land, etc., has been changed from its legal owner to another party who now legally owns it.

Transfer pricing

The price at which goods or services are transferred between one country and another within the same organisation.

Transformational leadership

A systematic form of leadership that enhances the motivation, morale and performance of followers through change, innovation, and group dynamics.

Transformations

Change in form, function, condition or outward appearance of a good or service. For example, a plastics company buys polymer pellets (transaction) which are then melted and poured into molds to make a child's toy (transformation).

Transitional employment

The arrangement of lessened or altered duties for an employee who has been absent from the workplace because of illness or injury, but has been given leave by their medical provider to return.

Transnational

Multinational. Refers to businesses, organisations, etc., which operate in or between several countries.

Transvection

Series of transformations and transactions that take place throughout the commercialization schedule (from producer to consumer). The transvection is a measure of efficiency in turning raw materials into finished goods. Used by marketers to evaluate and optimize efficiency of their channels.

Treasurer

A person in a company, organisation, club, etc., who is responsible for the management of funds and accounts.

Treasury bill (T-bill)

A certificate representing a short-term loan to the federal government for periods not exceeding one year.

Treasury bond

A certificate representing a long-term loan to the federal government for periods exceeding ten years.

Treasury note (T-note)

A certificate representing a median-term loan to the federal government for a duration of between two and ten years.

Tree diagram

A chart used to break any task, goal, or category into increasingly detailed levels of information. Family trees are the classic example of a tree diagram. In PathMaker, the structure of the tree diagram is identical to that of the cause & effect diagram.

Trial offer

A temporary offer by a company usually aimed at first-time buyers in which a customer can try a product or service free or at discounted rates for a short period of time.

Triple-dip Recession

A recession during which there is are two brief periods of economic growth, each followed by a slide back into recession, before final recovery.

Troubleshoot

To identify and solve problems which arise in the workplace.

Trust fund

Property or funds which are legally held in control of a trustee on behalf of an individual or organisation.

Trustafarian

An informal term for a wealthy young person, who gives the appearance of being unemployed and living a Bohemian lifestyle in less than comfortable circumstances, but who is living off a trust fund.

Trustbuster

A government agent whose job is to break up monopolies or corporate trusts under the anti-trust laws.

Trustee

An individual or organisation who is legally responsible for managing the financial affairs or another person or company.

Turd polishing

Australian equivalent of not being able to make a silk purse out of a pigs ear. An engineering term for fixing the defects in a product, process, system, etc., then repeating as new defects appear, rather than re-engineering it with fewer defects.

Turnover

The number of employees lost and gained over a given time period.

Turntablist

A person who uses vinyl records, a turntable of a record player and a DJ mixer all together as an instrument to create sounds.

Tycoon

A wealthy, prominent, successful business person, also referred to as a mogul, magnate, baron ,etc.

Type I error

Rejecting something that is acceptable. Also known as an alpha error.

Type II error

Accepting something that should have been rejected. Also known as β error.

Tyre kicker

A person who appears to be interested in purchasing an item, especially a secondhand car, but has no intention of buying it.

U

U chart
A control chart showing the count of defects per unit in a series of random samples.

Ultra vires
Latin for 'Beyond The Powers'. Legal term which refers to actions or deeds, especially performed by a corporation, that exceed official powers.

Unanimous
A complete agreement on a decision or opinion by everyone in a group.

Unauthorised
Without official endorsement or permission.

Unbundling
Dividing a company into separate companies, usually after a takeover, in order to sell some or all of the subsidiaries. Supplying a product, service or equipment in separate components.

Uncalled capital
The value of shares which have been issued by a company but which have not yet been paid for by the shareholders.

Unconsolidated
Describes subsidiary companies whose financial statements, shares, etc., are not included in the parent company's finances.

Uncontested
Without opposition or competition. A lawsuit which is not disputed by the person against whom it has been filed.

Undercut
To sell a product, service, etc., cheaper than the competition.

Undermanned
Describes a company, business, etc., which does not have enough workers to function properly. Understaffed.

Undershoot
To fall short of reaching a goal or target.

Undersubscribed
When a product, service, etc., is not being bought by enough people.

Underwriter
A person who assesses the risk and eligibility of an insurance company's potential client. On the Stock Market, an organisation, such as a bank, that agrees to purchase any unsold shares which are offered for sale by a company.

Undischarged bankrupt
A person who has officially been declared bankrupt but has not yet been given permission to start another business, and must not stop paying debts which are still owed.

Unearned income
Personal income which has not come from employment but from investments, dividends, interest, etc.

Unemployment
An economic situation in which jobless people, often those who have been made redundant from their jobs, are actively seeking employment.

Unfair dismissal
Term used when a person's employment is terminated by their employer without a good reason.

Unfair labour practice (ULP)
An action carried out by an employer or union that violates the Federal Service Labour-Management Relations Statute, part of the National Labour Relations Act (NLRA), and would be investigated by the National Labour Relations Board (NLRB).

Unfavourable trade balance
Describes when a country's value of its imports exceeds the value of its exports.

Unhappy camper
Someone who has complaints about their employers. An unsatisfied customer.

Unilateral
Performed by one person, group, side, party, etc-basically 'going alone'. For example a unilateral decision is one made without dependence or condition upon others who might have interests in the matter in question.

Unilateral contract
A one-sided agreement in which one party promises to do something (or refrain from doing something) in return for an action, not a promise, from a second party.

Union
Workers who organize a united group, usually related to the kind of work they do, to collectively bargain for better work conditions, pay or benefit increases, etc.

Unique visitor
Describes a person who visits a website, as one unit, even if they have made several visits to the same site in a particular period of time, usually 24 hours.

Unit trust
A fund which raises money from a number of investors, usually investing only a small amount each, which is then invested on their behalf by a fund manager in a range of shares, securities, bonds, etc.

Universal product code
Assigned 12-digit number used to identify a product. Translated into barcodes consisting of a series of vertical parallel bars, it can be used for scan entry, by an electronic cash register, or information for product sales and inventory tracking. The first set of digits are the same for all of the manufacturer's products and represent the name of the manufacturer. The next set refers to the product itself and are assigned by the manufacturer to the product of his choice.

Unjustifiable dismissal
Firing an employee in a way that the courts do not find justifiable (i.e. unfairly or in violation of the employment contract).

Unlimited company
In the UK, a company whose owners have unlimited liability, e.g. if the company goes into liquidation the owners are required to raise the funds to pay the company's debts.

Unlimited liability

The obligation of a company's owners or partners to pay all the company's debts, even if personal assets have to be used.

Unlisted

Refers to company whose shares are not traded on the Stock Exchange.

Unofficial strike

Also known as a Wildcat Strike. A form of industrial action which does not have the approval or permission of a trade union.

Unsolicited

Not requested or invited, for example junk mail.

Unsystematic risk

Also called Residual Risk. The risk that can affect a company's share prices, production, etc., such as a sudden strike by employees.

Unzip

On a computer, to return files to their original size after they have been compressed.

UPC

Universal Product Code. A bar code, using thick and thin vertical lines, which is printed on labels, packets, etc., to identify a specific product, and is used for stock control.

Upload

To transfer data or Programmes from a smaller computer, camera, etc., or a computer at a remote location, to a larger computer system.

Upselling

A sales technique in which the salesperson tries to persuade the customer to purchase more expensive and/or more goods than they originally intended.

Uptick

Also called Plus Tick. On the Stock Market, a transaction or quote at a price above the preceding transaction for the same security.

Uptime

The period of time which a computer, piece of machinery, etc., is operational and available for use.

Upwardly mobile

Describes someone who is moving towards a higher social and/or economic position.

Urban regeneration

Also called Urban Renewal, the redevelopment of run-down parts of a towns or cities, to include business and housing projects, typically funding by governments or agencies.

Url (uniform resource locator)

Internet service provider address of a document or website, usually a protocol consisting of a name(s). Also expressed as a series of numbers: Example: *stevetoms.net* is the base URL for this glossary, which references its IP (Internet Protocol) address of 75.53.135.140.

Usance

In international trade, the period of time allowed, which varies between countries, for the payment of a bill of exchange.

USB - universal serial bus

A device on a computer which is used for connecting other devices, such as telephones, scanners, printers, etc. Bus is derived from busbar, a metal conductor strip within a switchboard.

User friendly
Easy to learn or use by people who are not experts.

Username
In computing, refers to the name that uniquely identifies the person using a computer system or Programme and is usually used with a password.

Usp
Unique Selling Proposition – Differentiates and positions it in the mind of the consumer. Unlike an SCA (sustainable competitive advantage), a USP can be adapted, modified, and even changed depending on fluctuations in the market.

Utility
Ability of the product to satisfy customers needs and wants. The 4 major marketing utilities include form utility, time utility, place utility, and possession utility. More recent studies include psychological utility.

Utopia/utopian
An imaginery society or world or situation which is ideal and everyone has everything they want, from the highly revered English statesman, scholar, lawyer and writer, Sir Thomas More's 1516 century book Utopia, whose full Latin title loosely translates to mean 'On the Best State of a Republic and on the New Island of Utopia'. The opposite term Dystopia, was devised two centuries later.

U-value
Buildings and construction industry term referring to insulation effectiveness of materials.

V

Vacancy
A job opening which is offered by a company that wants to hire an employee. An available room in a hotel.

Vacancy rate
The percentage of unoccupied rental space or units, e.g hotel rooms, compared to total available rental area at a given time.

Valid
Legally or formally acceptable or binding. Unexpired, e.g. a passport.

Validity
In research studies, it means the data collected reflects what it was designed to measure. Often, invalid data also contains bias.

Valuation
The process of determining the current value of stock or other assets.

Value added
Each time work is done to inputs to transform them into something of greater usefulness as an end product.

Value engineering
In manufacturing, a method of producing a product at the lowest price but without sacrificing quality, safety, etc., and at the same time meeting the customers needs.

Value investor
An investor who buys shares, etc., which they believe to be underpriced, in order to make a profit by selling them when they price rises.

Value line index
An index representing 1700 equally-weighted companies from the NYSE, AMEX, and the over-the-counter markets.

Value proposition
Giving customers what they pay for — unique value that competitors don't offer or emphasize. In Houston, Rice Epicurean Supermarkets host gourmet cooking demonstrations, grocery delivery, unique gourmet products, and catering services.

Value share
A share, etc., which is considered to be underpriced and is therefore a good investment prospect.

Value-added reseller
VAR. A company which purchases a product and modifies or enhances it before reselling it to the consumer. This practice is common in the computer industry.

Valued policy
An insurance policy in which the insurer agrees to pay a claim for a specified amount in the event of loss, damage, etc., for items insured, such as works of art.

Vampiring

Star-power overshadowing an advertiser's promotional message. When Chrysler contracted Celine Dion to appear in an ad for its Pacifica model, it generated more sales for her music than sales of the auto.

Vanilla

Plain and ordinary without any extras. Basic.

Vapourware

Term used to describe computer software which is advertised before it has been, and may never be, developed, often to damage sales of a competitor's product which has already been launched.

Variable cost

In business, costs which vary according to the changes in activity, production, etc. of the company, such as overheads, labour and material costs.

Variables data

Data that is measured on a continuous and infinite scale such as temperature, distance, and pressure rather than in discreet units or yes/no options. Variables data is used to create histograms, some control charts, and sometimes run charts.

Variance

A measure of deviation from the mean in a sample or population.

Variation

Change in the output or result of a process. Variation can be caused by common causes, special causes, tampering, or structural variation.

VAT

Value Added Tax. A tax paid by consumers which is added to the price of certain goods and services.

VDU

Visual/Video Display Unit. A computer screen or monitor which displays text and/or pictures.

Vendee

A person or business who buys goods, property, etc.,

Vendor

Manufacturer, producer, or seller (can also include wholesalers and retailers and their affiliated sales agents).

Venture capital

Money invested in a new business which is expected to make a lot of profit but which also involves considerable risk.

Vertical disintegration

A situation in which a company that previously produced parts and materials is now buying them from other suppliers.

Vertical equity

A concept of economic fairness, for example people who are better off should contribute more taxes than those who are less well off.

Vertical integration

Strategy for growth in which a company adds new facilities to existing manufacturing or distribution facilities, reducing risk by extending control through its commercialization schedule (distribution channels). It primary purpose is to enable the firm to become more effective and efficient. Ex: By owning the mines, ships, and railroads tracks, Carnegie Steel became vertically integrated as a means to expand/grow.

Vertical integration

A situation in which a company acquires one or more of the companies which are involved in the production or distribution processes of its goods/services, for example a brewer which buys a pub chain, or a clothing retailer which buys a knitwear factory.

Vertical market/vertical sector

Vertical market sector-Often shortened to 'vertical' - this refers to an industrial activity or trade comprising producers, manufacturers, makers, providers and users, etc - basically the supply chain or all the linked purchasers - of the same products/services, for example media, coal production, healthcare, automotive, education, retail, etc. Imagine a bar chart in which each vertical bar is an industry; or imagine a series of vertical lines, each one connecting suppliers and customers in a supply chain for a single industry. A sub-section of a vertical market sector, such as car magazines (within the media vertical), or private schools (within education), or shoe-shops (within retail) is typically called a niche or a niche market.

Vested interest

When an individual, business or group has a special interest in something, such as property, an activity, etc., from which there is a personal or financial gain.

Veto

Latin for 'I Forbid'. To vote against. The right to block a law, etc.

Vexatious litigant

A person or party who regularly brings unsustainable lawsuits against another party in order to harass or annoy them.

Viable

Capable of being done or working successfully.

Vicarious liability

Having legal responsibility for the actions of another, e.g. the liabilty of an organisation for the actions of its employees.

Video game marketing

Activities that generate product sales via gaming consoles. This includes digital advertising while playing games, attending trade shows, watching movie trailers, TV commercials, and online or printed materials. Online gaming characters include Mario, Pac Man, and "Soap" MacTavish of Grand Theft Auto.

Vigorish

A slang term, also abbreviated to vig, for the commission or fee charged by a bookmaker or casino on a wager. Also the interest on a loan from a loan shark or unregulated loan provider. The term is Yiddish (Jewish) deriving from the Russian word vyigrysh, meaning winnings.

Viral marketing

Any marketing technique that induces people (or web sites) to pass on a marketing message to other people or sites, creating a growth in the message's visibility and effect. A classic example of this concept was Hotmail whereby each email sent via Hotmail included Hotmail's own advertisement in the footer (Get your Free Email....").

Virtual HR

The use of various types of technology to provide employees with self-serve options. Voice response systems, employee kiosks are common methods.

Virtual memory

On a computer, a technique of simulating additional memory by moving data between the computers memory and a hard disk.

Virtual reality
An artificial three-dimentional (3-D) image or experience, created by a computer, and which seems real to the person looking at it.

Virus
A computer Programme with a hidden code, designed to infect a computer without the owners knowledge, and which causes harm to the computer or destroys data, etc.

Vision
Often incorporated into an organizational mission (or vision) statement to clarify what the organization hopes to be doing at some point in the future. The vision should act as a guide in choosing courses of action for the organization.

Vocation
An occupation for which a person is strongly suited and/or to which they are dedicated.

Vocational
Relating to an occupation for which a person has undergone special training or has special skills.

Voice recognition
Technology which allows computers, mobile phones, etc., to be operated by being spoken to.

Voice-over
A presenter or actor in a TV commercial or Programme who is heard but who is not seen on the screen.

Void
A contract, agreement, document, etc., which is no longer valid or legal.

Voluntary bankruptcy
A situation in which a debtor voluntary files for bankruptcy because they cannot pay their creditors.

Voluntary benefits
Benefits that are paid for by the employee through payroll deductions. The employer pays for administration. Examples of these benefits include life insurance, dental, vision, disability income, auto insurance, long-term care coverage, medical supplement plans and homeowners insurance.

Voluntary liquidation
A situation where the owners/directors of a solvent company decide to cease business, sell the company's assets and pay all the creditors.

Volunteerism
How a company supports an employee who wishes to volunteer or otherwise offer unpaid services to a community organization, often by providing paid leave of sponsorship.

Vote of no confidence
A vote which shows that the majority of those voting have lost confidence in something, usually a government.

Voting shares
Called Voting Stock in the US. A company share which gives the shareholder the right to vote on matters regarding company policy, etc.

W

Wage differential
The difference in wage rates between different types of worker, often those with similar jobs but who work in different regions of a country, have different skills, hours of work, etc.

Wage drift
A situation when basic rates of pay are not as high as levels of wages actually paid. This is often because of increases in overtime, bonuses, profit share, etc.

Wage slave
Someone whose is totally dependent on the wages they earn.

Waiver
A formal statement in which someone gives up a right or privilege.

Walk back the cat
A metaphor for troubleshooting. When something goes wrong, the situation is analysed in chronological order to find out when the problem happened and why, and correct mistakes so they don't happen again. Like when a cat unravels a ball of string and you have to rewind the twisted yarn to find the flaw.

Walking papers
Also called Walking Ticket. A notification of dismissal from a job.

Wall street
A street in Lower Manhattan where the New York Stock Exchange and financial centre is situated.

WAN
Wide Area Network. A communications network which covers a wide area of a region or country, connecting computers, phones, etc.

Wants
To feel the need for, craving, desire, or wish to have or possess. It is often said that "wants are manifestations of unmet needs."

WAP
Wireless Application Protocol. An open network communications system which enables information to be sent between hand-held devices such as mobile phones, pagers, etc.

Warrant
A certificate which entitles the holder to buy a specific number of shares at a fixed price within a specified period of time. A legal document issued by a court of law authorising the police to make an arrest, search premises, etc.

Watch list
A list of investments being monitored because they are showing signs of unusual activity, often because the companies who own the shares may be takeover targets.

Watchdog
A person or organisation that monitors the practices of companies to ensure they are nor acting illegally.

WATS
Wide Area Telecommunications Service. In the US and Canada, a long distance telephone service which provides discounted calls for companies that place large volumes of long distance telephone calls.

Wayzgoose
A traditional August outing or party for printers, typically around St Bartholomwe's Day, 24th August, marking the end of summer, when work by candlelight began each year. The term persisted in the print industry in more general use referring to a company party, although its use is now rare since large-scale automation and workforce reduction.

Web traffic
Number of hits or unique visitors that a website receives. This traffic results from marketers' efforts to drive more people (potential customers) to their sites.

Webinar
Web-based seminar. A meeting, conference, etc., which is transmitted over the Internet, with each participant using their own computer to connect to the other participants.

Webmaster
A person who is responsible for maintaining a website.

Webzine
An electronic magazine which is published on the Internet.

Weighbridge
Known as a Weigh Station in the US. A vehicle weighing system which consists of a metal plate set into a road which vehicles, usually trucks with loads, are driven onto to be weighed to check if they are overladen.

Weighting
An allowance paid to workers who live in certain areas of the country, such as London, to compensate for higher living costs.

Well-being/wellbeing/well being
Significant term and consideration concerning personal health and happiness in the workplace, with implications for performance, quality, organizational effectiveness and profitability. Well-being, and specifically the promotion and strategic improvement of personal well-being in the workplace, is a major extension of earlier principles and issues of stress and stress management.

Wet lease
An arrangement in which an airline leases an aircraft, complete with crew, insurance, etc., to another company, usually for a short period of time.

Wheeling and dealing
Making a profit, sometimes dishonestly, buy buying and selling things, or acting as a go-between for two parties.

Whistleblower/Whistle-blower
A person who informs the public (usually via websites or news media) and/or relevant authorities (watchdogs, government, ombudsman, standards body, etc) about wrong-doings, failings, corruption, or other illegal activities within an organization. The wrong actions might be of a colleague,

superior, workgroup, or any number of individuals working in the organization, or otherwise working with the organization. Typically, but not essentially, the whistleblower is or was employed by the organization concerned, or becomes quickly unemployed or at least suspended.

White collar
Refers to employees who work in offices or business rather than manual workers.

White collar crime
An illegal act such as fraud, embezzlement, bribery, etc., committed by a worker in business or administrative function.

White goods
Large domestic electrical appliances, such as cookers, washing machines, fridges, etc.

White knight
A company, individual, etc., who offers favourable terms in a takeover, usually saving the acquired company from a hostile takeover.

White van man
A derogatory term for drivers of white commercial vans, who have a reputation for driving recklessly and intimidating car drivers by driving about three inches from their rear bumper.

Wholesale
Channel members in a distribution network (commercialization schedule) that sell to other wholesalers and retailers. Generally, it involves sales to other organizations that are not the intended end user (customer) for the product. Marketers enroll channel members to perform functions which they cannot perform as effectively or efficiently, such as transporting, grading, sorting, assorting, financing, or researching other channel members/customers. In the U.S., no sales taxes are collected at the wholesale level. Thus, a Sam's Club or Costco can operate as both wholesaler and retailer. For example, a Little League organization may have a tax I.D. number (to avoid paying sales tax) when purchasing hot dogs, buns, mustard, and ketchup at Sam's Club, because it will then transform these items into finished hot dogs for sale at the ballpark—where tax will be collected from the fan.

Wholesale
The sale of goods in large quantities, usually to retailers who then sell them for a profit.

Wholesale bank
A bank which provides services to large organisations, financial institutions, etc., rather than individual customers.

Wholesaler
A channel institution which purchases and sells in bulk from either original suppliers and/or other channel intermediaries, charging a margin for its services.

Widget
A small Programme which is run by certain computers. A small device, switch, gadget, etc., whose name is not known.

Wi-fi
Wireless Fidelity. A wireless technology which enables computers, mobile phones, video games, etc., to be operated by using radio frequency.

Wilshire 5000 equity index
A stock market index composed of approximately 7000 securities,

including most issues from NYSE, AMEX, and the over-the-counter markets.

Wind farm

A large area of land, which has strong winds, on which a group of wind turbines are placed in order to produce electricity by driving generators.

Windfall

A sudden, unexpected sum of money or piece of good fortune received by someone.

Win-win

Describes a situation or arrangement in which all parties benefit or profit.

With profits

Describes an insurance policy which pays the sum assured plus any bonuses which may have accumulated over the term of the policy.

Without prejudice

Written on a document in legal proceedings, negotiations, etc., meaning that any information contained in the document does not affect the legal rights of a party involved in a dispute.

Without recourse

A legal term written on a bill of exchange which signifies that the buyer accepts the risk of non-payment from a third party, rather than the seller.

Word-of-mouth (referral marketing)

WOM marketing is an alternative marketing strategy supported by research and technology that encourages consumers to dialogue about products and services through various online and offline tactics, often facilitated by brand ambassadors.

Work in progress

Also called Work In Process. Work on a product, contract, etc., that a company has invested in but is not yet completed. A piece of music, art, etc., which is unfinished but may be available for viewing or listening.

Work permit

A legal document which gives a person a right to employment in certain foreign countries.

Work/life employee benefits

Work/Life benefits are "non-traditional" employee benefits that assist employees in managing their lives. Employers purchase these services from vendors and they are offered to employees as benefits. These services can make the difference in attracting and retaining employees. Common life management benefits include : child and elder care referral services, employee assistance Programme (EAP), concierge, legal assistance, and emergency back-up childcare.

Workaholic

A person who is addicted to work.

Workers compensation

A form of insurance to reimburse employees who are injured or contract an illness in the course of preforming their job, in exchange for mandatory relinquishment of the employee's right to sue his or her employer for the sort of negligence. Laws vary by state, but employers are required to carry appropriate workers' compensation insurance, to ensure sufficient funding to cover the types of injures that are likely to occur in their workplace. Such insurance types include disability insurance, health insurance, life insurance, or a wage replacement provision.

Workforce planning
The assessment of the current workforce in order to predict future needs. This can consist of both demand planning and supply planning. Many e-recruitment software providers include modules for workforce planning.

Working capital
Current assets less current liabilities, representing the required investment, continually circulating, to finance stock, debtors, and work in progress.

Working time directive
Rules set by the European Union which limits the maximum number of hours in a working week, the minimum amount of annual leave and the minimum amount of rest period in a working day to which an employee is entitled.

Work-life Balance
The attempt to balance work and personal life in order to have a better quality of life. A person with a balanced life is an asset to his or her business, as he or she experiences greater fulfillment at work and at home.

World economic forum
WEF. Based in Geneva, Switzerland, an non-profit, international organisation which brings together politicians, business and education leaders from all over the world to discuss ways to improve economic and social growth, health and environment issues, etc.

World trade organisation
WTO. An international organisation, established in 1995, with more than 150 member nations, based in Geneva, Switzerland. The WTO monitors international trade, helping importers and exporters conduct their business, and provides assistance to developing countries.

World wide web
WWW. Also known as The Web, a computer network system in which documents are inter-linked using hypertext computer code, and allows information to be accessed using the Internet.

Wow factor
The instant appeal of a product, property, etc., which impresses and surprises people the first time they see it.

Wrap
The end of a film shoot when everything is finished, the set can be taken down and everyone can go.

Writ
A written order issued by a court of law which orders someone to do, or not do, something.

Writ of execution
A court order which ensures that a judgement is enforced.

Write-off
In accounting, to reduce the book value of an asset, sometimes to zero, or cancel a debt which has not been, or is unlikely to be, paid.

X

X-efficiency

A concept introduced by economist Harvey Liebenstein. A company's ability to use its workers, machines, technology, etc., to produce maximum output at lowest cost and as quickly as possible.

Xenology

The scientific study and/or research of alien cultures and biology.

Xerox machine

A piece of equipment which makes paper copies of documents, etc.

X-inefficiency

When a company is not using its employees, machinery, resources, etc., effectively, often because of lack of competition.

XML and HR-XML

Extensible Markup Language. A common system used for defining data. Unlike HTML, XML is not a fixed set of elements. XML allows information creators to apply descriptive markup (or "tags") around each discrete element of data. The HR-XML Consortium strives to spare employers and vendors the risk and expense of having to negotiate and agree upon data interchange mechanisms on an ad-hoc basis. By using XML, the Consortium provides the means for any company to transact with other companies without having to establish, engineer, and implement many separate interchange mechanisms.

Y

Yarnstorming

Also called yarnbombing, an intriguingly specialised type of peaceful demonstration and activism in which objects such as works of art, sculpture, railings, phone boxes, considered unattractive by the activists, are covered by knitting or crochet, usually at night, and mainly by young women.

Yellow pages

A telephone directory, usually printed on yellow paper, which lists businesses, organisations, retailers, etc., in alphabetical order in categories according to the service they provide.

Yellow sheets

Published every day in the US by the National Quotation Bureau, a list which shows information and prices of corporate bonds.

Yeoman

A servant or attendant in a royal or noble household.

Yield

The value found by dividing the amount of interest paid on a bond by the price, thus measuring the income from a bond (The term also refers to the dividend from stock divided by its price. Yield, however, is not a measure of total return since it does not include capital gains or losses.).

Yield to maturity

The return expected on a bond held until the maturity date.

Youth court

A court of law, which members of the public are not allowed to attend, that deals with juvenile (under 18 years of age) offenders.

Yuppie

Derives from Young Urban Professional. Term used since the 1980s to describe a young person who has a well-paid job and an affluent lifestyle.

Z

Zero defects

Philip Crosby's recommended performance standard that leaves no doubt regarding the goal of total quality. Crosby's theory holds that people can continually move closer to this goal by committing themselves70 to their work and the improvement process.

Zero-based budgeting

ZBB. A system in which a yearly budget for a department in a company starts at zero with no pre-authorised funds, and the department has to justify its budget requests.

Zero-rated

Describes goods or services on which the buyer pays no value-added-tax.

Zero-sum game

A situation in which what is lost by one person, company, etc., is matched by a gain by another/others. Used in economics and Game Theory to describe the relatively simple 'strictly competitive' situation whereby all the losses and gains balance each other to zero. Potential gains are finite; what is gained by one must be lost by another, and vice-versa.

Zip

In computing, compressing data to make a file smaller in order for it to be stored or sent to another computer. Also, slang for nothing.

Zone pricing

A pricing strategy by which all customers within a specific geographic zone or region are charged the same price; those more distant pay more due to higher shipping costs. Price zones are set by marketers, not by law.

Z-score

Developed by Dr Edward Altman of New York University in the 1960s, a measurement of the financial health of a company which predicts the probability of the company going bankrupt.

Management Theory and Principles

3 Dimensions of Strategic Change

In their book 'Managing Change for Competitive Success' (1991) Andrew Pettigrew and Richard Whipp distinguish between three dimensions of strategic change:

1. **Content (Objectives, Purpose and Goals)** : The content of change aims to answer the question **"WHAT"**
2. **Process (Implementation)** : The process of change aims to answer the question **"HOW"**
3. **Context (The Internal and External Environment)** : The context of change aims to answer the question **"WHERE"**

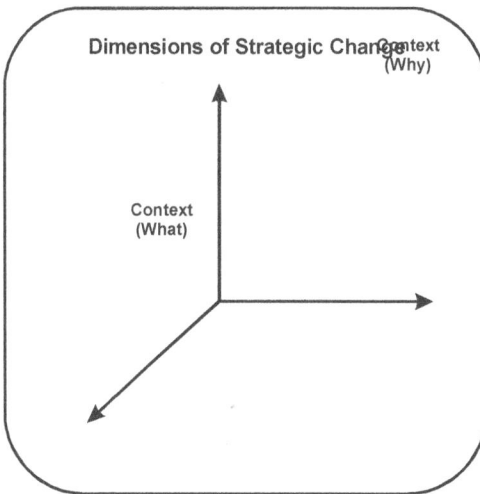

Dimensions of Strategic Change

Context
(Why)

Context
(What)

Pettigrew and Whipp emphasize the continuous interplay between these change dimensions. The implementation of change is an "iterative, cumulative and reformulation-in-use process." Successful change is a result of the interaction between the content or what of change (objectives, purpose and goals); the process or how of change (implementation); and the organizational context or where of change (the internal and external environment).

Based on substantial empirical research, they also present five central interrelated factors belonging to successfully managing strategic change:

1. Environmental assessment (continuous monitoring of both the internal and external environment [competition] of the organization through open learning systems)
2. Human resources as assets and liabilities (employees should know they are seen as valuable and feel trusted by the organization)
3. Linking strategic and operational change (Intentions are implemented and transformed through time, bundling of operational activities is powerful and can lead to new strategic changes)
4. Leading change (Move the organization forwards; creating the right climate for change, coordinating activities, steering. Setting the agenda not only for the direction of the change, but also for the right vision and values)
5. Overall coherence (a change strategy should be consistent (clear goals), consonant (with its environment), provide a competitive edge and be feasible.

The Dimensions of Strategic Change

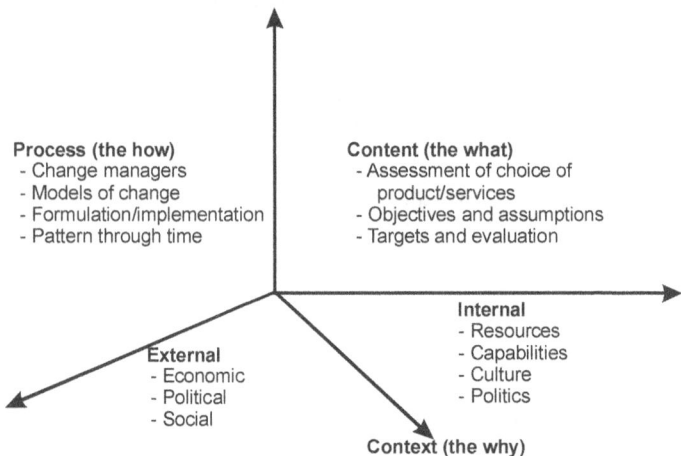

Process (the how)
- Change managers
- Models of change
- Formulation/implementation
- Pattern through time

Content (the what)
- Assessment of choice of product/services
- Objectives and assumptions
- Targets and evaluation

Internal
- Resources
- Capabilities
- Culture
- Politics

External
- Economic
- Political
- Social

Context (the why)

7-S Framework of McKinsey

The 7-S framework of McKinsey is a Value Based Management (VBM) model that describes how one can holistically and effectively organize a company. Together these factors determine the way in which a corporation operates. The 7's of McKinsey Framework are listed below:
1. **Shared Value :** The interconnecting center of McKinsey's model is: Shared Values. What does the organization stands for and what it believes in. Central beliefs and attitudes.
2. **Strategy :** Plans for the allocation of a firms scarce resources, over time, to reach identified goals. Environment, competition, customers.
3. **Structure :** The way the organization's units relate to each other: centralized, functional divisions (top-down); decentralized (the trend in larger organizations); matrix, network, holding, etc.

4. **System :** The procedures, processes and routines that characterize how important work is to be done: financial systems; hiring, promotion and performance appraisal systems; information systems.
5. **Staff :** Numbers and types of personnel within the organization.
6. **Style :** Cultural style of the organization and how key managers behave in achieving the organizations goals. Management Styles.
7. **Skill :** Distinctive capabilities of personnel or of the organization as a whole. Core Competences.

Element of 7S model	Application to digital marketing team	Key issues from practice and literature
Strategy	The significance of digital marketing in influencing and supporting organisations' strategy	Gaining appropriate budgets and demonstrating / delivering value and ROI from budgets. Annual planning approach. Techniques for using digital marketing to impact organisation strategy Techniques for aligning digital strategy with organisational and marketing strategy
Structure	The modification of organizational structure to support digital marketing.	Integration of team with other management, marketing (corporate communications, brand marketing, direct marketing) and IT staff Use of cross-functional teams and steering groups Insourcing vs. outsourcing
Systems	The development of specific processes, procedures or information systems to support digital marketing	Campaign planning approach-integration Managing/sharing customer information Managing content quality Unified reporting of digital marketing effectiveness In-house vs. external best-of-breed vs. external integrated technology solutions
Staff	The breakdown of staff in terms of their background and characteristics such as IT vs. Marketing, use of contractors/consultants, age and sex.	Insourcing vs. outsourcing Achieving senior management buy-in/involvement with digital marketing Staff recruitment and retention. Virtual working Staff development and training

Style	Includes both the way in which key managers behave in achieving the organizations' goals and the cultural style of the organization as a whole.	Relates to role of digital marketing team in influencing strategy ï¿½ it is it dynamic and influential or conservative and looking for a voice
Skills	Distinctive capabilities of key staff, but can be interpreted as specific skill-sets of team members.	Staff skills in specific areas: supplier selection, project management, Content management, specific e-marketing approaches (SEO,PPC, affiliate marketing, e-mail marketing, online advertising)
Superordinate goals	The guiding concepts of the digital marketing organisation which are also part of shared values and culture. The internal and external perception of these goals may vary	Improving the perception of the importance and effectiveness of the digital marketing team amongst senior managers and staff it works with (marketing generalists and IT)

What is 7-S Model?

The Seven-Ss (7-S Model) is a framework for analyzing organizations and their effectiveness. It looks at the seven key elements that make the organizations successful, or not: strategy; structure; systems; style; skills; staff; and shared values.

The Seven S
Framework fro Analyzing and Improving Organzation

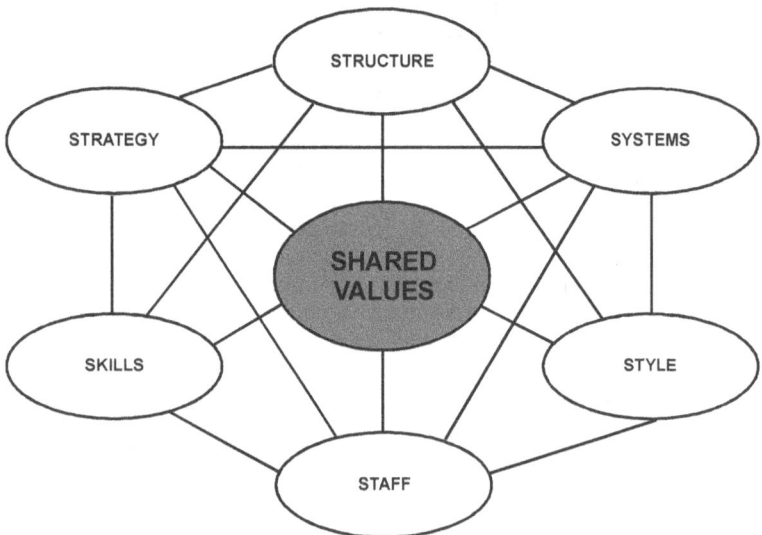

Consultants at McKinsey & Company developed the 7S model in the late 1970s to help managers address the difficulties of organizational change. The model shows that organizational immune systems and the many interconnected variables involved make change complex, and that an effective change effort must address many of these issues simultaneously.

7-S Model: A Systemic Approach to Improving Organizations

The 7-S model is a tool for managerial analysis and action that provides a structure with which to consider a company as a whole, so that the organization's problems may be diagnosed and a strategy may be developed and implemented.

The 7-S diagram illustrates the multiplicity interconnectedness of elements that define an organization's ability to change. The theory helped to change manager's thinking about how companies could be improved. It says that it is not just a matter of devising a new strategy and following it through. Nor is it a matter of setting up new systems and letting them generate improvements.

There is no starting point or implied hierarchy – different factors may drive the business in any one organization.

Shared Values

Shared values are commonly held beliefs, mindsets, and assumptions that shape how an organization behaves its corporate culture. Shared values are what engender trust. They are an interconnecting center of the 7Ss model. Values are the identity by which a company is known throughout its business areas, what the organization stands for and what it believes in, it central beliefs and attitudes. These values must be explicitly stated as both corporate objectives and individual values.

Structure

Structure is the organizational chart and associated information that shows who reports to whom and how tasks are both divided up and integrated. In other words, structures describe the hierarchy of authority and accountability in an organization, the way the organization's units relate to each other: centralized, functional divisions (top-down); decentralized (the trend in larger organizations); matrix, network, holding, etc. These relationships are frequently diagrammed in organizational charts. Most organizations use some mix of structures – pyramidal, matrix or networked ones – to accomplish their goals.

Strategy

Strategy are plans an organization formulates to reach identified goals, and a set of decisions and actions aimed at gaining a sustainable advantage over the competition.

Systems

Systems define the flow of activities involved in the daily operation of business, including its core processes and its support systems. They refer to the procedures, processes and routines that are used to manage the organization and characterize how important work is to be done. Systems include:

- Business System
- Business Process Management System (BPMS)
- Management information system

- Innovation system
- Performance management system
- Financial system/capital allocation system
- Compensation system/reward system
- Customer satisfaction monitoring system

Style

"Style" refers to the cultural style of the organization, how key managers behave in achieving the organization's goals, how managers collectively spend their time and attention, and how they use symbolic behavior. How management acts is more important that what management says.

Staff

"Staff" refers to the number and types of personnel within the organization and how companies develop employees and shape basic values.

Skills

"Skills" refer to the dominant distinctive capabilities and competencies of the personnel or of the organization as a whole.

80-20 Rule

The 80-20 rule (also known as the Pareto principle, the law of the vital few and the principle of factor sparsity) states that, for many events, 80% of the effects comes from 20% of the causes. Business management thinker Joseph M. Juran suggested the principle and named it after Italian economist Vilfredo Pareto, who observed that 80% of income in Italy went to 20% of the population. It is a common rule of thumb in business; e.g., "80% of your sales comes from 20% of your clients."

It is worthy of note that some applications of the Pareto principle appeal to a pseudo-scientific "law of nature" to bolster non-quantifiable or non-verifiable assertions that are "painted with a broad brush". The fact that hedges such as the 90/10, 70/30, and 95/5 "rules" exist is sufficient evidence of the non-exactness of the Pareto principle. On the other hand, there is adequate evidence that "clumping" of factors does occur in most phenomena.

The Pareto principle is only tangentially related to Pareto efficiency, which was also introduced by the same economist, Vilfredo Pareto. Pareto developed both concepts in the context of the distribution of income and wealth among the population.

The misnamed 80-20 rule (also known as the Pareto principle, the law of the vital few and the principle of factor sparsity) states that for many phenomena 80% of consequences stem from 20% of the causes. The idea has rule-of-thumb application in many places, but it's also commonly and unthinkingly misused.

Some hold that the principle is recursive, and may be applied to the top 20% of causes; thus there would be a "64-4" rule, and a "51.8-0.8" rule, and so on. This is a special case of the wider phenomenon of Pareto distributions.

Vilfredo Pareto

Vilfredo Pareto (born July 15, 1848 in France – died August 19, 1923 in Lausanne, Switzerland) made several important contributions to economics, sociology and moral philosophy, especially in the study of income distribution and in the analysis of individuals' choices. He introduced the concept of Pareto efficiency and helped develop the field of microeconomics with ideas such as indifference curves. His theories influenced Benito Mussolini and the development of Italian fascism.

The Pareto family moved to Italy in 1858. In 1870, Pareto received an engineering degree from the Turin Polytechnic Institute and he took employment with the Italian state railways. In 1886, he became a lecturer on economics and management at the University of Florence. In 1893, he was appointed as a lecturer in economics at the University of Lausanne in Switzerland where he remained for the rest of his life.

In 1906, he made the well-known observation that 20% of the population owned 80% of the property in Italy, later generalised (by Joseph M. Juran and others) into the so-called Pareto principle (for many phenomena 80% of consequences stem from 20% of the causes), and generalised further to the concept of a Pareto distribution.

The Pareto index is a measure of the inequality of income distribution.

The Pareto chart is a special type of histogram, used to view causes of a problem in order of severity from largest to smallest. It is a statistical tool that graphically shows the 20-80 rule.

Pareto's social policies were put on paper in his work, Mind and Society.

In his Trattato di Sociologia Generale he put forward the first Social cycle theory in sociology

Joseph M. Juran, The Real "Father" of the 80-20 Rule

Joseph M. Juran (born December 1904 in Romania) has been called the "father" of quality. Joseph M. Juran's major contribution to the world has been in the field of quality management. Perhaps most important, he is recognized as the person who added the human dimension to quality broadening it from its statistical origins.

In 1937, Dr. Juran conceptualized the Pareto principle, which millions of managers rely on to help separate the "vital few" from the "useful many" in their activities. This is commonly referred to as the 20-80 principle. In 2003, the American Society for Quality is proposing renaming the Pareto Principle the "Juran Principle." Its universal application makes it one of the most useful concepts and tools of modern-day management.

Dr. Juran wrote the standard reference work on quality control, the Quality Control Handbook, first published in 1951 and now in its fifth edition. This handbook is the reference for most quality departments and business improvement change agents since it provides important how-to information dedicated to improving an organization's performance by improving the quality of its goods and services.

His classic book, Managerial Breakthrough, first published in 1964, presented a more general theory of quality management. It was the first book to describe a step-by-step sequence for breakthrough improvement. This process has evolved into Six Sigma today and is the basis for quality initiatives worldwide.

In 1979, Dr. Juran founded Juran Institute, an organization aimed at providing research and pragmatic solutions to enable organizations from any industry to learn the tools and techniques for managing quality.

The Juran Trilogy, published in 1986, identified and was accepted worldwide as the basis for quality management. After almost 50 years of research, his trilogy defined three management processes required by all organizations to improve. Quality control, quality improvement and quality planning have become synonymous with Juran and Juran Institute, Inc.

Juran describes quality from the customer perspective as having two aspects: higher quality means a greater number of features that meet customers' needs. The second aspect relates to "freedom from trouble": higher quality consists of fewer defects.

As a result of the power and clarity of Joseph Juran's thinking and the scope of his influence, business leaders, legions of managers and his fellow theorists worldwide recognize Dr. Juran as one of "the vital few" a seminal figure in the development of management theory. Juran has contributed more to the field and over a longer period of time than any other person, and yet, feels he has barely scratched the surface of his subject. "My job of contributing to the welfare of my fellow man" writes Juran, is the great unfinished business.

How can the 80-20 Rule Help me in Life and Business?

The 80-20 Principle can and should be used by every intelligent person in their daily life. It can multiply the profitability of corporations and the effectiveness of any organization or individual.

The value of the Pareto Principle for a manager is that it reminds you to focus on the 20 percent that matters. Of the things you do during your day, only 20 percent really matter. Those 20 percent produce 80 percent of your results. Identify and focus on those things. When the fire drills of the day begin to sap your time, remind yourself of the 20 percent you need to focus on. If something in the schedule has to slip, if something isn't going to get done, make sure it's not part of that 20 percent.

- Have a product range? Have a look at how much of your profit comes from each item. Put your effort into the 20% that give you 80% of your sales – your winners.
- Selling products or services? Most likely, 80% of your sales come from 20% of your customers- the ones who make the big purchases and are repeat-buyers. Cherish that 20%.
- Have a sales force? Have a look at how much of your profit comes from each person. Make sure you reward and retain the 20% that are your winners.
- Have an affiliate Programme? Find the top 5-20% who give you 80% of your income, and make sure you support, encourage and reward your winners.

- Do advertising? Have a look at where the sales come from. Then identify the few ads that really pull, and the few places where you run them that really produce. Then refine your winning ads, and run them in those few places that give you the best results.
- Check your web traffic logs! Which keywords are bringing you the most traffic? Which search engines? Which websites? You'll find that a small number of keywords, search engines and websites give you the lion's share of your traffic. Nurture them, and build on those strengths!

These are only few examples of the use you can make of the Pareto Principle.

Action Centred Leadership

The concept of Action-Centred Leadership was created by leadership management guru John Adair whilst lecturing at the Royal Military Academy Sandhurst, and remains his best known work.

The Action-Centred Leadership model uses three circles to link the three key elements of leadership, the task needs, the team needs, and the individual needs, in a simple but effective tool for leadership development. According to The Action Centred Leadership approach a leader aims to achieve task by building teams and developing individuals. These three responsibilities have crosssections.

Responsibilities to the task include:
- Define the task
- Identify available resources
- Formulate a plan
- Delegate responsibility
- Set quality standards
- Maintain control
- Keep to schedule

- Report to higher authority
- Assess progress and adjust plans as appropriate

Responsibilities to the team include:

- Establish and communicate acceptable performance standards
- Establish and communicate acceptable ethical standards
- Maintain discipline and focus
- Proactively resolve conflicts
- Encourage team spirit
- Motivate the team
- Establish leadership roles within the team
- Establish and maintain effective communication

Responsibilities to the individual include:

- Understand individuals, their strengths, skills, personality, and needs
- Support and assist individuals
- Acknowledge effort and good work
- Identify individual training needs
- Encourage and develop individual creativity, freedom and authority

Often a leader will be operating in just one or two of the areas, the three circle model helps leaders plot exactly where they are and help develop their own leadership skills to take advantage more fully of the resources available from a whole team to get the task done.

ADL Matrix

Part of thinking about strategy involves thinking about the state of your industry; understanding how your organization fits into it; and, from this, figuring out your best way forward.

While there are many tools that help you do this, you can get particularly useful insights with the Arthur D Little (ADL) Matrix. Developed in the late 1970s by the highly respected Arthur D Little consulting company, it helps you think about strategy based on:

Using the ADL Matrix

If your business unit has a strong market presence and a newly emerging product line, you'll likely want to aggressively push its position and capture as much market share as you can. But this strategy does not apply so well to business lines with dominant competitive positions in declining markets. In this instance, you're better off putting your energy into new, growing markets and simply maintaining your current market position in the declining industry.

The ADL Matrix addresses these unique needs by recommending general strategies for different combinations of competitive position and industry maturity.

Industry Maturity

There are four categories of industry maturity (also referred to as the industry life cycle):

1. Embryonic: The introduction stage, characterized by rapid market growth, very little competition, new technology, high investment and high prices.

2. Growth: The market continues to strengthen, sales increase, few (if any) competitors exist, and company reaps rewards for bringing a new product to market.

3. Mature: The market is stable, there is a well-established customer base, market share is stable, there are lots of competitors, and energy is put toward differentiating from competitors.

4. Aging: Demand decreases, companies start abandoning the market, the fight for market share among remaining competitors gets too expensive, and companies begin leaving or consolidating until the marketing demise.

Competitive Position

The five categories for competitive position are as follows:

1. Dominant: This is rare and typically short-lived. There ïs little, if any, competition, usually a result of bringing a brand-new product to market or having built an extremely strong reputation in the market (think Microsoft).

2. Strong: Market share is strong and stable, regardless of what your competitors are doing.

3. Favorable: Your business line enjoys competitive advantages in certain segments of the market. However, there are many rivals of equal strength, and you have to work to maintain your advantage.

4. Tenable: Your position in the overall market is small, and market share is based on a niche, a strong geographic location, or some other product differentiation. Strong competitors are overtaking your market share by building their products and defining clear competitive advantages.

5. Weak: There is continual loss of market share, and your business line, as it exists, is too small to maintain profitability.

The resulting ADL Matrix looks like this, with the various strategies prescribed for each of the 20 combinations:

	Industry Maturity			
	Embryonic	Growth	Mature	Aging
Dominant	-Aggressive push for market share - Invest faster than market share dictates	- Maintain industry position and market share - Invest to sustain growth	- Maintain position, grow market share as the industry grows - Reinvest as necessary	- Maintain industry position - Reinvest as necessary
Strong	-Aggressive push for market share - Look for ways to improve competitive advantage - Invest faster than market share dictates	-Aggressive push for market share - Look for ways to improve competitive advantage - Invest to increase growth and position	- Maintain position, grow market share as the industry grows - Reinvest as necessary	- Maintain industry position or cut expenditures to maximize profit (harvest) - Minimum reinvestment
Favoirable	- Moderate to aggressive push for market share - Look for ways to improve competitive advantage - Invest selectively	- Look for ways to improve competitive advantage and market share - Selectively invest to improve position	- Develop a niche or other strong differentiating factor and maintain it. - Minimum or selective reinvestment	- Cut expenditures to maximize profit (harvest) or plan a phased withdrawal - Minimum investment or look to get out of current investment

Tenable	- Look for ways to improve industry position - Invest very selectively	- Develop a niche or other strong differentiating factor and maintain it - Invest selectivel	- Develop a niche or other strong differentiating factor maintain it or plan a phased withdrawal. - Selective reinvestment	- Phased withdrawal or abandon market - Get out of investments or divest
Weak	- Decide if potential benefits outweigh costs, otherwise get out of market - Invest or divest	- Look for ways to improve share and position, or get out of the market - Invest or divest	- Look for ways to improve share and position or plan a phased withdrawal - Selectively invest or divest	- Abandon market - Divest

Using the ADL Matrix

The ADL Matrix provides you with a generic strategy. You'll need to fine-tune the strategy and tailor it to your current business.

Step #1: Identify your industry maturity category.

Think about the following questions as you decide which stage is most descriptive:

What are you currently experiencing with market growth?

How many competitors do you have?

How large is your market?

Is your investment increasing or decreasing?

Are your sales increasing, decreasing or staying the same?

How is your product differentiated from competitor products?

Deciding on an industry life cycle stage isn't easy, and competitors' actions often have a bearing on this, making it hard to determine and predict. Strategy is not an exact science, so do the best you can.

Step #2: Determine your competitive position.

Choose the best fit. Be careful not to project what you want your position to be, but what it truly is. Take a long, hard look at where youre currently operating.

Tip: If you are having trouble finding the perfect match for maturity level or competitive position, look for the combination that most closely fits your situation.

Step #3: Plot your matrix position.

Consider the strategies suggested as a starting point for your strategic planning.

Tip: Look at the strategy recommended as well as those strategies immediately surrounding it. It can be difficult to pinpoint either of the dimensions, and your business may be on the cusp between two positions. By examining close options, you can choose the general strategic formula with the best fit.

Tip: It is important to remember that while the ADL Matrix points you in a general strategic direction; you will probably want to perform further, more detailed analysis before making a final strategic plan. So verify you strategic choice using one or more other strategy tools such as USP Analysis, Porters Five Forces or Bowmans Strategy Clock, and then work out what internal changes you will need to make to implement the strategy effectively. The McKinsey 7S Framework is among the tools that will help you with this.

Key Points of ADL Matrix

The ADL Matrix is a great tool for uncovering high level strategies that may be successful for your business.

By focusing on competitive position and industry maturity, the matrix helps you see the role your business plays in the larger marketplace. With this big picture view, complemented by other strategy tools, you will have a great starting place for building your strategic plan.

ADL Matrix

The ADL matrix from Arthur D. Little is a portfolio management method that is based on product life cycle thinking.

The ADL portfolio management approach uses the dimensions of environmental assessment and business strength assessment. The environmental measure is an identification of the industry's life cycle. The business strengths measure is a categorization of the corporation's SBU's into one of five (6) competitive positions: dominant, strong, favorable, tenable, weak (and non-viable). This yields a 5 (competitive positions) by 4 (life cycle stages) matrix. Positioning in the matrix identifies a general strategy.

In the ADL approach, the line of business or SBU is not especially defined by a product or organizational unit. The strategist must identify discrete businesses by finding commonalties among products and business lines using the following criteria as guidelines:

- Common rivals
- Prices
- Customers
- Quality/Style
- Substitutability
- Divestment or liquidation

This assessment of the industry life cycle stage of each business is made on the basis of:

- Business market share,
- Investment, and
- Profitability and cash flow.

The competitive position of a firm is based on an assessment of the following criteria:

- **Dominant:** Rare. Often results from a near monopoly or protected leadership.
- **Strong:** A strong business can usually follow a strategy without too much consideration of moves from rivals.
- Favorable: Industry is fragmented. No clear leader among stronger rivals.
- Tenable: Business has a niche, either geographical or defined by the product.
- Weak: Business is too small to be profitable or survive over the long term. Critical weaknesses.

Limitations of the ADL Matrix

- There is no standard length of life cycles,
- Determining the current industry life cycle phase is awkward,
- Competitors may influence the length of the life cycle.

Ansoff Matrix

To portray alternative corporate growth strategies, Igor Ansoff presented a matrix that focused on the firm's present and potential products and markets (customers). By considering ways to grow via existing products and new products, and in existing markets and new markets, there are four possible product-market combinations. Ansoff's matrix is shown below:

	Existing Products	New Products
Existing Markets	Market Penetration	Product Development
New Markets	Market Development	Diversification

Ansoff Matrix Growth Strategies

Ansoff's matrix provides four different growth strategies:

1. Market Penetration - the firm seeks to achieve growth with existing products in their current market segments, aiming to increase its market share.

2. Market Development – the firm seeks growth by targeting its existing products to new market segments.

3. Product Development – the firms develops new products targeted to its existing market segments.

4. Diversification - the firm grows by diversifying into new businesses by developing new products for new markets.

Selecting a Product-Market Growth Strategy

The market penetration strategy is the least risky since it leverages many of the firm's existing resources and capabilities. In a growing market, simply maintaining market share will result in growth, and there may exist opportunities to increase market share if competitors reach capacity limits. However, market penetration has limits, and once the market approaches saturation another strategy must be pursued if the firm is to continue to grow.

Market development options include the pursuit of additional market segments or geographical regions. The development of new markets for the product may be a good strategy if the firm's core competencies are related more to the specific product than to its experience with a specific market segment. Because the firm is expanding into a new market, a market development strategy typically has more risk than a market penetration strategy.

A product development strategy may be appropriate if the firm's strengths are related to its specific customers rather than to the specific product itself. In this situation, it can leverage its strengths by developing a new product targeted to its existing customers. Similar to the case of new market development, new product development carries more risk than simply attempting to increase market share.

Diversification is the most risky of the four growth strategies since it requires both product and market development and may be outside the core competencies of the firm. In fact, this quadrant of the matrix has been referred to by some as the "suicide cell". However, diversification may be a reasonable choice if the high risk is compensated by the chance of a high rate of return. Other advantages of diversification include the potential to gain a foothold in an attractive industry and the reduction of overall business portfolio risk.

The product/market grid of Ansoff is a model that has proven to be very useful in business unit strategy processes to determine business growth opportunities. The product/market grid has two dimensions: products and markets.

Over these 2 dimensions, four growth strategies can be formed:
- Market penetration,
- Market development,
- Product development, and
- Diversification.

Market Penetration

Company strategies based on market penetration normally focus on changing incidental clients to regular clients, and regular client into heavy clients. Typical systems are volume discounts, bonus cards and customer relationship management.

Market Development

Company strategies based on market development often try to lure clients away from competitors or introduce existing products in foreign markets or introduce new brand names in a market.

Product Development

Company strategies based on product development often try to sell other products to (regular) clients. This can be accessories, add-ons, or completely new products. Often existing communication channels are leveraged.

Diversification

Company strategies based on diversification are the most risky type of strategies. Often there is a credibility focus in the communication to explain why the company enters new markets with new products. This 4th quadrant (diversification) of the product/market grid can be further split up in four types:
- horizontal diversification (new product, current market)
- vertical diversification (move into firms supplier's or customer's business)
- concentric diversification (new product closely related to current product in new market)
- conglomerate diversification (new product in new market).

Although already decennia old, the product/market grid of Ansoff remains a valuable model for communication around business unit strategy processes and business growth.

Balanced Scorecard

The balanced scorecard is a strategic planning and management system used;
- To align business activities to the vision and strategy of the organization,
- Improve internal and external communications and,
- Monitor organization performance against strategic goals.

The balanced scorecard suggests us to view 4 critical perspectives of our business:

1. Learning & growth: includes training, learning, corporate culture and attitudes, self growth. Individuals are the main repository of knowledge of an organisation and the critical resource. Communication among workers is key, as is avoiding brain drain.

2. Business process: Metrics based on internal business processes allow management to monitor how well the business is running and wether it's products/services are well accepted by clients.

3. Customer: Indicators on customer satisfaction and tools to improve and monitor customer relations are critical

4. Financial: Timely and accurate financial data is still a key to manage the business. Data should be centralised and of fast and easy access, but financial data should not be the only indicator, thus the original intention of the word balanced.

The Balanced Scorecard automates and centralizes the issuance and tracking of objectives, targets, measures and initiatives.

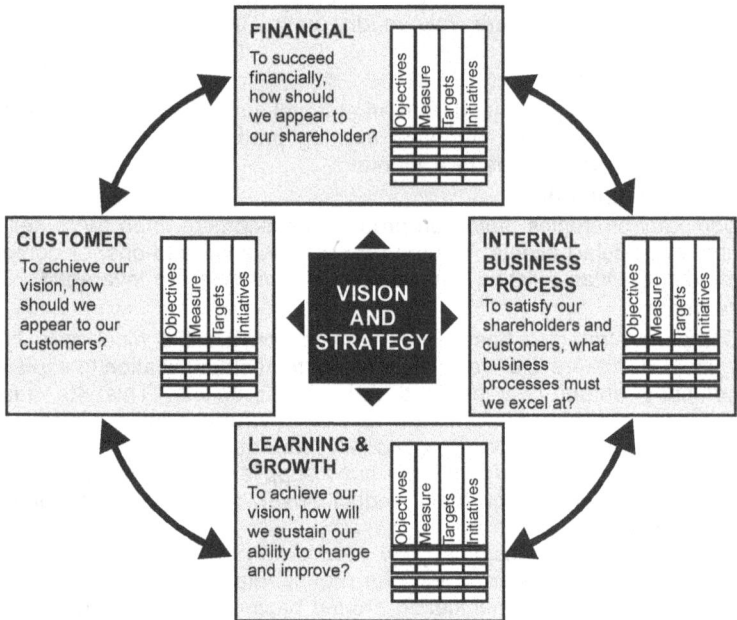

The Balanced Scorecard (BSC) began as a concept for measuring whether the smaller-scale operational activities of a company are aligned with its larger-scale objectives in terms of vision and strategy. It was developed and first used at Analog Devices in 1987. By focusing not only on financial outcomes but also on the human issues, the Balanced Scorecard helps provide a more comprehensive view of a business, which in turn helps organizations act in their best long-term interests. The strategic management system helps managers focus on performance metrics while balancing financial objectives with customer, process and employee perspectives. Measures are often indicators of future performance.

History of Balanced Scorecard

In 1992, Robert S. Kaplan and David P. Norton began publicizing the Balanced Scorecard through a series of journal articles. In 1996, they published the book The Balanced Scorecard. Since the original concept was introduced, Balanced Scorecards have become a fertile field of theory and research, and many practitioners have diverted from the original Kaplan & Norton articles. Robert S. Kaplan and David P. Norton themselves revisited Balanced Scorecards with the benefit of a decade's experience since the original article.

The Balanced Scorecard is a performance planning and measurement framework, with similar principles as Management by Objectives, which was publicized by Robert S. Kaplan and David P. Norton in the early 1990s. Having realized the shortcomings of traditional management control systems, Robert S. Kaplan and David P. Norton designed the Balanced Scorecard as a result of a one-year research project involving 12 companies. Since its introduction, the Balanced Scorecard has been awarded a prize by the American Accounting Association as the best theoretical contribution in 1997, and its industry and academic attention has placed it alongside approaches such as Activity Based Costing and Total Quality Management.

Balanced scorecard is a tool to execute and monitor the organisational strategy by using a combination of financial and non financial measures. It is designed to translate vision and strategy into objectives and measures across four balanced perspectives: financial, customers, internal business process and learning and growth. It gives a framework ensuring that the strategy is translated into a coherent set of performance measures.

Use of Balanced Scorecard

Implementing Balanced Scorecards typically includes four processes:
1. Translating the vision into operational goals;
2. Communicating the vision and link it to individual performance;
3. Business planning;
4. Feedback and learning, and adjusting the strategy accordingly.

The Balanced Scorecard is a framework, or what can be best characterized as a strategic management system that claims to incorporate all quantitative and abstract measures of true importance to the enterprise. According to Kaplan and Norton, The Balanced Scorecard provides managers with the instrumentation they need to navigate to future competitive success.

Many books and articles referring to Balanced Scorecards confuse the design process elements and the Balanced Scorecard itself. In particular, it is common for people to refer to a strategic linkage model or strategy map as being a Balanced Scorecard.

Balanced Scorecard is a performance management tool. Although it helps focus managers' attention on strategic issues and the management of the implementation of strategy, it is important to remember that the Balanced Scorecard itself has no role in the formation of strategy. In fact, Balanced Scorecards can comfortably co-exist with strategic planning systems and other tools.

Original Balanced Scorecard Methodology

The earliest Balanced Scorecards comprised simple tables broken into four sections – typically these "perspectives" were labeled "Financial", "Customer", "Internal Business Processes", and "Learning & Growth". Designing the Balanced Scorecard required selecting five or six good measures for each perspective.

Many authors have since suggested alternative headings for these perspectives, and also suggested using either additional or fewer perspectives. These suggestions were notably triggered by a recognition that different but equivalent headings would yield alternative sets of measures. The major design challenge faced with this type of Balanced Scorecard is justifying the choice of measures made. "Of all the measures you could have chosen, why did you choose these?" This common question is hard to ask using this type of design process. If users are not confident that the measures within the Balanced Scorecard are well chosen, they will have less confidence in the information it provides. Although less common, these early-style Balanced Scorecards are still designed and used today.

In short, early-style Balanced Scorecards are hard to design in a way that builds confidence that they are well designed. Because of this, many are abandoned soon after completion.

Improved Balanced Scorecard Methodology

In the mid 1990s, an improved design method emerged. In the new method, measures are selected based on a set of "strategic objectives" plotted on a "strategic linkage model" or "strategy map". With this modified approach, the strategic objectives are typically distributed across a similar set of "perspectives", as is found in the earlier designs, but the design question becomes slightly less abstract.

Managers have to identify five or six goals within each of the perspectives, and then demonstrate some inter-linking between these goals by plotting causal links on the diagram. Having reached some consensus about the objectives and how they inter-relate, the Balanced Scorecard is devised by choosing suitable measures for each objective. This type of approach provides greater contextual justification for the measures chosen, and is generally easier for managers to work through. This style of Balanced Scorecard has been commonly used since 1996 or so.

Several design issues still remain with this enhanced approach to Balanced Scorecard design, but it has been much more successful than the design approach it supersedes.

Popularity of Balanced Scorecard

Kaplan and Norton found that companies are using Balanced Scorecards to:
- Drive strategy execution;
- Clarify strategy and make strategy operational;
- Identify and align strategic initiatives;
- Link budget with strategy;
- Align the organization with strategy;
- Conduct periodic strategic performance reviews to learn about and improve strategy.

In 1997, Kurtzman found that 64 percent of the companies questioned were measuring performance from a number of perspectives in a similar way to the Balanced Scorecard.

Balanced Scorecards have been implemented by government agencies, military units, business units and corporations as a whole, non-profit organizations, and schools.

Many examples of Balanced Scorecards can be found via Web searches.

However, adapting one organization's Balanced Scorecard to another is generally not advised by theorists, who believe that much of the benefit of the Balanced Scorecard comes from the implementation method.

Variants, Alternatives and Criticisms About Balanced Scorecard

Since the late 1990s, various alternatives to the Balanced Scorecard have emerged, such as The Performance Prism, Results Based Management and Third Generation Balanced Scorecard. These tools seek to solve some of the remaining design issues, in particular issues relating to the design of sets of Balanced Scorecards to use across an organization, and issues in setting targets for the measures selected.

Applied Information Economics (AIE) has been researched as an alternative to Balanced Scorecards. In 2000, the Federal CIO Council commissioned a study to compare the two methods by funding studies in side-by-side projects in two different agencies. The Dept. of Veterans Affairs used AIE and the US Dept. of Agriculture applied Balanced Scorecards. The resulting report found that while AIE was much more sophisticated, AIE actually took slightly less time to utilize. AIE was also more likely to generate findings that were newsworthy to the organization, while the users of Balanced Scorecards felt it simply documented their inputs and offered no other particular insight. However, Balanced Scorecards are still much more widely used than AIE.

A criticism of Balanced Scorecards is that the scores are not based on any proven economic or financial theory, and therefore have no basis in the decision sciences. The process is entirely subjective and makes no provision to assess quantities (e.g., risk and economic value) in a way that is actuarially or economically well-founded.

Another criticism is that the Balanced Scorecard does not provide a bottom line score or a unified view with clear recommendations: it is simply a list of metrics.

Some people also claim that positive feedback from users of Balanced Scorecards may be due to a placebo effect, as there are no empirical studies linking the use of Balanced Scorecards to better decision making or improved financial performance of companies.

The Four Perspectives of The Balanced Scorecard

The grouping of performance measures in general categories (perspectives) is seen to aid in the gathering and selection of the appropriate performance measures for the enterprise. Four general perspectives have been proposed by the Balanced Scorecard:

1. Financial perspective;
2. Customer perspective;
3. Internal process perspective;
4. Learning and growth perspective.

The financial perspective examines if the companys implementation and execution of its strategy are contributing to the bottom-line improvement of the company. It represents the long-term strategic objectives of the organization and thus it incorporates the tangible outcomes of the strategy in traditional financial terms. The three possible stages as described by Kaplan and Norton (1996) are rapid growth, sustain and harvest. Financial objectives and measures for the growth stage will stem from the development and growth of the organization which will lead to increased sales volumes, acquisition of new customers, growth in revenues etc. The sustain stage on the other hand will be characterized by measures that evaluate the effectiveness of the organization to manage its operations and costs, by calculating the return on investment, the return on capital employed, etc. Finally, the harvest stage will be based on cash flow analysis with measures such as payback periods and revenue volume. Some of the most common financial measures that are incorporated in the financial perspective are EVA, revenue growth, costs, profit margins, cash flow, net operating income etc.

The customer perspective defines the value proposition that the organization will apply in order to satisfy customers and thus generate more sales to the most desired (i.e. the most profitable) customer groups. The measures that are selected for the customer perspective should measure both the value that is delivered to the customer (value position) which may involve time, quality, performance and service and cost and the outcomes that come as a result of this value proposition (e.g., customer satisfaction, market share). The value proposition can be centered on one of the three: operational excellence, customer intimacy or product leadership, while maintaining threshold levels at the other two.

The internal process perspective is concerned with the processes that create and deliver the customer value proposition. It focuses on all the activities and key processes required in order for the company to excel at providing the value expected by the customers both productively and efficiently. These can include both short-term and long-term objectives as well as incorporating innovative process development in order to stimulate improvement. In order to identify the measures that correspond to the internal process perspective, Kaplan and Norton propose using certain clusters that group similar value creating processes in an organization. The clusters for the internal process perspective are operations management (by improving asset utilization, supply chain management, etc), customer management (by expanding and deepening relations), innovation (by new products and services) and regulatory & social (by establishing good relations with the external stakeholders).

The learning and growth perspective is the foundation of any strategy and focuses on the intangible assets of an organization, mainly on the internal skills and capabilities that are required to support the value-creating internal processes. The learning and growth perspective is concerned with the jobs (human capital), the systems (information capital), and the climate (organization capital) of the enterprise. These three factors relate to what Kaplan and Norton claim is the infrastructure that is needed in order to enable ambitious objectives in the other three perspectives to be achieved. This of course will be in the long term, since an improvement in the learning and growth perspective will require certain expenditures that may decrease short-term financial results, whilst contributing to long-term success.

Key Performance Indicators (KPI) of Balanced Scorecard

According to each perspective of the Balanced Scorecard, a number of KPIs can be used such as:
Financial
- Cash flow
- ROI

- Financial Result
- Return on capital employed
- Return on equity

Customer
- Delivery Performance to Customer – by Date
- Delivery Performance to Customer – by Quality
- Customer satisfaction rate
- Customer Loyalty
- Customer retention

Internal Business Processes
- Number of Activities
- Opportunity Success Rate
- Accident Ratios
- Overall Equipment Effectiveness

Learning & Growth
- Investment Rate
- Illness rate
- Internal Promotions
- Employee Turnover
- Gender/Racial Ratios

Benchmarking Methods

Benchmarking is a systematic comparison of organizational processes and performance to create new standards or to improve processes.

Benchmarking models are used to determining how well a business unit, division, organization or corporation is performing compared with other similar organizations. A Benchmark is often used for improving communication, professionalizing the organization / processes or for budgetary reasons. Traditionally, performance measures have been compared with previous measures from the same organization at different times. Although this can be a good indication of the rate of improvement within the organization, it could be that although the organization is improving, the competition is improving faster.

Benchmarking (also "best practice benchmarking" or "process benchmarking") is a process used in management and particularly strategic management, in which organizations evaluate various aspects of their processes in relation to best practice, usually within their own sector. This then allows organizations to develop plans on how to adopt such best practice, usually with the aim of increasing some aspect of performance. Benchmarking may be a one-off event, but is often treated as a continuous process in which organizations continually seek to challenge their practices.

There are four types of benchmarking methods:
1. Internal (benchmark within a corporation, for example between business units)
2. Competitive (benchmark performance or processes with competitors)
3. Functional (benchmark similar processes within an industry)
4. Generic (comparing operations between unrelated industries)

Typically, benchmarking models involves the following benchmarking steps:
- scope definition
- choose benchmark partner(s)
- determine measurement methods, units, indicators and data collection method
- data collection
- analysis of the discrepancies
- present the results and discuss implications / improvement areas and goals
- make improvement plans or new procedures
- monitor progress and plan ongoing benchmark.

Benchmarking is a tough process that needs a lot of commitment to succeed. More than once benchmarking projects end with the 'they are different from us' syndrome or competitive sensitivity prevents the free flow of information that is necessary. However comparing performances and processes with 'best in class' is important and should ideally be done on a continuous basis (the competition is improving its processes also…).

Historically, benchmarking is based on Kaizen and competitive advantage thinking.

Advantages of Benchmarking

Benchmarking is a powerful management tool because it overcomes "paradigm blindness." Paradigm Blindness can be summed up as the mode of thinking, "The way we do it is the best because this is the way we've always done it." Benchmarking opens organizations to new methods, ideas and tools to improve their effectiveness. It helps crack through resistance to change by demonstrating other methods of solving problems than the one currently employed, and demonstrating that they work, because they are being used by others.

Collabourative Benchmarking

Benchmarking, originally invented as a formal process by Rank Xerox, is usually carried out by individual companies. Sometimes it may be carried out collabouratively by groups of companies (eg subsidiaries of a multinational in different countries). One example is that of the Dutch municipally-owned water supply companies, which have carried out a voluntary collabourative benchmarking process since 1997 through their industry association.

There is no single benchmarking process that has been universally adopted. The wide appeal and acceptance of benchmarking has led to various benchmarking methodologies emerging. The most prominent methodology is the 12 stage methodology by Robert Camp (who wrote the first book on benchmarking in 1989).

The 12 stage methodology consisted of:
1. Select subject ahead
2. Define the process
3. Identify potential partners
4. Identify data sources
5. Collect data and select partners
6. Determine the gap
7. Establish process differences
8. Target future performance

9. Communicate
10. Adjust goal
11. Implement
12. Review/recalibrate.

The following is an example of a typical shorter version of the methodology:

Identify your problem areas - Because benchmarking can be applied to any business process or function, a range of research techniques may be required. They include: informal conversations with customers, employees, or suppliers; exploratory research techniques such as focus groups; or in-depth marketing research, quantitative research, surveys, questionnaires, re engineering analysis, process mapping, quality control variance reports, or financial ratio analysis. Before embarking on comparison with other organizations it essential that you know your own organization's function, process; base lining performance provides a point against which improvement effort can be measured.

Identify other industries that have similar processes - For instance if one were interested in improving hand offs in addiction treatment s/he would try to identify other fields that also have hand off challenges. These could include air traffic control, cell phone switching between towers, transfer of patients from surgery to recovery rooms.

Identify organizations that are leaders in these areas - Look for the very best in any industry and in any country. Consult customers, suppliers, financial analysts, trade associations, and magazines to determine which companies are worthy of study.

Survey companies for measures and practices – Companies target specific business processes using detailed surveys of measures and practices used to identify business process alternatives and leading companies. Surveys are typically masked to protect confidential data by neutral associations and consultants.

Visit the "best practice" companies to identify leading edge practices – Companies typically agree to mutually exchange information beneficial to all parties in a benchmarking group and share the results within the group.

Implement new and improved business practices – Take the leading edge practices and develop implementation plans which include identification of specific opportunities, funding the project and selling the ideas to the organization for the purpose of gaining demonstrated value from the process.

Cost of Benchmarking

Benchmarking is a moderately expensive process, but most organizations find that it more than pays for itself. The three main types of costs are:

Visit Costs – This includes hotel rooms, travel costs, meals, a token gift, and lost labour time.

Time Costs – Members of the benchmarking team will be investing time in researching problems, finding exceptional companies to study, visits, and implementation. This will take them away from their regular tasks for part of each day so additional staff might be required.

Benchmarking Database Costs – Organizations that institutionalize benchmarking into their daily procedures find it is useful to create and maintain a database of best practices and the companies associated with each best practice now.

The cost of benchmarking can substantially be reduced through utilizing the many internet resources that have sprung up over the last few years. These aim to capture benchmarks and best practices from organizations, business sectors and countries to make the benchmarking process much quicker and cheaper.

Technical benchmarking or Product Benchmarking

The technique initially used to compare existing corporate strategies with a view to achieving the best possible performance in new situations, has recently been extended to the comparison of technical products. This process is usually referred to as "Technical Benchmarking" or "Product Benchmarking'. Its use is particularly well developed within the automotive industry ("Automotive Benchmarking"), where it is vital to design products that match precise user expectations, at minimum possible cost, by applying the best technologies available worldwide. Many data are obtained by fully disassembling existing cars and their systems. Such analyzes were initially carried out in-house by car makers and their suppliers. However, as they are expensive, they are increasingly outsourced to companies specialized in this area. Indeed, outsourcing has enabled a drastic decrease in costs for each company (by cost sharing) and the development of very efficient tools (standards, software).

Types of Benchmarking

Process benchmarking – the initiating firm focuses its observation and investigation of business processes with a goal of identifying and observing the best practices from one or more benchmark firms. Activity analysis will be required where the objective is to benchmark cost and efficiency; increasingly applied to back-office processes where outsourcing may be a consideration.

Financial benchmarking – performing a financial analysis and comparing the results in an effort to assess your overall competitiveness.

Performance benchmarking – allows the initiator firm to assess their competitive position by comparing products and services with those of target firms.

Product benchmarking – the process of designing new products or upgrades to current ones. This process can sometimes involve reverse engineering which is taking apart competitors products to find strengths and weaknesses.

Strategic benchmarking – involves observing how others compete. This type is usually not industry specific meaning it is best to look at other industries.

Functional benchmarking – a company will focus its benchmarking on a single function in order to improve the operation of that particular function. Complex functions such as Human Resources, Finance and Accounting and Information and Communication Technology are unlikely to be directly comparable in cost and efficiency terms and may need to be disaggregated into processes to make valid comparison.

Benefit-Cost Analysis (BCA)

Benefit-Cost Analysis (BCA) is a tool for organizing information on the relative value of alternative public investments like environmental restoration projects. When the value of all significant benefits and costs can be expressed in monetary terms, the net value (benefits minus costs) of the alternatives under consideration can be computed and used to identify the alternative that yields the greatest increase in public welfare. However, since environmental goods and services are not commonly bought or sold in the marketplace, it can be difficult to express the outputs of an environmental restoration project in monetary terms. A couple of things can be done to overcome this. Either specialized measurement techniques must be used to estimate the value of goods and services produced by the project techniques that can be expensive and whose results can reflect a much higher degree of uncertainty or alternative analytical methods must be used to allow the "apples and oranges" comparisons of monetary costs and non-monetized outputs.

The tools associated with BCA and value estimation have been developed to evaluate the overall economic efficiency of proposed actions, but the efficient use of resources is only one of many important social goals. Equity and justice are two others. For this reason, traditional BCA or alternative tools for assessing efficiency should not be used without also considering such factors as distributional effects (who pays vs. who benefits) and environmental justice (disproportionate share of negative impacts born by low-income and minority populations).

Traditional Benefit-Cost Analysis BCA

BCA analysis is commonly used to evaluate the economic feasibility of traditional public expenditures. Harbor deepening projects, for example, are usually evaluated using BCA since most of the costs and benefits of the deepening alternatives can be easily expressed in monetary terms. The costs are the monetary costs of mobilizing and operating a dredge for the initial deepening and for future maintenance dredging. The benefits are the transportation cost savings that result from being able to use larger, more efficient ships or from more fully loading the large ships that are already in use. However, there are many complicating factors in this apparently straightforward example.

First, a lot of money must be spent up front to deepen a harbor, but the benefits are realized little by little over time. That time span must be accounted for because a dollar spent today is worth more than a dollar received next year, even when you ignore the effects of inflation. This principle is what economists call the "time value of money." It reflects the fact that a dollar received today can be invested or saved in an interest bearing account and next year will be worth anywhere from $1.04 to $1.15 or more. In investment decisions, the time value of money is accounted for by using a discount rate to put the entire stream of benefits and costs on equal temporal footing expressing all benefits and costs in terms of their worth at a single point in time. Most economists agree that the discount rate used to evaluate public investments should be equal to the average rate of return of funds in the private sector. In its 1999 publication, "Discounting And The Treatment Of Uncertainty In Natural Resource Damage Assessment," NOAA's Damage Assessment and Restoration Programme explains it like this: "Each dollar spent on assessment, emergency restoration, or restoration represents a dollar that is not allocated to another use. These costs are discounted at a rate that represents the productivity of alternative uses of these funds in the economy." However, economists do not agree on the magnitude of the "opportunity" cost of capital–sometimes called the""social discount rate"–or even on how it should be measured. In the interim, most government agencies use the cost of government borrowing as a surrogate for the social discount rate.

Second, not all the costs of harbor deepening can easily be monetized. There are very real costs, for example, associated with the resuspension of contaminated sediments, the use of upland sites or ocean bottom for the disposal of materials, and the loss of marine life, such as loggerhead turtles, during the dredging process. But even when the expected environmental impacts of proposed alternatives are explicitly evaluated and quantified, the costs are usually not monetized. When they are treated separately in an environmental assessment, their full impact may not be appropriately reflected in the final ranking of alternatives.

Third, deep-draft navigation projects are funded in part by the federal government and in part by a non-federal sponsor usually a state port authority. The resulting transportation cost savings are shared by a number of parties port authorities; shipping companies; U.S. producers and foreign consumers of exported goods; and foreign producers and U.S. consumers of imported goods all share in the cost savings. Any consideration of the goodness of the fit between who is paying for the project and who is benefiting from it must happen outside the framework of BCA. The distributional effects of publicly funded projects must be considered from the standpoints of equity and justice.

Fourth, harbor deepening can result in significant externalities benefits or costs that are not directly generated by the investment under consideration, but that are the indirect result of that investment. When there are significant externalities, a plan may seem cost-effective only because project costs are passed on to someone else. Thus, calculated benefits, costs, and benefit-cost ratios can differ significantly from the project's true value to society.

For example, the improved efficiency of a deeper navigation channel often induces the flow of additional traffic as U.S. goods become more competitive in foreign markets and foreign goods become more competitive in U.S. markets. This induced traffic can result in externalities in the form of uncompensated social costs associated with the added noise, light, traffic, and pollution. These costs are as real as dredging costs, whether they show up in declining property values or quality of life. Either the social and environmental costs of these negative impacts or the cost of their avoidance should be included in benefit-cost analyses. However, they usually are not because they are hard to predict, hard to measure, and sometimes hard to express in monetary terms.

Finally, it is possible that many of the supposed benefits would have occurred without public expenditures for harbor deepening. Perhaps one of the most important and difficult components of BCA is the definition of the most likely future without-project condition, which forms the baseline against which all the with-project alternatives are measured.

Alternative Analytical Methods

If a correct application of BCA to a traditional civil works project like harbor deepening is problematic, its application to environmental restoration projects is even more so. Many outputs of environmental restoration projects cleaner water, greater species diversity, improved ecosystem health aren't commonly bought and sold in the marketplace. That doesn't make them less valuable, but it does greatly increase the difficulty of measuring their value and expressing it in monetary terms.

According to Orth et al. (1998), "[d]ecisions regarding potential investments in watershed resources can leave decision makers comparing 'apples to oranges' when the costs of watershed improvements are measurable in dollars but the benefits are not." There are two ways to address this problem: (1) estimate the monetary value of environmental benefits or (2) develop tools to help decision makers compare apples with oranges. Some tools for comparing apples and oranges will be described in the next three paragraphs.

When it's not possible or desirable to monetize the benefits of the project alternatives that are being evaluated, as would be needed for BCA, there are other economic tools that can help resource managers incorporate cost considerations into decision-making. Two of the most commonly used tools are closely related to BCA Cost-Effectiveness Analysis and Incremental Analysis.

Cost-Effectiveness Analysis (CEA) is used when there are two or more ways to achieve the same goal or to produce the same type and level of outputs. Given some environmental goal, such as enabling specified numbers and types of anadromous fish to pass a low dam, CEA helps users to identify the least-costly means of achieving that goal. When correctly applied, CEA takes into account the full stream of project costs, including construction, maintenance, and monitoring costs, as well as the time-value of money. Unlike BCA, CEA cannot be used to identify optimal plans when outcomes are dissimilar either in type or magnitude, but it does support the incorporation of cost considerations into decision-making.

Incremental Analysis (IA) is used primarily to evaluate alternatives that produce varying quantities of similar outputs. If, for example, the salinity of a wetland has been altered by a series of culverts and channel modifications, IA can be used to rank each increment of restoration (e.g., replacing culverts and restoring altered stream morphology) in terms of their cost-effectiveness. Like BCA and CEA, IA takes into account the full stream of project costs and the time value of money, and, like CEA, it does not require that the value of outputs be monetized. Unlike CEA, it does require that the outputs be quantified. In the example above, analysts would need an estimate of the salinity change associated with each increment of improvement.

Blue Ocean Strategy

Blue Ocean Strategy is a business strategy book that promotes a systematic approach "for making the competition irrelevant." The authors, W.Chan Kim and Rene Mauborgne, are professors of Strategy and Management at INSEAD (is an international graduate business school and research institution with campuses in France and in Singapore). A core idea is to create a leap in value for both the company and its buyers by breaking the differentiation/low cost trade-off and to align product value and profit propositions.

Blue Ocean Strategy is the result of a decade-long study of 150 strategic moves spanning more than 30 industries over a period of 120 years (1880-2000). In addition to retrospective case studies, the book offers theoretical approaches and practical tools to create and capture "blue oceans" of uncontested market space ripe for growth. Kim and Mauborgne argue that tomorrow's leading companies will succeed not by battling competitors, but by creating these blue oceans. This best seller sold more than a million copies in its first year of publication and is being published in 39 languages.

The Six Principles of Blue Ocean Strategy	
Formulation principles	*Risk factor each principle attenuates*
Reconstruct market boundaries	↓ Search risk
Focus on the big picture, not the numbers	↓ Planning risk
Reach beyond existing demand	↓ Scale risk
Get the strategic sequence right	↓ Business model risk
Execution principles	*Risk factor each principle attenuates*
Over come key organizational hurdles	↓ Organizational risk
Build execution into strategy	↓ Management risk
Red Ocean Versus Blue Ocean Strategy	
Red Ocean Strategy	*Blue Ocean Strategy*
Compete in existing market space.	Create uncontested market space.
Beat the competition.	Make the competition irrelevant.
Exploit existing demand.	Create and capture new demand.
Make the value-cost trade off.	Break the value-cost trade-off.
Align the whole system of a firm's activities with its strategic choice of differentiation of low cost.	Align the whole system of a firm's activities in pursuit of differentiation and low cost.

General Concept of Blue Ocean Strategy

The metaphor of red and blue oceans describes the market universe. Red oceans are all the industries in existence today the known market space. In the red oceans, industry boundaries are defined and accepted, and the competitive rules of the game are known. Here companies try to outperform their rivals to grab a greater share of product or service demand. As the market space gets crowded, prospects for profits and growth are reduced. Products become commodities or niche, and cutthroat competition turns the red ocean bloody. Hence, the term red oceans.

Blue oceans, in contrast, denote all the industries not in existence today the unknown market space, untainted by competition. In blue oceans, demand is created rather than fought over. There is ample opportunity for growth that is both profitable and rapid. In blue oceans, competition is irrelevant because the rules of the game are waiting to be set. Blue ocean is an analogy to describe the wider, deeper potential of market space that is not yet explored.

The corner-stone of Blue Ocean Strategy is 'Value Innovation'. A blue ocean is created when a company achieves value innovation that creates value simultaneously for both the buyer and the company. The innovation (in product, service, or delivery) must raise and create value for the market, while simultaneously reducing or eliminating features or services that are less valued by the current or future market. The authors critique Michael Porter's idea that successful business are either low-cost providers or niche-players. Instead, they propose finding value that crosses conventional market segmentation and offering value and lower cost.

This idea was originally proposed by Prof. Charles W. L. Hill from Michigan State University in 1988. Prof. Hill claimed that Porter's model was flawed because differentiation can be a means for firms to achieve low cost. Prof. Hill proposed that a combination of differentiation and low cost may be necessary for firms to achieve a sustainable competitive advantage.

Many others have proposed similar strategies. For example, Swedish professors Jonas Ridderstrale and Kjell Nordstrom in their 1999 book "Funky Business" follow a similar line of reasoning. For example, "competing factors" in Blue Ocean Strategy are similar to the definition of "finite and infinite dimensiones" in Funky Business. Just as Blue Ocean Strategy claims that a Red Ocean Strategy does not guarantee success, Funky Business explained that "Competitive Strategy is the route to nowhere". Funky Business argues that firms need to create "Sensational Strategies". Just like Blue Ocean Strategy, a Sensational Strategy is about "playing a different game" according to Ridderstrale and Nordstrom. Ridderstrale and Nordstrom also claim that the aim of companies is to create temporary monopolies. Kim and Mauborgne explain that the aim of companies is to create blue oceans, that will eventually turn red. This is the same idea expressed in the form of an analogy. Ridderstrale and Nordstrom also claimed in 1999 that "in the slow-growth 1990s overcapacity is the norm in most businesses". Kim and Mauborgne claim that blue ocean strategy make sense in a world that supply exceeds demand.

Preceding Work

The contents of the book are based on more than fifteen years of research and a series of Harvard Business Review articles as well as academic articles on various dimensions of the topic.

Kim and Mauborgne studied about one hundred fifty strategic moves made from 1880-2000 in more than thirty industries and closely examined the relevant business players in each . They analyzed the winning business players as well as the less successful competitors. Studied industries included hotels, cinemas, retail stores, airlines, energy, computers, broadcasting, construction, automotive and steel. They searched for convergence among the more and less successful players. Divergence across the two groups was also studied to discover the common factors leading to strong growth and the key differences separating those winners from the mere survivors and the losers. Kim and Mauborgne defined a consistent and common pattern across all the seemingly idiosyncratic success stories and first called it value innovation, and then Blue Ocean Strategy.

Research results were first published in 1997 in a Harvard Business Review article by Kim and Mauborgne titled "Value Innovation: The Strategic Logic of High Growth". The ideas, tools and frameworks were tested and refined over the years in corporate practice in Europe, the United States and Asia and presented in the following eight additional articles, before being published in the form of a book in 2005.

- 1997. "Fair Process: Managing in the Knowledge Economy". Harvard Business Review 75, January-February, 102-112.
- 1998. Procedural Justice, Strategic Decision Making and the Knowledge Economy." Strategic Management Journal, April.
- 1999. "Creating New Market Space." Harvard Business Review 77, January-February, 83-93.
- 1999. "Strategy, Value Innovation, and the Knowledge Economy." Sloan Management Review 40, no.3, Spring.
- 2000. "Knowing a Business Idea When You See One." Harvard Business Review 78, September-October, 129-141.
- 2002. "Charting Your Company's Future." Harvard Business Review 80, June, 76-85.
- 2003. "Tipping Point Leadership." Harvard Business Review 81, April, 60-69.
- 2004. "Blue Ocean Strategy." Harvard Business Review, October, 76-85.

The name "Blue Ocean Strategy" was introduced in the Harvard Business Review article published in October 2004. The book builds on and extends the work presented in these articles by providing a narrative arc that draws all these ideas together to offer a unified framework for creating and capturing blue oceans.

Examples of Blue Ocean Strategy

Some examples of companies that may have created new market spaces in the opinion of Kim and Mauborgne include ;

Cirque du Soleil: Blending of opera and ballet with circus format while eliminating star performer and animals;

Netjets: fractional jet ownership;

Southwest Airlines: offering flexibility of bus travel at the speed of air travel using secondary airports;

Curves: redefining market boundaries between health clubs and home exercise Programmes for women, and;

Home Depot: offering the prices and range of lumberyard, while offering consumers classes to help them with DIY projects.

Dyson: Vacuum Cleaners

Recent Application Examples of Blue Ocean Stratey

Reports of businesses using Blue Ocean Strategy concepts include:

1. Nintendo's Wii: An example of this strategy is the success of the Nintendo Wii and DS, which Nintendo designed to target audiences not traditionally known to play videogames. By simplifying its interface (through a touchscreen on the DS and motion controls on the Wii) and by marketing software which is designed to complement daily life rather than create escapist experiences(games such as Wii sports, Wii fit, Brain Training) Nintendo has manged to spark greater mainstream appeal than any previous consoles, news stories have detailed its appeal to those who have never played video games before. In addition both the Wii and the DS have faced supply issues throughout their lifetimes, forcing Nintendo to have to ramp up production rates repeatedly to try and keep up with demand for its systems.

2. China Mobile: China Mobile CEO Wang Jianzhou talked about China's hinterland as a classic "blue-ocean market," where the company is casting its net widely without worrying about getting tangled up with the nets of rivals.

3. Pitney Bowes: Michael Critelli, the departing CEO of Pitney Bowes, explained how Pitney Bowes created the Advanced Concept & Technology Group (ACTG), a unit responsible for identifying and developing new products outside. Critelli cited ACTG's development of a machine, which enables people to design and print their own postage from their desktops, as an example of a blue ocean strategic move.

4. Starwood: One group which has been exploring blue ocean thinking for the past three years is Starwood Hotels and Resorts. In an interview to INSEAD Knowledge, Robyn Pratt, Vice President, Six Sigma and Operational Innovation talks about how they are taking a step by step approach to implementing the concept.

Blue Ocean Strategy vs. Competition Based Strategies

Kim and Mauborgne argue that traditional competition-based strategies (red ocean strategies) while necessary, are not sufficient to sustain high performance. Companies need to go beyond competing. To seize new profit and growth opportunities they also need to create blue oceans.

The authors argue that competition based strategies assume that an industry's structural conditions are given and that firms are forced to compete within them, an assumption based on what academics call the structuralist view, or environmental determinism.To sustain themselves in the marketplace, practitioners of red ocean strategy focus on building advantages over the competition, usually by assessing what competitors do and striving to do it better. Here, grabbing a bigger share of the market is seen as a zero-sum game in which one company's gain is achieved at another company's loss. Hence, competition, the supply side of the equation, becomes the defining variable of strategy. Here, cost and value are seen as trade-offs and a firm chooses a distinctive cost or differentiation position. Because the total profit level of the industry is also determined exogenously by structural factors, firms principally seek to capture and redistribute wealth instead of creating wealth. They focus on dividing up the red ocean, where growth is increasingly limited.

Blue ocean strategy, on the other hand, is based on the view that market boundaries and industry structure are not given and can be reconstructed by the actions and beliefs of industry players. This is what the authors call reconstructionist view. Assuming that structure and market boundaries exist only in managers minds, practitioners who hold this view do not let existing market structures limit their thinking. To them, extra demand is out there, largely untapped. The crux of the problem is how to create it. This, in turn, requires a shift of attention from supply to demand, from a focus on competing to a focus on value innovation that is, the creation of innovative value to unlock new demand. This is achieved via the simultaneous pursuit of differentiation and low-cost. As market structure is changed by breaking the value/cost tradeoff, so are the rules of the game. Competition in the old game is therefore rendered irrelevant. By expanding the demand side of the economy new wealth is created. Such a strategy therefore allows firms to largely play a non-zero-sum game, with high payoff possibilities.

Tools and Frameworks of Blue Ocean Strategy

Blue Ocean Strategy has introduced a number of practical tools, methodologies and frameworks to formulate and execute Blue Ocean Strategies, attempting to make creation of blue oceans a systematic, repeatable process. Some of these are listed below;

Basic Tools of Blue Ocean Strategy

- The strategy canvas
- The Four Actions framework
- Eliminate-Reduce-Raise-Create Grid
- The initial litmus test for BOS: focus, divergence, compelling tagline

Frameworks / Methodologies Applicable to Strategy Execution

- Tipping Point Leadership approach
- Four Organizational Hurdles framework
- Kingpins approach, Fishbowl management, atomization
- Hot spots, cold spots and consigliere approach
- 3 E principles of Fair Process

Additional Tools / Methodologies / Frameworks for Strategy Formulation

- The six paths framework
- The sequence of Blue Ocean Strategy
- Buyer Utility map
- Buyer experience cycle
- The profit model of Blue Ocean Strategy
- Price corridor of the mass model
- Four Step Visualizing Strategy Process
- Pioneer-Migrator Settler Map
- Three tiers of noncustomers framework

Criticisms about Blue Ocean Modelling

While co-authors, Professor Kim and Affiliate Professor Mauborgne, propose approaches to finding uncontested market space, at the present there are few if any success stories of companies that applied their theories. This hole in their data persists despite the publication of Value Innovation concepts since 1997. A critical question is whether this book and its related ideas are descriptive rather than prescriptive. The authors present many examples of successful innovations, and then explain from their Blue Ocean perspective – essentially interpreting success through their lenses.

The research process followed by the authors has been criticized on several grounds. No control group was used. There is no way to know how many companies exploiting a blue ocean strategy concept failed. The theory therefore does not meet the falsifiability criteria in practice. A deductive process was not followed. The examples in the book are selected to "tell a winning story".

A whole chapter of the book explaining what the authors call "Tipping Point Leadership" is based on a conclusion that the drop in crime in New York city was caused by a change in policies, actions, and leadership. However, according to the book Freakonomics, crime rates dropped due to an increase in abortion rates several years earlier. Crime rates fell simultaneously in cities other than New York that had not applied what the authors call Tipping Point Leadership.

Brand and communication are taken for granted and do not represent a key for success. Kim and Maubourgne take the marketing of a value innovation as a given, assuming the marketing success will come as a matter of course.

The book only presents a snaphot overview of 3 industries: automobiles, computers and movie theaters.

It is argued that rather than a theory, Blue Ocean Strategy is an extremely successful attempt to brand a set of already existing concepts and frameworks with a highly "sticky" idea. The blue ocean/red ocean analogy is a powerful and memorable metaphor, which is responsible for its popularity. This metaphor can be powerful enough to stimulate people to action. However, the concepts behind the Blue Ocean Strategy (such as the competing factors, the consumer cycle, non-customers, etc.) are not new. Many of these tools are also used by Six Sigma practitioners and proposed by other management gurus.

Bricks and Clicks Model

Bricks-and-clicks is a business model by which a company integrates both offline (bricks) and online (clicks) presences. It is also known as click-and-mortar or clicks-and-bricks, as well as bricks, clicks and flips, flips referring to catalogues.

For example, an electronics store may allow the user to order online, but pick up their order immediately at a local store, which the user finds using locator software. Conversely, a furniture store may have displays at a local store from which a customer can order an item electronically for delivery.

The bricks and clicks model has typically been used by traditional retailers who have extensive logistics and supply chains. Part of the reason for its success is that it is far easier for a traditional retailer to establish an online presence than it is for a start-up company to employ a successful pure "dot com" strategy, or for an online retailer to establish a traditional presence (including a strong brand).

The success of the model in many sectors has destroyed the credibility of analysts who argued that the Internet would render traditional retailers obsolete through disintermediation.

Advantages of the Bricks and Clicks model

Click and mortar firms have the advantage in areas of existing products and services. In these cases there are major advantages in retaining ties to a physical company. This is because they are able to use their competencies and assets, which include:

Core competency. Successful firms tend to have one or two core competencies that they can do better than their competitors. It may be anything from new product development to customer service. When a bricks and mortar firm goes online it is able to use this core competency more intensively and extensively.

Existing supplier networks. Existing firms have established relationships of trust with suppliers. This usually ensures problem free delivery and an assured supply. It can also entail price discounts and other preferential treatment.

Existing distribution channels. As with supplier networks, existing distribution channels can ensure problem free delivery, price discounts, and preferential treatments.

Brand equity. Often existing firms have invested large sums of money in brand advertising over the years. This equity can be leveraged on-line by using recognized brand names. An example is Disney.

Stability. Existing firms that have been in business for many years appear more stable. People trust them more than pure on-line firms. This is particularly true in financial services.

Existing customer base. Because existing firms already have a base of sales, they can more easily obtain economies of scale in promotion, purchasing and production; economies of scope in distribution and promotion; reduced overhead allocation per unit; and shorter break even times.

A lower cost of capital. Established firms will have a lower cost of capital. Bond issues may be available to existing firms that are not available to dot coms. The underwriting cost of a dot com IPO is higher than an equivalent brick and click equity offering.

Learning curve advantages. Every industry has a set of best practices that are more or less known to established firms. New dot coms will be at a disadvantage unless they can redefine the industry's best practices and leap frog existing firms.

Pure dot coms, on the other hand, have the advantage in areas of new e-business models that stress cost efficiency. They are not burdened with brick and mortar costs and can offer products at very low marginal cost.

Business Process Reengineering (BPR)

Business process reengineering (BPR) is a management approach aiming at improvements by means of elevating efficiency and effectiveness of the processes that exist within and across organizations. The key to BPR is for organizations to look at their business processes from a "clean slate" perspective and determine how they can best construct these processes to improve how they conduct business.

Business process reengineering is also known as BPR, Business Process Redesign, Business Transformation, or Business Process Change Management.

History of Business Process Reengineering

In 1990, Michael Hammer, a former professor of computer science at the Massachusetts Institute of Technology (MIT), published an article in the Harvard Business Review, in which he claimed that the major challenge for managers is to obliterate non-value adding work, rather than using technology for automating it (Hammer 1990). This statement implicitly accused managers of having focused on the wrong issues, namely that technology in general, and more specifically information technology, has been used primarily for automating existing work rather than using it as an enabler for making non-value adding work obsolete.

Hammer's claim was simple: Most of the work being done does not add any value for customers, and this work should be removed, not accelerated through automation. Instead, companies should reconsider their processes in order to maximize customer value, while minimizing the consumption of resources required for delivering their product or service. A similar idea was advocated by Thomas H. Davenport and J. Short (1990), at that time a member of the Ernst & Young research center, in a paper published in the Sloan Management Review the same year as Hammer published his paper.

This idea, to unbiasedly review a companys business processes, was rapidly adopted by a huge number of firms, which were striving for renewed competitiveness, which they had lost due to the market entrance of foreign competitors, their inability to satisfy customer needs, and their insufficient cost structure. Even well established management thinkers, such as Peter Drucker and Tom Peters, were accepting and advocating BPR as a new tool for (re-)achieving success in a dynamic world. During the following years, a fast growing number of publications, books as well as journal articles, was dedicated to BPR, and many consulting firms embarked on this trend and developed BPR methods. However, the critics were fast to claim that BPR was a way to dehumanize the work place, increase managerial control, and to justify downsizing, i.e. major reductions of the work force (Greenbaum 1995, Industry Week 1994), and a rebirth of Taylorism under a different label.

Despite this critique, reengineering was adopted at an accelerating pace and by 1993, as many as 65% of the Fortune 500 companies claimed to either have initiated reengineering efforts, or to have plans to do so. This trend was fueled by the fast adoption of BPR by the consulting industry, but also by the study Made in America, conducted by MIT, that showed how companies in many US industries had lagged behind their foreign counterparts in terms of competitiveness, time-to-market and productivity.

Definition of BPR

Different definitions can be found. This section contains the definition provided in notable publications in the field.

Hammer and Champy (1993) define BPR as

"… the fundamental rethinking and radical redesign of business processes to achieve dramatic improvements in critical contemporary measures of performance, such as cost, quality, service, and speed."

Thomas H. Davenport (1993), another well-known BPR theorist, uses the term process innovation, which he says

"… encompasses the envisioning of new work strategies, the actual process design activity, and the implementation of the change in all its complex technological, human, and organizational dimensions."

Additionally, Davenport (ibid.) points out the major difference between BPR and other approaches to organization development (OD), especially the continuous improvement or TQM movement, when he states:

"Today firms must seek not fractional, but multiplicative levels of improvement 10x rather than 10%."

Finally, Johansson et al. (1993) provide a description of BPR relative to other process-oriented views, such as Total Quality Management (TQM) and Just-in-time (JIT), and state:

"Business Process Reengineering, although a close relative, seeks radical rather than merely continuous improvement. It escalates the efforts of JIT and TQM to make process orientation a strategic tool and a core competence of the organization. BPR concentrates on core business processes, and uses the specific techniques within the JIT and TQM toolboxes as enablers, while broadening the process vision."

In order to achieve the major improvements BPR is seeking for, the change of structural organizational variables, and other ways of managing and performing work is often considered as being insufficient. For being able to reap the achievable benefits fully, the use of information technology (IT) is conceived as a major contributing factor. While IT traditionally has been used for supporting the existing business functions, i.e. it was used for increasing organizational efficiency, it now plays a role as enabler of new organizational forms, and patterns of collabouration within and between organizations.

BPR derives its existence from different disciplines, and four major areas can be identified as being subjected to change in BPR – organization, technology, strategy, and people – where a process view is used as common framework for considering these dimensions. The approach can be graphically depicted by a modification of "Leavitt's diamond" (Leavitt 1965).

Business strategy is the primary driver of BPR initiatives and the other dimensions are governed by strategy's encompassing role. The organization dimension reflects the structural elements of the company, such as hierarchical levels, the composition of organizational units, and the distribution of work between them. Technology is concerned with the use of computer systems and other forms of communication technology in the business. In BPR, information technology is generally considered as playing a role as enabler of new forms of organizing and collabourating, rather than supporting existing business functions. The people / human resources dimension deals with aspects such as education, training, motivation and reward systems. The concept of business processes – interrelated activities aiming at creating a value added output to a customer – is the basic underlying idea of BPR. These processes are characterized by a number of attributes: Process ownership, customer focus, value-adding, and cross-functionality.

The Role of Information Technology

Information technology (IT) has historically played an important role in the reengineering concept. It is considered by some as a major enabler for new forms of working and collabourating within an organization and across organizational borders.

The early BPR literature, e.g. Hammer and Champy (1993), identified several so called disruptive technologies that were supposed to challenge traditional wisdom about how work should be performed.

1. Shared databases, making information available at many places
2. Expert systems, allowing generalists to perform specialist tasks
3. Telecommunication networks, allowing organizations to be centralized and decentralized at the same time
4. Decision-support tools, allowing decision-making to be a part of everybody's job
5. Wireless data communication and portable computers, allowing field personnel to work office independent
6. Interactive videodisk, to get in immediate contact with potential buyers
7. Automatic identification and tracking, allowing things to tell where they are, instead of requiring to be found
8. High performance computing, allowing on-the-fly planning and revisioning

In the mid 1990s, especially workflow management systems were considered as a significant contributor to improved process efficiency. Also ERP (Enterprise Resource Planning) vendors, such as SAP, positioned their solutions as vehicles for business process redesign and improvement.

Methodology of Business Process Reengineering

Although the labels and steps differ slightly, the early methodologies that were rooted in IT-centric BPR solutions share many of the same basic principles and elements. The following outline is one such model, based on the PRLC (Process Reengineering Life Cycle) approach developed by Guha et.al. (1993).

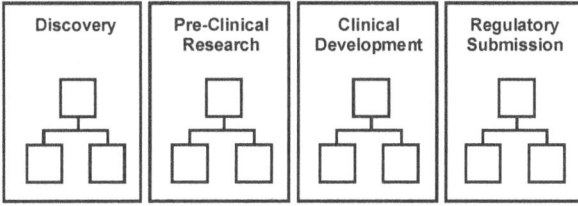

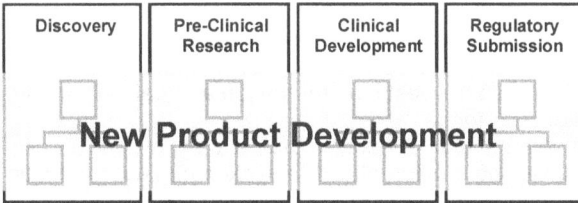

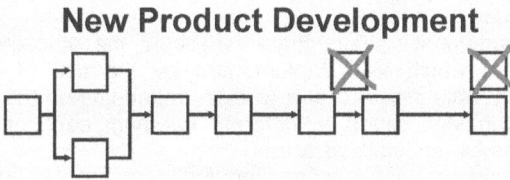

New Product Development

Benefiting from lessons learned from the early adopters, some BPR practitioners advocated a change in emphasis to a customer-centric, as opposed to an IT-centric, methodology. One such methodology, that also incorporated a Risk and Impact Assessment to account for the impact that BPR can have on jobs and operations, was described by Lon Roberts (1994). Roberts also stressed the use of change management tools to proactively address resistance to changea factor linked to the demise of many reengineering initiatives that looked good on the drawing board.

BPR – A Rebirth of Scientific Management?

By its critics, BPR is often accused to be a re-animation of Taylor's principles of scientific management, aiming at increasing productivity to a maximum, but disregarding aspects such as work environment and employee satisfaction. It can be agreed that Taylor's theories, in conjunction with the work of the early administrative scientists have had a considerable impact on the management discipline for more than 50 years. However, it is not self-evident that BPR is a close relative to Taylorism and this proposed relation deserves a closer investigation.

In the late 19th century Frederick Winslow Taylor, a mechanical engineer, started to develop the idea of management as a scientific discipline. He applied the premise that work and its organizational environment could be considered and designed upon scientific principles, i.e. that work processes could be studied in detail using a positivist analytic approach. Upon the basis of this analysis, an optimal organizational structure and way of performing all work tasks could be identified and implemented. However, he was not the one to originally invent the concept. In 1886, a paper entitled "The Engineer as Economist", written by Henry R. Towne for the American Society of Mechanical Engineers, had laid the bedrock for the development of scientific management.

The basic idea of scientific management was that work could be studied from an objective scientific perspective and that the analysis of the gathered information could be used for increasing productivity, especially of blue-collar work, significantly. Taylor (1911) summarized his observations in the following four principles:

1. Observation and analysis through time study to set the optimal production rate. In other words, develop a science for each mans task a One Best Way.
2. Scientifically select the best man for the job and train him in the procedures he is expected to follow.
3. Cooperate with the man to ensure that the work is done as described. This means establishing a differential rate system of piece work and paying the man on an incentive basis, not according to the position.
4. Divide the work between managers and workers so that managers are given the responsibility for planning and preparation of work, rather than the individual worker.

Scientific management's main characteristic is the strict separation of planning and doing, which was implemented by the use of a functional foremanship system. This means that a worker, depending on the task that he or she is performing, can report to different foreman, each of them being responsible for a small, specialized area.

Taylor's ideas had a major impact on manufacturing, but also administration. One of the most well-known examples is Ford Motor Co., which adopted the principles of scientific management at an early stage, and built its assembly line for the T-model based on Taylor's model of work and authority distribution, thereby giving name to Fordism.

Later on, Taylor's ideas were extended by the time and motion studies performed by Frank Gilbreth and his wife Lillian. Henry Gantt, a co-worker of Taylor, developed Taylor's idea further, but placed more emphasis on the worker. He developed a reward system that no longer took into account only the output of the work, but was based on a fixed daily wage, and a bonus for completing the task.

Taylor's work can be, and has been, criticized many times for degrading individuals to become machinelike. One of the most famous critiques of the situation that an application of scientific management could result in, is shown in Charles Chaplin's movie "Modern Times (film)". Despite that fact, Taylor was inspired by the vision of creating a workplace that is beneficial to all members of the organization, both management and workers.

When looking at Taylor's ideas retrospectively, we can conclude, that they very well fitted the organizations of the early 20th century. The kind of organization he proposed requires certain pre-conditions, which were satisfied in the technological and socio-economic environment of his time and the heritage from economic individualism and a Protestant view of work. However, despite the good intention of designing organizations where managers and workers could jointly contribute to the common achievements, Taylor missed the fact that he had been building his principles on wrong assumptions. There are some major critical points that can be brought forward against Taylor's concept.

The strict belief in man being totally rational, and the history of Protestant ethic, which considered work as being a manifestation of religious grace, made him disregard the crucial issue of human behaviour and the fact that money is insufficient as the single source of motivation (Tawney 1954).

The lack of considering the organizational environment as a conceivable factor, and the overemphasis on organizational efficiency. As Thompson (1969) notes:

"Scientific management, focusing primarily on manufacturing or similar production activities, clearly employs economic efficiency as its ultimate criterion and achieves conceptual closure of the organization by assuming that goals are known, tasks are repetitive, output of the production process somehow disappears, and resources in uniform qualities are available."

If accepting Thompson's critique as valid and relevant, it can be concluded that the strict hierarchical organization seems to be unfit to take on the challenges that are imposed by fierce competition and dynamic market structures. Due to the focus on improvement through repetition and resource uniformity, the applicability on organizations and processes without these characteristics, such as pharmaceutical R&D, can be questioned.

Peter Drucker noted a third problem related to scientific management, namely that there was no real concern about technology, i.e. that Taylor considered his theory as being general, and that it could be applied to any organization, independently of the technology used. Drucker (1972) stated:

"Scientific management was not concerned with technology. It took tools and technology as givens."

This point brings forward a clear argument against the application of Taylor's principles and methodologies for improving today's organizations. Considering that the rapid development in the IT field actually constitutes a driving force in itself, it appears to be unfit to employ organizational concepts that neglect the changing and enabling role of technology. On the other hand we can argue that the application of scientific management in the early 20st century, as we look at it retrospectively, must be considered as the contemporary use of a concept that would look and be applied in a different way today. Taylor did not neglect technology, he considered it as an important contributor to organizational performance, but given the pace of development, he could not consider it as a major driver of change.

Looking at the suggested relationship between BPR and Taylor's principles we can conclude that primarily Thompson's and Drucker's criticism build a strong case against BPR being a successor of Taylorism. An organizational concept that does not take into account changing business environments and rapid technological advancements is not fit for serving as an improvement method today. Also the BPR literature offers a harsh critique of the continuous application of tayloristic principles in the modern business world, thus rejecting the separation of planning and doing and the strict functional division of labour. BPR proponents claim that taking BPR for Taylorism is a major misunderstanding of the concept, and responsible for a considerable number of reengineering project failures. On the other hand, there is also a similarity which stems from the methodological approach: Both scientific management and BPR have a focus on productivity and efficient use of resources that can be achieved through an optimum process design and its subsequent deployment. The following quote, referring to scientific management can equally be used to describe the intention of reengineering:

"To conduct the undertaking toward its objectives by seeking to derive optimum advantage from all available resources." (Loyd 1994)

At the same time it cannot be denied, that the implementation of process-based organizations in practice often is accompanied by massive lay-offs and an emphasis on managerial control. A study by CSC Index from 1994 revealed that 73% of the companies applying BPR reduced their workforce with an average of 21%. Thomas Davenport, an early contributor to the BPR-field, provided a harsh critique against labeling substantial workforce reductions reengineering and in a paper from 1995 he stated that:

"Reengineering didn't start out as a code word for mindless bloodshed ... The [other] thing to remember about the start of reengineering is that the phrase massive layoffs was never part of the early vocabulary." (Davenport, 1995)

Successes of Business Process Reengineering

BPR, if implemented properly, can give huge returns. BPR has helped giants like Procter and Gamble Corporation and General Motors Corporation succeed after financial drawbacks due to competition. It helped American Airlines somewhat get back on track from the bad debt that is currently haunting their business practice. BPR is about the proper method of implementation..

General Motors Corporation implemented a 3-year plan to consolidate their multiple desktop systems into one. It is known internally as "Consistent Office Environment" (Booker, 1994). This reengineering process involved replacing the numerous brands of desktop systems, network operating systems and application development tools into a more manageable number of vendors and technology platforms. According to Donald G. Hedeen, director of desktops and deployment at GM and manager of the upgrade Programme, he says that the process "lays the foundation for the implementation of a common business communication strategy across General Motors." (Booker, 1994). Lotus Development Corporation and Hewlett-Packard Development Company, formerly Compaq Computer Corporation, received the single largest non-government sales ever from General Motors Corporation. GM also planned to use Novell NetWare as a security client, Microsoft Office and Hewlett-Packard printers. According to Donald G. Hedeen, this saved GM 10% to 25% on support costs, 3% to 5% on hardware, 40% to 60% on software licensing fees, and increased efficiency by overcoming incompatibility issues by using just one platform across the entire company.

Michael Dell is the founder and CEO of DELL Incorporated, which has been in business since 1983 and has been the world's fastest growing major PC Company. Michael Dell's idea of a successful business is to keep the smallest inventory possible by having a direct link with the manufacturer. When a customer places an order, the custom parts requested by the customer are automatically sent to the manufacturer for shipment. This reduces the cost for inventory tracking and massive warehouse maintenance. Dell's website is noted for bringing in nearly "$10 million each day in sales."(Smith, 1999). Michael Dell mentions: "If you have a good strategy with sound economics, the real challenge is to get people excited about what you're doing. A lot of businesses get off track because they don't communicate an excitement about being part of a winning team that can achieve big goals. If a company can't motivate its people and it doesn't have a clear compass, it will drift." (Smith, 1999) Dell's stocks have been ranked as the top stock for the decade of the 1990s, when it had a return of 57,282% (Knestout and Ramage, 1999). Michael Dell is now concentrating more on customer service than selling computers since the PC market price has pretty much equalized. Michael Dell notes: "The new frontier in our industry is service, which is a much greater differentiator when price has been equalized. In our industry, there's been a pretty huge gap between what customers want in service and what they can get, so they've come to expect mediocre service. We may be the best in this area, but we can still improve quite a bit in the quality of the product, the availability of parts, service and delivery time." (Smith, 1999) Michael Dell understands the concept of BPR and really recognizes where and when to reengineer his business.

Ford reengineered their business and manufacturing process from just manufacturing cars to manufacturing quality cars, where the number one goal is quality. This helped Ford save millions on recalls and warranty repairs. Ford has accomplished this goal by incorporating barcodes on all their parts and scanners to scan for any missing parts in a completed car coming off of the assembly line. This helped them guarantee a safe and quality car. They have also implemented Voice-over-IP (VoIP) to reduce the cost of having meetings between the branches.

A multi-billion dollar corporation like Procter and Gamble Corporation, which carries 300 brands and growing really has a strong grasp in re-engineering. Procter and Gamble Corporation's chief technology officer, G. Gil Cloyd, explains how a company which carries multiple brands has to contend with the "classic innovator's dilemma most innovations fail, but companies that don't innovate die. His solution, innovating innovation…" (Teresko, 2004). Cloyd has helped a company like Procter and Gamble grow to $5.1 billion by the fiscal year of 2004. According to Cloyd's scorecard, he was able to raise the volume by 17%, the organic volume by 10%, sales are at $51.4 billion up by 19%, with organic sales up 8%, earnings are at $6.5 billion up 25% and share earnings up 25%. Procter and Gamble also has a free cash flow of $7.3 billion or 113% of earnings, dividends up 13% annually with a total shareholder return of 24%. Cloyd states: "The challenge we face is the competitive need for a very rapid pace of innovation. In the consumer products world, we estimate that the required pace of innovation has doubled in the last three years. Digital technology is very important in helping us to learn faster." (Teresko, 2004) G. Gil Cloyd also predicts, in the near future, "as much as 90% of P&G's R&D will be done in a virtual world with the remainder being physical validation of results and options." (Teresko, 2004).

Critiques against Business Process Reengineering

The most frequent and harsh critique against BPR concerns the strict focus on efficiency and technology and the disregard of people in the organization that is subjected to a reengineering initiative. Very often, the label BPR was used for major workforce reductions. Thomas Davenport, an early BPR proponent, stated that:

"When I wrote about "business process redesign" in 1990, I explicitly said that using it for cost reduction alone was not a sensible goal. And consultants

Michael Hammer and James Champy, the two names most closely associated with reengineering, have insisted all along that layoffs shouldn't be the point. But the fact is, once out of the bottle, the reengineering genie quickly turned ugly." (Davenport, 1995).

Michael Hammer similarly admitted that:

"I wasn't smart enough about that. I was reflecting my engineering background and was insufficient appreciative of the human dimension. I've learned that's critical." (White, 1996)

Criticisms against the BPR

- lack of management support for the initiative and thus poor acceptance in the organization.
- exaggerated expectations regarding the potential benefits from a BPR initiative and consequently failure to achieve the expected results.
- underestimation of the resistance to change within the organization.
- implementation of generic so-called best-practice processes that do not fit specific company needs.
- overtrust in technology solutions.
- performing BPR as a one-off project with limited strategy alignment and long-term perspective.
- poor project management.

BPR Development after 1995

With the publication of critiques in 1995 and 1996 by some of the early BPR proponents, coupled with abuses and misuses of the concept by others, the reengineering fervor in the U.S. began to wane. Since then, considering business processes as a starting point for business analysis and redesign has become a widely accepted approach and is a standard part of the change methodology portfolio, but is typically performed in a less radical way as originally proposed.

More recently, the concept of Business Process Management (BPM) has gained major attention in the corporate world and can be considered as a successor to the BPR wave of the 1990s, as it is evenly driven by a striving for process efficiency supported by information technology. Equivalently to the critique brought forward against BPR, BPM is now accused of focusing on technology and disregarding the people aspects of change.

Capability Maturity Model (CMM)

The Capability Maturity Model model is an organizational model that describes 5 evolutionary stages (levels) in which an organization manages its processes.

Capability Maturity Model (CMM) describes 5 evolutionary stages in which an organization manages its processes. The thought behind the Capability Maturity Model, originally developed for software development, is that an organization should be able to absorb and carry its software applications. The model also provides specific steps and activities to get from one level to the next.

The 5 Stages of the Capability Maturity Model are:

1. Initial (processes are ad-hoc, chaotic, or actually few processes are defined).

Management Theory and Principles

2. Repeatable (basic processes are established and there is a level of discipline to stick to these processes)
3. Defined (all processes are defined, documented, standardized and integrated into each other)
4. Managed (processes are measured by collecting detailed data on the processes and their quality)
5. Optimizing (continuous process improvement is adopted and in place by quantitative feedback and from piloting new ideas ands technologies)

The Capability Maturity Model is useful not only for software development, but also for describing evolutionary levels of organizations in general and in order to describe the level of Value Based Management that an organization has realized or wants to aim for.

Capability Maturity Model

The Capability Maturity Model (CMM) is a process capability maturity model which aids in the definition and understanding of an organization's processes.

The CMM was originally described in the book Managing the Software Process (Addison Wesley Professional, Massachusetts, 1989). The CMM was conceived by Watts Humphrey, who based it on the earlier work of Phil Crosby. Active development of the model by the SEI (US Dept. of Defense Software Engineering Institute) began in 1986. The SEI was at Carnegie Mellon University in Pittsburgh.

The CMM was originally intended as a tool for objectively assessing the ability of government contractors' processes to perform a contracted software project. Though it comes from the area of software development, it can be (and has been and still is being) applied as a generally applicable model to assist in understanding the process capability maturity of organizations in diverse areas. For example, software engineering, system engineering, project management, risk management, system acquisition, information technology (IT), personnel management. It has been used extensively for avionics software and government projects around the world.

Though still thus widely used as a general tool, for software development purposes the CMM has been superseded by CMMI (Capability Maturity Model Integration). The old CMM was renamed to Software Engineering CMM (SE-CMM) and organizations accreditations based on SE-CMM expired on the 31st of December, 2007.

Other variants of the CMM include Software Security Engineering CMM SSE-CMM and People CMM. Other maturity models such as ISM3 have also emerged.

Maturity model

A maturity model is a structured collection of elements that describe certain aspects of maturity in an organization. A maturity model may provide, for example:

- a place to start
- the benefit of a communitys prior experiences
- a common language and a shared vision
- a framework for prioritizing actions
- a way to define what improvement means for your organization.

A maturity model can be used as a benchmark for assessing different organizations for equivalent comparison. The model describes the maturity of the company based upon the project the company is handling and the related clients.

Structure of Capability Maturity Model (CMM)

The CMM involves the following aspects:

1. Maturity Levels: It is a layered framework providing a progression to the discipline needed to engage in continuous improvement (It is important to state here that an organization develops the ability to assess the impact of a new practice, technology, or tool on their activity. Hence it is not a matter of adopting these, rather it is a matter of determining how innovative efforts influence existing practices. This really empowers projects, teams, and organizations by giving them the foundation to support reasoned choice.)

2. Key Process Areas: A Key Process Area (KPA) identifies a cluster of related activities that, when performed collectively, achieve a set of goals considered important.

3. Goals: The goals of a key process area summarize the states that must exist for that key process area to have been implemented in an effective and lasting way. The extent to which the goals have been accomplished is an indicator of how much capability the organization has established at that maturity level. The goals signify the scope, boundaries, and intent of each key process area.

4. Common Features: Common features include practices that implement and institutionalize a key process area. These five types of common features include: Commitment to Perform, Ability to Perform, Activities Performed, Measurement and Analysis, and Verifying Implementation.

5. Key Practices: The key practices describe the elements of infrastructure and practice that contribute most effectively to the implementation and institutionalization of the key process areas.

Levels of the CMM

There are five levels of the CMM. According to the SEI:

"Predictability, effectiveness, and control of an organization's software processes are believed to improve as the organization moves up these five levels. While not rigorous, the empirical evidence to date supports this belief."

Level 1 – Initial : At maturity level 1, processes are usually not documented and change based on the user or event. The organization does not have a stable environment and may not know or understand all of the components that make up the environment. As a result, success in these organizations depends on the institutional knowledge, the competence and heroics of the people in the organization, and the level of effort expended by the team. In spite of this chaotic environment, maturity level 1 organizations often produce products and services; however, they frequently exceed the budget and schedule of their projects. Due to the lack of formality, level 1 organizations, often over commit, abandon processes during a crisis, and are unable to repeat past successes. There is very little planning and executive buy-in for projects and process acceptance is limited. IT organizations at level 1 are often seen as a service instead of a partner.

Level 2 – Repeatable : At maturity level 2, some software development processes are repeatable, possibly with consistent results. The processes may not repeat for all the projects in the organization. The organization may use some basic project management to track cost and schedule.

Process discipline is unlikely to be rigorous, but where it exists it may help to ensure that existing practices are retained during times of stress. When these practices are in place, projects are performed and managed according to their documented plans.

Project status and the delivery of services are visible to management at defined points (for example, at major milestones and at the completion of major tasks).

Basic project management processes are established to track cost, schedule, and functionality. The minimum process discipline is in place to repeat earlier successes on projects with similar applications and scope. There is still a significant risk of exceeding cost and time estimates.

Level 3 – Defined : The organization's set of standard processes, which are the basis for level 3, are established and subject to some degree of improvement over time. These standard processes are used to establish consistency across the organization. Projects establish their defined processes by applying the organizations set of standard processes, tailored, if necessary, within similarly standardized guidelines.

The organization's management establishes process objectives for the organizations set of standard processes, and ensures that these objectives are appropriately addressed.

Level 4 – Managed : Using process metrics, management can effectively control the process (e.g., for software development). In particular, management can identify ways to adjust and adapt the process to particular projects without measurable losses of quality or deviations from specifications. Organizations at this level set quantitative quality goals for both software process and software maintenance. Subprocesses are selected that significantly contribute to overall process performance. These selected subprocesses are controlled using statistical and other quantitative techniques. A critical distinction between maturity level 3 and maturity level 4 is the predictability of process performance. At maturity level 4, the performance of processes is controlled using statistical and other quantitative techniques, and may be quantitatively predictable. At maturity level 3, processes are only qualitatively predictable.

Level 5 – Optimizing : Maturity level 5 focuses on continually improving process performance through both incremental and innovative technological improvements. Quantitative process-improvement objectives for the organization are established, continually revised to reflect changing business objectives, and used as criteria in managing process improvement. The effects of deployed process improvements are measured and evaluated against the quantitative process-improvement objectives. Both the defined processes and the organizations set of standard processes are targets of measurable improvement activities.

Process improvements to address common causes of process variation and measurably improve the organization's processes are identified, evaluated, and deployed.

Optimizing processes that are nimble, adaptable and innovative depends on the participation of an empowered workforce aligned with the business values and objectives of the organization. The organization's ability to rapidly respond to changes and opportunities is enhanced by finding ways to accelerate and share learning.

A critical distinction between maturity level 4 and maturity level 5 is the type of process variation addressed. At maturity level 4, processes are concerned with addressing special causes of process variation and providing statistical predictability of the results. Though processes may produce predictable results, the results may be insufficient to achieve the established objectives. At maturity level 5, processes are concerned with addressing common causes of process variation and changing the process (that is, shifting the mean of the process performance) to improve process performance (while maintaining statistical probability) to achieve the established quantitative process-improvement objectives.

Extensions of CMM

Recent versions of CMMI from SEI indicate a "level 0", characterized as "Incomplete". Many observers leave this level out as redundant or unimportant, but Pressman and others make note of it.

Anthony Finkelstein extrapolated that negative levels are necessary to represent environments that are not only indifferent, but actively counterproductive, and this was refined by Tom Schorsch as the Capability Immaturity Model.

Key Process Areas of Capability Immaturity Model CMM

The CMMI contains several key process areas indicating the aspects of product development that are to be covered by company processes.

Key Process Areas of the Capability Maturity Model Integration (CMMI)

Abbreviation	Name	Area	Maturity Level
REQM	Requirements Management	Engineering	2
PMC	Project Monitoring and Control	Project Management	2
PP	Project Planning	Project Management	2
SAM	Supplier Agreement Management	Project Management	2
CM	Configuration Management	Support	2
MA	Measurement and Analysis	Support	2
PPQA	Process and Product Quality Assurance	Support	2
PI	Product Integration	Engineering	3
RD	Requirements Development	Engineering	3
TS	Technical Solution	Engineering	3
VAL	Validation	Engineering	3
VER	Verification	Engineering	3
OPD	Organizational Process Definition	Process Management	3

Abbreviation	Name	Area	Maturity Level
OPF	Organizational Process Focus	Process Management	3
OT	Organizational Training	Process Management	3
IPM	Integrated Project Management	Project Management	3
ISM	Integrated Supplier Management	Project Management	3
IT	Integrated Teaming	Project Management	3
RSKM	Risk Management	Project Management	3
DAR	Decision Analysis and Resolution	Support	3
OEI	Organizational Environment for Integration	Support	3
OPP	Organizational Process Performance	Process Management	4
QPM	Quantitative Project Management	Project Management	4
OID	Organizational Innovation and Deployment	Process Management	5
CAR	Causal Analysis and Resolution	Support	5

History Capability Maturity Model

The Capability Maturity Model was initially funded by military research. The United States Air Force funded a study at the Carnegie-Mellon Software Engineering Institute to create an abstract model for the military to use as an objective evaluation of software subcontractors. The result was the Capability Maturity Model, published as Managing the Software Process in 1989. The CMM is no longer supported by the SEI and has been superseded by the more comprehensive Capability Maturity Model Integration (CMMI), of which version 1.2 has now been released.

Context of Capability Maturity Model

In the 1970s, technological improvements made computers more widespread, flexible, and inexpensive. Organizations began to adopt more and more computerized information systems and the field of software development grew significantly. This led to an increased demand for developersand managerswhich was satisfied with less experienced professionals.

Unfortunately, the influx of growth caused growing pains; project failure became more commonplace not only because the field of computer science was still in its infancy, but also because projects became more ambitious in scale and complexity. In response, individuals such as Edward Yourdon, Larry Constantine, Gerald Weinberg, Tom DeMarco, and David Parnas published articles and books with research results in an attempt to professionalize the software development process.

Watts Humphrey's Capability Maturity Model (CMM) was described in the book Managing the Software Process (1989). The CMM as conceived by Watts Humphrey was based on the work a decade earlier of Phil Crosby who published the Quality Management Maturity Grid in his book Quality is Free in 1979. Active development of the model by the SEI (US Dept. of Defense Software Engineering Institute) began in 1986.

The CMM was originally intended as a tool to evaluate the ability of government contractors to perform a contracted software project. Though it comes from the area of software development, it can be, has been, and continues to be widely applied as a general model of the maturity of processes (e.g., IT Service Management processes) in IS/IT (and other) organizations.

Note that the first application of a staged maturity model to IT was not by CMM/SEI, but rather Richard L. Nolan in 1973.

The model identifies five levels of process maturity for an organisation:
1. Initial (chaotic, ad hoc, heroic) the starting point for use of a new process.
2. Repeatable (project management, process discipline) the process is used repeatedly.
3. Defined (institutionalized) the process is defined/confirmed as a standard business process.
4. Managed (quantified) process management and measurement takes place.
5. Optimising (process improvement) process management includes deliberate process optimization/improvement.

Within each of these maturity levels are KPAs (Key Process Areas) which characterise that level, and for each KPA there are five definitions identified:
1. Goals
2. Commitment
3. Ability
4. Measurement
5. Verification

The KPAs are not necessarily unique to CMM, representing as they do the stages that organizations must go through on the way to becoming mature.

The assessment is supposed to be led by an authorised lead assessor. One way in which companies are supposed to use the model is first to assess their maturity level and then form a specific plan to get to the next level. Skipping levels is not allowed.

N.B.: The CMM was originally intended as a tool to evaluate the ability of government contractors to perform a contracted software project. It may be suited for that purpose. When it became a general model for software process improvement, there were many critics.

"Shrinkwrap" companies are also called "COTS" or commercial-off-the-shelf firms or software package firms. They include Claris, Apple, Symantec, Microsoft, and Lotus, amongst others. Many such companies rarely if ever managed their requirements documents as formally as the CMM described in order to achieve level 2, and so all of these companies would probably fall into level 1 of the model.

Origins of Capability Maturity Model

In the 1980s, several military projects involving software subcontractors ran over-budget and were completed much later than planned, if they were completed at all. In an effort to determine why this was occurring, the United States Air Force funded a study at the SEI. The result of this study was a model for the military to use as an objective evaluation of software subcontractors. In 1989, the Capability Maturity Model was published as Managing the Software Process. The basis for the model is the Quality Management Maturity Grid introduced by Philip Crosby in his 1979 book 'Quality is Free'.

Timeline of CMM

1987: SEI-87-TR-24 (SW-CMM questionnaire), released.
1989: Managing the Software Process, published.
1990: SW-CMM v0.2, released (first external issue).
1991: SW-CMM v1.0, released.
1993: SW-CMM v1.1, released.
1997: SW-CMM revisions halted in support for CMMI.
2000: CMMI v1.02, released.
2002: CMMI v1.1, released.
2006: CMMI v1.2, released.

Current State of Capability Maturity Model

Although these models have proved useful to many organizations, the use of multiple models has been problematic. Further, applying multiple models that are not integrated within and across an organization is costly in terms of training, appraisals, and improvement activities. The CMM Integration project was formed to sort out the problem of using multiple CMMs. The CMMI Product Team's mission was to combine three source models:

1. The Capability Maturity Model for Software (SW-CMM) v2.0 draft C
2. The Systems Engineering Capability Model (SECM)
3. The Integrated Product Development Capability Maturity Model (IPD-CMM) v0.98

Supplier Sourcing

CMMI is the designated successor of the three source models. The SEI has released a policy to sunset the Software CMM and previous versions of the CMMI. The same can be said for the SECM and the IPD-CMM; these models were superseded by CMMI.

Future direction of Capability Maturity Model

With the release of the CMMI Version 1.2 Product Suite, the possibility of multiple CMMI models was created. There is now a CMMI for Development (CMMI-DEV), V1.2[1] and a CMMI for Acquisition (CMMI-ACQ), V1.2. A version of the CMMI for Services is being developed by a Northrop Grumman-led team under the auspices of the SEI, with participation from Boeing, Lockheed Martin, Raytheon, SAIC, SRA, and Systems and Software Consortium (SSCI).

Suggestions for improving CMMI are welcomed by the SEI. For information on how to provide feedback.

In some cases, CMMI can be combined with other methodologies. It is commonly used in conjunction with the ISO 9001 standard. JPMorgan Chase & Co. tried combining CMM with Extreme Programmeming (XP), and Six Sigma. They found that the three systems reinforced each other well, leading to better development, and did not mutually contradict, Six Sigma and CMMI.

Controversial Aspects of Capability Maturity Model

The software industry is diverse and volatile. All methodologies for creating software have supporters and critics, and the CMM is no exception.

The CMM was developed to give Defense organizations a yardstick to assess and describe the capability of software contractors to provide software on time, within budget, and to acceptable standards. It has arguably been successful in this role, even reputedly causing some software sales people to clamour for their organizations' software engineers/developers to "implement CMM."

The CMM is intended to enable an assessment of an organization's maturity for software development. It is an important tool for outsourcing and exporting software development work. Economic development agencies in India, Brazil, Ireland, Egypt, Syria, and elsewhere have praised the CMM for enabling them to be able to compete for US outsourcing contracts on an even footing.

The CMM provides a good framework for organizational improvement. It allows companies to prioritize their process improvement initiatives.

Criticisms about Capability Maturity Model

CMM has failed to take over the world. It's hard to tell exactly how wide spread it is as the SEI only publishes the names and achieved levels of compliance of companies that have requested this information to be listed. The most current Maturity Profile for CMMI is available online.

CMM is well suited for bureaucratic organizations such as government agencies, large corporations and regulated monopolies. If the organizations deploying CMM are large enough, they may employ a team of CMM auditors reporting their results directly to the executive level. (A practice encouraged by SEI.) The use of auditors and executive reports may influence the entire IT organization to focus on perfectly completed forms rather than application development, client needs or the marketplace. If the project is driven by a due date, CMMs intensive reliance on process and forms may become a hindrance to meeting the due date in cases where time to market with some kind of product is more important than achieving high quality and functionality of the product.

Suggestions of scientifically managing the software process with metrics only occur beyond the Fourth level. There is little validation of the processes cost savings to business other than a vague reference to empirical evidence. It is expected that a large body of evidence would show that adding all the business overhead demanded by CMM somehow reduces IT headcount, business cost, and time to market without sacrificing client needs.

No external body actually certifies a software development center as being CMM compliant. It is supposed to be an honest self-assessment. Some organizations misrepresent the scope of their CMM compliance to suggest that it applies to their entire organization rather than a specific project or business unit.

The CMM does not describe how to create an effective software development organization. The CMM contains behaviors or best practices that successful projects have demonstrated. Being CMM compliant is not a guarantee that a project will be successful, however being compliant can increase a project's chances of being successful.

The CMM can seem to be overly bureaucratic, promoting process over substance. For example, for emphasizing predictability over service provided to end users. More commercially successful methodologies (for example, the Rational Unified Process) have focused not on the capability of the organization to produce software to satisfy some other organization or a collectively-produced specification, but on the capability of organizations to satisfy specific end user "use cases" as per the Object Management Group's UML (Unified Modeling Language) approach.

From the systemic perspective, the CMM(I) represents a (n+1) classical engineering approach which does not take under consideration numerous human cognitive, organizational and cultural factors, essential for the success of every projects. On the other hand, a process design is strongly connected with the process carrier systems and their requested functions and goals, these clear computational relations are especially important for the validation of the results of the CMM(I) applications. It seems, the CMM(I) requires yet a solid theoretical ontological and epistemological background in order to be a trustworthy standard, for an example only, the arbitrary initial choice of the levels and Key Process Areas are not sufficiently motivated.

Critical analysis of CMM has been published in at least two papers. Bach raises questions about the validity of CMM's assertions regarding what constitutes good software-development processes. Bollinger and McGowan discuss flaws in CMM's use of assembly-line process models. They show that manufacturing is fundamentally different than software development, as the former is primarily concerned with replication and the latter with design.

The Most Beneficial Elements of CMM Level 2 and 3

Creation of Software Specifications, stating what is going to be developed, combined with formal sign off, an executive sponsor and approval mechanism. This is NOT a living document, but additions are placed in a deferred or out of scope section for later incorporation into the next cycle of software development.

A Technical Specification, stating how precisely the thing specified in the Software Specifications is to be developed will be used. This is a living document.

Peer Review of Code (Code Review) with metrics that allow developers to walk through an implementation, and to suggest improvements or changes. (Note – This is problematic because the code has already been developed, and a bad design potentially cannot be fixed by "tweaking".) The Code Review gives complete code a formal approval mechanism.

Version Control – a very large number of organizations have no formal revision control mechanism or release mechanism in place.

The idea that there is a "right way" to build software, that it is a scientific process involving engineering design and that groups of developers are not there to simply work on the problem du jour.

Companies Appraised Against the CMMI

Many IT companies across the world are making forays up the CMMI level ladder. One must be very skeptical about a company claiming that they have obtained a certain level (the higher level, the more skeptical to be) of CMM at an "enterprise level." Usually this is used as a marketing technique that may indeed apply to some project done by the company at some time, but most unlikely achieved by the enterprise.

Competitive Advantage

Porter's Competitive advantage (CA) is a position that a firm occupies in its competitive landscape. Michael Porter posits that a competitive advantage, sustainable or not, exists when a company makes economic rents, that is, their earnings exceed their costs (including cost of capital). That means that normal competitive pressures are not able to drive down the firm's earnings to the point where they cover all costs and just provide minimum sufficient additional return to keep capital invested. Most forms of competitive advantage cannot be sustained for any length of time because the promise of economic rents drives competitors to duplicate the competitive advantage held by any one firm.

A firm possesses a Sustainable Competitive Advantage (SCA) when it has value-creating processes and positions that cannot be duplicated or imitated by other firms that lead to the production of above normal rents. An SCA is different from a competitive advantage (CA) in that it provides a long-term advantage that is not easily replicated. But these above-normal rents can attract new entrants who drive down economic rents. A CA is a position a firm attains that lead to above-normal rents or a superior financial performance. The processes and positions that engender such a position are not necessarily non-duplicable or inimitable.

Analysis of the factors of profitability is the subject of numerous theories of strategy including the five forces model pioneered by Michael Porter of the Harvard Business School.

In marketing and strategic management, sustainable competitive advantage is an advantage that one firm has relative to competing firms. The source of the advantage can be something the company does that is distinctive and difficult to replicate, also known as a core competency — for example Procter & Gamble's ability to derive superior consumer insights and implement them in managing its brand portfolio. It can also be an asset such as a brand (e.g. Coca Cola) or a patent, such as Viagra. It can also simply be a result of the industry's cost structure — for example, the large fixed costs that tend to create natural monopolies in utility industries. To be sustainable, the competitive advantage must be:

- distinctive, and
- proprietary

In the past decades, IT is becoming more and more important. Especially the internet plays a major role in todays world and not to forget in businesses. The ability to effectively manage information helps organizations dealing with changes in the environment, which can result in a competitive advantage over other firms. An example of gaining competitive advantage: Organizations make information available for each other in an efficient way in order to reduce all difficulties of purchasing, marketing and distribution.

In 2006, Jaynie L. Smith authored Creating Competitive Advantage (Doubleday). This book outlines how companies fail to understand their own existing competitive advantages and use them in sales/marketing. She provides a framework for how companies can evaluate their own operations and develop competitive advantage/competitive positioning statements to better hone their sales/marketing messages. Competitive advantage statements help distinguish companies by highlighting what they offer to the customer using tangible terms and concepts. The next step is to test those CA statements through independent market research. This allows a company to understand their customers' hierarchy of buying criteria in an objective indepenedent context. From there, companies can tailor their CA statements to speak directly to the buying interests of the customer.

COMPETITIVE ADVANTAGE

		Lower Cost	Differentiation
COMPETITIVE SCOPE	Broad Target	1. Cost Leadership	2. Differentiation
	Narrow Target	3. Cost Focus	3b. Differentiation Focus

Competitive Advantage

Competitive Advantage: a company is said to have a competitive advantage over its rivals when its profitability is greater than the average profitability of all other companies competing for the same set of customers.

Sustainable Competitive Advantage

Sustainable Competitive Advantage: a company has a sustained competitive advantage when its strategies enable it to maintain above-average profitability for a number of years.

Competitive advantages vary from situation to situation and from time to time. Some basic examples of CAs can be divided in 4 main global areas:

1. **Cost:** Low-cost operations
2. **Quality:** High quality, Consistent quality
3. **Time:** Delivery speed, On-time delivery, Development speed
4. **Flexibility:** Customization, Volume flexibility, Variety

Porter's Generic Competitive Strategies (Ways of Competing)

A firm's relative position within its industry determines whether a firm's profitability is above or below the industry average. The fundamental basis of above average profitability in the long run is sustainable competitive advantage. There are two basic types of competitive advantage a firm can possess: low cost or differentiation. The two basic types of competitive advantage combined with the scope of activities for which a firm seeks to achieve them, lead to three generic strategies for achieving above average performance in an industry: cost leadership, differentiation, and focus. The focus strategy has two variants, cost focus and differentiation focus.

1. **Cost Leadership :** In cost leadership, a firm sets out to become the low cost producer in its industry. The sources of cost advantage are varied and depend on the structure of the industry. They may include the pursuit of economies of scale, proprietary technology, preferential access to raw materials and other factors. A low cost producer must find and exploit all sources of cost advantage. if a firm can achieve and sustain overall cost leadership, then it will be an above average performer in its industry, provided it can command prices at or near the industry average.

2. **Differentiation :** In a differentiation strategy a firm seeks to be unique in its industry along some dimensions that are widely valued by buyers. It selects one or more attributes that many buyers in an industry perceive as important, and uniquely positions itself to meet those needs. It is rewarded for its uniqueness with a premium price.

3. **Focus :** The generic strategy of focus rests on the choice of a narrow competitive scope within an industry. The focuser selects a segment or group of segments in the industry and tailors its strategy to serving them to the exclusion of others.

The focus strategy has two variants: (a) In cost focus a firm seeks a cost advantage in its target segment, while in; (b) differentiation focus a firm seeks differentiation in its target segment. Both variants of the focus strategy rest on differences between a focuser's target segment and other segments in the industry. The target segments must either have buyers with unusual needs or else the production and delivery system that best serves the target segment must differ from that of other industry segments. Cost focus exploits differences in cost behaviour in some segments, while differentiation focus exploits the special needs of buyers in certain segments.

Core Competencies

A core competency is something that a firm can do well and that meets the following three conditions specified by Gary Hamel and C.K. Prahalad (1990):

1. Core competency provides consumer benefits
2. Core competency is not easy for competitors to imitate
3. Core competency can be leveraged widely to many products and markets.

A core competency can take various forms, including technical/subject matter know how, a reliable process, and/or close relationships with customers and suppliers (Mascarenhas et al. 1998). It may also include product development or culture such as employee dedication. Modern business theories suggest that most activities that are not part of a company's core competency should be outsourced.

If a core competency yields a long term advantage to the company, it is said to be a sustainable competitive advantage.

Development of the Core competency Concept

The concept of core competencies was developed in the management field. C.K. Prahalad and Gary Hamel introduced the concept in a 1990 Harvard Business Review article. They wrote that a core competency is "an area of specialized expertise that is the result of harmonizing complex streams of technology and work activity." As an example they gave Honda's expertise in engines. Honda was able to exploit this core competency to develop a variety of quality products from lawn mowers and snow blowers to trucks and automobiles. To take an example from the automotive industry, it has been claimed that Volvos core competency is safety. This however, is perhaps the end result of their competency in terms of customer benefit. Their core competency might be more about their ability to source and design high protection components, or to research and respond to market demands concerning safety.

Ever since Prahalad and Hamel introduced the term in the 1990's many researchers have tried to highlight and further illuminate the meaning of core competency. According to D. Leonard-Barton (1992), "Capabilities are considered core if they differentiate a company strategically." On the other hand Galunic and Rodan (1998) argue that "a core competency differentiates not only between firms but also inside a firm it differentiates amongst several competencies. In other words, a core competency guides a firm recombining its competencies in response to demands from the environment."

For example, Black and Decker's core technological competencies pertain to 200 to 600 W electric motors, and this motor is their core product. All of their end products are modifications of this basic technology (with the exception of their work benches, flash lights, battery charging systems, toaster ovens, and coffee percolators).

They produce products for three markets:
- the home workshop market: In the home workshop market, small electric motors are used to produce drills, circular saws, sanders, routers, rotary tools, polishers, and drivers
- the home cleaning and maintenance market: In the home cleaning and maintenance market, small electric motors are used to produce dust busters, etc.
- the kitchen appliance market: In the kitchen appliance market, small electric motors are used to produce can openers, food processors, blenders, bread makers, and fans.

Characteristics of Core Competencies

There are three tests for Core Competencies:
1. Potential access to a wide variety of markets – the core competency must be capable of developing new products and services
2. A core competency must make a significant contribution to the perceived benefits of the end product.
3. Core Competencies should be difficult for competitors to imitate. In many industries, such competencies are likely to be unique.

Core competencies are those capabilities that are critical to a business achieving competitive advantage. The starting point for analysing core competencies is recognising that competition between businesses is as much a race for competence mastery as it is for market position and market power. Senior management cannot focus on all activities of a business and the competencies required to undertake them. So the goal is for management to focus attention on competencies that really affect competitive advantage.

The Work of Hamel and Prahalad

The main ideas about Core Competencies where developed by C.K. Prahalad and Gary Hamel through a series of articles in the Harvard Business Review followed by a best-selling book – Competing for the Future. Their central idea is that over time companies may develop key areas of expertise which are distinctive to that company and critical to the company's long term growth.

'In the 1990s managers will be judged on their ability to identify, cultivate, and exploit the core competencies that make growth possible – indeed, they'll have to rethink the concept of the corporation it self.' C K Prahalad and G Hamel 1990

These areas of expertise may be in any area but are most likely to develop in the critical, central areas of the company where the most value is added to its products.

For example, for a manufacturer of electronic equipment, key areas of expertise could be in the design of the electronic components and circuits. For a ceramics manufacturer, they could be the routines and processes at the heart of the production process. For a software company the key skills may be in the overall simplicity and utility of the Programme for users or alternatively in the high quality of software code writing they have achieved.

Core Competencies are not seen as being fixed. Core Competencies should change in response to changes in the company's environment. They are flexible and evolve over time. As a business evolves and adapts to new circumstances and opportunities, so its Core Competencies will have to adapt and change.

Identifying Core Competencies

Prahalad and Hamel suggest three factors to help identify core competencies in any business:

What does the Core Competence Achieve?	Comments / Examples
Provides potential access to a wide variety of markets	The key core competencies here are those that enable the creation of new products and services. **Example:** Why has Saga established such a strong leadership in supplying financial services (e.g. insurance) and holidays to the older generation? Core Competencies that enable Saga to enter apparently different markets: - Clear distinctive brand proposition that focuses solely on a closely-defined customer group - Leading direct marketing skills – database management; direct-mailing campaigns; call centre sales conversion - Skills in customer relationship management
Makes a significant contribution to the perceived customer benefits of the end product	Core competencies are the skills that enable a business to deliver a fundamental customer benefit – in other words: what is it that causes customers to choose one

	product over another? To identify core competencies in a particular market, ask questions such as "why is the customer willing to pay more or less for one product or service than another?" "What is a customer actually paying for? **Example:** Why have Tesco been so successful in capturing leadership of the market for online grocery shopping? Core competencies that mean customers value the Tesco.com experience so highly: - Designing and implementing supply systems that effectively link existing shops with the Tesco.com web site - Ability to design and deliver a "customer interface" that personalises online shopping and makes it more efficient - Reliable and efficient delivery infrastructure (product picking, distribution, customer satisfaction handling)
Difficult for competitors to imitate	A core competence should be "competitively unique": In many industries, most skills can be considered a prerequisite for participation and do not provide any significant competitor differentiation. To qualify as "core", a competence should be something that other competitors wish they had within their own business. **Example:** Why does Dell have such a strong position in the personal computer market? Core competencies that are difficult for the competition to imitate: - Online customer "bespoking" of each computer built - Minimisation of working capital in the production process - High manufacturing and distribution quality – reliable products at competitive prices

A competence which is central to the business's operations but which is not exceptional in some way should not be considered as a core competence, as it will not differentiate the business from any other similar businesses. For example, a process which uses common computer components and is staffed by people with only basic training cannot be regarded as a core competence. Such a process is highly unlikely to generate a differentiated advantage over rival businesses. However it is possible to develop such a process into a core competence with suitable investment in equipment and training.

It follows from the concept of Core Competencies that resources that are standardised or easily available will not enable a business to achieve a competitive advantage over rivals.

Core Group Theory

Who Really Matters: The Core Group Theory of Power, Privilege and Success starts with a hilarious anecdote about an Exxon Oil employee conference to announce their new "core values". Enshrined as number one on their list of core values was this simple sentence: "The customer comes first". That night there was an executive dinner, and after a few drinks a brash young rising star named Monty proposed a toast. "I just want you to know," he said, "that the customer does not come first." Then Monty named the president of the division, "He comes first." He named the European president. "He comes second." And the North American president. "He comes third." The Far Eastern president "comes fourth." And so on for the fifth, sixth and seventh senior executives of that division, all of whom were in the room. "The customer," concluded Monty, "comes eight." An Exxon retiree who told me this story said: "There was an agonized silence for about ten seconds. I thought Monty would get fired on the spot. Then one of the top people smiled, and the place fell apart in hysterical laughter. It was the first truth spoken all day."

According to Art Kleiner, "The customer comes first" is one of the three great lies of the modern corporation. The other two being: "We make our decisions on behalf of the shareholders" and "Employees are our most important asset."

In Who Really Matters: The Core Group Theory of Power, Privilege and Success Art Kleiner tries to answer the question what is the actual objective of the modern corporation, making the bold statement that what comes first in every organization is keeping the Core Group (normally most of the top executives) satisfied. And yet, according to Kleiner Core Groups are not inherently bad or dysfunctional, but rather necessary and even the best hope we have for ennobling humanity, since organizations are natural amplifiers of human capability. An organization's Core Group is also the source of its energy, drive and direction. or more accurately, any organization goes wherever its people perceive that the Core Group needs and wants to go. Non-members depend upon the Core Group for direction, The Core Group and its members depend upon the non-members for their legitimacy.

You will not often find Core Groups mentioned in any organization chart. They exist in people's hearts and minds only. After some time, organizations will resemble how their Group act and looks like and automatically pivot and twist to give the members of the Core Group what they think they want and need, without even asking them. Great Core Groups hold an essential form of knowledge. They set the context that establishes this knowledge as significant. (Compare: Intellectual Capital).

How do Core Groups become so powerful? Kleiner explains the mechanism is based on guesswork and amplification. People who are not in the Core Group try to guess as good as they can what it is the Core Group wants. So even a casual remark in passing by a Core Group member can be amplified to a shift of direction of an entire division. As a consequence, Top Managers need to be very cautious in what they say. According to Kleiner, concepts like the Balanced Scorecard do not really change this. Although more objective measurements may be used and there is better strategic communication top-down, still a lot of guesswork remains: people assume that they should interpret the numbers according to what they perceive the Core Group really wants, and also people assume they should interpret the Core Group according to the numbers: if the measurements send a clear signal, then people assume that is where the Core Group wants the organization to go. Core Group dynamics also prevent organizations from changing easily according to Kleiner. Both the Core Group and the non-Core Group employees have an interest in maintaining the status quo.

Who Really Matters: The Core Group Theory of Power, Privilege and Success also gives interesting examples of Core Groups: Enron (...), HP, Government Agencies, and includes special chapters on the role labour unions, management consultants and schools play. Art Kleiner ends the book with reflections on Making a Better World, giving important tips and clues on what not to do and what should be done if one wants to influence or even change a Core Group and discussing Corporate Governance, Corporate Purpose and how Core Groups thinking relates to the world we and our children live in.

Are Core Groups and Core Group theory relevant within Value Based Management? Of course they are. Managing for Value (the second of the three components of VBM) should be seen in another perspective if Kleiner is right. Perhaps the "managing" in corporations often is indeed primarily aimed at satisfying the needs of the Core Group. Also executive compensation and corporate governance regulation become even more important then than they already are.

Art Kleiner suggests that is it is possible to create "Expanded-Core-Group Organizations". To do this, the following elements are suggested:

1. employee stock-ownership plans
2. financial literacy
3. non-hierarchical decision-making
4. comprehensive (financial and strategy) training Programmes

This is were Core Group theory is very much like Value Based Management thinking.

Core Group Theory and Vale Based Management

As far as the Value Creation part of VBM is concerned it is important whether one should aim primarily at maximizing shareholder value or stakeholder value or that in reality the Core Group comes first, principally a form of stakeholder value. Core Group dynamics can indeed explain how it is possible that companies adopting the maximizing shareholder philosophy often end up in becoming less responsive to shareholders in a meaningful way. If Core Group members lack adequate knowledge or experience or mistakenly(!) decide that the organization's first job is to keep up the stock price, the easiest way of doing that is the presentation of slowly but steadily growing positive quarterly figures. Through guesswork and amplification the entire organization will follow a Core Group that makes this severe mistake and will support the Core Group in providing a manipulated and wrong picture of the reality instead of what really should be done: taking decisions that maximize shareholder (or stakeholders) value.

Art Kleiner goes one step further saying: "we need a model that recognizes the primacy of the Core Groups while constraining them from abuses of power" and suggests we need a third model (besides stakeholder value and shareholder value): a model that recognizes the primacy of Core Groups while constraining them from abuses of power.

This is where we would slightly disagree with Kleiner: Core Groups are a mechanism, a model that explains who really matters, but not an end. Through writing Who Really Matters: The Core Group Theory of Power, Privilege and Success Art Kleiner has given us a brilliant insight in the dynamics why organizations often fail to implement Value Based Management or their corporate purpose. But Core Groups should not be what really matters. In other words: what really matters for organizations is whether they do what they were created and exist for: taking care of the desired value creation for its shareholders and/or stakeholders (Value Based Management).

For its description and analysis of how Core Groups work, this book should become a management classic and Kleiner's book is highly recommended for any top manager, strategy consultant or corporate governance specialist acting in the field of Value Based Management.

Who Really Matters The Core Group Theory of Power, Privilege and Success

During two decades spent watching organizations at work (and the struggles people had within them), I saw that most of the stated rhetoric about their purpose represents a set of lies:

- Corporations do not exist to return investment to shareholders. (If they did, they would be better at it).
- Non-profits do not exist to fulfill the requirements of their membership (except to the extent they need to do so to keep their membership).
- Government agencies do not exist to fulfill the public interest (especially when it's in the public interest for them to go out of existence).
- Employees are not any organization's greatest asset.
- The customer does not come first.

Who, Then, Does?

It varies, depending on the organization – but in every one of them, there is some "Core Group" of key people who matter more than anyone else when decisions are made. The Core Group of any organization won't be named in a formal hierarchy chart, contract, or constitution. It exists in peoples' hearts and minds. Its power is derived not from authority, but from legitimacy. Its influence is not always conscious, or even visibly apparent, but it is always present in the implementation of actual decisions.

Once you understand the Core Group nature of organizations, then you can understand the true nature of political parties (devoted first and foremost to getting jobs for their Core Group members), diversity in organizations (the glass ceiling is the boundary between the rest of the organization and the Core Group), and labour unions (who have collective-bargained their way into the Core Group of many companies, which is why they are so intensely hated by managers).

Core Groups aren't bad in themselves; every organization has them. Behind every great organization is a great Core Group. The trick is learning to find the organizations with great Core Groups, change the ones that can be changed, and avoid the dysfunctional ones – hopefully in time to avoid being capsized.

Cost Benefit Analysis

Cost-benefit analysis is a term that refers both to:

- a formal discipline used to help appraise, or assess, the case for a project or proposal, which itself is a process known as project appraisal; and
- an informal approach to making decisions of any kind.

Under both definitions the process involves, whether explicitly or implicitly, weighing the total expected costs against the total expected benefits of one or more actions in order to choose the best or most profitable option. The formal process is often referred to as CBA, or Cost-Benefit analysis in the United States.

Closely related, but slightly different, formal techniques include cost-effectiveness analysis and benefit effectiveness analysis.

Theory of Cost Benefit Analysis

Cost Benefit Analysis is an economic tool to aid social decision-making, and is typically used by governments to evaluate the desirability of a given intervention in markets. The aim is to gauge the efficiency of the intervention relative to the status quo. The costs and benefits of the impacts of an intervention are evaluated in terms of the public's willingness to pay for them (benefits) or willingness to pay to avoid them (costs). Inputs are typically measured in terms of opportunity costs – the value in their best alternative use. The guiding principle is to list all of the parties affected by an intervention, and place a monetary value of the effect it has on their welfare as it would be valued by them.

The process involves monetary value of initial and ongoing expenses vs. expected return. Constructing plausible measures of the costs and benefits of specific actions is often very difficult. In practice, analysts try to estimate costs and benefits either by using survey methods or by drawing inferences from market behaviour. For example, a product manager may compare manufacturing and marketing expenses to projected sales for a proposed product, and only decide to produce it if he expects the revenues to eventually recoup the costs. Cost-benefit analysis attempts to put all relevant costs and benefits on a common temporal footing. A discount rate is chosen, which is then used to compute all relevant future costs and benefits in present-value terms. Most commonly, the discount rate used for present-value calculations is an interest rate taken from financial markets (R.H. Frank 2000). This can be very controversial – for example, a high discount rate implies a very low value on the welfare of future generations, which may have a huge impact on the desirability of interventions to help the environment, and so on. Empirical studies have suggested that in reality, people's discount rates do decline over time. Because CBA aims to measure the public's true willingness to pay, this feature is typically built into studies.

During cost-benefit analysis, monetary values may also be assigned to less tangible effects such as the various risks which could contribute to partial or total project failure; loss of reputation, market penetration, long-term enterprise strategy alignments, etc. This is especially true when governments use the technique, for instance to decide whether to introduce business regulation, build a new road or offer a new drug on the state healthcare. In this case, a value must be put on human life or the environment, often causing great controversy. The cost-benefit principle says, for example, that we should install a guardrail on a dangerous stretch of mountain road if the dollar cost of doing so is less than the implicit dollar value of the injuries, deaths, and property damage thus prevented

(R.H. Frank 2000).

Cost-benefit calculations typically involve using time value of money formula. This is usually done by converting the future expected streams of costs and benefits to a present value amount.

Application of Cost Benefit Analysis

Cost-benefit analysis is mainly, but not exclusively, used to assess the value for money of very large private and public sector projects. This is because such projects tend to include costs and benefits that are less amenable to being expressed in financial or monetary terms (e.g. environmental damage), as well as those that can be expressed in monetary terms. Private sector organisations tend to make much more use of other project appraisal techniques, such as rate of return, where feasible.

The practice of cost-benefit analysis differs between countries and between sectors (e.g. transport, health) within countries. Some of the main differences include the types of impacts that are included as costs and benefits within appraisals, the extent to which impacts are expressed in monetary terms and differences in discount rate between countries.

Cost Benefit Analysis in UK

Basic cost-benefit techniques were applied to the development of the motorway network in the 1950s and 60s. Over the last 40 years, cost-benefit techniques have gradually developed to the extent that substantial guidance now exists on how transport projects should be appraised in the UK. The Department for Transport (DfT) and its agencies have made extensive use of a number of key cost-benefit indicators, including:

- PVB (present value of benefits);
- PVC (present value of costs);
- NPV (PVB less PVC);
- NPV/k (where k is the level of funds available) and
- BCR (benefit cost ratio).

In 1998 the New Approach to Appraisal (NATA) was introduced by the then Department for Transport, Environment and the Regions. This brought together cost-benefit results with those from detailed environmental impact assessments and presented them in a balanced way. NATA was first applied to national road schemes in the 1998 Roads Review, but subsequently rolled out to all modes of transport. It is now a cornerstone of transport appraisal in the UK and is maintained and developed by the Department for Transport.

Cost Benefit Analysis in EU

The EU's 'Developing Harmonised European Approaches for Transport Costing and Project Assessment' (HEATCO) project, part of its Sixth Framework Programmeme, has reviewed transport appraisal guidance across EU member states and found that significant differences exist between countries. HEATCO's aim is to develop guidelines to harmonise transport appraisal practice across the EU.

Cost Benefit Analysis in US

Much of the early development work on cost-benefit analysis as a discipline was the result of problems faced by the US Army Corps of Engineers in deciding how and where to build bridges in supporting combat operations.

Cost-benefit analysis is now a well established discipline in the US. California's Department of Transportation (Caltrans) provide detailed guidance on how Cost-benefit analysis should be applied to transport projects.

Evolutionary Biology of Cost Benefit Analysis

Cost-benefit analysis is used in evolutionary biology to assess the fitness costs and benefits of traits. For example, a behavioral ecologist may use the cost benefit approach to explain the evolution of play behavior in young animals. Costs would include injury and increased vulnerability of predation, while benefits may include improvement of a certain skill important in future success. Deviation from predictions based on the cost-benefit approach may highlight factors not considered by the researcher.

Accuracy Problems in Cost Benefit Analysis

The accuracy of the outcome of a cost-benefit analysis is dependent on how accurately costs and benefits have been estimated. A peer-reviewed study of the accuracy of cost estimates in transportation infrastructureplanning found that for rail projects actual costs turned out to be on average 44.7 percent higher than estimated costs, and for roads 20.4 percent higher (Flyvbjerg, Holm, and Buhl, 2002). For benefits, another peer-reviewed study found that actual rail ridership was on average 51.4 percent lower than estimated ridership; for roads it was found that for half of all projects estimated traffic was wrong by more than 20 percent (Flyvbjerg, Holm, and Buhl, 2005). Comparative studies indicate that similar inaccuracies apply to fields other than transportation. These studies indicate that the outcomes of cost-benefit analyses should be treated with caution, because they may be highly inaccurate. In fact, inaccurate cost-benefit analyses may be argued to be a substantial risk in planning, because inaccuracies of the size documented are likely to lead to inefficient decisions, as defined by Pareto and Kaldor-Hicks efficiency (Flyvbjerg, Bruzelius, and Rothengatter, 2003).

These outcomes (almost always tending to underestimation, unless significant new approaches are overlooked) are to be expected, since such estimates:
1. rely heavily on past like projects (frequently differing markedly in function or size, and certainly in the skill levels of the team members),
2. rely heavily on the project's members to identify (remember from their collective past experiences) the significant cost drivers,
3. rely on very crude heuristics ('rules of thumb') to estimate the money cost of the intangible elements, and
4. are unable to completely dispel the usually (unconscious) biases of the team members (who often have a vested interest in a decision to 'go ahead') and the natural psychological tendency to "think positive" (whatever that involves).

Another challenge to cost-benefit analysis comes from determining which costs should be included in an analysis (the significant cost drivers). This is often controversial as organizations or interest groups may feel that some costs should be included or excluded from a study.

In the case of the Ford Pinto (where, due to design flaws, the Pinto was liable to burst into flames in a rear-impact collision), the Ford company's decision was not to issue a recall. Ford's cost benefit analysis had estimated that: based on the number of cars in use and the probable accident rate, deaths due to the design flaw would run about $49.5 million (the amount Ford would pay out of court to settle wrongful death lawsuits). This was estimated to be less than the cost of issuing a recall ($137.5 million). In the event, Ford overlooked (or considered insignificant) the costs of the negative publicity so engendered, which turned out to be quite significant (since it led to the recall anyways and to measurable losses in sales).

Specifically in the field of Health Economics, cost-benefit analysis is viewed as an inadequate measure by extra-welfarists, as willingness-to-pay methods of determining the value of human life are subject to bias according to income inequity. This is due to the inherent nature of "ability to pay," which weighs heavily in the willingness-to-pay question (i.e. one's willingness-to-pay is constrained by one's ability-to-pay). For this reason, extra-welfaristscost-utility analysis and the QALY to analyze the effects of health policies. support use of

Weighing-scale approach to decision-making Cost-Benefit Analysis

Cost-benefit analysis (CBA) is the weighing-scale approach to decision-making. All the plusses (cash-flows and other intangible benefits) are put on one side of the balance and all the minuses (the costs and disadvantages) are put on the other. Whichever weighs the heavier wins.

Example of a Cost Benefit Analysis (CBA):

A company that would like to buy new software to improve its business might conduct a CBA to decide and make up its mind.

On the minus (cost) side would be:
- the price of the software,
- the cost of consultants to install and implement the software, and
- the cost of training for the users of the software.

However on the plus (benefits) side would be:
- improved business processes (leading to an annual cost decrease),
- due to better available information, being able to take better decisions (leading to additional cash-flows), and
- increased staff moral from using the state of the art tools for running the business.

A frequently made mistake in the CBA method is to use non-discounted amounts for calculating the costs and benefits. A method like NPV or Economic Value Added or CFROI is strongly recommended, because all of these account for the time value of money.

A frequent problem with CBA is that typically the cost are tangible, hard and financial, while the benefits are hard and tangible, but also soft and intangible. Caution should be taken here against people who claim that "if you can't measure it does not exist / it has no value". Especially in more strategic investments, frequently the intangible benefits clearly outweigh the financial benefits

Cultural Dimensions of Hofstede

The practical applications for Geert Hofstede's research on cultural differences (Prof. Geert Hofstede, Emeritus Professor, Maastricht University, AN Velp, Netherlands)

For those who work in international business, it is sometimes amazing how different people in other cultures behave. We tend to have a human instinct that 'deep inside' all people are the same – but they are not. Therefore, if we go into another country and make decisions based on how we operate in our own home country – the chances are we'll make some very bad decisions.

Geert Hofstede's research gives us insights into other cultures so that we can be more effective when interacting with people in other countries. If understood and applied properly, this information should reduce your level of frustration, anxiety, and concern. But most important, Geert Hofstede will give you the 'edge of understanding' which translates to more successful results.

Example of Cultural Dimensions

One example of cultural differences in business is between the Middle Eastern countries and the Western countries, especially the United States.

When negotiating in Western countries, the objective is to work toward a target of mutual understanding and agreement and 'shake-hands' when that agreement is reached – a cultural signal of the end of negotiations and the start of 'working together'.

In Middle Eastern countries much negotiation takes place leading into the 'agreement', signified by shaking hands. However, the deal is not complete in the Middle Eastern culture. In fact, it is a cultural sign that 'serious' negotiations are just beginning.

Imagine the problems this creates when each party in a negotiation is operating under diametrically opposed 'rules and conventions.'

This is just one example why it is critical to understand other cultures you may be doing business with – whether on a vacation in a foreign country, or negotiating a multi-million dollar deal for your company.

On each country page you will find the unique Hofstede graphs depicting the Dimension scores and other demographics for that country and culture – plus an explanation of how they uniquely apply to that country.

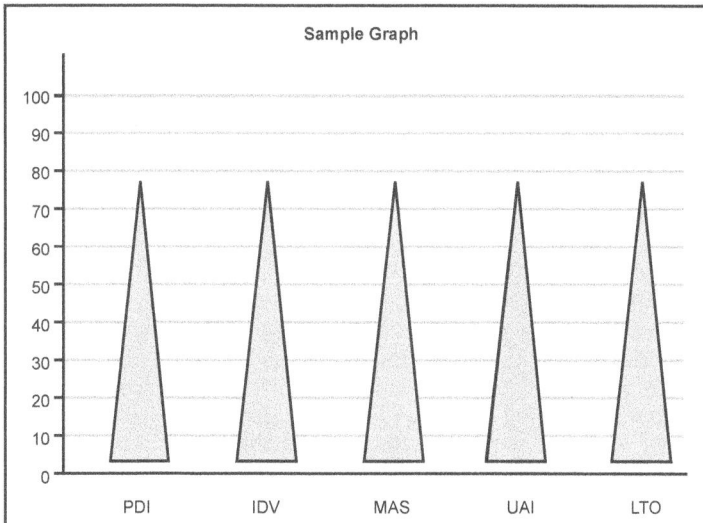

Sample Graph

Description for each of Hofstede's Dimensions listed below:

Power Distance Index (PDI): Power Distance Index (PDI) that is the extent to which the less powerful members of organizations and institutions (like the family) accept and expect that power is distributed unequally. This represents inequality (more versus less), but defined from below, not from above. It suggests that a society's level of inequality is endorsed by the followers as much as by the leaders. Power and inequality, of course, are extremely fundamental facts of any society and anybody with some international experience will be aware that 'all societies are unequal, but some are more unequal than others'.

Individualism (IDV): Individualism (IDV) on the one side versus its opposite, collectivism, that is the degree to which individuals are inte-grated into groups. On the individualist side we find societies in which the ties between individuals are loose: everyone is expected to look after him/herself and his/her immediate family. On the collectivist side, we find societies in which people from birth onwards are integrated into strong, cohesive in-groups, often extended families (with uncles, aunts and grandparents) which continue protecting them in exchange for unquestioning loyalty. The word 'collectivism' in this sense has no political meaning: it refers to the group, not to the state. Again, the issue addressed by this dimension is an extremely fundamental one, regarding all societies in the world.

Masculinity (MAS): Masculinity (MAS) versus its opposite, femininity, refers to the distribution of roles between the genders which is another fundamental issue for any society to which a range of solutions are found. The IBM studies revealed that (a) women's values differ less among societies than men's values; (b) men's values from one country to another contain a dimension from very assertive and competitive and maximally different from women's values on the one side, to modest and caring and similar to women's values on the other. The assertive pole has been called 'masculine' and the modest, caring pole 'feminine'. The women in feminine countries have the same modest, caring values as the men; in the masculine countries they are somewhat assertive and competitive, but not as much as the men, so that these countries show a gap between men's values and women's values.

Uncertainty Avoidance Index (UAI): Uncertainty Avoidance Index (UAI) deals with a society's tolerance for uncertainty and ambiguity; it ultimately refers to man's search for Truth. It indicates to what extent a culture Programmes its members to feel either uncomfortable or comfortable in unstructured situations. Unstructured situations are novel, unknown, surprising, different from usual. Uncertainty avoiding cultures try to minimize the possibility of such situations by strict laws and rules, safety and security measures, and on the philosophical and religious level by a belief in absolute Truth; 'there can only be one Truth and we have it'. People in uncertainty avoiding countries are also more emotional, and motivated by inner nervous energy. The opposite type, uncertainty accepting cultures, are more tolerant of opinions different from what they are used to; they try to have as few rules as possible, and on the philosophical and religious level they are relativist and allow many currents to flow side by side. People within these cultures are more phlegmatic and contemplative, and not expected by their environment to express emotions.

Long-Term Orientation (LTO) versus short-term orientation: This fifth dimension was found in a study among students in 23 countries around the world, using a questionnaire designed by Chinese scholars It can be said to deal with Virtue regardless of Truth. Values associated with Long Term Orientation are thrift and perseverance; values associated with Short Term Orientation are respect for tradition, fulfilling social obligations, and protecting one's 'face'. Both the positively and the negatively rated values of this dimension are found in the teachings of Confucius, the most influential Chinese philosopher who lived around 500 B.C.; however, the dimension also applies to countries without a Confucian heritage.

Defined as the body of beliefs, norms, and values shared by a group of people, culture presents the biggest challenge to businesses working internationally. It is a key factor in how all other areas of business work together. As stated by Geert Hofstede, "Culture is more often a source of conflict than of synergy. Cultural differences are a nuisance at best and often a disaster." A summary of Hofstede's major factors impacting international business relationships that also influence the practice of international management are shown below.

Value Dimension	Value Description	High Score	Low Score
Power Distance Index (PDI)	The degree of equality, or inequality, between people in the country's society	Indicates that inequalities of power and wealth have been allowed to grow within the society. These societies are more likely to follow a caste system that does not allow significant upward mobility of its citizens.	Indicates the society de-emphasizes the differences between citizen's power and wealth. In these societies equality and opportunity for everyone is stressed.
Individualism (IDV)	Degree to which a society reinforces individual or collective achievement and interpersonal relationships.	Indicates that individuality and individual rights are paramount within the society. Individuals may tend to form a larger number of looser relationships.	Typifies societies of a more collectivist nature with close ties between individuals. Reinforce extended families and collectives where everyone takes responsibility for fellow members of their group.
Masculinity (MAS)	Degree to which a society reinforces, or does not reinforce, the traditional	Indicates the country experiences a high degree of gender differentiation. Males dominate a significant portion of the society and	Indicates the country has a low level of differentiation and discrimination between genders.

301

	masculine work role model of male achievement, control, and power	power structure, with females being controlled by male domination.	Females are treated equally to males in all aspects of the society.
Uncertainty Avoidance Index (UAI)	Level of tolerance for uncertainty and ambiguity within the society – i.e. unstructured situations.	Indicates the country has a low tolerance for uncertainty and ambiguity Creates a rule-oriented society that institutes laws, rules, regulations, and controls in order to reduce the amount of uncertainty.	Indicates the country has less concern about ambiguity and uncertainty and has more tolerance for a variety of opinions. Reflected in a society that is less rule-oriented, more readily accepts change, and takes more and greater
Long-Term Orientation (LTO)	Degree to which a society embraces, or does not embrace, long-term devotion to traditional, forward thinking values.	Indicates the country prescribes to the values of long-term commitments and respect for tradition. This is thought to support a strong work ethic where long-term rewards are expected as a result of today's hard work. However, business may take longer to develop in this society, particularly for an "outsider".	Indicates the country does not reinforce the concept of long-term, traditional orientation. In this culture, change can occur more rapidly as long-term traditions and commitments do not become impediments to change.

Fayol's 14 Principles of Management

According to Henry Fayol management has 14 principles. Henry Fayol listed the 14 principles of management as follows in figure.

Henry Fayol synthesised 14 principles for organisational design and effective administration. Fayol's 14 principles are:

1. Specialisation/Division of Labour: A principle of work allocation and specialisation in order to concentrate activities to enable specialisation of skills and understandings, more work focus and efficiency.

2. Authority with Corresponding Responsibility: If responsibilities are allocated then the post holder needs the requisite authority to carry these out including the right to require others in the area of responsibility to undertake duties.

3. Discipline: The generalisation about discipline is that discipline is essential for the smooth running of a business and without it – standards, consistency of action, adherence to rules and values – no enterprise could prosper. "in an essence – obedience, application, energy, behaviour and outward marks of respect observed in accordance with standing agreements between firms and its employees".

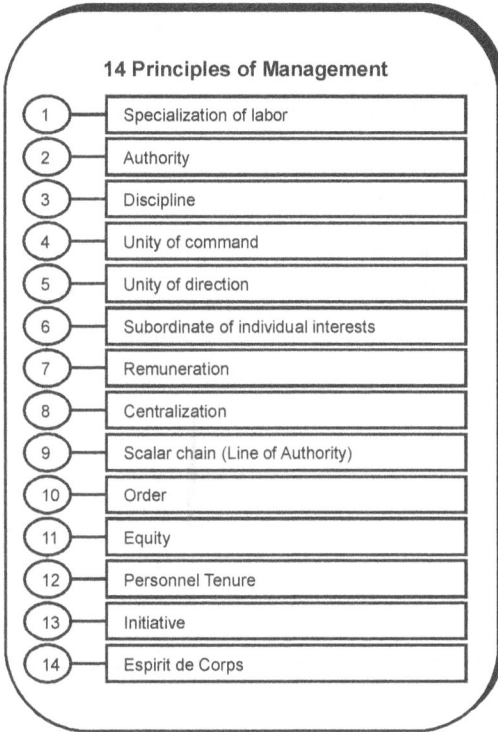

14 Principles of Management

1	Specialization of labor
2	Authority
3	Discipline
4	Unity of command
5	Unity of direction
6	Subordinate of individual interests
7	Remuneration
8	Centralization
9	Scalar chain (Line of Authority)
10	Order
11	Equity
12	Personnel Tenure
13	Initiative
14	Espirit de Corps

4. Unity of Command: The idea is that an employee should receive instructions from one superior only. This generalisation still holds – even where we are involved with team and matrix structures which involve reporting to more than one boss – or being accountable to several clients. The basic concern is that tensions and dilemmas arise where we report to two or more bosses. One boss may want X, the other Y and the subordinate is caught between the devil and the deep blue sea.

5. Unity of Direction: The unity of command idea of having one head (chief executive, cabinet consensus) with agree purposes and objectives and one plan for a group of activities) is clear.

6. Subordination of Individual Interest to the General Interest: Fayol's line was that one employee's interests or those of one group should not prevail over the organisation as a whole. This would spark a lively debate about who decides that the interests of the organisation as a whole are. Ethical dilemmas and matters of corporate risk and the behaviour of individual "chancers" are involved here. Fayol's work – assumes a shared set of values by people in the organisation – a unitarism where the reasons for organisational activities and decisions are in some way neutral and reasonable.

7. Remuneration of Staff: The general principle is that levels of compensation should be "fair" and as far as possible afford satisfaction both to the staff and the firm (in terms of its cost structures and desire for profitability/surplus).

8. Centralisation: Centralisation for Henry Fayol is essential to the organisation and a natural consequence of organising. This issue does not go away even where flatter, devolved organisations occur. Decentralisation – is frequently centralisaed-decentralisation !!! The modes of control over the actions and results of devolved organisations are still matters requiring considerable attention.

9. Scalar Chain / Line of Authority: The scalar chain of command of reporting relationships from top executive to the ordinary shop operative or driver needs to be sensible, clear and understood.

10. Order: The level of generalisation becomes difficult with this principle. Basically an organisation "should" provide an orderly place for each individual member – who needs to see how their role fits into the organisation and be confident, able to predict the organisations behaviour towards them. Thus policies, rules, instructions and actions should be understandable and understood. Orderliness implies steady evolutionary movement rather than wild, anxiety provoking, unpredictable movement.

11. Equity: Equity, fairness and a sense of justice "should"pervade the organisation – in principle and practice.

12. Stability of Tenure: Time is needed for the employee to adapt to his/her work and perform it effectively. Stability of tenure promotes loyalty to the organisation, its purposes and values.

13. Initiative: At all levels of the organisational structure, zeal, enthusiasm and energy are enabled by people having the scope for personal initiative. (Note: Tom Peters recommendations in respect of employee empowerment)

14. Esprit de Corps: Here, Fayol emphasises the need for building and maintaining of harmony among the work force, team work and sound interpersonal relationships.

In the same way that Alfred P Sloan, the executive head of General Motors reorganised the company into semi-autonomous divisions in the 1920s, corporations undergoing reorganisation still apply "classical organisation" principles – very much in line with Fayol's recommendations.

Fayol's definition of management roles and actions distinguishes between **Five Elements**:

1. **Prevoyance.** (Forecast & Plan). Examining the future and drawing up a plan of action. The elements of strategy.
2. **To organize.** Build up the structure, both material and human, of the undertaking.
3. **To command.** Maintain the activity among the personnel.
4. **To coordinate.** Binding together, unifying and harmonizing all activity and effort.
5. **To control.** Seeing that everything occurs in conformity with established rule and expressed command.

The Adam Smith Problem

The Adam Smith Problem is the suggestion that there is a conflict between Smith's moral theory based on sympathy and his economic theory based on self-interest.

In The Wealth of Nations Adam Smith claims that self-interest alone (in a proper institutional setting) can lead to socially beneficial results. But in his Theory of Moral Sentiments Smith argues that sympathy is required to achieve socially beneficial results. On the surface it appears that a contradiction exists. Economist August Oncken referred to this as 'the Adam-Smith-Problem'. Austrian economist Joseph Schumpeter also emphasized this apparent contradiction in his commentary on Smith's work.

Adam Smith himself cannot have seen any contradiction, since he produced a revised edition of Moral Sentiments after the publication of Wealth of Nations. Both sets of ideas are to be found in his Lectures on Jurisprudence. In recent years most students of Adam Smith's work have argued that no contradiction exists. In the Theory of Moral Sentiments, Adam Smith develops a theory of psychology in which individuals in society find it in their self-interest to develop sympathy as they seek approval of what he calls the "impartial spectator." The self-interest he speaks of is not a narrow selfishness but something that involves sympathy.

Some readers of The Wealth of Nations have assumed that when Smith speaks of "self-interest" he is referring to selfishness. Although in some contexts, such as buying and selling, sympathy generally need not be considered, Smith makes it clear that he regards selfishness as inappropriate, if not immoral, and that the self-interested actor has sympathy for others. In The Theory of Moral Sentiments Adam Smith argues that the self-interest of any actor includes the interest of the rest of society, since the socially-defined notions of appropriate and inappropriate actions necessarily affect the interests of the individual as a member of society. Context is also useful as Adam Smith was against the idea of corporations, or "joint stock companies."

In any case, Adam Smith apparently believed that moral sentiments and self-interest would always add up to the same thing. One possible line of reasoning he might have employed in reaching this conclusion is as follows: the invisible hand cannot operate if there is no society, for precluding a societal construct precludes division of labour, and thus, the efficiency which comes with its manifestation. Now for society to exist, justice is a necessary condition (as pointed out in Smith's Theory of Moral Sentiments). For justice to exist in any social setting, individuals must harbor the passions of gratitude and resentment governed by a sense of 'merit' and 'demerit' (again from Smith's Theory of Moral Sentiments). And finally, as Adam Smith himself would have so vehemently argued, the sense of 'merit' and 'demerit' is almost exclusively engendered by human sympathy. In conclusion, the invisible hand of the market is, at some level, contingent upon the ability of humans to sympathize: Smith's self-interest is indeed in consonance with the notion of sympathy.

The BCG matrix

Product Portfolio Method: The Boston Consulting Group Matrix (BCG matrix) method is based on the product life cycle theory that can be used to determine what priorities should be given in the product portfolio of a business unit. To ensure long-term value creation, a company should have a portfolio of products that contains both high-growth products in need of cash inputs and low-growth products that generate a lot of cash. It has 2 dimensions: market share and market growth. The basic idea behind it is that the bigger the market share a product has or the faster the product's market grows the better it is for the company.

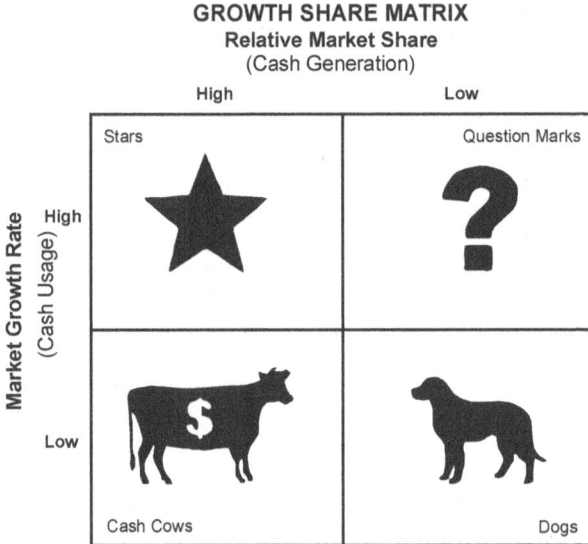

GROWTH SHARE MATRIX
Relative Market Share
(Cash Generation)

	High	Low
High	Stars ★	Question Marks ?
Low	Cash Cows $	Dogs

Market Growth Rate (Cash Usage)

Placing products in the BCG matrix results in 4 categories in a portfolio of a company:
1. **Stars (=high growth, high market share)**
   - use large amounts of cash and are leaders in the business so they should also generate large amounts of cash.
   - frequently roughly in balance on net cash flow. However if needed any attempt should be made to hold share, because the rewards will be a cash cow if market share is kept.
2. **Cash Cows (=low growth, high market share)**
   - profits and cash generation should be high , and because of the low growth, investments needed should be low. Keep profits high
   - Foundation of a company
3. **Dogs (=low growth, low market share)**
   - avoid and minimize the number of dogs in a company.
   - beware of expensive turn around plans.
   - deliver cash, otherwise liquidate

4. Question Marks (= high growth, low market share)

- have the worst cash characteristics of all, because high demands and low returns due to low market share
- if nothing is done to change the market share, question marks will simply absorb great amounts of cash and later, as the growth stops, a dog
- either invest heavily or sell off or invest nothing and generate whatever cash it can. Increase market share or deliver cash

The BCG Matrix method can help understand a frequently made strategy mistake: having a one-size-fits-all-approach to strategy, such as a generic growth target (9 percent per year) or a generic return on capital of say 9,5% for an entire corporation.

In such a scenario:

A. Cash Cows Business Units will beat their profit target easily; their management have an easy job and are often praised anyhow. Even worse, they are often allowed to reinvest substantial cash amounts in their businesses which are mature and not growing anymore.

B. Dogs Business Units fight an impossible battle and, even worse, investments are made now and then in hopeless attempts to 'turn the business around'.

C. As a result (all) Question Marks and Stars Business Units get mediocre size investment funds. In this way they are unable to ever become cash cows. These inadequate invested sums of money are a waste of money. Either these SBUs should receive enough investment funds to enable them to achieve a real market dominance and become a cash cow (or star), or otherwise companies are advised to disinvest and try to get whatever possible cash out of the question marks that were not selected.

Limitations of BCG Matrix

Some limitations of the Boston Consulting Group Matrix include:

- High market share is not the only success factor
- Market growth is not the only indicator for attractiveness of a market
- Sometimes Dogs can earn even more cash as Cash Cows

The BCG Growth-Share Matrix

The BCG Growth-Share Matrix is a portfolio planning model developed by Bruce Henderson of the Boston Consulting Group in the early 1970's. It is based on the observation that a company's business units can be classified into four categories based on combinations of market growth and market share relative to the largest competitor, hence the name "growth-share". Market growth serves as a proxy for industry attractiveness, and relative market share serves as a proxy for competitive advantage. The growth-share matrix thus maps the business unit positions within these two important determinants of profitability.

This framework assumes that an increase in relative market share will result in an increase in the generation of cash. This assumption often is true because of the experience curve; increased relative market share implies that the firm is moving forward on the experience curve relative to its competitors, thus developing a cost advantage. A second assumption is that a growing market requires investment in assets to increase capacity and therefore results in the consumption of cash. Thus the position of a business on the growth-share matrix provides an indication of its cash generation and its cash consumption.

Relative Market Share
(Cash Generation)

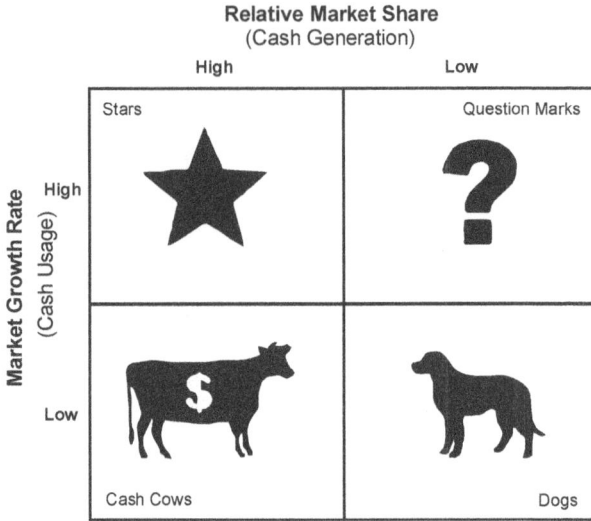

Henderson reasoned that the cash required by rapidly growing business units could be obtained from the firm's other business units that were at a more mature stage and generating significant cash. By investing to become the market share leader in a rapidly growing market, the business unit could move along the experience curve and develop a cost advantage. From this reasoning, the BCG Growth-Share Matrix was born.

The Four Categories of BCG Matrix

Dogs – Dogs have low market share and a low growth rate and thus neither generate nor consume a large amount of cash. However, dogs are cash traps because of the money tied up in a business that has little potential. Such businesses are candidates for divestiture.

Question marks – Question marks are growing rapidly and thus consume large amounts of cash, but because they have low market shares they do not generate much cash. The result is a large net cash comsumption. A question mark (also known as a "problem child") has the potential to gain market share and become a star, and eventually a cash cow when the market growth slows. If the question mark does not succeed in becoming the market leader, then after perhaps years of cash consumption it will degenerate into a dog when the market growth declines. Question marks must be analyzed carefully in order to determine whether they are worth the investment required to grow market share.

Stars – Stars generate large amounts of cash because of their strong relative market share, but also consume large amounts of cash because of their high growth rate; therefore the cash in each direction approximately nets out. If a star can maintain its large market share, it will become a cash cow when the market growth rate declines. The portfolio of a diversified company always should have stars that will become the next cash cows and ensure future cash generation.

Cash cows – As leaders in a mature market, cash cows exhibit a return on assets that is greater than the market growth rate, and thus generate more cash than they consume. Such business units should be "milked", extracting the profits and investing as little cash as possible. Cash cows provide the cash required to turn question marks into market leaders, to cover the administrative costs of the company, to fund research and development, to service the corporate debt, and to pay dividends to shareholders. Because the cash cow generates a relatively stable cash flow, its value can be determined with reasonable accuracy by calculating the present value of its cash stream using a discounted cash flow analysis.

Under the growth-share matrix model, as an industry matures and its growth rate declines, a business unit will become either a cash cow or a dog, determined soley by whether it had become the market leader during the period of high growth.

While originally developed as a model for resource allocation among the various business units in a corporation, the growth-share matrix also can be used for resource allocation among products within a single business unit. Its simplicity is its strength – the relative positions of the firm's entire business portfolio can be displayed in a single diagram.

Limitations of BCG Matrix

The growth-share matrix once was used widely, but has since faded from popularity as more comprehensive models have been developed. Some of its weaknesses are:

1. Market growth rate is only one factor in industry attractiveness, and relative market share is only one factor in competitive advantage. The growth-share matrix overlooks many other factors in these two important determinants of profitability.
2. The framework assumes that each business unit is independent of the others. In some cases, a business unit that is a "dog" may be helping other business units gain a competitive advantage.
3. The matrix depends heavily upon the breadth of the definition of the market. A business unit may dominate its small niche, but have very low market share in the overall industry. In such a case, the definition of the market can make the difference between a dog and a cash cow.
4. While its importance has diminished, the BCG matrix still can serve as a simple tool for viewing a corporation's business portfolio at a glance, and may serve as a starting point for discussing resource allocation among strategic business units.

The Clarkson Principles of Stakeholder Management

Origin and Purpose of Clarkson Principles of Stakeholder Management: The year after his retirement from the faculty of the University of Toronto in 1988, Max Clarkson (1922-1998) founded the Centre for Corporate Social Performance and Ethics in the Faculty of Management, now the Clarkson Centre for Business Ethics & Board Effectiveness, or CC(BE) 2 . Four conferences hosted by the Centre between 1993 and 1998 brought together management scholars to share ideas on stakeholder theory, an emerging field of study examining the relationships and responsibilities of a corporation to employees, customers, suppliers, society, and the environment. The Alfred P. Sloan Foundation funded the project, from which the Clarkson Principles emerged.

Critical Content of Clarkson Principles of Stakeholder Management

After an introduction to the stakeholder concept with comments on shareowners and the legal and moral duty of managers, seven (7) principles of Stakeholder Management are set forth, each with a paragraph or two expanding on its meaning. These principles represent an early stage general awareness of corporate governance concerns that have been widely discussed in connection with the business scandals of 2002.

Implementation of Clarkson Principles of Stakeholder Management

In many ways, the Clarkson Principles are meta-principles that encourage management to embrace specific stakeholder principles and then to implement them in accordance with the norms listed above. Their current use seems largely hortatory, unlike principles or codes that call for formal adoption by managers or corporations.

Principles of Stakeholder Management

The large, professionally managed corporation is the distinctive economic institution of the twentieth century. It has proved uniquely effective in mobilizing resources and knowledge; increasing productivity; and creating new technologies, products and services. Corporations have proliferated and grown because they meet the needs of various members of society: customers, workers and communities, as well as investors. The worldwide spread of corporate activity has produced an increasingly integrated and interdependent global economy.

The success of the corporation, however, inevitably gives rise to questions and criticisms. Corporations are spontaneous and voluntary associations in which diverse individuals and interests collabourate for the creation and distribution of wealth. Some critics question whether organizations with the vast scale and scope of contemporary multinationals can be effectively controlled and directed toward these purposes. Others are concerned about the limited range of interests directly represented in corporate governance, and the lack of openness in corporate decision-making. And, as multinational corporations expand their activities and linkages, both corporate managers and their critics search for principles for action that transcend national borders and cultural values, and modes of operation that will achieve the broad purposes of the corporation on a long-term and sustainable basis, without undue conflict with diverse human and social norms.

The Principles of Stakeholder Management presented in this document (Table 1) have been developed in response to these concerns and needs. They are addressed to managers: those individuals at any level who are responsible for the performance and impact of the corporation. They are consistent with the basic organizational structure and purpose of the modern business enterprise; they do not suggest that the corporation be turned into a polity (i.e., a unit of political government), nor into an agency of the state. In sum, these guidelines are intended to make managers more aware of the diverse constituencies that they are obligated to serve and increase the openness of management processes. There are many reasons to believe that adoption of a stakeholder approach to management will contribute to the long-term survival and success of a firm. Positive and mutually supportive stakeholder relationships encourage trust, and stimulate collabourative efforts that lead to relational wealth," i.e., organizational assets arising from familiarity and teamwork. By contrast, conflict and suspicion stimulate formal bargaining and limit efforts and rewards to stipulated terms, which result in time delays and increased costs. In addition, more and more executives are recognizing that a reputation for ethical and socially responsible behavior can be the basis for a competitive edge in both market and public policy relationships. Finally, in spite of the specification and measurement difficulties involved, many research studies have found evidence of positive associations (and few have found negative associations) between various socially and ethically responsible practices and conventional economic and financial indicators of corporate performance (profitability, growth, etc.) Thus, there is no reason to think that the conscientious and continuing practice of stakeholder management will conflict with conventional financial performance goals.

The Stakeholder Concept

The constituencies that are affected (favorably or adversely) by the operation of the corporation are referred to here as its stakeholders. The implication of the term is that such parties have a stake in the corporation: something at risk, and therefore something to gain or lose, as a result of corporate activity. Many stakeholders (e.g., investors, employees) are linked to the corporation through explicit contracts. With many others (e.g., customers), contractual relations may be largely implicit, and subject to specific interpretation only in problematic circumstances. Still other interests (third parties outside the network of explicit and implicit contracts) are non-contractual and often involuntary, and the parties involved may even be unaware of their relationship to the corporation until some specific event, favorable or unfavorable, draws it to their attention. Impacts on third parties are often referred to as "externalities," because they occur outside the range of the firms internal and market relationships. Examples of third party impacts are economic benefits or environmental harms that may be experienced by communities as a result of corporate operations. Such impacts, although clearly external to the firm as an organization, are nonetheless real, and perhaps significant: they are, therefore, within the normal purview of responsible management. The notion that important aspects of corporate performance can be ignored by managers because they are external (perhaps as a result of being deliberately externalized) is incorrect.

The Status of Shareowners

Shareowners have a special status among stakeholders in that their potential gain or loss from their involvement with the corporation is determined as a residual: it depends upon what is left over after all other stakeholder claimants have received their specified distributions. If a firm is, or is expected to be, profitable, its shareowners may receive dividends or appreciation in the value of their shares; if a firm incurs, or is expected to incur, losses, its shareowners will correspondingly lose. (Of course, other contractual stakeholders may be included in profit-sharing arrangements, and even non-contractual third parties (e.g., philanthropies) may benefit or suffer because of variations in corporate profitability.)

The distinctive position of shareowners among stakeholders is not due to their fractional ownership interest in the corporate entity, which is essentially a legal artifact; and owning stock is not riskier than other forms of association with the corporation. Indeed, the possibility of job loss (to employees), product failure (to customers), etc., may be much more significant to the parties involved than the impact of any single corporate bankruptcy on a well-diversified shareowner. But employee and customer risks (like the risks of lenders) arise because the corporation may fail to fulfill its contractual obligations. By contrast, shareowner risks are an inherent feature of their ownership contract. They have agreed to take whatever is left over, or the current market value of whatever is expected to be left over in the future.

The Legal and Moral Duty of Managers

Managers occupy a special place within the corporate structure. They are responsible for negotiating contracts with the firm's voluntary constituents and for accommodating the firm's involuntary stakeholders, in order to turn these disparate individuals and groups into a cooperative, wealth-enhancing network (or, at least, to minimize the number and severity of unavoidable conflicts). They attempt to accomplish this task by distributing among stakeholders the rewards and burdens that arise from corporate activity in ways that encourage (or at least do not discourage) their participation and by developing organizational processes and cultures that enhance stakeholder satisfaction.

The responsibilities of managers require and presume discretionary authority, and, as a condition of this authority, managers owe the corporation a duty of loyalty. This duty is, to some extent, a matter of law. But the moral responsibility of managers exceeds the normal market standard of indifference (i.e., not knowingly doing harm) and embraces all of the stakeholders of the firm, not merely the shareowners. Managers have an obligation to deal openly and honestly with the firm's various stakeholders and to avoid purely self-serving actions which their privileged access to information and discretionary authority may make possible. Managerial policies and processes should emphasize the interdependence among all stakeholders and should demonstrably reflect the application of a common standard of fairness.

Table 1: Principles of Stakeholder Management

Principle 1	Managers should acknowledge and actively monitor the concerns of all legitimate stakeholders, and should take their interests appropriately into account in decision-making and operations.
Principle 2	Managers should listen to and openly communicate with stakeholders about their respective concerns and contributions, and about the risks that they assume because of their involvement with the corporation.
Principle 3	Managers should adopt processes and modes of behavior that are sensitive to the concerns and capabilities of each stakeholder constituency.
Principle 4	Managers should recognize the interdependence of efforts and rewards among stakeholders, and should attempt to achieve a fair distribution of the benefits and burdens of corporate activity among them, taking into account their respective risks and vulnerabilities.

Principle 5	Managers should work cooperatively with other entities, both public and private, to insure that risks and harms arising from corporate activities are minimized and, where they cannot be avoided, appropriately compensated.
Principle 6	Managers should avoid altogether activities that might jeopardize inalienable human rights (e.g., the right to life) or give rise to risks which, if clearly understood, would be patently unacceptable to relevant stakeholders.
Principle 7	Managers should acknowledge the potential conflicts between (a) their own role as corporate stakeholders, and (b) their legal and moral responsibilities for the interests of stakeholders, and should address such conflicts through open communication, appropriate reporting and incentive systems and, where necessary, third party review.

Commentary on Principles of Stakeholder Management (Table 1)

Principle 1: Managers should acknowledge and actively monitor the concerns of all legitimate stakeholders, and should take their interests appropriately into account in decision-making and operations.

The first requirement of stakeholder management is an awareness of the existence of multiple and diverse stakeholders, and an understanding of their involvement and interest in the corporation. Many stakeholders (investors, employees, customers) are readily identified because of their express or implied contractual relationship to the firm. Others may identify themselves because of the impact, positive or negative, of the firm's activities on their own well-being. And, of course, some third parties may claim a stake in the firm when no such relationship, in fact, exists. Managers are not obligated to respond favorably to every request or criticism; they are, however, obligated to examine all such claims carefully before passing judgment on their validity.

The salience of specific stakeholder concerns varies among different areas of managerial decision-making, and according to the time horizon involved. Current working conditions are of greatest concern to employees; the cost and quality of products are of greatest concern to customers. Long-term survival and growth may be of greatest concern to investors and to the communities within which the firm operates. In taking particular decisions and actions, managers should give primary consideration to the interests of those stakeholders who are most intimately and critically involved.

Principle 2: Managers should listen to and openly communicate with stakeholders about their respective concerns and contributions, and about the risks that they assume because of their involvement with the corporation.

Communication, both internal and external, is a critical function of management, and effective communication involves receiving, as well as sending, messages. Hence, to understand stakeholder interests and to integrate various stakeholder groups into an effective wealth-producing team, managers must engage in dialogue. A commitment to engage in dialogue, however, does not constitute a commitment to collective decision-making: there are obvious limits as to the amount and content of information (particularly information about strategic options under consideration) that can be appropriately shared with particular stakeholder groups. Nevertheless, the more open managers can be about critical decisions and their consequences, and the more clearly managers understand and appreciate the perspectives and concerns of affected parties, the more likely it is that problematic situations can be satisfactorily resolved. Open communication and dialogue are, in themselves, stakeholder benefits, quite apart from their content or the conclusions reached.

Principle 3: Managers should adopt processes and modes of behavior that are sensitive to the concerns and capabilities of each stakeholder constituency.

Stakeholder groups differ not only in their primary interests and concerns, but also in their size, complexity, and level of involvement with the corporation. Some groups are dealt with through formal, and even legally prescribed, mechanisms, such as collective bargaining agreements and shareowner meetings. Others are reached through advertising, public relations, or press releases; still others (e.g., government officials) are reached largely through official proceedings and personal contacts. Both the mode of contact and the type of information presented, or the opportunity for dialogue, can appropriately vary among different stakeholder groups, although the descriptions of situations and explanations of actions offered by managers should be consistent among all stakeholders. Extreme caution is required when managers deal with stakeholder groups that have limited capacity to assimilate and evaluate complex situations and options.

Principle 4: Managers should recognize the interdependence of efforts and rewards among stakeholders, and should attempt to achieve a fair distribution of the benefits and burdens of corporate activity among them, taking into account their respective risks and vulnerabilities.

A business firm's a purposive organization in which all voluntary stakeholders collabourate for mutual benefit. Involuntary or consequential stakeholders (e.g., communities or third parties) may also be affected by the operation of the enterprise. And both voluntary and involuntary stakeholders are vulnerable, and differently vulnerable, to the effects of uncertainty and change over time. Successful managers will see that all stakeholders receive sufficient benefits to assure their continued collabouration in the enterprise, and that their burdens and risks are no greater than they are willing to bear. Again, the openness and demonstrable fairness of the distribution of benefits and burdens among stakeholders are, in themselves, stakeholder benefits. Managers may need to make special efforts to demonstrate stakeholder interdependence and the collabourative nature of the enterprise to non-contractual and involuntary stakeholders.

Principle 5: Managers should work cooperatively with other entities, both public and private, to insure that risks and harms arising from corporate activities are minimized and, where they cannot be avoided, appropriately compensated.

Corporate wealth creation necessarily gives rise to consequences that may not be fully mediated through the marketplace. Some of these may be beneficial and welcome; others may be harmful. Monitoring and ameliorating undesirable consequences (i.e., negative externalities) often requires cooperation with other firms, private sector organizations, public agencies and units of government. Managers should be proactive in developing contacts with relevant groups and in forging coalitions aimed at reducing harmful impacts and compensating affected parties. The often true observation that one firm cannot solve this problem alone should be a stimulus to multi-party cooperation, not an excuse for neglect and inaction.

Principle 6: Managers should avoid altogether activities that might jeopardize inalienable human rights (e.g., the right to life) or give rise to risks which, if clearly understood, would be patently unacceptable to relevant stakeholders.

The ultimate consequences of most human endeavors (particularly endeavors involving large expenditures, diverse interests and long time periods) can never be fully anticipated in advance. Hence, managerial decisions and corporate operations necessarily give rise to multiple and diverse risks. Managers should communicate openly with stakeholders concerning the risks involved with their specific roles in the corporate enterprise, and should negotiate appropriate risk-sharing (and benefit-sharing) contracts wherever possible. When stakeholders knowingly agree to accept a particular combination of risks and rewards, then the arrangement is usually considered satisfactory. However, some projects may have consequences for which no conceivable compensation would be adequate, or risks that cannot be fully understood or appreciated by critical stakeholders. In these circumstances, managers have a responsibility to restructure projects to eliminate the possibility of unacceptable consequences, or to abandon them entirely if necessary.

Principle 7: Managers should acknowledge the potential conflicts between (a) their own role as corporate stakeholders, and (b) their legal and moral responsibilities for the interests of all stakeholders, and should address such conflicts through open communication, appropriate reporting and incentive systems and, where necessary, third party review.

Up to this point, we have spoken of managers as if they were disinterested coordinators of stakeholder interactions. However, managers also form a distinct stakeholder group, with privileged access to information and unique influence on corporate decisions. As stakeholders, managers are naturally interested in the security of their jobs, the level of their rewards, and the scope of their discretion in the use of corporate resources. Other stakeholder groups (shareowners and boards of directors, in particular) have devised a variety of arrangements intended to align the interests of managers with those of the corporation as a whole, and to prevent opportunistic abuse of managerial positions.

However, the tension between the interests of managers as stakeholders, on one hand, and those of other stakeholder groups and of the corporation itself as an on-going entity, on the other, is unavoidable. Responsible managers will recognize this, and will therefore accept and encourage organizational practices intended to control this source of intra-organizational conflict. Managers gain credibility when they establish procedures to monitor their own performance and, when appropriate, to facilitate third party review. Credibility matters when managers ask other stakeholders to align their interests with those of the corporation, and to act responsibly rather than opportunistically. Without mutual credibility, stakeholder trust diminishes and the collabourative character of the organization may be jeopardized.

The Competitive Advantage of Nations

The Diamond Model of Michael Porter for the Competitive Advantage of Nations offers a model that can help understand the competitive position of a nation in global competition. This model can also be used for other major geographic regions.

Traditionally, economic theory mentions the following factors for comparative advantage for regions or countries:

1. Land
2. Location
3. Natural resources (minerals, energy)
4. Labour, and
5. Local population size.

Because these factor endowments can hardly be influenced, this fits in a rather passive (inherited) view towards national economic opportunity.

Porter says sustained industrial growth has hardly ever been built on above mentioned basic inherited factors. Abundance of such factors may actually undermine competitive advantage! He introduced a concept of "clusters," or groups of interconnected firms, suppliers, related industries, and institutions that arise in particular locations.

As a rule Competitive Advantage of nations has been the outcome of 4 interlinked advanced factors and activities in and between companies in these clusters. These can be influenced in a pro-active way by government.

These interlinked advanced factors for Competitive Advantage for countries or regions in Porters Diamond framework are:

1. Firm Strategy, Structure and Rivalry (The world is dominated by dynamic conditions, and it is direct competition that impels firms to work for increases in productivity and innovation)

2. Demand Conditions (The more demanding the customers in an economy, the greater the pressure facing firms to constantly improve their competitiveness via innovative products, through high quality, etc)

3. Related Supporting Industries (Spatial proximity of upstream or downstream industries facilitates the exchange of information and promotes a continuous exchange of ideas and innovations)

4. Factor Conditions (Contrary to conventional wisdom, Porter argues that the "key" factors of production (or specialized factors) are created, not inherited. Specialized factors of production are skilled labour, capital and infrastructure. "Non-key" factors or general use factors, such as unskilled labour and raw materials, can be obtained by any company and, hence, do not generate sustained competitive advantage. However, specialized factors involve heavy, sustained investment. They are more difficult to duplicate. This leads to a competitive advantage, because if other firms cannot easily duplicate these factors, they are valuable).

The role of government in Porter's Diamond Model is "acting as a catalyst and challenger; it is to encourage – or even push – companies to raise their aspirations and move to higher levels of competitive performance . They must encourage companies to raise their performance, stimulate early demand for advanced products, focus on specialized factor creation and to stimulate local rivalry by limiting direct cooperation and enforcing anti-trust regulations.

Porter introduced this model in his book: The Competitive Advantage of Nations, after having done research in ten leading trading nations. The book was the first theory of competitiveness based on the causes of the productivity with which companies compete instead of traditional comparative advantages such as natural resources and pools of labour. This book is considered required reading for government economic strategists and is also highly recommended for corporate strategist taking an interest in the macro-economic environment of corporations.

Overview of The Competitive Advantage of Nations (The Diamond Model)

Porter is a famous Harvard business professor. He conducted a comprehensive study of 10 nations to learn what leads to success. Recently his company was commissioned to study Canada in a report called "Canada at the Crossroads".

Porter believes standard classical theories on comparative advantage are inadequate (or even wrong).

According to Porter, a nation attains a competitive advantage if its firms are competitive. Firms become competitive through innovation. Innovation can include technical improvements to the product or to the production process.

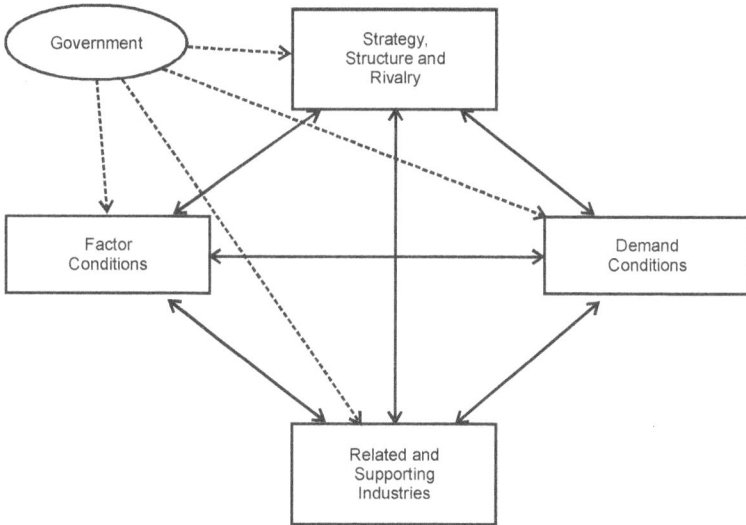

The Diamond – Four Determinants of National Competitive Advantage

Four attributes of a nation comprise Michael Porter's "Diamond" of national advantage. They are:

1. factor conditions (i.e. the nation's position in factors of production, such as skilled labour and infrastructure),
2. demand conditions (i.e. sophisticated customers in home market),
3. related and supporting industries, and
4. firm strategy, structure and rivalry (i.e. conditions for organization of companies, and the nature of domestic rivalry).

Factor Conditions

Factor conditions refers to inputs used as factors of production – such as labour, land, natural resources, capital and infrastructure. This sounds similar to standard economic theory, but Porter argues that the "key" factors of production (or specialized factors) are created, not inherited. Specialized factors of production are skilled labour, capital and infrastructure.

"Non-key" factors or general use factors, such as unskilled labour and raw materials, can be obtained by any company and, hence, do not generate sustained competitive advantage. However, specialized factors involve heavy, sustained investment. They are more difficult to duplicate. This leads to a competitive advantage, because if other firms cannot easily duplicate these factors, they are valuable.

Porter argues that a lack of resources often actually helps countries to become competitive (call it selected factor disadvantage). Abundance generates waste and scarcity generates an innovative mindset. Such countries are forced to innovate to overcome their problem of scarce resources. How true is this?

Switzerland was the first country to experience labour shortages. They abandoned labour-intensive watches and concentrated on innovative/high-end watches.

Japan has high priced land and so its factory space is at a premium. This lead to just-in-time inventory techniques (Japanese firms can't have a lot of stock taking up space, so to cope with the potential of not have goods around when they need it, they innovated traditional inventory techniques).

Sweden has a short building season and high construction costs. These two things combined created a need for pre-fabricated houses.

Demand Conditions

Michael Porter argues that a sophisticated domestic market is an important element to producing competitiveness. Firms that face a sophisticated domestic market are likely to sell superior products because the market demands high quality and a close proximity to such consumers enables the firm to better understand the needs and desires of the customers (this same argument can be used to explain the first stage of the IPLC theory when a product is just initially being developed and after it has been perfected, it doesnt have to be so close to the discriminating consumers).

If the nation's discriminating values spread to other countries, then the local firms will be competitive in the global market.

One example is the French wine industry. The French are sophisticated wine consumers. These consumers force and help French wineries to produce high quality wines. Can you think of other examples? Or counter-examples?

Related and Supporting Industries

Porter also argues that a set of strong related and supporting industries is important to the competitiveness of firms. This includes suppliers and related industries. This usually occurs at a regional level as opposed to a national level. Examples include Silicon valley in the U.S., Detroit (for the auto industry) and Italy (leather-shoes-other leather goods industry).

The phenomenon of competitors (and upstream and/or downstream industries) locating in the same area is known as clustering or agglomeration. What are the advantages and disadvantages of locating within a cluster? Some advantages to locating close to your rivals may be:

- potential technology knowledge spillovers,
- an association of a region on the part of consumers with a product and high quality and therefore some market power, or
- an association of a region on the part of applicable labour force.

Some disadvantages to locating close to your rivals are:
- potential poaching of your employees by rival companies and
- obvious increase in competition possibly decreasing mark-ups.

Firm Strategy, Structure and Rivalry

Strategy

(a) **Capital Markets:** Domestic capital markets affect the strategy of firms. Some countries capital markets have a long-run outlook, while others have a short-run outlook. Industries vary in how long the long-run is. Countries with a short-run outlook (like the U.S.) will tend to be more competitive in industries where investment is short-term (like the computer industry). Countries with a long run outlook (like Switzerland) will tend to be more competitive in industries where investment is long term (like the pharmaceutical industry).

(b) **Individuals' Career Choices:** Individuals base their career decisions on opportunities and prestige. A country will be competitive in an industry whose key personnel hold positions that are considered prestigious.

Does this appear to hold in the U.S. and Canada? What are the most prestigious occupations? What about Asia? What about developing countries?

Structure

Porter argues that the best management styles vary among industries. Some countries may be oriented toward a particular style of management. Those countries will tend to be more competitive in industries for which that style of management is suited.

For example, Germany tends to have hierarchical management structures composed of managers with strong technical backgrounds and Italy has smaller, family-run firms.

Rivalry

Porter argues that intense competition spurs innovation. Competition is particularly fierce in Japan, where many companies compete vigorously in most industries.

International competition is not as intense and motivating. With international competition, there are enough differences between companies and their environments to provide handy excuses to managers who were outperformed by their competitors.

The Diamond as a System

The points on the diamond constitute a system and are self-reinforcing.

Domestic rivalry for final goods stimulates the emergence of an industry that provides specialized intermediate goods. Keen domestic competition leads to more sophisticated consumers who come to expect upgrading and innovation. The diamond promotes clustering.

Porter provides a somewhat detailed example to illustrate the system. The example is the ceramic tile industry in Italy.

Porter emphasizes the role of chance in the model. Random events can either benefit or harm a firm's competitive position. These can be anything like major technological breakthroughs or inventions, acts of war and destruction, or dramatic shifts in exchange rates.

One might wonder how agglomeration becomes self-reinforcing.

When there is a large industry presence in an area, it will increase the supply of specific factors (ie: workers with industry-specific training) since they will tend to get higher returns and less risk of losing employment.

At the same time, upstream firms (ie: those who supply intermediate inputs) will invest in the area. They will also wish to save on transport costs, tariffs, inter-firm communication costs, inventories, etc.

At the same time, downstream firms (ie: those use our industry's product as an input) will also invest in the area. This causes additional savings of the type listed before.

Finally, attracted by the good set of specific factors, upstream and downstream firms, producers in related industries (ie: those who use similar inputs or whose goods are purchased by the same set of customers) will also invest. This will trigger subsequent rounds of investment.

Implications of The Competitive Advantage of Nations for Governments

The government plays an important role in Porter's diamond model. Like everybody else, Porter argues that there are some things that governments do that they shouldn't, and other things that they do not do but should. He says, "Government's proper role is as a catalyst and challenger; it is to encourage – or even push – companies to raise their aspirations and move to higher levels of competitive performance"

Governments can influence all four of Porter's determinants through a variety of actions such as

Subsidies to firms, either directly (money) or indirectly (through infrastructure).

Tax codes applicable to corporation, business or property ownership.

Educational policies that affect the skill level of workers.

They should focus on specialized factor creation. (How can they do this?)

They should enforce tough standards. (This prescription may seem counterintuitive. What is his rationale? Maybe to establish high technical and product standards including environmental regulations.)

The problem, of course, is through these actions, it becomes clear which industries they are choosing to help innovate. What methods do they use to choose? What happens if they pick the wrong industries?

Criticisms about The Diamond Model

Although Porter theory is renowned, it has a number of critics.

Porter developed this paper based on case studies and these tend to only apply to developed economies.

Porter argues that only outward-FDI is valuable in creating competitive advantage, and inbound-FDI does not increase domestic competition significantly because the domestic firms lack the capability to defend their own markets and face a process of market-share erosion and decline. However, there seems to be little empirical evidence to support that claim.

The Porter model does not adequately address the role of MNCs. There seems to be ample evidence that the diamond is influenced by factors outside the home country.

The Delta Model

The Delta Model is a strategy (organizing) framework that was developed by Dean Wilde, along with other members of Dean & Company, and Arnoldo Hax of the MIT/Sloan School of Management. It is aimed at assisting managers in the articulation and implementation of effective corporate and business strategies.

The emergence of the Internet, with the previously unimagined potentials for communication, and the technologies surrounding e-business and e-commerce, made available some new options tools that allowed the feasibility of new business approaches. Hax and Wilde II integrate the Competitive Advantage and Value Chain frameworks from Porter with the Resource-Based View on the Firm and complement those with new Extended Enterprise perspectives and with offering Total Customer Solutions.

The Delta Model Contains the Following Elements:

1. Strategic Triangle: used for defining strategic positions that reflect fundamentally new sources of profitability (three strategic options: best product, customer solutions, and system lock-in),

2. Aligning these strategic options with a firm's activities and provides congruency between strategic direction and execution (three fundamental processes are always present and are the repository of key strategic tasks: operational effectiveness, customer targeting, and innovation), and

3. Adaptive processes: core processes of the company must be aligned to the chosen strategy in order to make progress against the strategic agenda and avoid a commodity-like outcome. The Delta Model identifies the core processes of the business and provides a guide for how they need to function differently to achieve different strategic positions capable of continually responding to an uncertain environment.

4. Metrics (Aggregate Metrics that should be supplemented with Granular Metrics).

Hax and Wilde believe a firm owes itself to its customers. They are the ultimate repository of all the firm's activities. At the heart of management and, certainly, at the heart of strategy, resides the customer. We have to serve the customer in a distinctive way if we expect to enjoy superior performance. The name of the game is to attract, to satisfy, and to retain the customer.

The intimacy and connectivity of the networked economy offer opportunities to create competitive positions based upon the structure of the customer relationship.

System Lock-In
System Economics
Market Dominance
Achieving Complementor Share

**Enabled
Through
Effective Use
of Technology**

Total Customer Solutions
Customer Economics
Cooperation
Achieving Customer Share

Best Product
Product Economics
Rivalry
Achieving Product Share

A business can establish an unbreakable link, deep knowledge, and close relationship that we refer to as customer bonding. These bonds can be directly formed with the customer, or indirectly formed through the complementors that the customer wishes to access.

Both are powerful sources of margin and sustainability. The bonds represent investments made by customers and complementors in and around the business product.

The Strategy Delta

Arnoldo C. Hax and Dean L. Wilde II, The Delta Model Toward a Unified Framework of Strategy, MIT Sloan School of Management Working Paper Number 4261-02.

What is the fundamental unit of strategy? Michael Porter's hugely influential work seeks to make sense of strategy within the bounds of particular industries, whether the Swiss watch industry or the Dutch flower industry. Another approach is propounded by Gary Hamel and C.K. Prahalad. This theoretical school sees the company as the basic strategic unit. A company's strategy is regarded as a function of its resources human and otherwise. Over the last decade, a great deal of intellectual energy has been expended on refining these two world views, merging them, or coming up with coherent alternatives.

Entering this theoretical fray are Arnoldo C. Hax, the Alfred P. Sloan Professor of Management at MIT's Sloan School of Management, and Dean L. Wilde II, chairman and founder of strategy consultants Dean & Company. The Delta Model developed by Professor Hax and Mr. Wilde puts forward three strategic options that can lead to what they call customer bonding. These are best product, total customer solutions, and system lock-in.

The best-product strategy is built on having a low-cost or differentiated product. However, this option is limited because it does not build substantial customer bonding. The business-to-business total customer solutions strategy is based on reducing customer costs and increasing customer profits. Companies compete on the basis of customer economics. Finally, system lock-in embraces others in the supply chain customers, suppliers, and complementors. Complementors are firms that produce products or services that enhance a company's own product and service portfolio. Proprietary computer standards is one example of how a complementor can execute system lock-in. More than 100,000 applications are designed to work with Microsoft's Windows operating system, whereas only one-quarter of that number of applications exist for Apple's Macintosh system, according to the authors.

The Hax and Wilde team add some compelling financial performance data to the discussion about customer-centered strategy. Their research looked at more than 100 major companies whose strategic positions clearly fitted one of the three categories system lock-in, best product, or total customer solution. Those that competed on the basis of system lock-in were substantially more successful in terms of market value added (MVA) and market-to-book value. For example, companies with a system lock-in had a mean MVA of 57.15, compared with 14.26 for companies competing on the basis of having a best product and 22.38 for those competing on the basis of a total customer solution.

The authors argue that three daptive processes namely, operational effectiveness, customer targeting, and innovation are the primary means by which the three different strategic options can be pursued and executed.

The Deming Cycle

The Deming cycle, or PDSA cycle, is a continuous quality improvement model consisting of a logical sequence of four repetitive steps for continuous improvement and learning: Plan, Do, Study (Check) and Act. The PDCA cycle is also known as the Deming Cycle, or as the Deming Wheel or as the Continuous Improvement Spiral. It originated in the 1920s with the eminent statistics expert Mr. Walter A. Shewhart, who introduced the concept of PLAN, DO and SEE. The late Total Quality Management (TQM) guru and renowned statistician Edwards Deming modified the Shewart cycle as: PLAN, DO, STUDY, and ACT.

Along with the other well-known American quality guru-Joseph Juran, Edwards Deming went to Japan as part of the occupation forces of the allies after World War II. Deming taught a lot of Quality Improvement methods to the Japanese, including the usage of statistics and the PLAN, DO, STUDY, ACT cycle.

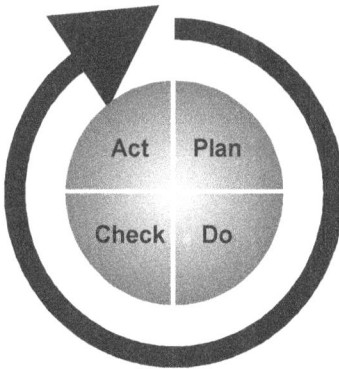

The graphic above shows Deming's Plan-Do-Check-Act (PDCA) cycle. (Deming himself called it the 'Shewhart Cycle' but Deming's work in Japan has lead to it commonly being named after him.) In BPE, everything is done with the discipline of PDCA. At all levels of the organization we:

Plan what we are going to do. In this step we assess where we are, where we need to be, why this is important, and plan how to close the gap. Identify some potential solutions.

Do try out or test the solutions (sometimes at a pilot level).

Check to see if the countermeasures you tried out had the effect you hoped for, and make sure that there are no negative consequences associated with them. Assess if you have accomplished your objective.

Act on what you have learned. If you have accomplished your objective, put controls into place so that the issue never comes back again. If you have not accomplished your objective, go through the cycle again, starting with the Plan step.

Frequently, a particular project will define sub-objectives, run thorough the PDCA cycle one or more times to accomplish the sub-objective, then define the next objective and go through the cycle again. Thus, many projects end up "turning the wheel" many times before completion. In ongoing management activities, we find a similar use of the cycle.

What we are trying to avoid by using the PDCA discipline is the "Ready, Fire, Aim" fallacy where people jump to the solution without identifying the problem and assessing if their proposed solution fixes it, or even results in another problem. The Act step makes sure we don't have to fix it again in a couple of years.

Problems With Deming Cycle

The Deming Cycle's application was intended for quality control purposes and proposed continuous improvement in quality of products/experiments.[4] The simple cycle works well in this application, but it is debatable that it should be applied to major organizational improvement. ISO recognized the need to provide better guidance in this regard and published the ISO standard ISO 9004:2000, which replaced the use of the term continuous improvement with continual improvement. The change is not trivial, it recognizes that organizational quality system performance improvement requires significant effort and needs pauses to consolidate change (hence continual and not continuous improvement) (ISO 9004:2000).

The Deming Cycle has an inherent circular paradigm, it assumes that everything starts with Planning. Plan has a limited range of meaning. Shewart intended that experiments and quality control should be planned to deliver results in accordance with the specifications, which is good advice. However, Planning was not intended to cover aspects such as creativity, innovation, invention or Complex Adaptive Systems. In these aspects particularly when based upon imagination, it is often impossible or counterproductive to plan.

The Deming Cycle approaches often do not get to the root cause of a problem, especially in adaptive situations which call for an experiential approach but demand much more rigour in analysis and data collection. An adaptive challenge exists where there are no visible solutions to problems, and can exist, for example in areas where chaos, uncertainty, and ambiguity exists, such as new frontiers, and existing complex systems such as Healthcare.

Do and Act have the same meaning in English. Dictionaries (Shorter Oxford) provide the following relevant definitions:

Do: verb 1 perform or carry out (an action). 2 achieve or complete (a specified target). 3 act or progress in a specified way. 4 work on (something) to bring it to a required state.

Act: verb 1 take action; do something. 2 take effect or have a particular effect. 3 behave in a specified way.

The 'Act' in the Deming Cycle is meant to be interpreted to have a different meaning to 'Do', otherwise it could be as easily have been PDCD or PACA. In PDCA, 'Act' is meant to apply actions to the outcome for necessary improvement, in other words 'Act' means 'Improve' (applying PDCA to itself could result in PDCI).

The Deming Cycle is a set of activities (Plan, Do, Check, Act) designed to drive continuous improvement. Initially implemented in manufacturing, it has broad applicability in business. First developed by Walter Shewhart, it is more commonly called the Deming cycle in Japan where it was popularized by Edwards Deming.

The Strategic Triangle of 3C's

Kenichi Ohmae's 3C's model stands for the corporation, the customer, and the competition. The 3C's model (three C's framework) of Kenichi Ohmae, a famous Japanese strategy guru, stresses that a strategist should focus on three key factors for success. "In the construction of any business strategy, three main players must be taken into account:
1. The corporation itself,
2. The customer, and
3. The competition.

Only by integrating the three C's (Customer, Competitor, and Company) in a strategic triangle, sustained competitive advantage can exist. Kenichi Ohmae refers to these key factors as the three C's or the strategic triangle.

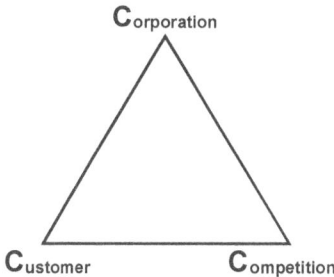

3C's model: Customer-based strategies are the basis of all strategy. "There is no doubt that a corporation's foremost concern ought to be the interest of its customers rather than that of its stockholders and other parties. In the long run, the corporation that is genuinely interested in its customers is the one that will be interesting to investors".

Segmenting by Objectives

Here, the differentiation is done in terms of the different ways different customers use the product. Take coffee, for example. Some people drink it to wakeup or keep alert, while others view coffee as a way to relax or socialize (coffee breaks).

Segmenting by Customer Coverage

This type of strategic segmentation normally emerges from a trade-off study of marketing costs versus market coverage. There appears always to be a point of diminishing returns in the cost-versus-coverage relationship. The corporation's task, therefore, is to optimize its range of market coverage, be it geographical or channel, so that its cost of marketing will be advantageous relative to the competition.

Resegmenting the Market

In a fiercely competitive market, the corporation and its head-on competitors are likely to be dissecting the market in similar ways. Over an extended period of time, therefore the effectiveness of a given initial strategic segmentation will tend to decline. In such a situation it often pays to pick a small group of key customers and reexamine what it is that they are really looking for.

Changes in Customer Mix

Such a market segment change occurs where the forces at work are altering the distribution of the user-mix over time by influencing demography, distribution channels, customer size, etc. This kind of change calls for shifting the allocation of corporate resources and/or changing the absolute level of resources committed in the business, failing which severe losses in the market share can occur.

3C's framework: Corporate-based strategies. They aim to maximize the corporation's strengths relative to the competition in the functional areas that are critical to success in the industry.

Selectivity and Sequencing: In order to win the corporation does not need to have a clear lead in every function from sourcing to functioning. If it can gain a decisive edge in one key function, it will eventually be able to pull ahead of the competition in other functions that may now be no better than mediocre.

A Case of Make or Buy

In case of rapidly rising wage costs, it becomes a critical decision for a company to subcontract a major share of its assembly operations. Its competitors may not be able to shift production so rapidly to subcontractors and vendors, and the resulting difference in cost structure and/or in the company's ability to cope with demand fluctuations could have have significant strategic implications.

Improving Cost-Effectiveness

This can be done in three basic methods. The first is by reducing basic costs much more effectively than the competition. The second method is simply to exercise greater selectivity in terms of orders accepted, product offered, or functions to be performed which means cherry-picking the high-impact operations so that as others are eliminated, functional costs will drop faster than sales revenues. The third method is to share a certain key function among the corporation's other businesses or even with other companies. Experience indicates that there are many situations in which sharing resources in one or more basic sub-functions of marketing can be advantageous.

3 C's model: Competitor-based strategies according to Kenichi Ohmae can be constructed by looking at possible sources of differentiation in functions ranging from purchasing, design, and engineering to sales and servicing.

The Power of an Image

Both Sony and Honda outsell their competitors as they invested more heavily in public relations and promotion and managed these functions more carefully than did their competitors. When product performance and mode of distribution are very difficult to differentiate, image may be the only source of positive differentiation. But as the case of the Swiss watch industry reminds us, a strategy built on image can be risky and must be monitored constantly.

Capitalizing on Profit – and Cost- Structure Differences

Firstly, the difference in source of profit might be exploited, for e.g. profit from new product sales, profit from services etc. Secondly, a difference in the ratio of fixed cost to variable cost might also be exploited strategically for e.g. a company with a lower fixed cost ratio can lower prices in a sluggish market and win market share. This hurts the company with a higher fixed cost ratio as the market price is too low to justify its high-fixed-cost-low-volume operation.

Tactics for Flyweights

If such a company chooses to compete in mass-media advertising or massive R&D efforts, the additional fixed costs will absorb such a large portion of its revenue that its giant competitors will inevitably win. It could though calculate its incentives on a graduated percentage basis rather than on absolute volume, thus making the incentives variable by guaranteeing the dealer a larger percentage of each extra unit sold. The Big Three, of course, cannot afford to offer such high percentages across the board to their respective franchised stores; their profitability would soon be eroded if they did.

Hito-Kane-Mono

A favourite phrase of Japanese business planners is hito-kane-mono, or people, money, and things (fixed assets). They believe that streamlined corporate management is achieved when these three critical resources are in balance without any superfluity or waste. For example cash over and beyond what competent people can intelligently expend is wasted. Again too many managers without enough money will exhaust their energies and involve their colleagues in time-wasting paper warfare over the allocation of the limited funds. Of the three critical resources, funds should be allocated last. Based on the available mono-plant, machinery, technology, process know-how, functional strengths and so on-the corporation should first allocate management talent. Once these hito have developed creative, imaginative ideas to capture the business's upward potential, the kane, or money, should be allocated to the specific ideas and Programmes generated by individual managers.

www.ingramcontent.com/pod-product-compliance
Lightning Source LLC
Chambersburg PA
CBHW072051020426
42334CB00017B/1465